SWEETEN IT WITH
AGAVE

HEALTHY, DELICIOUS, AND LOW GLYCEMIC DESSERTS

**A NATURALLY
SUGAR-FREE
COOKBOOK**

JEN BACCELLIERI

H.W.
Publishing

DEDICATED TO MI AMOR, WHO HAS BEEN SO LOVING AND PATIENT
DURING THIS FIRST BOOK JOURNEY,

TO MY FELLOW HOLISTIC HEALTH COLLEAGUES, WHO COMMIT
THEIR LIVES TO SERVING THE HEALTH AND WELL-BEING OF OTHERS,

AND TO MY MOTHER ANN, WHO TAUGHT ME HOW TO LOVE FOOD.

Library of Congress Control Number: 2011903732
ISBN: 978-0-578-06472-7

Book design: Tania Kac
Production: Pam Uhlenkamp
Copy Editor: Katy Klutznick

For more information about this book and to join our online agave community, visit:
www.SweetenItWithAgave.com

Published by H.W. Publishing

Printed in the United States of America.

TABLE OF CONTENTS

INTRODUCTION IX

PART 1
CHOOSING AGAVE NECTAR 13

    CHAPTER 1: WHAT IS AGAVE? THE BASICS 13
        What is the Agave Plant? 13
        What is Agave Nectar? 14
        What is the Difference Between Agave Varieties? 15
        The Science of Sugar 17
        Agave Nectar Compared to High-Fructose Corn Syrup 19
        Choosing a Quality Agave Nectar 22
        Raw vs. Cooked Agave Nectar 22
        Nutritional Facts 23
        Substituting Agave Nectar in Standard Recipes 24

    CHAPTER 2: THE BENEFITS OF USING AGAVE NECTAR 27
        Why Switch to Agave Nectar? 28
        Glycemic Index: Agave Nectar vs. White Sugar
           and Other Sweeteners 28
        Sugar Addiction: Replacing Sugar with Agave Nectar 29
        Agave Nectar in Children's Diets 30

    CHAPTER 3: THE BENEFITS OF USING QUALITY INGREDIENTS . 33
        Why Organic? 34
        Why Whole Grain Flours? 39
        Why Good Fats? 41
        Why Quality Salts? 43

    CHAPTER 4: GETTING STARTED WITH THE BASICS 45
        Stocking Your Kitchen 46
        Helpful Appliances and Tools to Have on Hand 47
        How to Measure 48
        The Ingredients 49
        Guide to Gluten-Free Recipes by Chapter 50

CHAPTER 5: CONVERSION CHARTS AND BAKING GUIDES ... 53

    Create Your Own Recipes and Conversions 54

    Common Abbreviations... 54

    Top Tips for Baking at High Altitudes......................... 55

    Converting Sweeteners to Agave Nectar 56

    Fahrenheit, Celsius, and Gas Number Conversions 57

    Liquid Measurement Conversions 58

    Dry Measurement Conversions............................... 59

    Formulas for Conversion..................................... 59

    Baking Pan Conversion Chart 60

    Baking Pan Sizes 62

    Ingredient Equivalents....................................... 63

    I'm Missing an Ingredient! Ingredient Substitutions 64

PART 2
THE RECIPES 71

CHAPTER 6: BEVERAGES 73

    Cold Drinks... 74

    Natural Sodas 81

    Hot Drinks.. 88

CHAPTER 7: FLAVORED AGAVE NECTAR AND EXTRACTS..... 93

    Making Your Own Flavored Agave 94

    Sample Combinations 94

    Making Your Own Extracts 95

CHAPTER 8: SYRUPS, SAUCES, AND FROSTINGS 99

    Syrups and Sauces 100

    Frostings 108

CHAPTER 9: JAMS, JELLIES, PRESERVES, AND MARMALADES..113

    Understanding the Differences 114

    Base Recipes.. 115

    Sample Recipes 120

CHAPTER 10: BREADS.......................................127

    Top Tips for Making Great Breads 128

    Yeasted Breads 130

    Yeast-Free Breads... 148

    Gluten-Free Breads..153

CHAPTER 11: MUFFINS **159**

   Top Tips for Making Great Muffins 160

   Muffins 161

   Pastry Muffins. 170

   Gluten-Free Muffins 173

CHAPTER 12: CAKES, BIRTHDAY CAKES,
CUPCAKES, AND CHEESECAKES. **185**

   Top Tips for Making Great Cakes 186

   Cakes and Birthday Cakes 193

   Cheesecakes 207

   Gluten-Free Cakes 209

CHAPTER 13: COOKIES AND BARS **215**

   Top Tips for Making Great Cookies and Bars 216

   Cookies 218

   Bars and Brownies. 230

   Gluten-Free Cookies and Brownies 233

CHAPTER 14: PUDDINGS AND CUSTARDS **239**

   Understanding the Differences 240

   Top Tips for Making Great Puddings and Custards 240

   Puddings and Custards 242

CHAPTER 15: PIES AND TARTS **259**

   Top Tips for Baking Great Pies and Tarts 260

   3 Ways to Make Whole Grain Pie Crusts 262

   Whole Grain Pie Crust Recipes 270

   Gluten-Free Pie Crust Recipes 273

   Pie Fillings 278

   Raw Pie Crusts and Fillings 291

CHAPTER 16: COBBLERS, CRISPS, AND CRUMBLES **303**

   Understanding the Differences 304

   Cobblers 304

   Crisps 307

   Crumbles 309

CHAPTER 17: ICE CREAM **313**

   Dairy Ice Cream 314

   Dairy-Free Ice Cream 318

CHAPTER 18: RAW FOOD TREATS **325**
    Raw Chocolate 326
    Superfood Balls 328
    Raw Candies and Treats 332

CHAPTER 19: CANDIES WITH A HEALTHY TWIST **339**
    Making Your Own Chocolate 340
    Truffles 342
    Candies 346

CHAPTER 20: SNACKS **355**
    Snack Bars and Energy Bars 356
    Other Snacks 364

**CHAPTER 21: FUN FOODS FOR KIDS
AND THE YOUNG AT HEART** **369**
    Fun Foods 370
    Popsicles 375
CHAPTER 22: BREAKFAST FOODS **385**
    Cold Cereal 386
    Hot Cereal 390
    French Toast 395
    Pancakes 396
    Waffles 401

GLOSSARY OF INGREDIENTS **407**

RESOURCES **425**

ENDNOTES **426**

INDEX **430**

Symbols Used in This Book

If you are avoiding gluten, wheat, and dairy in your diet, look for the recipes in this book with the following symbols. But don't limit yourself. Recipes can be adjusted—see page 64 for a guide to substitutions!

 Wheat Free

 Gluten Free

 Dairy Free

INTRODUCTION

My career in holistic health began when my passion for medicinal plants and healing compelled me to pursue an undergraduate degree in Ethnobotany and Healing Arts through The Friends World Program of Long Island University. I traveled to remote villages in Central and South America and India, learning traditional healing modalities and about herbs and foods from tribal healers, scholars, and social workers. After graduation, I attended the Southwest School of Botanical Medicine in Arizona, where I gained certification as an herbalist. At the Southwest School, I further developed my knowledge of plants, learning to identify them in the wild and create herbal remedies. I also began to educate others about herbal remedies. While working with people, I began to notice a pattern: one's relationship with food is the foundation of one's health. A person whose diet is dominated by soda, processed foods, and refined sugar is a person who is likely to be suffering from health problems. I realized that herbal remedies enhance treatment but rarely override the importance of good nutrition. To get to the root of an individual's problem, I had to delve deeper. I attended the Institute for Integrative Nutrition, where I explored the potential of using food to heal the body. There I studied with some of the top nutrition gurus of our generation. After three years of study and practicum, I became a certified holistic health counselor, natural chef, and cooking instructor.

In 2002, I founded *The Art of Living Wellness Center*. After personally struggling with and conquering my own sugar addiction, I discovered my niche in treating clients with an addiction to sugar. Over the last ten years, I have greatly expanded my knowledge of whole foods, nutrition, and natural medicine and have worked with more than a thousand sugar-addicted clients. As with any addiction, simply telling a person to stop is ineffective. Throughout the course of a six-month health program, I seek to transition clients away from harmful sugars and chemicals to more healthful alternatives. I also help clients achieve a more balanced diet that includes whole foods. Nearly every client who has completed my program has left free of addiction to sugar or other sweeteners. In addition, they were able to meet their overall health goals and develop a new, positive relationship to food.

Of all the natural sweeteners, I find agave nectar to be the best-tasting alternative to sugar; it is also the easiest to substitute for sugar. Fairly new to the market, agave nectar is still relatively unknown by many. It is nonaddictive and has a low glycemic index, and its light flavor makes it an excellent option for cooking and baking. Like any sweetener, though, agave nectar should be used sparingly, making up only a small portion of your balanced diet. My purpose for this book is to create a comprehensive, educational guide to agave nectar and demonstrate the ways in which it can play a central role in a naturally sugar-free lifestyle. Since there are questionable brands of agave nectar on the market, some of which have been rumored to contain high-fructose corn syrup, finding a reputable brand is important. After much research, I have selected the most widely available, highest quality, and most economical source on the market: Madhava. I have personally toured Madhava's facilities in Colorado and have spoken extensively with the owner of the company. Madhava uses a world-recognized third-party organization to oversee the operations of the plants in Mexico and is committed to providing a high-quality, organic, and pure product to consumers. In addition, they have supplied independent lab analysis of their products. The company also maintains ethical and fair-trade business practices. Madhava employs many Hnahnu (nah-nu) people in Mexico, who are descended from the Aztecs. This provides local people with a livable wage in a traditional trade in their home region. Another reason I prefer Madhava agave over other brands is because their agave nectar is lower in fructose and has a lower glycemic index. As with any product, new brands will continue to appear on the market; be sure, if you have doubts, to contact suppliers with questions about the quality of any new product.

The information in this book will help you seamlessly embrace a healthy lifestyle without compromising delicious taste. I have created more than 300 diverse recipes for you to enjoy. These unique recipes will demonstrate how to bake with agave, using ingredients with the highest standard of nutritional integrity. All recipes are free of processed foods like white flour and low-quality fats, like canola oil. All of the flours used in the recipes are whole grain and many recipes are wheat free, dairy free, and gluten free (see page 50). If you are uncertain about the benefits of using whole grains, organic food, and high-quality fats and salts, please see Chapter 3 for a thorough explanation. All of the recipes are appropriate for those who are interested in substituting agave for sugar (such as diabetics) or for parents who simply want to nurture their children with more healthful sweets.

At the end of each chapter, you'll find space to make notes on your creative adaptations to the recipes in this cookbook. Thus, you may use this as a workbook, fleshing out your own ideas, improvisations, and winning recipes!

In conjunction with this book, I have created a cutting-edge website that will allow participants to co-create new versions of recipes or submit original recipes for community review. This will enable us to learn from one another and create even better recipes collectively. As the caretaker of this project, I plan to include the best new and revised recipes in subsequent editions of this book. My aim is to facilitate a lively interchange that will include the creative genius of our entire community.

I hope you will enjoy learning about agave nectar and will be surprised to discover that healthful sweets can also be enjoyable treats!

PART I

CHOOSING AGAVE NECTAR

CHAPTER I

WHAT IS AGAVE? THE BASICS

What Is the Agave Plant?

Agave is a succulent plant found in the American southwest, Central America, and South America. It thrives in hot, arid climates and is commonly produced in the central desert region

of Mexico. While agave looks like a cactus, it is actually a close relative of the lily and amaryllis families. Throughout the centuries, the agave plant has had many traditional uses. The most famous is the production of the popular alcoholic drink tequila, which, along with blue agave nectar, is made from the *Agave tequilana* plant. During an agave shortage in the 1990s, growers explored alternative species of agave for production. Today, the Nekutli company generates their agave nectar with a wild species called *Agave salmiana* (commonly named Maguey), which is hand gathered by the Hnahnu people.

For millennia, the Hnahnu people have maintained a deep traditional knowledge of the life cycle, characteristics, and uses of the agave plant. Agave was used in many products necessary for their survival, including fibers for weaving, construction materials, soap, small furniture, foods, beverages, paper, medicinal products, firewood, toys, and ornaments. The Hnahnu are not the only people to have explored agave's offerings. In Ayurvedic medicine (traditional Indian medicine), agave is considered a demulcent, an herb that creates a protective barrier for irritated or inflamed tissue. Agave has been used to soothe and restore the stomach and intestines, protect them from infection and irritation, and provide relief from digestive ailments such as ulcers and inflammatory conditions. It is also used as a laxative and an antiseptic.[1] A study published in the *Journal of Ethnopharmacology* confirms that the agave plant has anti-inflammatory effects.[2] Agave also held a prominent place among Aztecs, who prized its antibacterial effect on wounds and drank it as a ceremonial fermented beverage called *pulque*.[3] Aztecs also honored Mayahuel, the goddess of the agave plant, weaving, and female fertility, by drinking pulque[4]. And pulque was used in many Aztec rituals, ceremonies, celebrations, and festivals.[5] Today, Mexicans still enjoy this lightly fermented drink.

Pre-biotic Qualities of Agave

The main carbohydrate in agave is a naturally occurring inulin. Inulins are a type of fructan (a group of fructose molecules) that have many health benefits in their natural form.

Agave nectar is composed of 3 to 5 percent inulin and contains a form of fructan found in vegetables, including green beans, onions, asparagus, and artichokes. The International Society for Horticultural Science has shown that fructans from agave have pre-biotic properties, meaning they selectively stimulate the growth and activities of beneficial bacteria, found in the gut, such as Bifidobacteria and Lactobacilli, and thereby inhibit the growth of harmful bacteria.

When tested against commercial inulin, agave fructans were found to stimulate the beneficial bacteria more efficiently than commercial samples.[6] Recent studies indicate that the presence of fructans in the digestive tract protects against osteoporosis by increasing absorption of magnesium and calcium; this may also protect against colon cancer and diabetes.[7] It should be noted that naturally occurring inulin contained in agave and other vegetables should not be confused with the commercially processed additive "Inulin/FOS" now added to commercial yogurts.

What Is Agave Nectar?

Agave nectar, or agave syrup, is a natural liquid sweetener made from juice extracted from the center cavity or the pressed core of the agave plant. There are two varieties of agave currently used to produce agave nectar sold in the United States:

- *Agave tequilana* — the most common and widely known variety. The core of the plant is used to make blue agave nectar and tequila.

- *Agave salmiana* — the less common variety. *Aguamiel* juice is collected from the center cavity of the plant and is used to make agave nectar. Left on its own, the juice would naturally ferment into pulque, the traditional, mildly alcoholic drink mentioned above. The core of the plant can also be used to make agave nectar.

Madhava, a major producer of agave, uses both blue agave and the less common *Agave salmiana*, which is hand gathered according to Fair Trade standards by the indigenous Hnahnu people of Mexico. The production of agave nectar helps to support the local economy and allows family members, who may otherwise be forced to seek work in cities, to remain in their ancestral villages.

There are currently two methods of making agave nectar from the juice of the plant:

- Non-GMO natural enzymes with low-heat vacuum evaporation of water

- Thermal hydrolysis with higher heat and low-heat vacuum evaporation of water

Both achieve the same goal, which is to separate the naturally occurring inulin (a complex polysaccharide that is not sweet) into *fructose* and *glucose* (monosaccharides that are sweet).

Agave Tequilana core (left)
Agave Salmiana core (right)

What Is The Difference Between Agave Varieties?

Agave Tequilana

Agave Salmiana

Agave Tequilana

Agave tequilana is a signature crop of Mexico and is used predominantly for the production of tequila; more recently, however, it has also been used to make blue agave syrup.

It is produced primarily in central Mexico at moderate elevations. Agave syrup can only be produced from mature, flowering *Agave tequilana* plants that are about eight to ten years old. The core, called the piña, is cut in pieces and slowly baked in large vats at approximately 165°F. This converts the inulin into natural sugars. The sugary juice that is produced is called aguamiel.

Tequila is made by fermenting and distilling the aguamiel. To make blue agave nectar, the aguamiel is filtered and boiled down, after which natural enzymes are added to convert the fructans into monosaccharides.[8] You may notice a slight difference in taste between *Agave tequilana* and *Agave salmiana*, but this difference will not affect recipes.

Agave Salmiana

Agave salmiana is a less common, wild species traditionally used by the Hnahnu. Their Aztec ancestors revered it as a sacred plant that could purify the body and soul. *Agave salmiana* grows in desert regions of central Mexico at high elevations. Mature plants reach their prime after around eight years, when their shoots begin to flower.

Agave nectar can be made in two ways with this plant: using the core as with blue agave or via a unique process developed by the Hnahnu, where the juice is collected by hand from a cavity in the center of live plants. This raw *Agave salmiana* juice, also referred to as aguamiel, has been consumed for centuries as a sweet drink. Each plant will produce about eight liters of aguamiel twice a day for about six to eight months before its production is exhausted.

Once removed from the plant, if not immediately processed, the aguamiel will rapidly ferment naturally into pulque. Today, more than 800 Hnahnu gather the aguamiel, using traditional methods, twice daily for the production of agave nectar.

Agave nectar is made from the aguamiel of *Agave salmiana* plants by straining the juice before it ferments, gently heating it to 118 to 120°F, and removing water through vacuum evaporation. As with blue agave, natural enzymes are added to convert the complex natural sugars into simple sugars, or fructans and monosaccharides. This process is similar to the process by which bees convert nectar into honey.

By repeatedly ingesting and regurgitating plant nectar, honey bees mix their own natural enzymes with the nectar to create honey. These natural enzymes separate the complex sugars in the nectar into the monosaccharides fructose, glucose and aguamiel. This mixture is high in natural yeasts and water content and, like raw aguamiel in the agave plant, will rapidly ferment if water does not evaporate. Bees then furiously flap their wings to create a strong draft in the hive that evaporates the water and concentrates the mixture into honey.[9]

Agave syrup looks similar to corn syrup and honey but is naturally refined and has a relatively low glycemic index of about 32. One tablespoon of agave nectar contains about 60 calories and 16 grams of carbohydrate. Agave nectar consists primarily of the monosaccharides fructose and glucose, and is 1.4 times sweeter than white sugar. It has a clear, sweet, neutral taste, which provides a great alternative to refined sugar or processed artificial sweeteners in baking and cooking. It is less viscous than honey and therefore pours more easily and dissolves quickly into cooked and raw dishes and cold beverages. Agave nectar will not crystallize when stored for extended periods.

Today, there are many varieties of agave nectar on the market, such as raw, dark, amber, or light. Not all brands of agave nectar are alike and there are subtle distinctions in flavor and slight differences in the glycemic index of each variety. Generally, darker agave nectars contain a higher vitamin and mineral content than lighter varieties.

Table 1: Varieties of Agave Nectar

	Taste	Ideal Uses
Dark	Deep caramel notes	Desserts, sauces, marinades, savory dishes, baked beans, meat, poultry, and seafood
Amber	Lighter caramel notes	Desserts, sauces, savory dishes, roasted vegetables, pancakes and waffles, candies, hot and cold cereals
Light	Clear, neutral taste	Delicately flavored desserts, smoothies, juices, fruit, hot and cold cereals, tea and coffee
Raw (processed below 118°F)	Clear, neutral taste	Delicately flavored desserts, smoothies, juices, fruit, hot and cold cereals, tea and coffee

The Science of Sugar

What, exactly, is sugar? And how is it metabolized? Understanding the answers to these questions helps when comparing natural sweeteners. **Saccharides** are carbohydrates. **Monosaccharides** (single, simple sugar molecules) are the simplest molecules that comprise all carbohydrates and dissolve in water.[10] Common monosaccharides include *fructose*, *galactose*, and *glucose*. Monosaccharides do not require any further digestion in order to be absorbed by the body. Glucose and fructose are two of the most important monosaccharides in human nutrition and are found in their unbound form in many fruits, vegetables, and sweeteners like agave nectar and honey. While fructose and other nutrients, such as lipids and proteins, are transported to the liver and metabolized for energy or storage, glucose is transported directly into the bloodstream. Glucose is the most abundant carbohydrate and is a fundamental nutrient used for fuel in the body. The term "blood sugar" literally refers to the level of glucose in the bloodstream. Naturally occurring fructose and glucose are found in varying quantities in various foods. Fruits naturally high in fructose include apples and grapes, while sweet cherries and prunes are naturally high in glucose.[11]

GLUCOSE   GALACTOSE   FRUCTOSE

Disaccharides are two monosaccharides that are bound together to make a two-sugar molecule with one water molecule removed. The disaccharide *lactose*, the primary sugar in milk, is composed of the monosaccharides *glucose* and *galactose* bound together. Refined white table sugar contains the disaccharide *sucrose*, which is a bond of glucose and fructose molecules.[12] Disaccharides, like monosaccharides, will dissolve in water.[13] Disaccharide sweeteners include maple syrup, date sugar, sorghum syrup, and maltose (malt sugar). Fruits naturally higher in sucrose include dates, apples, and bananas.[14]

Glucose   +   Fructose
(joined by an oxygen bond) =

SUCROSE

Galactose   +   Glucose
(joined by an oxygen bond) =

LACTOSE

Polysaccharides are formed when either monosaccarides or disaccharides are bound together by glycosidic bonds (a multiple-sugar molecule). Complex starches such as those found in rice, potatoes, wheat, and corn are composed of polysaccharides. When we eat carbohydrate-rich foods, the disaccharides and polysaccharides must be broken into simple sugars before our bodies can use them as energy. Starches are insoluble in water; to be digested they must undergo hydrolysis and be catalyzed by an enzyme called amylase, which breaks the glycosidic bonds. Humans and other animals have amylase, which enables them to digest starches.[15] Polysaccharide sweeteners include brown rice syrup and barley malt syrup.

WHEAT STARCH

Agave Nectar Compared to High-Fructose Corn Syrup

Many people have confused agave syrup with high-fructose corn syrup (HFCS), even suggesting that both syrups are made the same way. This myth stems from a misunderstanding of how agave syrup is made and the basic scientific facts. Agave nectar, fresh fruits, dried fruits, honey, fruit juices, and HFCS all contain fructose but that is their only similarity. Agave nectar and HFCS are not produced in the same way, do not have the same chemical composition, and are *not* the same product.

HFCS is made by soaking corn in water with sulphur dioxide. It is then milled through screens and washed repeatedly to remove all of the starch. The starch and water slurry is then treated with enzymes, potentially mercury-contaminated hydrochloric acid and/or caustic soda[16], to separate the complex starches (cornstarch) from other fibrous parts of the kernel. This process converts the complex starch molecules into simple sugars, or monosaccharides, and creates syrup made almost entirely of glucose.[17]

So, how is fructose created if there is no natural fructose in corn? A portion of the glucose syrup made from the starch is separated and then further processed with isomerase enzymes, pressure, heat, and controlled acidity in order to convert one kind of monosaccharide (glucose) into another form (fructose). The resulting fructose solution is then combined back into the glucose syrup in different proportions to create varieties of HFCS ranging from 42 percent, 55 percent, or 90 percent fructose. Because corn syrup is initially glucose, this man-made fructose syrup is considered "high-fructose" corn syrup.[18]

It isn't the process of converting complex starches into sugars that makes HFCS a less-than-ideal sweetener for the health-conscious consumer: many natural sweeteners, including honey, agave nectar, amasake, barley malt syrup, and brown rice syrup all use natural enzymatic action to convert complex starches into sugars. I don't recommend HFCS, however, because it is made from mass-produced, nonorganic, genetically modified corn that is highly processed with caustic chemicals and stripped of its nutrients under high heat and pressure. The resulting sweetener retains none of the vitamins, minerals, or nutritive properties of the whole food in its original form. When we consume refined sweeteners, devoid of trace vitamins and minerals, existing nutrient stores in our bodies are then depleted in order to metabolize them.[19] This can heavily deplete one's body over time.

Why choose agave over HFCS? Because, unlike high-fructose corn syrup, agave nectar has naturally occurring fructose and glucose. No harsh chemicals, genetically engineered foods, or artificial enzymes are used in its production, and it retains trace minerals. Organic agave nectar has a natural fructose content similar to fruits and other natural sweeteners, like honey. Below is a comparison of the common carbohydrates found in fruits, fruit juices, dried fruits, and the sweeteners fructose, glucose, and sucrose.

Table 2: Comparison of Saccharides in Agave Nectar to Fruits and Other Sweeteners [20]

Food/Drink/Isolated Sweetener Per 100 grams	% Fructose	% Glucose	% Sucrose
Pomegranate	5	5	0
Banana	5	5	2
Apple	6	2	2
Pear	6	3	1
Sweet Cherry	15	7	0
Grape Juice (unsweetened)	7	7	0
Grapes	8	7	0
Dried Figs	23	25	0
Raisins	28	30	0
Golden Raisins	33	38	0
Prunes	12	25	0
Dates	32	34	1
Honey (this figure is from 1987, before bees were commonly fed HFCS) [21]	42	33	1
Organic Amber Agave Nectar (Madhava) [22]	56	16	0
Organic Light Agave Nectar (Madhava)[23]	63	12	0
Organic Blue Agave Nectar (Wholesome Sweeteners)[24]	70	21	0
High-Fructose Corn Syrup (55)	42	31	0
High-Fructose Corn Syrup (90)	72	7	0
Pure Refined Fructose Powder	93	0	0
White Sugar	0	0	100

As seen in Table 2, agave nectar is made up of 56 to 70 percent fructose (depending on the variety), which is similar to its counterparts, honey and HFCS. It is more important, however, to put these figures into context. While it may be tempting to look to numbers to simplify the complexities of human nutrition, numbers can be misleading in determining what we consider "good" for us. It is helpful to consider a bigger picture: how are sweeteners manufactured? In what quantities are they consumed? What is the quality of each ingredient a sweetener is combined with? What do scientific studies reveal when examining the effects of sweeteners on our health?

Based on fructose content alone, we might determine that raisins, dates, and honey all pose serious health risks when compared to, say, a grape — so different are their fructose contents. Yet, humans have long consumed dried fruits and honey safely; neither food has been linked to epidemic cases of obesity. Looking only at fructose content is not nearly as valuable or informative as looking at all sweeteners in a broader context.

Table 3: Comparison of Fructose, Calories, and Glycemic Index of Foods[25]

Food Item	Fructose Content (in grams)	Calories	Glycemic Index
1 large banana	7	121	51
1 large apple	14	116	44
1 cup of grapes	12	104	49
1 cup grape juice	19	152	n/a
1 large pear	14	133	42
5 dried figs	10	105	61
1.5 ounce box of raisins	13	129	66
5 dates	38	332	62
1 Tablespoon honey	9	64	58
1 Tablespoon Madhava agave nectar	12	60	31
1 cup chamomile tea sweetened with 1 teaspoon honey	3	23	n/a
1 cup chamomile tea sweetened with 1 teaspoon Madhava organic amber agave nectar	4	22	n/a
½ cup vanilla pudding sweetened with honey (25% more honey needed to achieve the same sweetness in the recipe)	9	197	n/a
½ cup vanilla pudding sweetened with Madhava organic amber agave nectar	10	178	n/a
1 can coca-cola sweetened with high-fructose corn syrup	33	136	63

Table 3 compares the fructose content, calories, and glycemic index of various fruits and sweeteners. Note, in some cases, eating a serving of pudding sweetened with agave nectar contains less fructose than a small box of raisins. A single can of soda contains 33 grams of fructose, considerably more than other food items. A tablespoon of agave nectar contains slightly more fructose than a tablespoon of honey, yet it has a significantly lower glycemic index and fewer calories. These statistics help reveal how excessive fructose consumption may contribute to many health issues, especially when you consider the high intake of soda among Americans. Again, always consider things in context. Fruit and sweeteners, like agave nectar and honey, when used in moderation, are safe additions to a healthful diet.

Choosing a Quality Agave Nectar

It is always important to choose organic agave nectar from a reputable company focused on quality. It has been rumored that some commercial varieties of agave nectar contain cheap fillers, including HFCS; this practice occurs with other sweet products, like honey and maple syrup, too. Many pancake syrups labeled "maple" or "honey" flavor are actually sugar and corn syrup with artificial flavors. In recent years, honey bees have been fed sugar and HFCS to increase and economize the production of honey. Unfortunately, this is a common phenomenon in the sweetener industry, making it that much more important to stay informed. These questionable business practices reflect negatively even on the companies that sell 100 percent pure organic agave, maple syrup, and honey. As consumers, it is incumbent upon us to seek out pure products that are produced with integrity.

Fortunately, companies exist that do care about quality. I personally recommend Madhava and its products. Madhava has played a key role in the formation of the International Organic Agave Association. The IOAA provides on-site inspections and certifications in the agave production industry. The American Botanical Society has been invited to participate in these audits. Madhava has also freely provided other important data, including:

- Independent lab analysis from Warren Labs [26]
- Auditing from a strict third-party business called AIB International, a company "committed to protecting the safety of the food supply chain." [27]
- In-house quality control procedures

Other companies also sell 100 percent pure organic agave nectar without additives. When in doubt, do your homework and contact the company to ask them directly about their product.

Raw vs. Cooked Agave Nectar

The definition of "raw" agave is widely misunderstood to mean uncooked juice extracted directly from the plant or leaves of the agave. The industry standard for raw foods is processing at a maximum temperature of 118° Fahrenheit. Before the raw foods movement became popular, agave nectar was generally prepared at about 140° Fahrenheit. When demand for raw agave nectar emerged, agave producers experimented with preparing the syrup at lower temperatures. Raw, unprocessed aguamiel extracted directly from plants is not a liquid sweetener. In fact, aguamiel ferments rapidly and becomes pulque within 12 hours of extraction. To make agave nectar, aguamiel must be quickly transported to a processing facility. Agave nectar classified as raw is made from aguamiel with the standard heating process conducted at temperatures at or below 118° Fahrenheit and is richer in vitamins, minerals, and enzymes than other varieties.

Nutrition Facts

One serving (1 tablespoon) of agave nectar weighs 21 grams and contains 16 grams of total carbohydrates, a small portion of which is not digestible. One serving contains 68 units of caloric energy (calories), but a few of these calories are comprised of indigestible fructans. The total number of digestible calories per serving is close to 60.[28]

Table 4: Nutritional Profile of Agave Nectar

Serving Size: **1 Tablespoon**	
Calories	60
Total Fat	0g
Sodium	0g
Total Carbohydrate	16g
Sugars	16g
Protein	0g

Agave nectar is approximately 40 percent sweeter than sugar and contains trace minerals, including calcium, potassium, magnesium, and iron. It also contains Vitamins C, E, B2, B5, and B6.

Table 5: Agave Nectar Specifications[29]

(Analysis conducted by Warren Analytical Labs and Madhava)

Physical and Chemical	
Brix	75.1-75.7
pH	5-5.1
Moisture (%)	22.6-22.9
Protein (g/100g)	0.07
Dry Matter (%)	77.1-77.4
Density (g/ml)	1.38
Sodium (ppm)	8.8-13.2
Cholesterol (%)	0
Total Carbohydrates (%dm)	99.9
Inulin (g/100g)	0.67
Calories (/100g)	314
Calcium (mg/100g)	1
Iron (mg/100g)	0.05
Sodium (mg/100g)	1
Niacin (mg/100g)	<.03

Table 5: Agave Nectar Specifications[29]

Physical and Chemical (Cont.)	
Panothenic Acid-B5 (mg/100g)	<.04
Riboflavin-B2 (mg/100g)	0.01
Vitamin B6 (mg/100g)	<.001
Vitamin E (mg/100g)	<.5
Vitamin C (mg/100g)	1
Ash (% dm)	.06-.1
Fat (%)	0
Conductivity (uS)	14.1-14.6

Microbiological	
Total Aerobic Plate Count (CFU/g)	27-35
Yeast and Mold Count (CFU/g)	10
Total Coliforms (CFU/g)	0
E. Coli (CFU/g)	0
Staphylococcus Aureus (CFU/g)	0
Bacilus Cereus (CFU/g)	0
Salmonella (CFU/g)	0
Listeria (CFU/g)	0

Substituting Agave Nectar in Standard Recipes

Agave nectar can be easily incorporated into recipes that call for sugar or other sweeteners. Light varieties of agave have a more delicate and neutral taste. Dark varieties work well for recipes enhanced by deeper caramel and molasses flavors, such as baked beans, pumpkin pie, or banana bread. In general, most desserts taste best when light, mild-flavored agave is substituted; but try both to determine your personal preference. When substituting agave nectar in recipes, keep in mind that agave is sweeter than sugar and other sweeteners, so less is needed. This helps offset the slightly higher cost of agave and also reduces the calories in standard recipes. Be sure to compensate for the added liquid when substituting agave for dry sweeteners in your recipes. Keep the following tips in mind when you convert recipes:

✓ Use less agave nectar than sugar by volume.

✓ Decrease liquids by 33 percent or increase dry ingredients by 33 percent if you are replacing a dry sweetener with agave.

✓ Like honey, agave nectar burns more easily than sugar. If the original recipe calls for sugar, you may need to reduce the baking temperature by up to 50°Fahrenheit.

Sample Ingredient Conversion:

Chocolate Chip Cookies

½ cup unsalted butter

⅔ cup granulated sugar

1 teaspoon pure vanilla extract

¾ cup all-purpose flour

⅛ teaspoon baking powder

½ cup chunky chocolate pieces

2 eggs

We can improve this recipe in three ways, creating more healthful, satisfying, and delicious cookies:

✓   Replace the sugar with agave nectar.

✓   Replace the white flour (all-purpose flour) with whole grain flour.

✓   Replace the butter with healthful organic butter or another optimal source of fat (see "Fats" section on page 41).

Here is a revised recipe that will yield delicious chocolate chip cookies made with high-quality, healthful ingredients:

½ cup unsalted organic butter or organic palm shortening

~~⅔ cup granulated sugar~~   ½ cup agave nectar

1 teaspoon pure vanilla extract

~~¾ cup all-purpose flour, plus~~   ¾ cup oat flour

~~3 Tablespoons all-purpose flour~~

⅛ teaspoon baking powder

~~½ cup chunky chocolate pieces~~   ½ cup grain-sweetened chocolate chips

2 eggs

With practice, you will become comfortable substituting high-quality, healthful ingredients for typical flours, sugars, and oils. You may also find yourself eating fewer treats, because healthful treats are more satisfying and filling than processed foods. Most importantly, many people find that agave does not produce the same cravings and addiction as sugar. Be creative and explore. Allow yourself to learn by making a few mistakes and have fun. Try adding ingredients that appeal to your personal tastes and don't worry too much about adhering to the original recipe. You might fail, but you also might discover an amazing new recipe!

Please see *Converting Sweeteners to Agave* on the next page for exact conversion measurements.

Converting Sweeteners to Agave Nectar

Old Recipe with Sugar	New Recipe with Agave
1 Tablespoon (3 teaspoons)	2 teaspoons
2 Tablespoons (⅛ cup)	4 teaspoons (or 1 T + 1 t)
3 Tablespoons	2 Tablespoons
⅛ cup (2 Tablespoons)	4 teaspoons (or 1 T + 1 t)
¼ cup	8 teaspoons (or 2 T + 2 t)
⅓ cup	¼ cup
½ cup	⅓ cup
⅔ cup	7 Tablespoons or ¼ cup plus 3 Tablespoons
¾ cup	½ cup
1 cup (16 Tablespoons)	⅔ cup
2 cups	1 ⅓ cup
3 cups	2 cups

Old Recipe with Honey	New Recipe with Agave
1 Tablespoon (3 teaspoons)	¾ Tablespoon (2 ¼ teaspoons)
2 Tablespoons (⅛ cup)	1 ½ Tablespoons (4 ½ teaspoons)
3 Tablespoons	2 ¼ Tablespoons
⅛ cup (2 Tablespoons)	1 ½ Tablespoons
¼ cup	3 Tablespoons
⅓ cup	6 Tablespoons or ¼ cup plus 2 Tablespoons
½ cup	¼ cup
⅔ cup	½ cup
¾ cup	½ cup + 1 Tablespoon
1 cup (16 Tablespoons)	¾ cup
2 cups	1 ½ cups
3 cups	2 ¼ cups

Old Recipe with Corn Syrup	New Recipe with Agave
1 Tablespoon (3 teaspoons)	½ Tablespoon
2 Tablespoons (⅛ cup)	1 Tablespoon
3 Tablespoons	1 ½ Tablespoons
⅛ cup (2 Tablespoons)	1 Tablespoon
¼ cup	2 Tablespoons
⅓ cup	¼ cup
½ cup	2 Tablespoons plus 2 teaspoons
⅔ cup	5 Tablespoons plus 1 teaspoon
¾ cup	¼ cup plus 2 Tablespoons
1 cup (16 Tablespoons)	½ cup
2 cups	1 cup
3 cups	1 ½ cups

CHAPTER 2

THE BENEFITS OF USING AGAVE NECTAR

Why Switch to Agave Nectar? 28

Glycemic Index: Agave Nectar vs.
White Sugar and Other Sweeteners 28

Sugar Addiction: Replacing Sugar
with Agave Nectar 29

A Gentler Sweet in Children's Diets 30

Why Switch to Agave Nectar?

Not all sweeteners are alike — some are gentle on the body and others are not; therefore, it is important to be aware of the differences. There are many great reasons to include agave nectar in your diet. Agave is a more healthful alternative to refined sweeteners, like white sugar, brown sugar (white sugar with molasses added), artificial sweeteners, and high-fructose corn syrup. In addition, agave is easily digested and absorbed and does not cause radical spikes in blood sugar. Perhaps most importantly, agave is mild tasting, delicious, and easy to use in baking.

Many nutrition counselors favor sweeteners like brown rice syrup and barley malt syrup because they contain complex sugars (polysaccharides) and carbohydrates. These are easier on the body than refined sugars because they take longer to break down and are not absorbed directly into the bloodstream.[30] However, an overabundance of polysaccharides in the intestinal tract has been associated with a number of digestive problems. If these sugars are not adequately broken down and absorbed, they can stimulate an overgrowth of harmful microorganisms which in turn damage the intestinal wall and prevent absorption of vital nutrients. Those suffering from intestinal disorders, like Irritable Bowel Syndrome (IBS), may choose honey or agave which are made of the simple sugars (monosaccharides) fructose and glucose and are absorbed directly into the bloodstream.[31]

Fructose and glucose are isolated from complex starches through enzymatic action. The inulin in agave nectar is comprised of beneficial fructans, which promote good bacteria in the gut and inhibit the growth of harmful microorganisms. Agave nectar supports both stable blood sugar *and* digestive health. This makes agave an ideal choice for those suffering from diabetes, depression, mood swings, food allergies, heart disease, food addiction, and obesity. Agave nectar easily replaces other sweeteners without causing the typical cravings or "sugar buzz." It also dissolves easily into baked goods and beverages, without imparting the aftertaste of artificial sweeteners or the strong flavors of honey and grain-based syrups. Sweetening foods and drinks with agave can ease your transition into a healthier lifestyle in which you can enjoy occasional sweets without the side effects and mood swings of refined sugar.

Glycemic Index: Agave vs. White Sugar and Other Sweeteners

One of agave nectar's most important features is its relatively low glycemic index (GI). The glycemic index measures a food's effect on the level of blood sugar in the body. Carbohydrates that break down quickly during digestion are classified with a high GI, while foods that break down more slowly and release glucose at a more gradual rate are classified as low GI. According to the University of Sydney, one of the foremost authorities on glycemic index, individuals consuming a diet of low GI foods (with little effect on blood sugar) are at reduced risk for obesity, heart disease, and diabetes.[32] The American Diabetes Association also featured a study supporting this theory, conducted by the Clinical Nutrition Research Unit of Uppsala University, in which they determined that Type-2 diabetic patients have improved glycemic control, lipid profile, and fibrinolytic activity when following a diet with low-GI foods. The study concluded that the low-GI diet had therapeutic value to Type-2 diabetic patients.[33] A meta-analysis published by Barclay, et al. concludes, "low-GI diets are independently associated with a reduced risk of certain chronic diseases. In diabetes and heart disease, the protection is comparable with that seen for whole grain and high fiber intakes."[34] Agave does not stimulate digestive insulin secretion, drastically raise blood sugar levels, or create a sugar "rush."

Today, products on the market for diabetics often contain artificial sweeteners that are considered unsafe by some experts. Many studies conducted on artificial sweeteners have indicated an increased risk of cancer among rats, though the medical community has not yet demonstrated unequivocally that this risk extends to humans.[35] When considering widely varied, conflicting information, it is important to remember that any sweetener should be used in moderation and to choose those that are natural and have the least potentially harmful effects. While it is not advisable for diabetics to consume large quantities of any sweetener, agave, used in moderation, is a useful alternative to conventional sweeteners. Agave nectar delivers the added benefits of better flavor with no aftertaste and more uniform weight and consistency, which is easier to substitute in recipes. Simply put, agave nectar is an ideal sweetener for individuals mindful of the glycemic index of foods.

Table 6: Glycemic Index Comparison [36]

Sweetener	Glycemic Index
Sugar (sucrose)	58-84
Agave nectar	11-32 (varies depending on the producer and plant type)
Honey	44-58
Maple Syrup	54
Apple	44
Dates	31-62
Banana	47-62
Maltitol	73
High Fructose Corn Syrup	Similar to sucrose (precise values have not been published)

Sugar Addiction: Replacing Sugar with Agave Nectar

Once considered a luxury food, consumption of refined white sugar has steadily increased since its inception in the 1700s. During the industrial revolution sugar became readily accessible; by 1874, the annual consumption of white sugar increased to an average of 37 pounds per person in the U.S. By 1887, annual consumption rose to 61 pounds per person.[37] From 1860-1960 the fat consumption in western civilization increased by less than 50 percent while sugar consumption had more than doubled.[38] Perhaps most troubling, by 2005 Americans annually consumed over 120 pounds of sugar per person, well exceeding government standards of safe consumption.[39]

Sugar has become one of the most socially normalized addictions. Millions of people experience uncontrollable cravings and the cyclical blood sugar swings caused by excessive sugar consumption. Refined sugar can be habit forming and challenging to eliminate, so much so, that it has been compared to drug addiction. Studies show that diets rich in sugar contribute to many health problems, including nutritional deficiency, diabetes, hypoglycemia, tooth decay, hyperactivity in children, heart disease, and obesity.[40]

Sugar appears in many products on the market today from sodas and ice cream to cookies, cereals, baked goods, and other desserts. But sugar is also found where we least expect it.

Sugar is added to ketchup, salad dressings, breads, meats, canned foods, frozen foods, juices, yogurt, sauces, and soups — just to name a few. Nearly any commercial product you can imagine is likely to contain sugar or high-fructose corn syrup. Even products in health food stores often contain sugar labeled as "evaporated cane juice." Take time to read labels. Awareness is the key to choosing foods that are free of sugars. Recently, many products have emerged that are sweetened with agave nectar instead of sugar, such as ketchup, ice cream, granola, and energy bars. If you are unable to find agave-sweetened products, you can either make them yourself or buy unsweetened products and add your own sweetener.

One of the most significant benefits of agave I have observed in my nutrition counseling practice is that, unlike sugar, it does not cause addiction, mood swings, or obvious spikes in blood sugar. I have witnessed the amazement of more than a thousand clients as they have made the switch to agave nectar. Clients who had reported feeling jittery, spacey, moody, and having low energy after eating sugary foods found that they experienced a balanced calm after eating foods sweetened with agave. Clients also noted the "satisfying sweetness" of agave and a reduction of sugar cravings.

"My daily sugar habit gave me constant migraines, but I was so addicted to sugar that I preferred headaches to quitting! When I finally realized that sugar was making me chronically sick, I substituted agave everywhere I'd been using sugar. My craving for sweets diminished after a month. Now, two years later, I'm sugar- and migraine-free, thanks to agave. As a sweet freak, I can comfortably say that agave helped save my health without sacrificing my sanity." Andrea, age 30, Boulder, CO

The fact that agave nectar has a low glycemic index may contribute to its nonaddictive qualities. A medical hypothesis from Thornley, et al. says, "GI may be the key mediator of the addictive potential of food." They conclude, "Just as slow release forms of nicotine help smokers recover from addiction, low GI foods may reduce cravings in obese or overweight populations."[41]

Agave Nectar in Children's Diets

If you are a parent, you are likely aware of the high quantity of sugar that exists in many children's diets today. Many studies have shown a direct correlation between sugar consumption and the dramatic rise of childhood obesity, hyperactivity, and attention deficit hyperactivity disorder (ADHD). In *Feeding the Brain: How Food Affects Children*, Keith Connor states that "Children who consume more than 25 percent of their daily calories as sugar show poorer attention and concentration, one of the key symptoms of ADHD. Compared with a group of children consuming less sugar calories, those who consumed more sugar also exhibited more aggressive behaviors.[42] Particularly concerning is the connection between the rise in consumption of soft drinks and obesity which are reaching epidemic proportions in pediatric medicine today."[43]

Today, many cookbooks address the possibilities of sugar substitution, offering healthful alternatives, such as stevia, applesauce, brown rice syrup, honey, and mashed fruit. I recommend these sweeteners for their health benefits, but they often yield mediocre results in terms of taste, texture, and appearance. Kids can tell the difference and may not be very excited about "healthy" treats that aren't tasty. After trying just a few of these alternative sweets, they may roll their eyes and beg to have their after-school snacks at a friend's house, where they know they can have a "real" cookie. This book presents a more effective strategy: Try offering nutritious desserts that appeal to your child's palate and he'll actually eat them! The recipes in this book will inspire you to create yummy sweets and drinks for your children that are sweetened with agave nectar. Agave does not have a strong flavor, yet imparts a delicious sweetness that kids enjoy. You can relax knowing you are offering a wholesome treat, while they enjoy the treats without feeling like they are missing out. In fact, kids can often tell the difference between how they feel after eating sugar and how they feel after eating an agave-sweetened treat. You can foster their awareness of this by creating a game to find out how they feel after eating sugar versus agave. This is a great exercise for adults, too.

Kid's Exercise: What Do You Notice in Your Body?

Explain to your child that you want to experiment with treats and you would like to play a game together.

Day 1: Have a sugary snack, like a cookie, pudding, cake, or ice cream.

Together, write down what you like about the treat and what you don't. Explain that in this exercise, we are looking not only at how things taste, but how they feel, too.

After eating the treat, keep a log of how your bodies feel, noticing overall energy, concentration, feeling "light-headed" versus calm and grounded (fluctuations in blood sugar), feeling good versus feeling bad, and feeling satisfied versus wanting more.

Record how you feel in the log below:

- 10 minutes after
- 30 minutes after
- 1 hour after

Day 2: Prepare an equivalent kind of treat from this cookbook using agave sweetener. If you had a cookie on day one, then make cookies. If you had ice cream, make ice cream.

Together, write down what you like about it, and what you don't.

Record how you feel in the log below:

- 10 minutes after
- 30 minutes after
- 1 hour after

Continue the exercise, alternating between sugar and agave for as long as you like. Evaluate your logs together, honestly exploring what your child thinks of the agave-sweetened treats. Allowing your child to make her own observations will help her discover the connections between what she eats and how she feels firsthand.

CHAPTER 3

THE BENEFITS OF USING QUALITY INGREDIENTS

Why Organic?..................... 34

Why Whole Grain Flours?.......... 39

Why Good Fats? 41

Why Quality Salts? 43

Why Organic?

Perhaps the number one thing to consider when committing to good health is diet. Chronic and prevalent health conditions are regularly linked to poor nutrition. Many cookbooks will advocate for a healthful or trendy ingredient by providing recipes with substitutions for that ingredient, while, at the same time, combining them with poor-quality ingredients, like canola oil, soy, white flour, or sugar. This book goes one step further, integrating agave nectar into recipes created in the larger context of holistic nutrition, which includes whole and organic foods, superfoods, healing herbs, whole grain flours, and high-quality fats and salts. You will find delicious options that take health into consideration—desserts *can* be satisfying *and* contain nutritious ingredients. Some of the ingredients may be new to you; I invite you to explore the *Resources* section (page 425) and the *Ingredients Glossary* (page 407), which describe these ingredients and offer information on finding them online or in health food stores.

Organic food production and consumption have exploded over the last decade, gaining popularity because organic foods are free of toxins that adversely affect our health. The quality, taste, and nutritional value of organic foods far exceed that of mass-produced products, and the cost has become comparable, especially when purchasing foods that are in season. We save money by eliminating mass-produced, packaged, and "convenience" food products sold in small quantities. Times are changing, and this chapter will address the key reasons behind the continued growth of the organic foods movement. When we choose organic in the marketplace, we cast a vote in favor of the health of our bodies as well as the health of our planet.

What Is Organic?

The organic movement evolved from the observation that better soils yield more nutritious foods. Organic farmers adhere to several basic tenets of production. They maintain and plant in nutrient-rich soil, eliminate chemical fertilizers and contaminants, and manage the land to support a biodiverse, healthy ecosystem.

Organic gardeners use numerous methods to accomplish these goals, which may include:

- **Composting**
- **Planting ground covers such as clover to retain water and maintain nitrogen content**
- **Reintroducing beneficial insects to their habitat**
- **Planting crops along field borders to retain water naturally**

It is well established that these methods protect and retain topsoil. They also improve nutrient levels that carry over to subsequent crops. Organically farmed, nutrient-rich soil naturally retains more moisture and requires less water. Organically produced plants are more resistant to disease, and beneficial insects help control threatening insects without the use of chemical pesticides. Composting and introduction of diverse plants and animals maintains carbon and nutrient content in the soil. In this way, organic gardening may actually help reduce carbon dioxidemiss emissions by sequestering carbon back into the soil, preventing its release into the atmosphere.

The USDA National Organic Standards Board (NOSB) Definition of Organic:

- Organic agriculture is an ecological production management system that promotes and enhances biodiversity, biological cycles and soil biological activity. It is based on minimal use of off-farm inputs and on management practices that restore, maintain and enhance ecological harmony.
- Organic is a labeling term that denotes products produced under the authority of the Organic Foods Production Act. The principal guidelines for organic production are to use materials and practices that enhance the ecological balance of natural systems and that integrate the parts of the farming system into an ecological whole.
- Organic agriculture practices cannot ensure that products are completely free of residues; however, methods are used to minimize pollution from air, soil and water.
- Organic food handlers, processors and retailers adhere to standards that maintain the integrity of organic agricultural products. The primary goal of organic agriculture is to optimize the health and productivity of interdependent communities of soil life, plants, animals and people.[44]

Top Ten Reasons For Going Organic (From www.Organic.org)

1. **You protect future generations throughout the world**
2. **You pay the real cost of real food**
3. **You gain more vitamins and minerals from your food**
4. **You protect water quality**
5. **You enjoy great flavor and nutrition**
6. **You keep chemicals off your plate and out of your body**
7. **You reduce global warming and save energy**
8. **You help prevent soil erosion**
9. **You help small farmers**
10. **You help restore and maintain biodiversity**

Our personal reasons for choosing organic are as varied as our tastes in music. We may choose organic to avoid chemical contaminants because we believe chemical exposure is detrimental to maintaining a healthy body. We may be concerned about the health of the earth our children and grandchildren will inherit. We may prefer flavorful and nutritious foods, and find that organic and locally-grown foods are more fresh and ripe than mass-produced foods shipped from remote destinations before reaching their peak of ripeness. The rising popularity of organic products has leveraged economies of scale to bring costs down in recent years as well. And if cost is a concern, you can prioritize certain organic foods to get the most "bang" out of your organic buck.

Organic Foods to Prioritize

Dairy and Meats

Given the choice, make organic meat, butter, and dairy products a priority in your diet. These foods, if not organic, are high in pesticides, chemicals, antibiotics, growth hormones, and even radioactive isotopes absorbed by plants from nutrient-deficient soil.[45] These toxins then accumulate in the fatty tissues of animals that ingest them.[46] Organic plants absorb vital nutrients from healthy soil and dairy products rendered from animals fed on organic grasses are rich in fat-soluble vitamins. Choosing organic dairy and meats is especially important for young children, whose bodies are still growing and are highly susceptible to the impacts of toxins. While I don't specify "organic butter" in these recipes, use organic butter whenever possible. I also strongly recommend seeking out sources of raw, unpasteurized, nonhomogenized dairy products, whenever you can get them. Pasteurization destroys the naturally occurring enzymes in dairy products, that help the body to assimilate the calcium in milk. After pasteurization, chemicals and synthetic vitamins are reintroduced to enhance the flavor and restore some of the nutrients lost during pasteurization. It's worth the extra money to find organic, grass-fed, unpasteurized dairy products in your state. [47] See *Resources* on page 425 for more information.

Organic Fruits and Vegetables

Purchase and support organic agriculture whenever possible. If you are unable to purchase only organic produce, it's helpful to know which commercially produced fruits and vegetables are the safest. Certain plants are highly absorbent and therefore more likely to contain elevated levels of chemicals. The following list will help you determine which fruits and vegetables to prioritize on your shopping list.

Table 7: Prioritizing Organic Produce [48]

PRODUCE HIGHEST IN PESTICIDES (TOP PRIORITY TO BUY ORGANIC)	PRODUCE LOWEST IN PESTICIDES (LOWER PRIORITY TO BUY ORGANIC)
Apple	Asparagus
Bell Pepper	Avocado
Carrot	Broccoli
Celery	Cabbage
Cherries	Eggplant
Grapes (Imported)	Kiwi
Kale	Mango
Lettuce	Onion
Nectarine	Papaya
Peach	Pineapple
Pear	Sweet Corn
Strawberries	Sweet Peas
	Tomato
	Watermelon

Organic Offers Higher Nutritional Value

When we choose whole, natural foods, we benefit from their maximum nutrition and healing properties. The cancer-fighting antioxidants in fresh foods such as Vitamin C and Vitamin E have been shown to detoxify the body. Recent reports confirm that organic crops contain 25 to 80 percent more of these valuable nutrients than their commercially produced counterparts.[49] See Table 8 below.

Table 8: Antioxidant Content in Organic and Commerical Produce

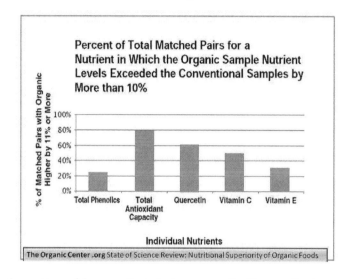

Antioxidants fight the action of free radicals in human cells. Free radicals are simply stray atoms that have lost electrons due to damage from radiation, chemical pollutants, or a chemical process.[50] The "rogue" electrons seek atoms to bond with, which wreaks havoc on the tissues and systems in the body (see the "Fats" section on page 41). Dr. Mark Percival notes that free radicals significantly contribute to aging and over-50 degenerative diseases.[51] Fortunately, antioxidants in all forms (flavonoids, carotenoids, phytosterols, and others) have been proven to bind with free radicals and stabilize them. This explains their demonstrated anti-mutagenic, anti-carcinogenic, and anti-aging properties. [52]

A study published by the Organic Food Center in 2008 exhaustively examined the specific components of organic plants using matched pairs of plants produced by commercial standards. The team concluded that "the consumption of organic fruits and vegetables . . . offered significant health benefits, roughly equivalent to an additional serving of a moderately nutrient dense fruit or vegetable on an average day." [53]

Armed with this information, we can confidently replace expensive supplements with fresh, wholesome, and organic foods. The 2008 report confirmed the higher nutrient content in organic produce, quelling debate over the nutritional advantage of organic foods. This study also found that organic produce contains "fewer undesirable compounds like mycotoxins, gycoalkaloids, cadmium and nickel."[54] Though studies examining the relative benefits of organic produce have been underemphasized in recent years, the Journal of Environmental Quality states, "Soon there will be enough high quality studies to reach the threshold of eight valid matched pairs for several more nutrients." [55]

The Pleasure of Real Food

Organic produce has a richer, sweeter, and deeper taste than commercial produce. Vital nutrients absorbed from the sun, water, and nutrient-rich soil contribute immeasurably to its texture and flavor. If you have ever tasted an organic, locally-grown tomato in the summer compared to a commercial tomato in the winter, you understand the difference. Even the contrast between conventional and organic raisins can be drastic. From a taste perspective alone, organic and locally grown produce is often the superior choice.

Organic for the Environment and Future Generations

Many varieties of fruits and vegetables that our parents enjoyed have disappeared from today's grocery aisles. Traditional and heirloom produce is slowly experiencing a resurgence among small, sustainable farms, but it may be years before wide-scale, sustainable organic farming can deliver a wide variety of traditional foods to every market in the U.S. By supporting the pioneers of organic gardening today, we are fostering a new paradigm for the next generation. Below is a short list of the challenges left for the next generation.

Global Warming

The Rodale Institute was among the first organizations to suggest that organic gardening can be used to mitigate global warming by decreasing fossil fuel emissions and sequestering carbon in the soil. Other prominent sources now provide evidence confirming this thesis. One USDA document states that the "environmental benefits of organic farming include reduced energy consumption, reduced erosion, higher carbon sequestration, no depletion of fertility, and reduced nutrient leaching." [56]

Water Scarcity

In addition to polluting our bodies, unsustainable farming practices are contaminating our water supply with pesticides and run-off from fertilizers. Purchasing organic products supports sustainable farming practices which can greatly alleviate this problem. Organic farms do not leach nitrates into our waterways or into our drinking water, which can pose significant risks for children, especially babies who may present with "blue baby" syndrome. The U.S. Department of Health's Agency for Toxic Substances and Disease Registry finds that, "In agricultural areas, nitrogen-based fertilizers are a major source of contamination for shallow groundwater aquifers that provide drinking water." [57] The Food and Agriculture Organization of the United Nations Agriculture and Consumer Protection Department further states that, "eliminating the use of synthetic nitrogenous fertilizer greatly lowers the risk of nitrogen contamination of water." [58]

Biodiversity

After leaving the White House, Lady Bird Johnson embarked upon a campaign to restore wildflower populations along highways and roads in Texas. This movement is now flourishing nationwide. But why did the wildflowers disappear? In the years immediately following the development of our transportation infrastructure, it was believed that natural flora was detrimental. During the 1950s, the use of herbicides replaced paid labor to protect pavement by eradicating potentially invasive plant life. [59] A report by the Transportation Research

Board confirms that chemical eradication with herbicides was still widely used during the 80s.[60] Fortunately, many states have now banned the use of herbicides.[61] We now recognize the benefits of wildflowers, which attract insects that pollinate neighboring crops and ingest damaging insects. Wildflower reemergence is both practically and aesthetically beneficial. Reintegrating native species has become widespread in recent years because it resolves erosion along highways and eliminates one major source of pollution in drinking water.

Organic farming also has far-reaching effects on the biodiversity of our environment. These practices support animal populations which have drastically declined in industrialized countries such as birds, bats, and beneficial insects. These species play an important role in naturally controlling pests without the use of chemical pesticides.[62] The mass production of corn, wheat, and soy in recent years has edged out diverse varieties of vegetables and fruits that may cost more to produce commercially or spoil during shipping over long distances. The unique characteristics of these little-known varieties are highly favored among organic gardeners, who share and collect the heirloom seeds of diverse crops that have never been genetically modified for mass-production. We support the diversity of varieties available for future generations when we buy organic produce.

Soil Erosion

Recent studies have revealed the mechanisms by which synthetic nitrogen fertilizers damage farmlands and surrounding waterways. This realization is eye-opening to chemical engineers whose intent was to increase carbon absorption and soil fertility with synthetic nitrogen. The distinctions between synthetic nitrogen and organic, carbon-rich nitrogen in compost is not currently understood and warrants further study; however, the existing evidence shows that synthetic fertilizer reduces both nitrogen and carbon in topsoil. The result, according to researchers at the University of Illinois, is that "injured soil becomes prone to compaction, which makes it vulnerable to runoff and erosion and limits the growth of stabilizing plant roots." Their study demonstrates the need to eradicate industrial farming practices, which erode top soil, leach nitrates into waterways, and deplete moisture from existing farmland.[63]

There is mounting evidence that the use of pesticides to eradicate unwanted pests through chemical means damages our soil. Organic gardener and author Elizabeth Stell states, "Pesticides kill soil organisms as well as pests, but killing soil organisms impairs soil health and therefore makes grasses even more susceptible to insects and diseases."[64]

To learn more about organic foods and farming, check out the *Resources* on page 425.

Why Whole Grain Flours?

I could not overlook the importance of whole grains while writing a book promoting the use of agave nectar instead of sugar. The recipes in this book have replaced white flour (also called unbleached wheat flour) with whole grain flours such as oat, barley, brown rice, millet, kamut, and whole wheat. Each whole grain has its own set of nutritional and healing benefits, which you may research in the *Glossary of Ingredients* on page 407. Using whole grain flours certainly adds an interesting challenge to baking that may take some time to master; but whole grains are well worth it — they contain more fiber, vitamins, and minerals. Nutritional deficiencies can cause cravings, so you may notice a decrease in your desire to eat sweets when you bake with wholesome ingredients.[65] Whole grain flours support a lifestyle of embracing whole, natural foods.

You may be wondering, "What's wrong with processed wheat flour or white flour?" White flour is made by stripping away the outer parts (the bran and the germ) from the whole wheat berry to isolate the inner white part of the grain (the endosperm). This process removes the vitamins, nutrients, and fiber. The end product is devoid of nutritional value.[66] In fact, digestion of refined white flour actually requires the body to flush out toxins and process simple starches and further depletes its existing vitamin and mineral reserves.[67] Food producers compound the irony by adding artificial vitamins and minerals back into the product to "enrich" it because otherwise it could not legally be sold as "food."[68] What explains the rising popularity of white flour over the last century? The answer is simple—longevity. White flour is lifeless and therefore has a much longer shelf life, making it significantly cheaper than whole grain flours. Given its detrimental health effects, you may want to consider choosing only whole grain flours in your diet.

Another important consideration is the long-term impact of white flour consumption on the body. The body's response to a teaspoon of sugar and a slice of white bread are, in terms of the endocrine response, largely similar — simple carbohydrates immediately enter the bloodstream as sugars when consumed and cause the pancreas to deliver a quick shot of insulin.[69] A regular diet of sugar and white flour may lead to chronic constipation, low energy, depression, and unstable blood sugar, which can lead to hypoglycemia or diabetes.[70]

In addition to depleting the body of vital nutrients and causing a blood-sugar imbalance, consumption of refined white flour can produce symptoms like low energy, weight gain, eczema, and acne, among others. These symptoms are triggered primarily by the gluten in processed wheat, which is genetically engineered and vastly different from its ancient form (see *Gluten-free Flours* below). Several ancient varieties of wheat, such as kamut and spelt, have not been mass produced or genetically engineered; the starch molecules in these products are essentially unchanged, thereby causing fewer allergic reactions.[71]

It is important to note that because whole grain flours retain the beneficial essential oils in the germ, they tend to spoil more quickly than heavily refined flours. Using a grain mill or Vita-mix to grind whole wheat berries into fresh flour ensures freshness and also retains the highest nutrient content. If you choose to buy prepared whole grain flours, refrigerate or freeze them to prevent rancidity.

This book provides the tools to start practicing baking and cooking with whole grain flours. Using whole grain flours will enhance a healthful lifestyle, providing vital nutrients to you and your family.

Gluten-Free Flours

Within the category of whole grains, there is another distinct group: gluten-free whole grain flours (see Table 9 on next page). Gluten is a protein found in wheat, rye, spelt, kamut, and barley. Oats are technically gluten free but are commonly adulterated with gluten during processing; to be certain buy oats labeled gluten free. Studies have shown that individuals with Celiac disease, autism, or attention deficit hyperactivity disorder have significantly reduced symptoms when avoiding gluten in their diet.[72] Others find that even without the diagnosis of these conditions, they prefer eating gluten-free foods to avoid symptoms such as lethargy, achy joints and muscles, depression, skin problems, allergies, weight gain, and digestive complaints. You may want to consider finding out whether or not you are sensitive to gluten by eliminating it entirely from your diet for two weeks and noticing whether or not you experience any changes in your body. You can then reintroduce gluten and pay attention to changes. If you feel better without gluten, then try the gluten-free recipes in this book. They are marked with this symbol: (GF)

Why Good Fats?

Fats, particularly animal fats like butter and lard, have received a bad rap in the United States over the past century. Obesity in the U.S. skyrocketed during the past several decades, especially among children; but this cannot be blamed entirely on fats.[73] Most Americans, including mainstream dieticians and medical professionals, accept the common doctrine associating animal fat with obesity, heart disease, and cancer; the majority of the data, however, strongly suggest otherwise — especially studies comparing the diets of indigenous people around the world with the diets of people living in industrialized societies.[74] In fact, when considered holistically, the greater body of research strongly suggests that obesity and other health problems are caused by refined sugar, highly processed flour products, and bad fats. Diets too low in fat can actually be harmful and consumption of certain kinds of fats — "good" fats — is absolutely essential to brain function, immunity, stable blood sugar, and overall good health.[75]

Not all fats are created equal. Some are rich in vital nutrients, while others contain harmful properties. Additionally, healthful fats can deteriorate through processing or improper storage. Fats can be generally defined as organic substances comprised of fatty acids which do not dissolve in water. Fat molecules are formed by fatty acid chains of carbon and hydrogen atoms. Fats are separated into three categories based on the structure of their chains — *saturated,* monounsaturated, and polyunsaturated. The bonds between carbon and hydrogen in saturated fats are stable, which make the fats solid at room temperature. Unsaturated fats contain unstable bonds which make them liquid at room temperature; when these bonds break down, fat becomes rancid.[76]

Contrary to popular belief, high-quality **saturated fats** are actually more healthful than unsaturated fats for several reasons. When looking at the picture of an unsaturated fat molecule (see Fig.1), the double bond between the atoms (trailing down to the right) becomes unstable when exposed to heat and breaks apart, forming free radicals. Unsaturated fats (i.e., free radicals) oxidize and turn the oil rancid. When you consume rancid oil, the free radicals bond with existing fat cells and cause major health issues. For example, free radicals will disrupt DNA and RNA function thereby compromising the immune system.

In addition to their relative stability, high-quality saturated fats contain vital fat-soluble nutrients such as vitamins A, D, E, and K. They also contain antioxidants which

Table 9:
Gluten-Free Flours
Amaranth
Arrowroot
Bean
Buckwheat
Chickpea
Coconut
Corn
Flax seed
Millet
Oats (check label)
Potato flour and starch
Quinoa
Rice
Sorghum
Tapioca
Teff

Figure 1: Saturated and Unsaturated Fatty Acid Chain[77]

protect against damage from free radicals. Finally, stable saturated fats aid the body's absorption of fat-soluble vitamins in other foods. Examples of saturated fats: butter, butterfat contained in dairy products (milk, cream, and cheese), coconut oil, and animal fats (goose and chicken fats). The highest nutritional content can be found in certified organic dairy products produced from grass-fed animals.[79]

Monounsaturated fats have one double bond, while **polyunsaturated fats** have multiple double bonds. Monounsaturated fats are found in vegetable oils which are liquid at room temperature. Olive oil is high in monounsaturated fat and becomes solid when refrigerated. It also withstands heat better than polyunsaturated fats. Polyunsaturated fats include sunflower, safflower, and canola oil. These vegetable oils are the most unstable and their molecules break down or "oxidize" easily in the presence of heat and light. They are often degraded by chemical extraction and refinement done at high heat which depletes the nutrients and turns the fat rancid.[80]

The most damaging form of commercial, polyunsaturated fats are **hydrogenated fats**, or **transfats**, which are available in the forms of margarine and vegetable shortening. Hydrogenation is the process whereby polyunsaturated oil is mixed with traces of metal and treated with hydrogen gas at high pressure. This creates an artificial bond between the hydrogen atoms and the available carbon atoms, which makes the fat solid at room temperature. This process makes the fat rancid. The fat must then be bleached and artificially flavored to mask its rancid flavor and appearance. These fats are highly unstable and have been directly linked with heart disease and cancer.[81]

Table 10: Recommended Oils for Baking

Oils	% Saturated Fat	% Monounsaturated Fat	% Polyunsaturated Fat
Organic Butter	63	29	4
Coconut Oil	92	6	2
Palm Oil	45	41	8
Olive Oil	13	74	8
Grapeseed Oil	11	16	72
Cocoa Butter	57	29	1
Sesame Oil	14	39	41

Table 11: Heat-Sensitive Oils to Avoid

Oils	% Saturated Fat	% Monounsaturated Fat	% Polyunsaturated Fat
Canola Oil	7	59	29
Corn Oil	13	24	59
Soybean Oil	15	24	58
Sunflower Oil	12	20	63
Safflower	10	13	72
Margarine	17	49	34

(all fat composition data retrieved from Wikipedia.com)

The best sources of saturated fats are organic, grass-fed dairy products, including butter, cheese, ghee, organic coconut oil, and palm oil. All saturated fats are very stable at high heat except butter, which burns easily because it contains milk solids. The fat content in butter is extremely stable, which is why clarified butter or "ghee" is excellent for cooking and frying.

The best sources of mono- and polyunsaturated fats are organic, minimally processed, cold-pressed vegetable oils. Be sure to choose cold-pressed oils in dark or opaque containers and store them in a cool place to prevent spoilage. Ideally, these oils should be used within six months of purchase. Polyunsaturated oils are the most unstable and spoil easily. The polyunsaturated fats listed should be avoided if possible, *especially* hydrogenated fats. Despite its recent popularity, canola oil is also important to avoid as it is made from rapeseeds which are highly processed, laden with pesticides, and extremely volatile. Organic canola oil is available, but not recommended due to the deleterious compounds naturally occurring in rapeseeds.[82]

The topic of good versus bad fats is complex and warrants further reading. Good fats are essential to good health and support many vital functions of the body. They are also indispensable in baking delicious, satisfying whole grain breads and desserts.

Why Quality Salts?

Throughout this book you will notice that I refer to "high-quality salt." Table salt and higher quality natural mineral salts differ significantly enough to warrant mention. Choosing quality ingredients for cooking and baking is important — and this applies to salt as well. Mainstream nutritional doctrine often dictates the restriction of salt in our diets. However, most experts agree that some sodium is essential to human life. Its presence in our bodies regulates many biochemical processes at the molecular level, such as maintaining fluid balance in cells, muscular functioning, nerve stimulation, and maintenance of proper acid-alkaline balance in the blood.[83] Many other minerals such as calcium, iodine, magnesium, potassium, and phosphorus operate in tandem to support these essential body functions, and our diets must include these vital nutrients in the proper balance to support good health. While many foods contain trace amounts of sodium and other complementary minerals, nonorganic foods grown in depleted soil are less likely to contain trace minerals such as calcium and magnesium. Therefore, while our ancestors may not have needed supplementary salt or minerals in their diets, our modern diets are often lacking in crucial nutrients. This may explain in part why we crave additional salt in our foods.[84]

Excessive intake of sodium, as with that of any nutrient, can lead to health problems. It has been associated with cardiovascular disease, hypertension, and kidney disorders.[85] Natural, unrefined sea salt in its raw form contains about 82-86 percent sodium chloride, 12-16 percent macrominerals, like magnesium, and up to 80 distinct trace minerals. In particular, the presence of sodium and magnesium in proper balance support proper absorption of each nutrient and do not inhibit proper bodily functions (magnesium plays a critical role in cardiovascular functioning). The role of these trace minerals in human health is only beginning to be examined and understood as is the distinction of natural, organic minerals versus their synthetic counterparts. Some research suggests that traces of organic iodine found in natural sea salt remain in the body far longer than synthetic iodine contained in refined salt.[86]

Refined salt, by contrast, is chemically processed at extremely high temperatures, which removes most of the beneficial, naturally occurring trace elements. Harmful additives such as aluminum compounds are then added to make the end product dry and pourable. Naturally occurring iodine is then replaced with potassium iodide and stabilized with dextrose, discoloring the salt. Finally the product is bleached to pure white. Even some "natural" salts mined from land sources are relatively low in trace minerals due to absence of nutrients at the source. The USDA standard for "table salt" is no less than 97.5 percent sodium chloride (NaCl) compared to most unrefined natural sea salts, which contain 82-86 percent NaCl. This significant concentration of sodium in table salt can cause severe imbalances in the body which can result in cravings and health problems.

The highest quality sea salts are extracted from the sea and dried naturally in the sun and contain less than 95 percent NaCl. There is also a natural, unrefined salt called "Real Salt", that is mined from natural land sources near Redmond, Utah and contains about 98 percent NaCl. Unrefined salt is naturally grey, pink, or red in color, reflecting the existence of trace minerals and nutrients. Many products labeled "sea salt" are actually refined and contain additives, so check the label carefully. Table 11 compares the mineral content in commercially available, unrefined natural salts. Check the glossary for more information.

Table 12: Mineral Content In Commerically Available Salts

Mineral Content	Celtic Sea Salt Light Grey Celtic [87]	Redmond Trading Co. RealSalt (Utah) [88]	Himalayan Pink Salt [89]	Refined Table Salt [90]
Bromide	0.024100%	0.002060%	0.000210%	0.0%
Calcium	0.090000%	0.497000%	0.405000%	0.09%
Chloride	53.750000%	60.070000%	59.093000%	0.0%
Copper	0.000004%	0.000028%	0.000056%	0.0005%
Fluoride	0.000560%	0.001380%	0.010000%	0.0%
Iron	0.003510%	0.052200%	0.003890%	0.0005%
Magnesium	0.460000%	0.091500%	0.016000%	0.012%
Phosphorus	0.000008%	0.008910%	0.000010%	0.0%
Potassium	0.120000%	0.103000%	0.350000%	0.0%
Sodium	32.890000%	37.900000%	38.261000%	99% (NaCl)
Strontium	0.005700%	0.005280%	0.001400%	0.0%
Sulfur / Sulfate	1.040000%	0.260000%	1.240000%	0.17%
Zinc	0.000106%	0.000093%	0.000238%	0.0%
Chemical Additives (bleach, anti-caking agents such as aluminum silicate, etc.)	0.0%	0.0%	0.0%	.75%
Total Sodium Chloride (NaCl):	**86.460000%**	**97.970000%**	**97.35000%**	**99%**

CHAPTER 4

GETTING STARTED WITH THE BASICS

Stocking Your Kitchen 46

Helpful Appliances and Tools to
Have on Hand. 47

How to Measure. 48

The Ingredients 49

Guide to Gluten-Free Recipes
by Chapter 50

Stocking Your Kitchen:
Products You'll Use in this Book

A well-stocked and organized kitchen can help create an enjoyable cooking experience. For bulk goods like flours and nuts, I highly recommend keeping them in well-labeled, airtight, glass jars to ensure freshness and ease of identification. The following list is a great guide to stocking your pantry and kitchen for the recipes in this book.

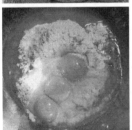

DRY GOODS PANTRY
- Agave nectar
- Amaranth flour
- Arrowroot
- Baking powder (sulfur-free)
- Baking soda
- Barley flour
- Brown rice flour
- Brown rice syrup
- Buttermilk powder
- Carob powder
- Cocoa powder
- Coconut flour
- Coconut milk
- Coconut, shredded
- Corn flour
- Cornmeal
- Cream of Tartar
- Date sugar
- Guar gum
- Kamut flour
- Maple syrup
- Millet flour
- Molasses (Black Strap, unsulfured)
- Oat flour
- Quinoa flour
- Salt (pink and grey varieties have the highest mineral content)
- Sorghum flour
- Spelt flour
- Tapioca flour
- Teff flour
- Whey powder
- White rice flour
- Whole wheat flour
- Whole wheat pastry flour
- Xanthan gum

SUPERFOODS
- Cacao powder (raw)
- Chia seeds
- Flax seeds
- Goji berries
- Hemp seeds
- Maca powder
- Medicinal mushroom powders (Reishi, Cordyceps, etc.)
- Spirulina

OILS
- Cocoa Butter
- Coconut
- Coconut Butter
- Ghee (Clarified Butter)
- Grapeseed
- Olive
- Sesame

PERISHABLE GOODS
- Eggs
- Flaxseed oil
- Fruit
- Milk (raw dairy, rice milk, nutmilk, oat milk, coconut, etc.)
- Nuts
- Organic butter
- Yeast
- Yogurt

Helpful Appliances and Tools to Have on Hand

- Baking sheets
- Blender or Vita-mix
- Bread pans
- Cake pans of various sizes
- Candy thermometer
- Chocolate molds
- Chopping boards
- Cookie cutters
- Cooling racks
- Double boiler or small metal bowl
- Electric mixer
- Flour sifter
- Food processor
- Grain grinder or Vita-mix
- Griddle
- KitchenAid Adjust-A-Cup® (awesome for measuring agave)
- Measuring cups (starting at ⅛ cup)
- Measuring spoons (starting at ¼ teaspoon)
- Microplane grater for citrus zests
- Mixing bowls (large, medium, small)
- Muffin cups
- Muffin tins
- Oven mitts and potholders
- Parchment Paper
- Pie pan (ceramic or glass)
- Pizza pan and stone
- Pizzelle maker
- Popsicle molds
- Ramekins
- Rolling pin
- Set of glass storage containers
- Set of metal bowls
- Spatula
- Stick blender
- Waffle iron

NONSTICK COOKWARE AND BAKEWARE

There is much controversy around the use of nonstick cookware and bakeware. I recommend using stainless steel, glass, or silicone instead of nonstick. Nonstick surfaces contain PFOA, a chemical that doesn't break down into less harmful chemicals over time. Once PFOA enters the body it does not leave. PFOA is found in other products as well. As a result, PFOA has been found in humans, due to exposure to these products. The impact of this exposure is unknown, so it is wise to make choices to avoid PFOA when possible. Choosing cookware that is free of potentially damaging chemicals is a safe bet.

PLASTIC VS. GLASS STORAGE CONTAINERS

I recommend using glass storage containers instead of plastic, which is known to leach harmful chemicals into food. Glass storage containers can be purchased in sets and have the added advantage of being transparent, so you can see what's inside easily. Glass containers are also handy because there are brands that are oven-safe, making it easy to bake directly in them and cover with a lid for transport and air-tight storage.

How to Measure:
The Equipment

GRADUATED MEASURING CUPS

Dry measuring cups are usually made of plastic or metal. I recommend the ones that come in sets of 1 cup, ½ cup, ⅓ cup, ¼ cup, ⅛ cup, ⅔ cup, and ¾ cup. Some sets include only 4 sizes. Having more sizes is often useful. Measuring cups are excellent for measuring dry ingredients accurately, because they can easily be leveled off.

LIQUID MEASURING CUPS

Liquid measuring cups look like little pitchers. They are available in 1-, 2-. 4-, and 8-cup measures. You will find them in glass or plastic, with the measures indicated in cups, ounces, and milliliters. I recommend glass. Larger measuring cups are great, because they can double as mixing bowls.

MEASURING SPOONS

Typically, you find measuring spoons in sets of four (1 tablespoon, 1 teaspoon, ½ teaspoon, and ¼ teaspoon). I recommend finding a set with a broader range. Look for one that includes the following sizes: 1 tablespoon, 1/2 tablespoon, 1 teaspoon, ½ teaspoon, ¼ teaspoon, ⅛ teaspoon. Having a 2-tablespoon measure can be handy as well; these are sold separately in odd-size measuring spoon sets.

ADJUSTABLE LIQUID AND DRY MEASURE

I am a big fan of adjustable measuring devices, such as the *Adjust-A-Cup*®. One side measures solid and dry ingredients in cup increments, while the other side measures liquids in cups, ounces, or milliliters. These work well for measuring agave nectar, oils, and shortening.

The Ingredients

BUTTER

Butter is commonly sold in ¼-pound sticks that measure ½ cup or 8 tablespoons. In the U.S., the wrapping usually has tablespoons and teaspoons clearly marked on the stick. If the butter has not been packed this way, set the butter out until soft, then pack butter into a measuring spoon, measuring cup, or Adjust-a-Cup®.

ORGANIC VEGETABLE SHORTENING

Shortening is easy to measure in measuring cups because of its soft consistency.

AGAVE NECTAR

The best solution for measuring agave, as well as other thick or sticky ingredients, is the Adjust-A-Cup® made by KitchenAid. With this tool, you can measure wet or dry ingredients conveniently and with very little mess — a must-have in every agave-using household!

FLOUR

Properly measuring flour is an important step for achieving great results with your recipes. Flour usually settles during packing and shipping, so you may need to "fluff" it with a fork before measuring. Use a dry measuring cup and run a knife or other straight edge across the top to get a perfect measure. Ideally, you might even sift the flour first, then measure; though, if you're in whip-it-up mode, this will take a bit of extra time. DO NOT pack flour into the measuring cup. This will lead to an inaccurate measure.

CORRECT METHOD TO MEASURE FLOUR

1. Sift the flour or fluff flour with a fork.
2. Fill the measuring cup to heaping full.
3. Level cup with a straight-edged knife.

COMMON FLOUR MEASURING MISTAKES

Using flour without sifting or fluffing can lead to inaccurate measures. The same is true for tapping the measuring cup. This will pack the flour down and cause you to use more flour than is called for in your recipe.

Guide to Gluten-Free Recipes by Chapter

BEVERAGES 73
All recipes in this chapter are gluten free

**FLAVORED AGAVE NECTARS
AND EXTRACTS** 93
All recipes in this chapter are gluten free

SYRUPS, SAUCES, AND FROSTINGS 99
All recipes in this chapter are gluten free

**JAMS, JELLIES, PRESERVES,
AND MARMALADES** 113
All recipes in this chapter are gluten free

BREADS

Banana Chocolate Chip Bread (yeast free) . .148

Brown Rice Bread (yeasted) 154

Pizza Crust (yeasted) 155

Potato Millet Bread (yeasted) 153

Pretzels (yeasted) 156

MUFFINS

Banana Coconut Muffins 181

Banana Rice Bran Muffins 175

Buckwheat Muffins .182

Carrot Rice Muffins .178

Corn Muffins 179

Cranberry Muffins 180

Gluten-Free Muffin Base Recipe 173

Nutty Rice Bran Muffins 176

Rice Bran Muffins 175

CAKES

Almond Orange Cake 211

Angel Food Cake 212

Chocolate Bundt Cake 213

Chocolate Zucchini Cake 210

Ricotta Cheesecake 208

White Cake Base Recipe 209

COOKIES AND BARS

Brownies 235

Coco-Cocoa Cookies 223

Flourless Almond Cookies 234

KC's Chocolate Chip Coconut Cookies . . 233

Macaroons 235

Vegan Almond Macaroons 236

PUDDINGS AND CUSTARDS 239
All recipes in this chapter are gluten free

PIES AND TARTS

Coconut Crust 275

Empanadas 290

Millet Sorghum Corn Crust 274

Sweet Amaranth Crust 274

Pie and Tart Fillings—all are gluten free . . . 278

Raw Pie Crusts 291

Raw Pie Fillings 295

Tapioca Rice Crust 273

COBBLERS, CRISPS, AND CRUMBLES

Peach Cobbler 306

ICE CREAM 313
All recipes in this chapter are gluten free

RAW FOOD TREATS **325**
All recipes in this chapter are gluten free

CANDIES WITH A HEALTHY TWIST

Chocolate Covered Cherries and
Strawberries 341

Chocolate Framboise Rose Truffles 342

Chocolate Lavender Truffles 345

Chocolate Mint Truffles 344

Chocolate Peanut Butter Cups 346

Easy Nutty Fudge 353

Gluten-free Halvah 352

Nougat Caramel Candy Bar 347

Peppermint Patties 348

Pomegranate Chocolate Truffles 343

Sesame Almond Candy 349

Sesame Crunch Candy 350

Simple Chocolate Base Recipe 340

Tahini Candy 352

SNACKS

Almond Flax Nut Bar 359

Banana Coconut Snack 365

Coconut Melon Snack 365

Fried Bananas with Chocolate Sauce 366

Green Power Bar 360

Homemade Protein Bar Base Recipe 358

Maca Power Bar 359

Sweet Chipotle Cashew Crunch 364

**FUN FOODS FOR KIDS AND THE
YOUNG AT HEART**

All recipes are gluten-free EXCEPT page 371

BREAKFAST FOODS

Amaranth Apple Waffles 402

Buckwheat Pancakes 397

Buttermilk Teff Waffles 405

Cardamom Grits 392

Fermented Buckwheat Pancakes 400

French Toast 395

Hot Quinoa Breakfast 393

Millet Waffles 405

Quick Rice Cereal 392

Quinoa Waffles 404

Sesame Yogurt Waffles 403

Sweet Morning Grits 391

Sweet Rice Pancakes 399

Whole Grain Buttermilk Pancakes 398

Symbols Used in This Book

If you are avoiding gluten, wheat, and dairy in your diet, look for the recipes in this book with the following symbols. But don't limit yourself. Recipes can be adjusted—see page 64 for a guide to substitutions!

 Wheat Free

 Gluten Free

 Dairy Free

CHAPTER 5

CONVERSION CHARTS AND BAKING GUIDES

Create Your Own Recipes
and Conversions 54

Top Tips for Baking at High Altitudes . .55

Converting Sweeteners to
Agave Nectar 56

Fahrenheit, Celsius, and Gas 57
Number Conversions

Liquid Measurement Conversions . . 58

Dry Measurement Conversions. 59

Formulas for Conversion 59

Baking Pan Conversion Chart 60

Baking Pan Sizes 62

Ingredient Equivalents 63

I'm Missing an Ingredient!
Ingredient Substitutions 64

Create Your Own Recipes and Conversions

My objective is not only to give you a plethora of new recipes, but also to offer tools that will enable you to improvise, create, and adapt recipes to your particular needs. Let's say you're in Europe, where measurements are in different units; or maybe you need to convert temperature from Celsius to Fahrenheit. Perhaps you're in the middle of a recipe and realize you're out of cornstarch. This chapter has information on conversions, substitutions, and how to stock your kitchen for all your baking adventures!

Common Abbreviations:

t = teaspoon

T = Tablespoon

c = cup

oz = ounce

pt = pint

qt = quart

gal = gallon

lb = pound

= pound

Top Tips for Baking at High Altitudes

At high altitude (3,000 feet and above), the air pressure is lower, which can make baking a bit more challenging. Here are some simple steps to ensure that your recipes turn out well.

✓ Adjust Baking Soda or Baking Powder:

Use the following chart as a guide to help you adjust your baking soda or baking powder so that your baked goods rise properly.

Table 13: Baking Soda and Baking Powder Altitude Adjustments

Baking Powder or Baking Soda	3,000 – 5,000 ft.	5,000- 6,500 ft.	6,500 – 8,000 ft.	+ 8,000 ft.
1 teaspoon	$7/8$	$1/2$	$1/4$	$1/4$
1 $1/2$ teaspoons	1 $1/4$	$3/4$	$1/2$	$1/2$
2 teaspoons	1 $1/2$	1	$3/4$	$3/4$
2 $1/2$ teaspoons	1 $3/4$	1 $1/4$	1	1
3 teaspoons	2	1 $1/4$	1	1
3 $1/2$ teaspoons	2 $1/2$	1 $1/2$	1	1

✓ Eggs:

For recipes that call for eggs, add one extra-large egg. This will add protein and moistness to cakes. Be sure to use room-temperature eggs and do not overbeat.

✓ Agave Nectar:

Agave is an excellent sweetener for recipes baked at high altitude because it adds moistness, which is helpful in high-altitude climates.

✓ Adjust Oven Temperature:

It may be necessary to increase your baking temperature slightly because leavening and evaporation proceed more rapidly at higher altitudes. Higher temperatures also help set the structure of cakes more quickly, which prevents collapsing.

From 3,000 - 6,500 ft., increase by 15 to 25 percent: For more delicate cakes, though, lean toward lower temperatures and experiment.

At 6,500 ft. and over, increase by 25 percent: You will likely need to experiment with finding the best temperature for your location. Make sure you have an oven thermometer so you can monitor the exact temperature of your oven.

✓ Adjust Baking Time:

Decrease baking time by 5-8 minutes per 30 minutes of baking time; higher temperatures mean shorter baking times.

✓ Adjust Flour:

At 3,000 feet, add 1 more tablespoon of flour per recipe.

For each additional 1,500 feet, add one more tablespoon. The addition of a little flour helps to strengthen the structure of baked goods. Flours with a high protein content like amaranth, quinoa, or millet flour may yield better results at high altitudes.

Converting Sweeteners to Agave Nectar

Old Recipe with Sugar	New Recipe with Agave
1 Tablespoon (3 teaspoons)	2 teaspoons
2 Tablespoons (⅛ cup)	4 teaspoons (or 1 T + 1 t)
3 Tablespoons	2 Tablespoons
⅛ cup (2 Tablespoons)	4 teaspoons (or 1 T + 1 t)
¼ cup	8 teaspoons (or 2 T + 2 t)
⅓ cup	¼ cup
½ cup	⅓ cup
⅔ cup	7 Tablespoons or ¼ cup plus 3 Tablespoons
¾ cup	½ cup
1 cup (16 Tablespoons)	⅔ cup
2 cups	1 ⅓ cup
3 cups	2 cups

Old Recipe with Honey	New Recipe with Agave
1 Tablespoon (3 teaspoons)	¾ Tablespoon (2 ¼ teaspoons)
2 Tablespoons (⅛ cup)	1 ½ Tablespoons (4 ½ teaspoons)
3 Tablespoons	2 ¼ Tablespoons
⅛ cup (2 Tablespoons)	1 ½ Tablespoons
¼ cup	3 Tablespoons
⅓ cup	6 Tablespoons or ¼ cup plus 2 Tablespoons
½ cup	¼ cup
⅔ cup	½ cup
¾ cup	½ cup + 1 Tablespoon
1 cup (16 Tablespoons)	¾ cup
2 cups	1 ½ cups
3 cups	2 ¼ cups

Old Recipe with Corn Syrup	New Recipe with Agave
1 Tablespoon (3 teaspoons)	½ Tablespoon
2 Tablespoons (⅛ cup)	1 Tablespoon
3 Tablespoons	1 ½ Tablespoons
⅛ cup (2 Tablespoons)	1 Tablespoon
¼ cup	2 Tablespoons
⅓ cup	¼ cup
½ cup	2 Tablespoons plus 2 teaspoons
⅔ cup	5 Tablespoons plus 1 teaspoon
¾ cup	¼ cup plus 2 Tablespoons
1 cup (16 Tablespoons)	½ cup
2 cups	1 cup
3 cups	1 ½ cups

Fahrenheit, Celsius, and Gas Number Conversions

The Formula:
To Convert Fahrenheit to Celsius: Subtract 32, multiply by 5, then divide by 9.
To Convert Celsius to Fahrenheit: Multiply by 9, divide by 5, then add 32.

Fahrenheit (F)	Celsius (C)	Gas Number	Oven Terms
225°F	110°C	¼	Very Cool
250°F	120°C	½	Very Slow
275°F	135°C	1	Very Slow
300°F	150°C	2	Slow
325°F	165°C	3	Slow
350°F	175°C	4	Moderate
375°F	190°C	5	Moderate
400°F	205°C	6	Moderately Hot
425°F	220°C	7	Hot
450°F	230°C	8	Hot
475°F	245°C	9	Hot
500°F	260°C	10	Extremely Hot
550°F	290°C	10	Broiling

Liquid Measurement Conversions

Liquid Measurement	Equivalent Measurement	Equivalent Measurement	Equivalent Measurement	Metric Equivalent	Decimal Equivalent
⅛ cup	1 ounce		2 Tablespoons	30 mL	.125 cup
¼ cup	2 ounces		4 Tablespoons	60 mL	.25 cup
⅓ cup	2.6 ounces		5 Tablespoons + 1 teaspoon	80 mL	.333 cup
⅜ cup	3 ounces		6 Tablespoons	90 mL	.375 cup
½ cup	4 ounces		8 Tablespoons	120 mL	.5 cup
¾ cup	6 ounces		12 Tablespoons	180 mL	.75 cup
1 cup	8 fluid ounces	½ pint	16 Tablespoons	240 mL	1 cup
2 cups	16 fluid ounces	1 pint		475 mL	2 cups
4 cups	32 fluid ounces	1 quart		950 mL	4 cups
2 pints	32 fluid ounces	1 quart		950 mL	4 cups
4 quarts	128 fluid ounces	1 gallon		3.8 liters	16 cups
8 quarts	one peck				
4 pecks	one bushel				
Dash	less than ¼ teaspoon				
1 teaspoon	⅙ fluid ounce	5 grams		5 mL	.333 Tablespoon
1 Tablespoon	½ fluid ounce	15 grams	3 teaspoons	15 mL	.5 fluid ounce
2 Tablespoons	1 fluid ounce	30 grams	⅛ cup	30 mL	.125 cup
8 Tablespoons	4 fluid ounces	¼ pint	½ cup	120 mL	.5 cup

Note: In cases where precise measures are not crucial, it may be more convenient to round these conversions off as follows:

1 cup = 250 mL

1 pint = 500 mL

1 quart = 1 liter

1 gallon = 4 liters

Dry Measurement Conversions

Dry Measurement	Equivalent Measurement	Equivalent Measurement	Equivalent Measurement	Equivalent Measurement
3 teaspoons	1 Tablespoon	½ ounce	14.2 grams	
1 Tablespoon	3 teaspoons	½ ounce	14.2 grams	
2 Tablespoons	⅛ cup	1 fluid ounce	28.3 grams	
1/8 cup	2 Tablespoons	1 fluid ounce	28.3 grams	
1/4 cup	4 Tablespoons	2 fluid ounces	56.7 grams	
1/3 cup	5 ⅓ Tablespoons (or 5 Tablespoons + 1 teaspoon)	2.6 fluid ounces	75.6 grams	
1/2 cup	8 Tablespoons	4 ounces	113.4 grams	1 stick butter
3/4 cup	12 Tablespoons	6 ounces	.375 pound	170 grams
1 cup	16 Tablespoons	8 ounces	.5 pound	226.8 grams
2 cups	32 Tablespoons	16 ounces	1 pound	453.6 grams
4 cups	64 Tablespoons	32 ounces	2 pounds	907.2 grams

Formulas For Conversion

If you are using these recipes outside the U.S., you will need to do some math to convert them into your local measurements.

To convert:	Multiply:
quarts into liters	multiply the quarts by 0.94635
liters into quarts	multiply the liters by 1.056688
liquid ounces into milliliters	multiply the ounces by 29.573
milliliters into ounces	multiply the milliliters by 0.0338
weight ounces into grams	multiply the ounces by 28.3495
grams into weight ounces	multiply the grams by 0.035274

Baking Pan Conversion Chart

The following table will help determine substitutions of pans and dishes of similar approximate size if you do not have the specific sized baking pan called for in a recipe.

3-CUP BAKING DISH OR PAN:

8" x 1-¼" round pan

10-CUP BAKING DISH OR PAN:

8" x 2 ½" springform pan

9" x 9" x 2" square pan

11 ¾" x 7 ½" x 1 ¾" baking pan

13" x 9" x 2" rectangular pan

15 ½" x 10 ½" x 1" jellyroll pan

10" round cake pan

10" springform pan

Two 8" round cake pans

Two 9" round cake pans

4-CUP BAKING DISH OR PAN:

8" x 1 ½" round layer cake pan

9" x 1 ½" round pie pan

11" x 1" round tart pan

8" x 4" loaf pan

9" round cake pan

11-CUP BAKING DISH OR PAN:

9" x 3" springform pan

10" x 2" round cake pan

Two 8" round cake pans

9" tube pan

10" springform pan

6-CUP BAKING DISH OR PAN:

8" round cake pan

7 ½" x 3" tube pan

8" x 8" x 2" square pan

8 ½" x 4 ½" x 2 ½" loaf pan

9" x 1 ½" round layer cake pan

9" x 2" round pie plate (deep dish)

9" x 9" x 1 ½" rectangular pan

10" x 1 ½" round pie plate

11" x 7" x 2" rectangular baking dish

12-CUP BAKING DISH OR PAN:

Two 9" round cake pans

9" x 3" tube pan

10" x 2 ½" springform pan

10" x 3 ½" bundt pan

13" x 9" x 2" metal baking pan

14" x 10 ½" x 2 ½" roasting pan

Baking Pan Conversion Chart (Cont.)

7-CUP BAKING DISH OR PAN:

8" x 2" round cake pan

9" x 9" x 2" rectangular pan

15-CUP BAKING DISH OR PAN:

13" x 9" x 2" rectangular pan

10" x 15" x 1" jellyroll pan

10" bundt pan

Two 9" round cake pans

Two 8" round cake pans

8-CUP BAKING DISH OR PAN:

8" x 8" x 2" square pan

9" x 2" round cake pan

9" x 5" x 3" loaf pan

9" x 9" x 1 ½" square pan

9 ¼" x 2 ¾" ring mold

9 ½" x 3 ¼" brioche pan

11" x 7" x 1 ½" baking pan

9" x 2" deep-dish pie plate

10" round pie plate

16-CUP BAKING DISH OR PAN:

9" x 3 ½" springform pan

10" x 4" fancy tube mold

9-CUP BAKING DISH OR PAN:

9" x 3" tube pan

18-CUP BAKING DISH OR PAN:

10" x 4" tube pan

Substituting Glass Pans:

When using glass pans, reduce the oven temperature by 25°F or about 4°C.

When Using Pans with Removable Bottoms:

With lighter, more liquid batters, line the bottom with foil or use a solid-bottomed pan.

Baking Pan Sizes

CAKE PANS

- 8" x 2" round cake pan ~ 6 cups
- 9" x 2" round cake pan ~ 8 cups
- 10" x 2" round cake pan ~ 11 cups
- 8" x 8" x 2" square cake pan ~ 8 cups
- 9" x 9" x 2" square cake pan ~ 10 cups
- 10 ½" tube pan ~ 15 cups
- 9" x 2 ½" springform cake pan ~ 10 cups
- 10" x 4" tube pan ~ 16 cups

PIE PANS

- 9" x 1½" round pie pan ~ 5 cups
- 10" x 2" round pie pan ~ 5 cups
- 10" x 2" fluted tart pan ~ 6 cups

RECTANGULAR PANS

- 11" x 7" x 2" rectangular pan ~ 6 cups
- 13" x 9" x 2" rectangular pan ~ 15 cups

LOAF PANS

- 9" x 5" x 3" loaf pan ~ 8 cups
- 5 ½" x 3" x 2 ½" mini loaf pan ~ 2 cups

MUFFIN PANS

- 1 ¾" x ¾" mini muffin cups ~ 2 Tablespoons
- 2 ¾" x 1 ¼" muffin cup ~ ¼ cup

Ingredient Equivalents

Ingredients	Measurement	Ounces
Almonds, ground	1 cup	2.8 ounces
Apple	1 medium apple = 1 cup sliced apple 1 lb apples = 3 cups peeled and sliced	
Banana, 3 medium	1 cup mashed	
Butter	½ cup (1 stick) (8 Tablespoons)	4 ounces
Chocolate chips	2 cups (1 package of chips)	12 ounces
Cocoa powder, unsweetened	1 cup	2.8 ounces
Coconut, shredded	1 cup	2.5 ounces
Cornmeal, coarse	1 cup	4.9 ounces
Cornmeal, fine	1 cup	6.3 ounces
Cornstarch	1 cup	4.4 ounces
Cream cheese	1 cup	8.2 ounces
Dates, pitted	1 ¼ cups cut up	8 ounces
Egg, 1 egg yolk	1 Tablespoon + 1 teaspoon	.7 ounce
Egg, 1 egg white	2 Tablespoons + 1 teaspoon	1 ounce
Egg, 1 large egg	4 Tablespoons	2 ounces
Organic shortening	1 cup	7 ounces
Heavy cream	1 cup	8.4 ounces
Lemon, 1	2-4 Tablespoons juice 1 teaspoon zest	
Lime, 1	2 Tablespoons juice 1 teaspoon zest	
Milk	1 cup	8 ounces
Oat flour	1 cup	4.4 ounces
Oats, rolled	1 cup	3 ounces
Orange, 1	⅓-½ cup juice 2 Tablespoons zest	
Potato starch	1 cup	5.5 ounces
Sour cream/yogurt	1 cup	8.6 ounces
Walnut/pecan halves	1 cup	3.5 ounces
Walnuts, chopped	1 cup	4.3 ounces
White rice flour	1 cup	5.3 ounces
Whole wheat flour	1 cup	4.3 ounces
Yeast, 1 package	1 Tablespoon	

I'm Missing An Ingredient! Ingredient Substitutions

If you find you are in the middle of baking and are missing an ingredient, or you want to avoid certain ingredients and are looking for substitutions, use this chart to help modify your recipe. Take into account differences in moisture, flavor, texture, and weight.

Ingredient	Quantity	Substitution
Allspice	1 teaspoon	➤ ½ teaspoon cinnamon **plus** ½ teaspoon ground cloves
Arrowroot	1 teaspoon	➤ 2 teaspoons flour ➤ 1 ½ teaspoons cornstarch ➤ 1 teaspoon tapioca flour ➤ 3 teaspoons kudzu/kuzu powder
Baking powder	1 teaspoon	➤ ¼ teaspoon baking soda **plus** ½ teaspoon cream of tartar **plus** ¼ teaspoon cornstarch ➤ ¼ teaspoon baking soda **plus** ½ cup sour milk **or** buttermilk **or** yogurt (decrease liquid called for in recipe by ½ cup) **How to make a batch of baking powder from scratch:** Combine ¼ cup baking soda with ½ cup cream of tartar, and ¼ cup cornstarch. Store in an airtight container.
Baking soda	½ teaspoon	➤ 2 teaspoons baking powder (Replace acidic liquid in recipe with non-acidic liquid)
Brown sugar	1 cup	➤ ⅔ cup agave **plus** ¼ cup molasses (decrease liquid in recipe by 25%)
Butter	1 cup	➤ ⅞ cup organic vegetable shortening, coconut oil, coconut ghee, or ghee

I'm Missing An Ingredient! Ingredient Substitutions (Cont.)

Ingredient	Quantity	Substitution
Buttermilk	1 cup	➤ 1 cup sour milk **or** yogurt **or** sour cream ➤ 1 cup water **plus** 1/4 cup buttermilk powder ➤ 1 Tablespoon lemon juice **or** white vinegar **plus** enough whole milk to make 1 cup (let stand 5 minutes)
Buttermilk powder	½ cup	➤ ½ cup sweet dairy whey ➤ ½ cup goat milk powder ➤ ½ cup buttermilk powder **plus** 3 ½ cups of water = 4 cups buttermilk
Carob powder/ carob chips	3 Tablespoons	➤ 3 Tablespoons cocoa powder **or** raw cacao powder ➤ 1 square (1 ounce) unsweetened chocolate minus 2 T of dry ingredient in recipe ➤ 3 Tablespoons grain-sweetened chocolate chips
Chocolate, semisweet	1 ounce (3 Tablespoons)	➤ 1 ounce unsweetened chocolate **plus** 2 teaspoons agave nectar ➤ 1 ounce grain-sweetened chocolate chips ➤ 3 Tablespoons cocoa powder **plus** 1 Tablespoon butter or coconut oil **plus** 2 teaspoons agave nectar ➤ 3 Tablespoons carob powder **plus** 2 Tablespoons water **plus** 2 teaspoons agave nectar
Chocolate, unsweetened	1 square (1 ounce)	➤ 3 Tablespoons cocoa powder **plus** 1 Tablespoon butter or coconut oil ➤ 3 Tablespoons carob powder **plus** 2 Tablespoons water ➤ 3 Tablespoons semisweet chocolate **minus** 2 teaspoons agave nectar

I'm Missing An Ingredient! Ingredient Substitutions (Cont.)

Ingredient	Quantity	Substitution
Cocoa powder, Dutch processed	3 Tablespoons	➤ 3 Tablespoons natural cocoa powder *plus* ⅛ teaspoon baking soda
Cocoa powder, natural	3 Tablespoons	➤ 3 Tablespoons (18 grams) Dutch processed cocoa powder *plus* ⅛ teaspoon cream of tartar *or* lemon juice *or* vinegar
Coconut	1 Tablespoon, grated, dry	➤ 1 ½ Tablespoons fresh, grated
	1 cup grated, dry	➤ 1 ⅓ cups flaked coconut
Coconut cream	1 cup	➤ 1 cup cream
Coconut milk	1 cup	➤ 1 cup another kind of milk
Cornstarch	1 Tablespoon	➤ 2 Tablespoons flour *or* tapioca flour ➤ 1 Tablespoon arrowroot
Corn syrup	1 cup	➤ ½ cup agave
Cream cheese	1 cup	➤ 1 cup ricotta cheese beaten until smooth ➤ 1 cup cottage cheese beaten until smooth
Cream of Tartar	½ teaspoon	➤ 1 ½ teaspoons lemon juice *or* vinegar
Cream, half & half (10-12% fat)	1 cup	➤ ⅞ cup whole milk *plus* 1 Tablespoon melted butter ➤ 3 Tablespoons oil *plus* milk to equal 1 cup
Cream, heavy (36-40% fat)	1 cup	➤ ¾ cup milk *plus* ⅓ cup melted butter ➤ ⅔ cup buttermilk *plus* ⅓ cup oil ➤ 1 cup yogurt *or* ricotta beaten until smooth (this mixture cannot be heated because it will separate)
Cream, whipping	1 cup	➤ ¾ cup milk *plus* ⅓ cup melted butter (for cooking only, will not whip)

I'm Missing An Ingredient! Ingredient Substitutions (Cont.)

Ingredient	Quantity	Substitution
Egg	1 whole large egg (approximately 3 Tablespoons)	➢ 3 Tablespoons **plus** 1 teaspoon frozen egg, thawed ➢ 1 egg white **plus** 2 teaspoons oil ➢ 1 Tablespoon ground flax seed soaked in 3 Tablespoons water ➢ ¼ cup silken tofu, pureed ➢ 1 egg in every 3 can be replaced with 1 Tablespoon cornstarch
Egg white	1 egg white (2 Tablespoons)	➢ 2 Tablespoons frozen egg white, thawed
Egg yolk	1 egg yolk (1 Tablespoon)	➢ 1 ¼ Tablespoon frozen egg yolk, thawed
Essential oils	½ teaspoon	➢ 2 teaspoons extract (Start with adjusting at a ratio of 1 part essential oil to 4 parts extract, then if you want more flavor, add 1 drop at a time of essential oil)
Guar gum	1 teaspoon	➢ 1 teaspoon xanthan gum ➢ 1 teaspoon ground flax seed ➢ 1 teaspoon ground chia seed
Kudzu/kuzu powder	1 Tablespoon	➢ 1 teaspoon arrowroot ➢ 1 teaspoon tapioca flour ➢ 1 ½ teaspoons cornstarch
Lemon juice	1 teaspoon	➢ ½ teaspoon white vinegar

I'm Missing An Ingredient! Ingredient Substitutions (Cont.)

Ingredient	Quantity	Substitution
Lemon zest	1 teaspoon	➤ ½ teaspoon lemon extract ➤ 1 teaspoon orange **or** lime zest
Milk, whole (3.5%)	1 cup	➤ 1 cup buttermilk **plus** ½ teaspoon baking soda (decrease baking powder by 2 teaspoons in a baking recipe) ➤ 1 cup fruit juice **or** 1 cup potato water (in baking) ➤ 1 cup water **plus** 11/2 teaspoons butter (for baking recipes only) ➤ 1 cup dairy-free milk
Peppermint extract	1 Tablespoon	➤ ¼ cup chopped fresh mint
Pumpkin pie spice	1 teaspoon	➤ ½ teaspoon cinnamon, ¼ teaspoon ginger, ⅛ teaspoon allspice, and ⅛ teaspoon nutmeg
Rum	¼ cup	➤ 1 Tablespoon rum extract **plus** enough liquid to make ¼ cup
Shortening	1 cup	➤ 1 cup butter (decrease salt in recipe by ½ teaspoon) **or** organic shortening (coconut or palm) **or** coconut oil
Sour cream	1 cup	➤ 1 cup yogurt (add 1 Tablespoon cornstarch to each cup to prevent separating) ➤ ¾ cup sour milk **or** buttermilk **plus** ⅓ cup melted butter ➤ 1 cup creme fraiche ➤ ⅞ cup whole milk **plus** 1 Tablespoon lemon juice **plus** 2 Tablespoons melted butter

I'm Missing An Ingredient! Ingredient Substitutions (Cont.)

Ingredient	Quantity	Substitution
Tapioca starch (also called Tapioca flour, Cassava flour, Yucca starch, Almidon de Yucca)	1 Tablespoon	➢ 1 Tablespoon arrowroot flour ➢ 1 ½ Tablespoon cornstarch ➢ 3 Tablespoons kudzu/kuzu powder *Note: If a recipe calls for tapioca flour in large quantities, don't use a substitute. Substitutes are appropriate for thickening purposes only.
Pure vanilla extract	1 teaspoon	➢ 1" vanilla bean split and simmered in liquid of recipe
Whey, sweet dairy	½ cup	➢ ½ cup buttermilk powder ➢ ½ cup goat milk powder
Wine	1 cup	➢ 1 cup water **plus** 3 Tablespoons lemon juice **plus** 1 Tablespoon agave nectar
Xanthan gum/ zanthan gum	1 teaspoon	➢ 1 teaspoon guar gum ➢ 1 teaspoon ground flax seed ➢ 1 teaspoon ground chia seed
Yeast, active dry	1 package (¼ ounce)	➢ 1 cake (6/10 ounce), compressed (⅔ ounce)
Yogurt, plain	1 cup	➢ 1 cup buttermilk **or** sour cream **or** sour milk ➢ 1 cup cottage cheese blended until smooth
Vinegar	½ teaspoon	➢ 1 teaspoon lemon juice

PART 2

CHAPTER 6

BEVERAGES

Cold Drinks

Nut and Seed Milk
Base Recipe 74

Latte di Mandorle
(Almond Milk) 75

Golden Milk 76

Raw Almond Chocolate Milk. . . . 76

Raw Cashew Chocolate Milk . . . 77

Pumpkin Cream Drink. 77

Smoothie Base Recipe 78

Coconut Milk #1 79

Coconut Milk #2 80

Natural Sodas

Juice Soda Base Recipe 81

Sparkling Apple Cider 81

Citrus Soda 81

Live Water Crystal Soda
Base Recipe. 82

Traditional Root Beer 83

Ginger Beer 84

Fresh Lemonade. 84

Instant Lemonade/Limeade 85

Punch 85

Superfood Raw Coffee Slush . . . 86

Refreshing Aloe Tonic Drink 86

Chia Sports Drink. 87

Chia Fresca 87

Hot Drinks

Spiced Apricot Cider 88

Chocolate Milk 88

Hot Chocolate 89

Hot Mint Chocolate. 89

Mexican Chocolate Elixir 90

Cold Drinks

Nut and Seed Milk Base Recipe

Nut and seed milks are easy to make and have a superior taste to store-bought brands. For best results choose nuts and seeds that are raw, fresh, and have been stored in the freezer to prevent rancidity. Broken nuts are cost effective and will not affect the quality of the milk. The following recipe is delicious by itself or blended in a smoothie with fruit. It will keep in the refrigerator for about 2 days. Use the leftover pulp in cookies and pie crusts for a unique taste and texture.

ADDITIONAL TOOLS NEEDED:

*1 nutmilk bag **or** cheesecloth with a fine sieve*

INGREDIENTS:

- ½ cup nuts or seeds, preferably unroasted
  Use any or a combination of almonds, cashews, Brazil nuts, hazelnuts, pecans, pine nuts, pistachio nuts, walnuts, pumpkin seeds, sesame seeds, and sunflower seeds.
- 3 cups water
- 1 teaspoon extract (optional)
  Try vanilla, almond, lemon, hazelnut, etc. This helps to preserve the milk and adds subtle flavor.
- 2-3 Tablespoons agave nectar
- Pinch high-quality salt
- 1 Tablespoon flax seed (optional)

OPTIONAL ADDITIONS:

- ½ - 1 teaspoon powdered spices (nutmeg, cinnamon, cardamom, clove, allspice, anise, or coriander)
- zests from citrus fruits, like lemon, orange, and lime.
- 1 teaspoon raw cacao powder, cocoa powder, or carob powder

DIRECTIONS:

1. Thoroughly rinse and sort nuts or seeds. Cover nuts/seeds with water. Let sit for 3-4 hours or, preferably, overnight.
2. Strain off soaking water.
3. Pour nuts and/or seeds into a blender. Add 3 cups fresh water and remaining ingredients.
4. Blend on high until completely blended, about 2 minutes.
5. Pour into a nutmilk bag or cheesecloth-lined strainer that is positioned over a large bowl. Squeeze the milk through to separate from the pulp.

Makes 3 servings

Latte di Mandorle (Almond Milk)

This dish dates back to the time of the Romans. When milk was difficult to transport and store, almond milk was a practical alternative. My grandmother Eileen made this delicate dessert at Christmas. Served up in parfait glasses, it's an elegant end to a holiday feast.

ADDITIONAL TOOLS NEEDED:

*1 nutmilk bag **or** cheesecloth with a fine sieve*

INGREDIENTS:

- 1 ½ lbs almonds, blanched*
- 3 cups water

- 5 ½ cups water
- ⅓ cup agave nectar
- 1 Tablespoon lemon zest
- 1 stick cinnamon
- ½ cup long grain white rice
- Pinch high-quality salt
- 1 teaspoon almond extract

DIRECTIONS:

1. Add almonds to a bowl and cover with 3 cups of water. Let sit overnight.
2. Drain water and add almonds to a blender. Add 5 1/2 cups fresh water and blend on high for 1 minute.
3. Secure a nutmilk bag or cheesecloth-lined fine sieve over a large saucepan. Add the contents of the blender into your straining device and squeeze the liquid out into the saucepan. The byproduct, almond pulp, can be dehydrated and ground into flour or added to muffins.
4. Add lemon zest, cinnamon stick, rice, and a pinch of salt to the almond milk, and cook on low heat, stirring occasionally. Cook until the rice is soft, about 30 minutes.
5. Remove the saucepan from the heat, and add 1 teaspoon of almond extract. Stir and ladle into parfait glasses. Chill before serving.

Makes about 4 servings

* Blanched means skins removed.

Golden Milk

Turmeric is one of nature's powerful healers. Most notably, it has been shown to cleanse the liver and reduce inflammation. This delicious golden milk can be safely consumed daily as part of a healthy diet.

INGREDIENTS:
- ½ cup water
- ½ teaspoon turmeric powder
- 1 cup milk (cow, goat, almond, rice, coconut, oat, etc.)
- 1 Tablespoon almond extract (optional)
- 1 Tablespoon agave nectar

DIRECTIONS:
1. Boil water and turmeric in small saucepan over medium-high heat for 8 minutes.
2. In a separate saucepan, bring the milk and almond extract to boiling point. Remove from heat.
3. Combine the two liquids. Add agave and stir to dissolve. Serve warm.

Makes 1-2 servings

Raw Almond Chocolate Milk

INGREDIENTS:
- 2 cups almond milk
- 3 Tablespoons raw cacao powder
- 2 Tablespoons almond butter
- 2 Tablespoons agave nectar
- 2 teaspoons pure vanilla extract

DIRECTIONS:
1. Combine all ingredients in a blender and blend until smooth.
2. Let sit for 5 minutes to allow flavors to expand.
3. For an icy treat add ½ - 1 cup ice and blend until smooth.
4. Serve immediately.

Makes 2 servings

Raw Cashew Chocolate Drink

INGREDIENTS:
- 1 cup almond milk
- 1 cup water
- ¼ cup raw cacao powder **or** raw carob powder
- 2 Tablespoons raw coconut butter
- ¼ cup raw agave nectar
- 1 Tablespoon raw cashew butter
- 1 teaspoon pure vanilla extract

DIRECTIONS:
1. Combine all ingredients in a blender and blend on high for 1 minute.
2. For an icy treat add 1 cup ice and blend until smooth.
3. Serve immediately.

Makes 2 servings

Pumpkin Cream Drink

This is a great drink for the fall when pumpkins are in season.

INGREDIENTS:
- 2 cups coconut milk
- ¼ cup agave nectar
- ½ teaspoon pure vanilla extract
- 2 cups cooked pumpkin
- 1 cup yogurt
- ¼ teaspoon pumpkin pie spice
- Additional pumpkin pie spice for sprinkling

DIRECTIONS:
1. Combine all ingredients in a blender and blend until smooth.
2. Top with additional pumpkin pie spice. Serve immediately.

Makes 2 servings

Smoothie Base Recipe

A smoothie makes for a great breakfast on the go or a wonderful afternoon snack.
The frozen banana and/or mango give the smoothie a creamy consistency.

INGREDIENTS
- ½ cup frozen fruit
- 1 frozen banana and/or 1 cup frozen mango
- 1 cup milk (cow, goat, almond, rice, coconut, oat, etc.)
- 1 Tablespoon agave nectar

OPTIONAL ADDITIONS:
Add in one or more of the following:

- 2 Tablespoons golden flax seeds
- ¼ - ½ cup hemp seeds (great vegetable protein)
- 1 Tablespoon maca powder (great for energy)
- 1 Tablespoon raw cacao powder or chunks (high in antioxidants)
- 1 Tablespoon sunflower seeds (ideally soaked overnight)
- 1-2 Tablespoons nut or seed butter (like tahini or almond)
- 1 teaspoon – 1 Tablespoon spirulina/blue green algae/chlorella (great for vegetarians)
- 2 Tablespoons goji berries (ideally soaked overnight)
- 1 teaspoon bee pollen (great for energy)
- 1 Tablespoon flaxseed oil
- 1 package frozen, unsweetened açaí paste or powder
- 2 teaspoons medicinal mushroom powder like reishi, shitake, maitake, turkey tail, or cordyceps (amazing for building and maintaining a strong immunity)
- 1 teaspoon probiotic powder (helps establish positive bacteria in the gut)
- 1 avocado
- ¼ cup barley malt powder
- 2 Tablespoons unsweetened whey protein powder (great protein source)
- ¼ cup fresh spinach or other leafy greens
- ½ cup nuts
- 1 Tablespoon coconut oil or coconut butter
- 4 sprigs of cilantro

DIRECTIONS:
Combine all ingredients in a blender and blend until smooth.

Coconut Milk #1

You can buy coconut milk, but making it from a live coconut is truly delightful. You will need a cleaver or a machete to break through the hard shell. I usually keep a machete on hand just for cracking coconuts. It's a little tricky until you get the hang of it.

INGREDIENTS:
- 3 young coconuts
- 2 teaspoons agave nectar (optional)

DIRECTIONS:
1. Crack open the coconut using a cleaver or machete. To cut the coconut open, make a quick and strong hit about 1 ½ inches from the top center of the coconut and do this on all sides until you can pry it open like a lid. Remember to be cautious when using a machete or cleaver.
2. Pour the coconut water through a strainer into a blender.
3. Next, scrape the coconut meat from the inside of the coconut with a large, strong spoon. Remove any chunks of shell and try to avoid scraping it too hard so you don't get the brown hull. Try to get as much of the white meat as possible. If you want it a little sweeter, add optional agave nectar.
4. Add coconut to blender and purée until smooth.

Makes about 3 servings

Coconut Milk #2

ADDITIONAL TOOLS NEEDED:
1 nutmilk bag **or** *cheesecloth with a fine sieve*

INGREDIENTS
- Young coconut
- Agave nectar to taste

DIRECTIONS
1. Preheat oven to 325°F.
2. Pierce the eyes of a fresh coconut, drain the liquid inside, and place the coconut on a rack in the oven. Bake for about 30 minutes.
3. Remove the coconut from the oven and let it cool. Crack it with a hammer so that the shell breaks into several pieces.
4. Remove all the coconut meat from the shell with a butter knife (safer in case it slips as you are prying the meat off the shell). Wash the meat and cut into 1-2" chunks and set aside.
5. Place the meat in a blender, add enough hot water to just cover all of the meat, and blend until finely grated.
6. Place a sieve covered with cheesecloth (a nutmilk bag works even better if you have one) over a bowl and pour the coconut pulp into the sieve. Squeeze the coconut pulp to extract as much liquid as possible into the bowl. You may need to wait until it's cool enough to squeeze or wear rubber gloves.
7. Discard the squeezed coconut pulp (or toss into a banana bread) and refrigerate the coconut milk. Add agave if desired. Use within 5-7 days. One coconut will make 2-3 cups of coconut milk.

How to Make Your Own Coconut Milk from Shredded Coconut:
1. Blend 1 cup of unsweetened shredded coconut for 2 minutes, then add 1 cup boiling water. Be careful when blending hot liquids.
2. Blend for about 30 seconds and allow the mixture to cool for 5 minutes.
3. Proceed from Step 6 in making coconut milk from fresh coconuts.

Natural Sodas

The overconsumption of high-fructose corn syrup and sugar-sweetened sodas is a huge concern today. The following homemade sodas are easy and fun to make and free of harmful sweeteners.

Juice Soda Base Recipe

Try this soda with any of these juices: apple, blueberry, grape, orange, grapefruit, cherry, pomegranate, or cranberry.

1. Fill glass with ½ sparkling mineral water or carbonate water and ½ juice of your choice.
2. Add agave to taste (1-2 teaspoons).

Makes 1 serving

Sparkling Apple Cider

1. Add ¼ teaspoon vitamin C powder (ascorbic acid) to 2 cups of apple juice or apple cider.
2. Add 1 teaspoon agave nectar.
3. Add 4 cups sparkling soda.
4. Mix well and adjust flavorings to your liking.

Makes about 4 servings

Citrus Soda

1. Squeeze a lemon or lime into a glass.
2. Add agave nectar to taste, 1-2 teaspoons.
3. Add sparkling mineral water or carbonated water.
4. Stir well.

Makes 1 serving

Live Water Crystal Soda Base Recipe

INGREDIENTS:
- 1 quart of water **or** sparkling mineral water
- 2 Tablespoons water crystals (put in a muslin bag)
- 2 Tablespoons agave nectar
- ½ cup dried fruit (raisins, figs, plums, prunes, apricots, peaches, currants, etc.)

DIRECTIONS:
1. In a 2-quart jar, add water, sparkling mineral water, and dried fruit (or juice).
2. Add the muslin bag with the water crystals.
3. Let ferment for 1-4 days at room temperature.
4. Remove the muslin bag, bottle your soda in quart jars and begin the next batch of soda immediately. If you don't want to make soda right away, place your muslin bag in a jar of water with 2 Tablespoons of agave in it to keep the crystals alive until you make your next batch. Feed your crystals every 2 weeks or so.

OPTIONAL ADDITIONS:
- Add a slice of lemon, ginger, sprigs of mint, lemon balm, lemon verbena, or your favorite spices.
- Instead of adding dried fruit and water, you can simply add organic juice such as apple, cranberry, orange, pomegranate, grape, grapefruit, or blueberry.

Makes about 4 servings

Japanese Water Crystals (Water Kefir)

Japanese water crystals are a probiotic mix of healthful bacteria and yeast suspended in a polysaccharide matrix. These "crystals" are used to ferment the sugar out of fruit juices. This process produces a wonderful carbonated probiotic drink. Water kefir can be purchased online and reused indefinitely. Keep your crystals in a small muslin bag so they are easy to strain.

Traditional Root Beer

INGREDIENTS:
- 5 quarts water
- 1 ounce sassafras root bark*
- 1 ounce sarsaparilla root
- 1 ounce cherry bark
- ½ ounce licorice root
- ½ teaspoon freshly ground nutmeg
- ½ stick of cinnamon
- ½ cup raisins
- ½ teaspoon high-quality salt
- ½ cup molasses
- 6 ¼ cups agave nectar

- 1 Tablespoon pure vanilla extract
- 1 teaspoon wintergreen or birch extract **or** ½ teaspoon pure essential oil of wintergreen

DIRECTIONS:
1. Put 5 quarts of water into a heavy brew pot and bring to a boil.
2. Add all ingredients except vanilla and wintergreen or birch extract.
3. Bring to a gentle boil then cover and simmer for one hour.
4. Remove from heat, strain your mixture into another pot and add vanilla and wintergreen (or birch extract).
5. Stir to blend flavors, then bottle in 1-quart jars.
6. To make the root beer: mix 1 part syrup to 4 parts sparkling water or to taste.

Author's note: Sassafras has been used in folk medicine for centuries — it is what gives root beer its traditional taste. Safrole, found in the flowering tree of sassafras, was deemed carcinogenic by the Food and Drug Administration as a result of studies done on rats in the 1960s. Artificial root beer flavors are now available, but I personally tend to trust old remedies more. Do your homework and be your own judge. If you like, you can substitute sassafras with another 1 ounce of sarsaparilla root.

Makes about 5 quarts

Ginger Beer

INGREDIENTS:
- 2 ½ cups peeled and coarsely chopped ginger
- 3 long strips of lemon peel from 1 lemon
- 4 cups water
- 1 ⅓ cup agave nectar
- 3 quarts chilled natural sparkling water **or** sparkling mineral water

DIRECTIONS:
1. Place ginger, lemon peel, and water in a 4-quart saucepan. Bring to a boil over high heat.
2. Simmer at a low boil, uncovered, for about 10 minutes.
3. Strain with a large mesh strainer and return liquid to pot.
4. Add agave, stir, and continue to boil until reduced to about 3 cups, another 15 minutes.
5. Cool the syrup, pour into a glass container, seal tightly, and chill at least 1 hour until cold or up to 1 week.
6. To make a 16 ounce serving of ginger ale: Mix ¼ cup ginger syrup with 1 cup sparkling water and pour over ice. Additional ginger syrup and/or agave may be added to taste.

Makes 3 cups of syrup

Fresh Lemonade

INGREDIENTS:
- 1 cup lemon juice, freshly squeezed from 4-6 lemons
- ¾ cup agave nectar
- 3-4 cups cold water, depending on your desired strength

DIRECTIONS:
1. Pour lemon juice and agave into a pitcher.
2. Add 3-4 cups of cold water or to taste. Stir well.
3. Refrigerate 30-40 minutes.
4. Serve with ice and sliced lemons.

Makes 3-4 servings

Instant Lemonade /Limeade

INGREDIENTS:
- 1 lemon, cut into quarters (**or** 1 lime or ½ grapefruit)
- 5 cups water
- ¼ cup agave nectar (**or** to desired sweetness)

DIRECTIONS:
1. Combine all ingredients in a blender and blend until smooth.
2. Strain in a mesh strainer and serve cold over ice.

Makes 5 servings

Punch

INGREDIENTS:
- 6 cups apple cider or juice
- 1 cinnamon stick
- 5 dried hibiscus flowers for red coloring (optional)
- ¼ teaspoon nutmeg
- 3 Tablespoons agave nectar
- 3 Tablespoons lemon juice
- 2 ¼ cup unsweetened pineapple juice

DIRECTIONS:
1. In large saucepan, heat the cider, cinnamon stick, and hibiscus flowers. Bring to a boil.
2. Reduce heat, cover, and simmer 5 minutes.
3. Uncover and add nutmeg, agave, lemon juice, and pineapple juice.
4. Simmer 5 minutes longer. Strain and serve in punch bowl.

Makes 6 servings

Superfood Raw Coffee Slush

INGREDIENTS:
- 2 cups nutmilk **or** coconut milk
- 1 ½ Tablespoons raw cacao powder **or** raw carob powder
- 1 Tablespoon maca powder
- 1 Tablespoon mesquite powder
- 2 Tablespoons agave nectar
- 1 Tablespoon roasted barley powder **or** roasted dandelion root powder
- 1 cup ice

DIRECTIONS:
1. Combine all ingredients except ice in a blender. Blend to mix well.
2. Add ice and blend until slushy.

Makes 2-3 servings

Refreshing Aloe Tonic Drink

If you come across aloe vera gel cubes at the market try adding a few to this drink!

INGREDIENTS:
- 2 cups water
- 1 Tablespoon agave nectar
- 1 Tablespoon lemon **or** lime juice, fresh squeezed
- 2 Tablespoons aloe vera juice*

DIRECTIONS:
1. In a pitcher combine all ingredients and stir well.
2. Serve on ice.

See glossary of ingredients for tips on choosing a good-quality aloe vera juice.

Makes 2 servings

Chia Sports Drink

This is an excellent sports drink. It's filled with electrolytes and essential fatty acids, which are anti-inflammatory and help decrease recovery time after a workout. Try taking it with you to the gym for the ultimate recharge.

INGREDIENTS:
- 16 ounces coconut water, fresh or store bought
- 2 Tablespoons chia seeds
- 2 Tablespoons fresh squeezed lime **or** lemon juice
- 2 Tablespoons agave nectar

DIRECTIONS:
Combine all ingredients, stir, and enjoy!

Makes 2 servings

Chia Fresca

This is an adaption from a traditional Central American drink.

INGREDIENTS:
- 2 quarts water
- 1 cup freshly squeezed lime juice
- ¾ cup agave nectar
- ¼ cup chia seeds
- Several sprigs of fresh mint for garnish (optional)

DIRECTIONS:
1. Combine water, lime juice, and agave. Stir in the chia seeds.
2. Garnish with mint leaves.
3. Serve in tall glasses over ice.

OPTIONAL VARIATIONS:
- Make an "aqua fresca" by blending fresh fruits with water and then add the chia seeds.
- Or use fresh or store-bought juice and add the chia. Great combinations include: mango and lime, cantaloupe and lime, or lemon and apple.

Makes about 8 servings

Hot Drinks

Spiced Apricot Cider

INGREDIENTS:
- 2 cups apricot nectar
- 2 ½ cups water
- ¼ cup lemon juice
- 2 Tablespoons agave nectar
- 2 whole cloves
- 2 cinnamon sticks, each about 3 inches long

DIRECTIONS:
1. In a saucepan, combine all ingredients and stir. Cover and cook on low for 2 hours.
2. Remove cloves and cinnamon sticks before serving.

Makes 4 servings

Chocolate Milk

INGREDIENTS:
- 1 cup unsweetened milk (cow, goat, almond, rice, coconut, oat, etc.)
- 1 ½ Tablespoon chocolate syrup (see page 103)

DIRECTIONS:
1. Gently heat milk, being careful not to boil or scald it.
2. Add chocolate syrup. Stir well.
3. Serve as hot chocolate or place in the fridge for a nice, cold chocolate milk drink.

Makes 1 serving

Hot Chocolate

INGREDIENTS:
- ½ cup unsweetened cocoa powder
- ¼ cup agave nectar
- 1 teaspoon pure vanilla extract
- ½ cup cold water
- 3 cups milk (cow, goat, rice, oat, almond, etc.)
- Whipped cream (optional)
- Shaved chocolate (optional)

DIRECTIONS:
1. In a large, heavy saucepan, combine the cocoa powder, agave, vanilla, and water.
2. Heat the mixture over low heat, whisking, until the cocoa powder is dissolved and the mixture is a smooth paste.
3. Gradually add the milk and simmer, whisking for 2 minutes.
4. For a special touch, top with whipped cream and shaved chocolate.

OPTIONAL VARIATIONS:
- **Mexican Hot Chocolate:** Add a pinch of cayenne pepper.
- **Irish Hot Chocolate:** Add 1 ounce Bailey's Irish Cream.
- **Warm Hug:** Add 1 ounce Peppermint Schnapps.

Makes 3 servings

Hot Mint Chocolate

INGREDIENTS:
- ½ cup hot water infused with 5 mint teabags
- ½ cup unsweetened cocoa powder
- ¼ cup agave nectar
- 1 teaspoon pure vanilla extract
- 3 cups milk (cow, goat, rice, oat, almond, etc.)
- Whipped cream (optional)
- Shaved chocolate (optional)

DIRECTIONS:
1. Add 5 mint tea bags to ½ cup of hot water and let stand for 10-12 minutes.
2. In a large, heavy saucepan, combine the cocoa powder, agave, vanilla, and mint tea infusion, and heat the mixture over low heat, whisking, until the cocoa powder is dissolved and the mixture is a smooth paste.
3. Gradually add the milk and simmer, whisking for 2 minutes.
4. For a special touch, top with whipped cream and shaved chocolate.

Makes 3 servings

Mexican Chocolate Elixir

This recipe is an adaption of an ancient Mayan drink.

INGREDIENTS:
- 1 ⅓ cup milk (cow, goat, almond, rice, oat, etc.)
- 1 cup cocoa powder
- 1 Tablespoon ground ancho chili pepper **or** 1 teaspoon chipotle chili **or** any red chili pepper
- 1 cinnamon stick **or** 1 teaspoon ground cinnamon
- ¼ teaspoon ground achiote (annatto) seeds (optional)
- 1 ½ cups (9 ounces) high-quality unsweetened chocolate
- ½ cup agave nectar
- 2 teaspoons raw cacao nibs
- 1 Tablespoon cornmeal
- 1 teaspoon pure vanilla extract
- Whipped cream
- Extra ancho chili for dusting

DIRECTIONS:
1. In a heavy saucepan, heat the milk over medium-high heat until warm, stirring occasionally.
2. Turn heat to low and add cocoa powder, chili, cinnamon stick, and optional achiote seed. Simmer for 15-20 minutes.
3. Remove from heat and strain out the spices. Add hot mixture to a blender.
4. Add chocolate and allow to melt.
5. Add agave, raw cacao nibs, cornmeal, and vanilla. Blend on high for a minute. Be cautious when blending hot liquids. If mixture is too thick, thin with water or milk.
6. Serve topped with whipped cream and ancho chili sprinkled on top.

Makes about 2 servings

My Beverage Creations:

Use this section to write down some of your favorite customized beverage recipes from this chapter.

Recipe:

. . . .

INGREDIENTS:

DIRECTIONS:

Serves _____

My Beverage Creations:

Use this section to write down some of your favorite
customized beverage recipes from this chapter.

Recipe:

INGREDIENTS:

....

....

....

....

....

....

....

DIRECTIONS:

....

....

....

....

....

....

Serves _____

CHAPTER 7

FLAVORED AGAVE NECTARS AND EXTRACTS

Making Your Own Flavored Agave

Base Recipe 94

Sample Combinations 94

Making Your Own Extracts

Base Extract Recipe 95

Flavored Agave Nectars

Edible essential oils can be added to agave nectar to create sweet-flavored syrups. It is extremely important that you select food-grade essential oils and avoid artificial oils and perfumes. The following fragrant syrups can be used on pancakes, in tea, drizzled over fruit or ice cream, or eaten as a delicious treat.

Base Recipe

1-2 drops of essential oil to ¼ cup of agave nectar

SAMPLE COMBINATIONS

Orange Agave Nectar

- ¼ cup agave nectar
- 2 drops orange essential oil

Chocolate Agave Nectar

- ¼ cup agave nectar
- 2 drops cocoa essential oil

Rose Agave Nectar

- ¼ cup agave nectar
- 1 drop rose essential oil

Lemony Agave Nectar

- ¼ cup agave nectar
- 1 drop lemon essential oil
- 1 drop lemongrass essential oil

Peppermint Agave Nectar

- ¼ cup agave nectar
- 1 drop peppermint essential oil

Geranium Ginger Agave Nectar

- ¼ cup agave nectar
- 1 drop geranium essential oil
- 1 drop ginger essential oil

Lemon Balm Lime Agave Nectar

- ¼ cup agave nectar
- 1 drop lemon balm essential oil
- 1 drop lime essential oil

Orange Clary Sage Agave Nectar

- ¼ cup agave nectar
- 1 drop orange essential oil
- 1 drop clary sage essential oil

Cayenne Black Pepper Agave Nectar

- ¼ cup agave nectar
- 1 drop cayenne essential oil
- 1 drop black pepper essential oil

The following is a list of some edible food-grade essential oils:			
• Anise	• Coriander	• Lavender	• Peppermint
• Basil	• Cumin	• Lemon	• Rose
• Bergamot	• Dill	• Lemon Balm	• Rosemary
• Black pepper	• Fennel	(Melissa)	• Sage
(not spicy, just	• Garlic	• Lemongrass	• Spearmint
aromatic)	• Geranium	• Lime	• Tangerine
• Cardamom	• German	• Mandarin	• Thyme
• Cinnamon	chamomile	• Marjoram	• Ylang-ylang
• Clary Sage	• Ginger	• Nutmeg	
• Clove	• Grapefruit	• Orange	
• Cocoa	• Jasmine	• Parsley	

Making Your Own Extracts

Essential oils are the essence of aromatic plants. Edible essential oils (such as anise, caraway, dill seed, peppermint, rosemary, and a host of others) are usually obtained by boiling the seeds, leaves, or other plant parts with water and condensing the vapors. Citrus essential oils are simply squeezed out of the rinds. When you choose an essential oil, look for therapeutic-grade so you are getting the highest quality oil.

Extracts are essential oils dissolved in ethyl alcohol, glycerol, or propylene glycol and may also contain water, a sweetening agent, or a food color. Purchased extracts are generally not as strong as the undiluted essential oil. See "Base Extract Recipe" above for making your own extracts.

Base Extract Recipe:

- 4 Tablespoons grain alcohol
- 1 Tablespoon edible essential oil
- 2 teaspoons agave nectar

Mix well and store in a dark, cool place.

My Flavored Agave Creations:

Use this section to write down some of your favorite customized flavored agave recipes from this chapter.

Recipe:

INGREDIENTS:

DIRECTIONS:

Serves _____

My Flavored Agave Creations:

Use this section to write down some of your favorite customized flavored agave recipes from this chapter.

Recipe:
. . . .

INGREDIENTS:

DIRECTIONS:

Serves _____

My Flavored Agave Creations:

Use this section to write down some of your favorite customized flavored agave recipes from this chapter.

Recipe:

INGREDIENTS:

DIRECTIONS:

Serves _____

CHAPTER 8

SYRUPS, SAUCES, AND FROSTINGS

Syrups and Sauces

Easy Fruit Syrup 100

Blackberry Sauce 101

Raspberry Sauce 101

Strawberry Sauce 102

Cranberry Orange Sauce 103

Chocolate Syrup 103

Carob Sauce 103

Cocoa Glaze for Cake 104

Apple Cider Sauce 105

Sweet Flax Sauce 105

Whipped Cream 106

Nutmeg Cream 106

Marzipan 107

Frostings

Fluffy Frosting 108

Vanilla Meringue Frosting 108

Peanut Butter Frosting 109

Creamy Coconut Frosting 109

Cocoa Nut Frosting 110

Carob Banana Frosting 110

Cream Cheese Frosting 110

Syrups and Sauces

Easy Fruit Syrup

Fruit syrups make wonderful toppings for angel food cake, pancakes, hot grain cereal, waffles, and whatever else you can think of!

Light Syrup:

- ⅔ cup agave nectar
- 3 cups water
- 1 cup fruit (strawberries, raspberries, blueberries, apples, pears, peaches, etc.)

Medium Syrup:

- ⅔ cup agave nectar
- 2 cups water
- 1 cup fruit

Heavy Syrup:

- ⅔ cup agave nectar
- 1 cup water
- 1 cup fruit

DIRECTIONS:
1. Boil agave and water for 5 minutes.
2. Add fruit and boil until fruit is heated through, about 10 minutes.
3. Store in a glass jar in the refrigerator.

Makes 3-4 cups

Blackberry Sauce

INGREDIENTS:
- ⅔ cup agave nectar
- ¼ cup water
- 2 cups blackberries
- 1 ½ Tablespoons fresh lemon juice
- 1 ½ teaspoons Crème de Cassis liqueur (optional)

DIRECTIONS:
1. Heat agave and water, stirring every minute or so. Cook for 5 minutes.
2. Add blackberries and lemon juice and cook 10 minutes more.
3. Add Crème de Cassis liqueur (optional).
4. Strain and serve over ice cream, pancakes, or waffles.

Makes about 4 cups

Raspberry Sauce

INGREDIENTS:
- ⅔ cup agave nectar
- ¼ cup water
- 2 cups raspberries
- 1 ½ Tablespoons fresh lemon juice
- 1 ½ teaspoons Framboise liqueur (optional)

DIRECTIONS:
1. Heat agave and water, stirring every minute or so. Cook for 5 minutes.
2. Add raspberries and lemon juice and cook 10 minutes more.
3. Add Framboise liqueur (optional).
4. Strain and serve over ice cream, pancakes, or waffles.

Makes about 4 cups

Strawberry Sauce

INGREDIENTS:
- ⅔ cup agave nectar
- ¼ cup water
- 2 cups strawberries, cut into small pieces
- 1 ½ Tablespoons fresh lemon juice
- 1 ½ teaspoons Fragoli wild strawberry liqueur (optional)

DIRECTIONS:
1. Heat agave and water, stirring every minute or so. Cook for 5 minutes.
2. Add strawberries and lemon juice, and cook 10 minutes more.
3. Add Fragoli wild strawberry liqueur (optional).
4. Strain and serve over ice cream, pancakes, or waffles.

Makes about 4 cups

Cranberry Orange Sauce

Perfect for holiday meals!

INGREDIENTS:
- 1 12-ounce bag of fresh cranberries
- 1 cup agave nectar
- 1 cup orange juice or water
- Orange zest (optional)

DIRECTIONS:
1. Add all ingredients to a saucepan and simmer on low heat for 15 minutes or until cranberries are totally soft.
2. Crush the cranberries with the back of a spoon.
3. Pour into a dish and set in the refrigerator for an hour or more. The sauce will thicken as it cools.

Makes about 4 cups

Chocolate Syrup

This is a great topping on ice cream or brownies.

INGREDIENTS:
- ¾ cup unsweetened cocoa powder
- 1 cup agave nectar
- ¼ teaspoon high-quality salt
- 1 teaspoon pure vanilla extract

DIRECTIONS:
1. Combine cocoa and agave in a saucepan and blend until all lumps of cocoa are gone.
2. Add salt and mix well.
3. Cook over medium heat, bringing it to a gentle boil for 2 minutes. Stir until thick.
4. Remove from heat, add vanilla, and cool completely.
5. Store in a mason jar in refrigerator.

Makes about 1 ½ cups

Carob Sauce

INGREDIENTS:
- 1 cup carob powder
- 1 cup agave nectar
- ¼ teaspoon high-quality salt
- 2 teaspoons pure vanilla extract

DIRECTIONS:
1. Boil together carob powder, agave, and salt. Stir constantly with a whisk.
2. Simmer over low heat for 10-15 minutes.
3. Add vanilla and remove from heat. Stir to thoroughly combine.
4. Store in an airtight glass jar.

Makes about 2 cups

Cocoa Glaze for Cake

INGREDIENTS:
- 1 ½ cups heavy cream
- 1 cup agave nectar
- 1 ½ cups cocoa powder
- 3 Tablespoons tapioca flour
- 3 Tablespoons butter
- 1 Tablespoon pure vanilla extract

DIRECTIONS:

To make glaze:

1. Heat cream in a saucepan over low heat, and stir in the agave.
2. Sift together the cocoa and tapioca flour and add to cream and agave mixture.
3. Add the butter and stir mixture over low heat for about 10 minutes or until smooth. Be careful not to boil. Stir in vanilla.
4. Strain glaze through fine sieve.

To glaze a cake:

1. Trace the cake pan you used for your cake on a piece of cardboard. Cut out the cardboard shape and place under your cake. Place cardboard and cake on a cooling rack positioned over a baking sheet.
2. Pour warm chocolate glaze generously over cake to coat completely. Refrigerate for 30 minutes or until the glaze is set. If you want to do a second coat, reheat remaining glaze and repeat process.
3. Chill to set glaze. Keep cake refrigerated until ½ hour before serving.

Cocoa Cream Frosting: Chill remaining glaze for about 30 minutes or until it is just beginning to get firm. Whip with an immersion blender or hand mixer until it is light and fluffy. Fill a piping bag with frosting and decorate cake.

Makes enough glaze to cover one 9" cake

Apple Cider Sauce

This sauce is delicious on vanilla ice cream or apple cake.

INGREDIENTS:
- 2 cups apple cider
- 2 teaspoons arrowroot flour
- 4 teaspoons cold water
- 1 Tablespoon butter
- 1 Tablespoon agave nectar

DIRECTIONS:
1. Boil cider in a small, heavy saucepan over high heat until reduced to 1 cup, about 15-20 minutes.
2. In a separate bowl or cup, mix arrowroot and cold water. Gradually add arrowroot to the cider while stirring. Cook until slightly thickened, about 1 minute.
3. Remove from heat and swirl in butter until melted, then add agave.
4. Sauce can be used either warm or chilled.

Makes about 2 cups

Sweet Flax Sauce

This makes an excellent and highly nutritious topping to muesli or hot grain cereals in the morning topped with fresh fruit.

INGREDIENTS:
- 3 Tablespoons flaxseed oil
- 1 cup cottage cheese
- 1 Tablespoon milk (cow, goat, almond, rice, coconut, oat, etc.)
- 1 Tablespoon agave nectar

DIRECTIONS:
1. Blend all ingredients until smooth.
2. Store in a glass jar in the refrigerator and use within 1 week.

Makes about 1 ½ cups

Whipped Cream

INGREDIENTS:
- 2 cups heavy cream
- 2 Tablespoons agave nectar or to taste
- 1 Tablespoon pure vanilla extract

DIRECTIONS:
1. In a large bowl, whip cream with a whisk or hand blender until slightly stiff.
2. Add agave. Continue to whip until cream forms soft peaks. Don't whip beyond the soft-peak stage or you might end up with butter.
3. Use immediately. Stores in the refrigerator for about 24 hours.

OPTIONAL ADDITIONS:
- A few drops of extracts such as almond or lemon.
- 1/4 teaspoon of floral waters such as rosewater or orange flower water.

Makes 3 1/2 cups

Nutmeg Cream

This cream is delicious on cobblers and crisps.

INGREDIENTS:
- ½ cup whipping cream
- 2 Tablespoons agave nectar
- 2 Tablespoons butter
- ¼ teaspoon nutmeg

DIRECTIONS:
1. Combine all ingredients in saucepan and bring to a light boil.
2. Simmer, stirring often, for 5 minutes or until mixture thickens slightly.
3. Place in the refrigerator until cool, then whip with a hand mixer or immersion blender until stiff.

Makes about 2 cups

Marzipan

(Almond Paste)

When you buy almond paste, it almost always has sugar in it. Try making your own and having some on hand for making delicious cookies and candies.

INGREDIENTS:
- 1 cup whole almonds, blanched* *or* 1 ⅓ cups slivered almonds
- 2 Tablespoons water
- 2 teaspoons butter
- 2 Tablespoons agave nectar
- ½ teaspoon almond extract (optional)

DIRECTIONS:
1. Preheat oven to 300°F.
2. Place almonds in a single layer on a cookie sheet.
3. Bake for 10 minutes, stirring occasionally to prevent browning. Cool 5 minutes.
4. Place almonds in a food processor using a steel blade, and process for 1 minute until almonds are ground.
5. Add water, butter, agave, and almond extract. Process for about 15 seconds until paste forms a ball. Use immediately or wrap in waxed paper and keep in a sealed container in the refrigerator. It can also be frozen.

Makes about 1 cup of almond paste

* Blanched means skins removed.

Frostings

Fluffy Frosting

This is a wonderful frosting for cakes and cupcakes.

INGREDIENTS:
- 2 egg whites
- ¼ teaspoon cream of tartar
- ½ cup agave nectar
- 1 teaspoon pure vanilla extract

DIRECTIONS:
1. Using a mixer or immersion blender, beat egg whites until stiff, then add the cream of tartar.
2. Heat agave to a boil.
3. Drizzle hot agave over stiffly beaten egg whites. Add vanilla.
4. Beat until the consistency is thick enough to spread.

Makes 2-3 cups

Vanilla Meringue Frosting

INGREDIENTS:
- ¼ teaspoon high-quality salt
- 2 egg whites
- 1 ½ cups agave nectar
- 2 teaspoons pure vanilla extract

DIRECTIONS:
1. Add salt to egg whites and beat with a mixer or hand mixer or whisk by hand.
2. Add the agave in a thin stream over egg whites while beating vigorously. Continue to beat until frosting is stiff.
3. Mix in vanilla until combined. Frost cake as desired.

Makes 2-3 cups

Peanut Butter Frosting

INGREDIENTS:
- 2 ¼ Tablespoons agave nectar
- ¼ cup butter, softened
- ¾ cup creamy peanut butter
- 1 teaspoon pure vanilla extract

DIRECTIONS:

1. Combine agave and butter and mix well.
2. Stir in peanut butter and vanilla.
3. Spread over banana bread, brownies, or serve as dip for sliced apples.

Makes about 1 cup

Creamy Coconut Frosting

INGREDIENTS:
- 1 cup coconut milk (do not use 'lite' coconut milk)
- 1 cup agave nectar
- ⅛ teaspoon high-quality salt
- 5 teaspoons arrowroot flour
- 1 teaspoon tapioca flour
- 1 Tablespoon water
- 1 ¼ cup coconut oil

DIRECTIONS:
1. In a medium saucepan, heat the coconut milk, agave, and salt and simmer on low.
2. In a bowl, mix arrowroot, tapioca, and water and form a paste. Add the paste to the coconut milk, stirring constantly.
3. Increase heat and bring mixture to a boil, stirring constantly.
4. Remove from heat and add coconut oil. Use an immersion blender or hand mixer to blend ingredients.
5. Place in freezer for about 30 minutes or until the frosting firms.
6. Beat frosting with immersion blender or hand mixer again until fluffy.
7. Spread over cakes or cupcakes.

Makes about 3 ½ cups

Cocoa Nut Frosting

INGREDIENTS:

- 3 Tablespoons agave nectar
- 3 Tablespoons butter, softened
- ⅔ cup buttermilk powder
- ⅓ cup cocoa powder **or** carob powder
- 4 Tablespoons cream cheese, softened
- ½ cup chopped nuts

DIRECTIONS:

1. Beat agave and butter together with a hand mixer or immersion blender.
2. Stir in buttermilk powder and either cocoa powder or carob powder.
3. Add cream cheese, mixing until smooth.
4. Spread over cake and top with nuts.

Makes about 2 cups

Carob Banana Frosting

INGREDIENTS:

- 1 ½ cups very ripe mashed banana
- 1 cup carob powder
- 3 Tablespoons unsalted butter, softened
- ½ teaspoon pure vanilla extract
- 2 teaspoons agave nectar

DIRECTIONS:

1. In a large bowl, combine all ingredients.
2. Using either a hand mixer or an immersion blender, beat until smooth.
3. Spread over cakes and cupcakes.

Makes about 3 cups

Cream Cheese Frosting

INGREDIENTS:

- Two 8-ounce packages cream cheese, softened
- ½ cup butter, melted (softened)
- 1 teaspoon pure vanilla extract
- ¾ cups agave nectar
- 1 Tablespoon milk (optional)

DIRECTIONS:

1. In a large bowl, combine all ingredients.
2. Using either a hand mixer or an immersion blender, beat until smooth.
3. Refrigerate until ready to use.

To color frosting: Many health food stores sell a natural food-based dye that you can add to the frosting or you can make your own.

- *For a rich pink color, add 7 Tablespoons of raspberries.*
- *For a purple/blue color, add 5 Tablespoons of blueberries.*

Makes about 2 cups

My Syrup, Sauce, and Frosting Creations:

*Use this section to write down some of your favorite
customized syrup, sauce, and frosting recipes from this chapter.*

Recipe:

INGREDIENTS:

....

....

....

....

....

....

....

DIRECTIONS:

....

....

....

....

....

....

Serves _____

My Syrup, Sauce, and Frosting Creations:

*Use this section to write down some of your favorite
customized syrup, sauce, and frosting recipes from this chapter.*

Recipe:

INGREDIENTS:

DIRECTIONS:

Serves _____

CHAPTER 9

JAMS, JELLIES, PRESERVES, AND MARMALADES

Understanding the Differences .114

Base Recipes

Fruit Jam made with Pomona's Universal Pectin Kit 115

Jelly made with Pomona's Universal Pectin Kit 116

No-Cook Freezer Jam with Agar-Agar 117

Instant Easy Fruit Jam with Agar-Agar 118

Raw Jam 119

Sample Recipes

Apple Butter 120

Apricot Agar-Agar Jam 121

Rose Apple Jelly 122

Mint Jelly 123

Berry Jam 124

Citrus Marmalade 125

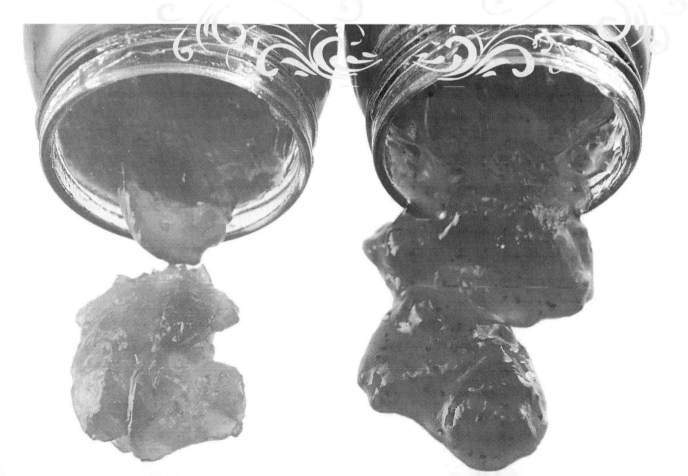

Understanding the Differences

Jams, jellies, preserves, and marmalades are usually made with sugar, but agave acts as a wonderful substitute that sets up fine with the thickening agents.

Jam is made with whole fruit that is smashed, blended, and cooked down to a pulp to release the pectin. The final product is a spreadable paste. **Preserves** are just like jam except they contain chunks of fruit or whole fruit. **Jellies** are made with fruit juice, pectin, and a sweetener. They are clear and free of fruit bits. Jellies can be made with ingredients other than fruit, including herbs, tea, wine, liqueurs, flowers, and vegetables. **Marmalades** are preserves made with the rind, pulp, and juice of citrus fruits. They do not usually include added pectin because there is natural pectin in the rind of citrus. They are used as spreads and glazes.

Fruits and herbs typically (and not so typically) used:

Blueberry, strawberry, boysenberry, raspberry, blackberry, currant, chokecherry, fig, grape, orange, grapefruit, kumquat, peach, apricot, cherry, plum, pear, mango, pomegranate, persimmon, lemon, apple, rhubarb, pineapple, ripe elderberries, prickly pear.

OPTIONAL ADDITIONS:
Try adding in other flavors to make your own unique jams, preserves, jellies, and marmalades.

- Lemon, orange, or lime zest
- Ginger, mint, lemon balm, or vanilla bean
- Floral waters, such as rosewater or orange flower
- Essential oils, such as mint or rose
- Extracts, such as vanilla

Canning:

If you have never canned before, it will be necessary to acquire some canning equipment, including home canning jars and lids, a utensil set for picking up the hot jars, a stainless steel water bath canning pot, and a canning rack. Read the instructions that come with your jars to learn how to safely and properly prepare your jars for canning.

Thickening Agents:

Traditionally, jams, jellies, marmalades, and preserves were thickened with naturally occurring fruit pectin in citrus and apple peel. Today, people more commonly use pectin powders since they simplify the process. The following recipes use three different sources of thickening: Pomona's Universal Pectin kit, agar-agar seaweed, and naturally occurring pectin found in apple and citrus peels. If using a pectin powder, I prefer to use the brand Pomona's instead of typical pectin packets because they work well with no-sugar jams and jellies. Detailed instructions for preparing different fruits are included with the kit.

Base Recipes

Fruit Jam made with Pomona's Universal Pectin Kit

· ·

Canning is necessary.

INGREDIENTS:
- 4 cups fruit, cleaned, peeled, and pitted, if necessary
- ¼ cup lemon **or** lime juice
- 2 teaspoons calcium water (instructions included in kit)
- ½ cup agave nectar
- 2 teaspoons fruit pectin powder

DIRECTIONS:
1. Crush the fruit in a saucepan or purée in a food processor or blender. Bring to a boil for 5 minutes.
2. Add lemon or lime juice.
3. Add calcium water and stir.
4. In a small bowl, mix agave and pectin powder. Add the agave-pectin mixture to the saucepan and stir vigorously for 2 minutes. The mixture should be totally dissolved in the jam. Allow the mixture to come back to a boil and remove from heat.
5. For immediate use, store in a sealed container in the refrigerator for up to 4 weeks.
6. To can: Pour hot jam into hot sterilized jars leaving ¼" headspace. Wipe the rims clean with a cloth. Seal and process in a boiling water canner for 5 minutes plus one more minute for each additional 1,000 feet of altitude over 5,000 feet. Check the seals — lids should be sucked down. Cool and store in a cool, dry, dark place. Refrigerate after opening.

Makes about 4-5 half-pint jars

Jelly made with Pomona's Universal Pectin Kit

Canning is necessary.

INGREDIENTS:
- 4 cups fruit juice (see below)
- ¼ cup lemon **or** lime juice
- 4 teaspoons calcium water (instructions included in kit)
- 1 cup agave nectar
- 4 teaspoons pectin powder

DIRECTIONS:
1. You can either use premade juice or make your own by mashing fruit (cleaned, peeled, and pitted, if necessary) through a strainer and collecting juice, running fruit through a juicer, or by boiling the fruit with 1/2 cup of water and straining.
2. Measure 4 cups of fruit juice into a large saucepan and add lemon or lime juice.
3. Add calcium water and stir. Bring to a boil.
4. In a small bowl, mix agave and pectin powder. When the fruit juice has come to a boil, add the agave-pectin mixture and stir vigorously for 2 minutes. The mixture should be totally dissolved in the juice. Allow the mixture to come back to a boil and remove from heat.
5. For immediate use, store in a sealed container in the refrigerator for up to 4 weeks.
6. To can: Pour hot jelly into hot sterilized jars leaving ¼-inch headspace. Wipe the rims clean with a cloth. Seal and process in a boiling water canner for five minutes plus one more minute for each additional 1,000 feet of altitude over 5,000 feet. Check the seals — lids should be sucked down. Cool and store in a cool, dry, dark place. Refrigerate after opening.

Makes about 4-5 half-pint jars

No Cook Freezer Jam with Agar-Agar

Canning is necessary.

INGREDIENTS:
- 3 cups chopped fruit (at room temperature)
- 1 Tablespoon lemon juice
- 3 cups cold water
- 2 Tablespoons agar-agar flakes
- ¼ cup agave nectar

DIRECTIONS:
1. Wash, hull, and finely chop the fruit.
2. In a mixing bowl, stir the lemon juice into the fruit. Set aside.
3. Place 3 cups of water in a small saucepan and stir in the agar-agar flakes. Turn on heat and bring the agar-agar to a simmer over medium-low heat until agar-agar is completely dissolved, about 2-5 minutes.
4. Stir the agave into the agar-agar mixture.
5. Continue stirring and add the agar-agar mixture to the fruit (do not add the fruit to the agar-agar). Stir until well combined. You can taste the mixture at this time and add more agave — up to 3 Tablespoons, if desired.
6. For immediate use, store in a sealed container in the refrigerator for up to 4 weeks.
7. To can: Pour hot jam into hot sterilized jars leaving ¼-inch headspace. Seal and process in a boiling water canner for five minutes plus one more minute for each additional 1,000 feet of altitude over 5,000 feet. Let cool in the refrigerator for 10-12 hours before freezing. Label and freeze the jam for up to 6 months.
8. When ready to use, thaw the jam in the refrigerator. It will keep about 3 weeks in the refrigerator.

Makes about 4 half-pint jars

Instant Easy Fruit Jam with Agar-Agar

Canning is not necessary.

INGREDIENTS:
- 1 cup fruit (apricot, peach, blackberry, raspberry, etc.)
- 1 Tablespoon agave nectar
- ¼ cup apple juice
- 1 Tablespoon agar-agar flakes **or** ¼ teaspoon agar-agar powder **or** ¼ stick of agar-agar (found in health food stores and Asian markets)

DIRECTIONS:
1. Clean, peel, and pit the fruit, if necessary. Make a pulp by adding fruit to a food processor and pulsing with the agave and apple juice.
2. Add fruit pulp to a saucepan and add agar-agar. Bring to a boil and simmer for 5 minutes or until agar-agar is totally dissolved.
3. Test the jam for firmness (agar's thickening effect varies according to its fineness) by putting a large metal spoon with a small amount of jam in the freezer for a couple of minutes until the jam is chilled. If the jam is the right thickness, your recipe is done. If the jam is too watery, stir in more agar, simmer the jam for another 5-10 minutes, and test it again. If the jam is too thick, stir in some fruit juice or water and test it again immediately.
4. Add to a half-pint jar, and store in the refrigerator for up to 3 weeks.

Makes about 1 half-pint jar

Raw Jam

A dehydrator is necessary.

INGREDIENTS:
- 2 cups fruit
- ½ cup raw agave nectar

DIRECTIONS:
1. Clean, peel, and pit the fruit, if necessary.
2. Combine fruit and agave in a blender and blend until smooth.
3. Pour onto a Teflex sheet and dehydrate at 105°F, stirring once in a while, for a couple of hours or until it is the consistency you want.
4. Use it on your favorite raw bread or crackers.

Makes 2 half-pint jars

Sample Recipes

Apple Butter

Canning is necessary.

INGREDIENTS:
- 4 lbs of cooking apples (Granny Smith or Gravenstein apples work well)
- 2 cups water
- 1 cup apple cider vinegar
- Approximately 2 ⅔ cups agave nectar (see below)
- ¼ teaspoon high-quality salt
- 2 teaspoons cinnamon
- ½ teaspoon ground cloves
- ½ teaspoon allspice
- Grated rind and juice of 1 lemon

DIRECTIONS:
1. Cut the apples into quarters. Don't core the apples and leave the skins on. Add to a large saucepan and add water and vinegar. Cook covered for 20 minutes, then remove from heat.
2. Ladle the cooked apple mixture into a food mill and process to make a pulp. You can also use a Chinois sieve and with the use of a pestle, force the pulp into a large bowl below. Measure the final pulp and add ⅓ cup of agave to every 1 cup of apple pulp. Add salt, cinnamon, ground cloves, allspice, lemon rind, and lemon juice.
3. Return the mixture to a large saucepan and cook on medium heat, stirring constantly for about 20 minutes or until the mixture is thick and smooth.
4. To can: Pour hot jelly into hot sterilized jars leaving ¼-inch headspace. Wipe the rims clean with a cloth. Seal and process in a boiling water canner for five minutes plus one more minute for each additional 1,000 feet of altitude over 5,000 feet. Check the seals — lids should be sucked down. Cool and store in a cool, dry, dark place. Refrigerate after opening.

Makes about 3 half-pint jars

Apricot Agar-Agar Jam

Canning is not necessary.

INGREDIENTS:
- 1 cup fresh apricots, pitted
- ¼ cup unsweetened peach juice **or** apricot juice
- 1 Tablespoon agave nectar
- 1 Tablespoon agar-agar flakes **or** ¼ teaspoon agar-agar powder **or** ¼ stick of agar-agar (found in health food stores and Asian markets)
- ¼ teaspoon freshly grated nutmeg

DIRECTIONS:
1. Make a fruit pulp by adding apricots to a food processor and pulsing with the juice and agave.
2. Add fruit pulp to a saucepan and add agar-agar and nutmeg. Bring to a boil and simmer for five minutes or until agar-agar is totally dissolved.
3. Test the jam for firmness.
4. Add to a half-pint jar and store in the refrigerator for up to three weeks.

Makes about 2 half-pint jars

Rose Apple Jelly

Made with Pomona's Universal Pectin Kit

Canning is necessary.

INGREDIENTS:
- 3 lbs apples
- 8 cups rose petals, packed
- 2 ⅔ cups hot water
- ¼ cup lemon juice
- 2 teaspoons calcium water (instructions included in kit)
- 1 cup agave nectar
- 2 teaspoons pectin powder

DIRECTIONS:
1. Cut the apples into quarters. Don't core the apples and leave the skins on. Add to a large saucepan and add enough water to just cover. Cook uncovered for 35-40 minutes or until apples are beginning to fall apart.
2. Carefully transfer the hot apples and juice to a sieve suspended over a large bowl. Avoid mashing the apples so no solids get through the sieve. The objective is to let the perfectly clear apple juice drip into the bowl below. Allow the apples to drain for about 1 ½ hours undisturbed.
3. In a glass bowl, add rose petals and 2 ⅔ cups hot water. Allow to sit undisturbed for 30 minutes.
4. In a large saucepan, bring 4 cups of the apple juice to a boil and add lemon juice.
5. Add calcium water and stir. Bring to a boil.
6. In a small bowl, mix agave and pectin powder. When the fruit juice has come to a boil, add the agave-pectin mixture and stir vigorously for 2 minutes. The mixture should be totally dissolved in the juice. Allow the mixture to come back to a boil. Next, add rose petals and soaking liquid. Cook over a gentle heat for 10-15 minutes, then remove from heat.
7. To can: Pour hot jelly into hot sterilized jars leaving ¼-inch headspace. Wipe the rims clean with a cloth. Seal and process in a boiling water canner for five minutes plus one more minute for each additional 1,000 feet of altitude over 5,000 feet. Check the seals — lids should be sucked down. Cool and store in a cool, dry, dark place. Refrigerate after opening.

Makes about 4-5 half-pint jars

Mint Jelly

. . . .

Made with Pomona's Universal Pectin Kit

Canning is necessary.

INGREDIENTS:
- 3 lbs apples
- 2 cups minced mint leaves
- ½ cup hot water
- 2 teaspoons calcium water (instructions included in kit)
- ⅓ cup agave nectar
- 2 teaspoons pectin powder
- 1-2 drops of food grade essential oil of peppermint (optional for extra mint flavor)

DIRECTIONS:
1. Cut apples into quarters. Don't core the apples and leave the skins on. Add to a large saucepan and add enough water to just cover them. Cook uncovered for 35-40 minutes or until apples are beginning to fall apart.
2. Carefully transfer the hot apples and juice to a sieve suspended over a large bowl. Avoid mashing the apples so no solids get through the sieve. The objective is to let the perfectly clear apple juice drip in to the bowl below. Allow the apples to drain for about 1 ½ hours, undisturbed.
3. In a glass bowl, add mint leaves and ½ cup hot water. Allow to sit undisturbed for 30 minutes.
4. In a large saucepan, measure 4 cups of the apple juice and bring to a boil.
5. Add calcium water and stir. Bring to a boil.
6. In a small bowl, mix agave and pectin powder. When the fruit juice has come to a boil, add the agave-pectin mixture and stir vigorously for 2 minutes. The mixture should be totally dissolved in the juice. Allow the mixture to come back to a boil, then add mint leaves and soaking liquid. Cook over a gentle heat for 10-15 minutes, then remove from heat.
A variation of the recipe would be to simply add the mint water and omit the mint leaves. At the very end, add essential oil of peppermint and stir well.
7. To can: Pour hot jelly into hot sterilized jars leaving ¼-inch headspace. Wipe the rims clean with a cloth. Seal and process in a boiling water canner for 5 minutes plus one more minute for each additional 1,000 feet of altitude over 5,000 feet. Check the seals — lids should be sucked down. Cool and store in a cool, dry, dark place. Refrigerate after opening.

Makes about 4-5 half-pint jars

Berry Jam

Made with Pomona's Universal Pectin Kit

Canning is necessary.

INGREDIENTS:
- 2 cups strawberries
- 2 cups raspberries
- ¼ cup lemon **or** lime juice
- 2 teaspoons calcium water (instructions for making calcium water included in kit)
- ½ cup agave nectar
- 2 teaspoons fruit pectin powder

DIRECTIONS:
1. Crush the berries in a saucepan. You can also purée them in a food processor or blender. Bring to a boil for 5 minutes.
2. Add lemon or lime juice.
3. Add calcium water and stir.
4. In a small bowl, mix agave and pectin powder. Add the agave-pectin mixture to the saucepan and stir vigorously for 2 minutes. The mixture should be totally dissolved in the jam. Allow the mixture to come back to a boil, then remove from heat.
5. For immediate use, store in a sealed container in the refrigerator for up to 4 weeks.
6. To can: Pour hot jam into hot sterilized jars leaving ¼-inch headspace. Wipe the rims clean with a cloth. Seal and process in a boiling water canner for 5 minutes plus one more minute for each additional 1,000 feet of altitude over 5,000 feet. Check the seals — lids should be sucked down. Cool and store in a cool, dry, dark place. Refrigerate after opening.

Makes about 4-5 half-pint jars

Citrus Marmalade

Canning is necessary.

When peeling citrus fruits for marmalades, be sure to include some of the pith (the white membrane just under the skin, where most of the pectin is found).

INGREDIENTS:
- ¾ cup grapefruit peel, about 1 grapefruit
- ¾ cup orange peel, about 1 orange
- ⅓ cup lemon peel, about 1 lemon
- 1 quart cold water
- Pulp of 1 grapefruit
- Pulp of 4 medium-sized oranges
- Pulp of 1 lemon
- 2 cups boiling water
- 2 cups agave nectar

DIRECTIONS:
1. Wash and peel fruit. Measure the peel and cut into thin strips.
2. Add strips into a small saucepan. Add cold water and simmer, covered, until tender, about 30 minutes. Drain and set aside in a bowl.
3. While the strips are simmering, prepare the fruit pulp. Remove seeds, peel, and membrane from 1 grapefruit, 3 oranges, and 1 lemon. Cut into fine pieces.
4. Add 2 cups of water back into the saucepan and bring to a boil. Add strips, citrus fruit, and agave.
5. Boil rapidly over high heat, stirring frequently, for about 20 minutes.
6. For immediate use, store in a sealed container in the refrigerator for up to 4 weeks.
7. To can: Pour hot marmalade into hot sterilized jars leaving ¼-inch headspace. Wipe the rims clean with a cloth. Seal and process in a boiling water canner for 5 minutes plus one more minute for each additional 1,000 feet of altitude over 5,000 feet. Check the seals — lids should be sucked down. Cool and store in a cool, dry, dark place. Refrigerate after opening.

Makes about 3 or 4 half-pint jars

My Jam, Jelly, Preserves, and Marmalade Creations:

Use this section to write down some of your favorite customized jam, jelly, preserves, and marmalade recipes from this chapter.

Recipe:

INGREDIENTS:

....

....

....

....

....

....

....

DIRECTIONS:

....

....

....

....

....

....

Serves _____

CHAPTER 10

BREADS

Top Tips for Making Bread..... 128

Yeasted

Whole Grain Bread 130

Spelt Oat Bread 131

Spelt Herb Bread 132

Dill Bread 133

Pumpernickel Bread 134

Oat Bran Bread. 135

Kamut Buttermilk Bread.......... 136

Dark Rye Bread. 137

Orange Rye Bread 138

Corn Bread 139

Carob Bread 140

Peasant Bread. 141

Challah 142

English Muffins 143

Stollen 144

Pizza Crust. 145

Pretzels....................... 146

Cinnamon Rolls. 147

Yeast-Free

Banana Bread 148

Apricot Bread 149

Carrot Bread. 150

Corn Bread with Corn
and Green Chile. 151

Amaranth Cornbread 152

Gluten-Free

Potato Millet Bread (yeasted)...... 153

Brown Rice Bread (yeasted) 154

Pizza Crust (yeasted). 155

Pretzels (yeasted). 156

Banana Chocolate Chip
Bread (yeast-free) 157

Top Tips For Making Great Breads

If you have never made bread before, you are in for a treat. Bread making does come with varying degrees of complexity — from the most basic to the most artistic levels. Whatever you are inspired to do, remember that baking bread doesn't have to be difficult and the rewards are well worth the effort. When you make your own bread, you can control the quality of the flours and other ingredients. You can also make several loaves at once and then slice and freeze it. If you don't get perfect bread the first time you try, don't give up. With a little practice and the following tips, you will be well on your way to fragrant kitchen smells and your very own delicious homemade bread.

Yeast:

Always use fresh yeast. If the yeast is old, there is a risk that your bread won't rise. It's also important when making yeasted breads to pay attention to the temperature of the liquid that you are feeding to the yeast. Yeast that is live and active will foam when added to warm water. If the liquid you place the yeast in is too hot, it will kill the yeast. Liquid that is too cold will not activate the yeast and the bread will not rise properly. For best results use a liquid that is just above warm but not scalding (see box to the right).

Yeast and Temperature

- At lower than 50°F (10°C), yeast is inactive.
- At 60°F - 70°F (15°C - 21°C), yeast action is slow.
- At 90°F - 100°F (32°C - 38°C), yeast is at its optimum temperature for fermentation.
- At higher than 104°F (40°C), yeast action starts to slow.
- At 138°F (58°C), yeast is killed.

Mixing Ingredients:

Before you start, make sure you are working on a clean surface and have assembled all the ingredients and measuring tools in front of you. Get organized first — if you're running around gathering ingredients, you can easily forget an ingredient or skip a step. Typically, your yeast-liquid mixture will be activating in the background as you assemble the dry ingredients. Next you'll stir in your wet ingredients and mix the dough with a wooden spoon or your hands. When the ingredients are well integrated, the dough can be set aside to rise.

Allowing the Dough to Rise:

When your dough is mixed you will need to cover it. I prefer natural fiber bread towels or any other clean, thin cloth that is slightly damp. This allows the dough to breathe while keeping moisture in. Place the dough in a warm area to help insure that it rises. If you notice that your bread dough isn't rising, try finding a slightly warmer environment. You can also place the dough in a gas oven with the pilot light on or in an electric oven with the light on and let the dough rise there. When your dough has doubled, you may want to punch it down and allow it to rise once more. A second rise will help to distribute the yeast and create a more even texture. A second rise will also relax the gluten in the bread and may even improve flavor.

Kneading:

This part of bread making can be intimidating but with practice you will learn the "feel" of the dough. Bread-making machines save time, but breads made in them may not turn out quite as well as breads made by hand. Throughout history, humans have made bread with nothing more than a bowl, a wooden board, and a pair of hands. It's a lot of fun to work the dough, so I recommend keeping it simple, without machines, and getting flour up to your elbows in the spirit of old-world bread making.

The Surface: Start off by lightly flouring your surface. Formica or marble counters won't absorb moisture from the dough, whereas wood may absorb moisture and require additional flour in the kneading process.

Technique: Scrape the dough onto a smooth, floured surface. Push the dough down and forward with the heels of your hands. Fold it back on itself, give the dough a quarter turn, and repeat. Keep kneading the dough for about 4-5 minutes, then cover it. Let it rest about 5 minutes, then knead again for 1-2 minutes. Allow the dough to rise for 30-45 minutes or shape it into a loaf (depending on the recipe and type of flours used).

Shaping:

There are numerous shapes to choose from. The size and shape will determine the bake time, so be sure to adjust the recipe if you are using a smaller shape.

Standard Loaf Pan: The easiest is to use a bread-loaf pan. Form a loaf that is a similar shape to a bread pan, then press the dough into the shape of the pan. This will create a shape that is great for sandwiches.

Bloomer: A cylindrical bread with slightly tapered ends, it is flat on the bottom and has diagonal slashes across the top.

Cob or Boulé: A round bread, known as cob in Britain and boulé in France.

Baguette: A long, rounded bread. Baguette is a French term for "stick" and it is typically 2-4 inches in diameter and 1-2 feet long.

Braided: Made by dividing the dough into 3 equal parts, making uniform strands or ropes, and braiding them together.

Rolls: Small rounds that are made by simply rolling little balls of dough in the palm of your hand and baking on an oiled cookie sheet about 1 ½ inches apart to allow for rising. Since they are smaller, decrease baking time to only 20-25 minutes.

Bread Sticks (Grissini): A pencil-shaped bread said to have originated near Turin, Italy. Breadsticks can either be dry and cracker-like or soft like bread. Bread sticks are often twisted and topped with salt or sesame seeds. They make a great accompaniment to soup.

Yeasted Breads

Whole Grain Bread

INGREDIENTS:
- 2 cups warm water
- 2 ¼ teaspoons dry active yeast (1 package)
- ⅓ cup agave nectar
- 1 cup kamut flour
- 1 cup whole spelt flour
- 1 cup oat flour
- 1 teaspoon high-quality salt
- 1 cup oat bran
- ¾ cup buttermilk powder
- Extra flour and neutral-tasting oil (grapeseed, untoasted sesame oil, coconut oil, **or** ghee) for kneading and greasing pan

DIRECTIONS:
1. In a large bowl, combine warm water and yeast.
2. Add agave and dissolve in the yeast mixture. Stir until yeast is dissolved and allow yeast to foam for 10 minutes.
3. Add kamut, spelt, oat flour, and salt and mix. Add in oat bran and buttermilk powder. Stir until a sticky dough forms.
4. Cover the bowl with a damp kitchen towel and let the dough rise in a warm area for about 30 minutes or until doubled in size.
5. Preheat oven to 350°F. If using a baking stone, place it in the oven to preheat.
6. Punch the dough down. Knead dough on lightly floured surface. Add more flour if necessary until dough no longer sticks to your hands. Knead the dough for about 10 minutes. Divide the dough into 2 equal pieces and form into loaves. Place the loaves into 2 lightly greased 9" x 5" loaf pans for a more square shape or shape dough as desired and place directly onto an oiled cookie sheet or baking stone. Cover with damp towel and let rise again until doubled.
7. Bake for 40-45 minutes or until the top is golden brown and the bottom of the loaf sounds hollow when tapped.
8. With a butter knife, loosen the sides, then gently remove from pans and place on cooling rack.

Makes about 2 loaves

Spelt Oat Bread

INGREDIENTS:
- 2 cups boiling water
- 1 cup rolled oats
- ⅜ cup agave nectar
- 2 Tablespoons butter
- 2 teaspoons high-quality salt
- 2 ¼ teaspoons dry active yeast (1 package)
- ½ cup warm water
- 2 cups spelt flour
- 2 cups oat flour
- Extra flour and neutral-tasting oil (grapeseed, untoasted sesame oil, coconut oil, **or** ghee) for kneading and greasing pan

TOPPING:
- 2 Tablespoons agave
- 2 Tablespoons rolled oats

DIRECTIONS:
1. In a large mixing bowl, combine boiling water, oats, agave, butter, and salt. Let stand for 1 hour.
2. In a small bowl, dissolve the yeast in warm water and allow yeast to foam for 10 minutes.
3. Pour the yeast mixture into the oat mixture and stir.
4. Add spelt flour and mix well. Stir in oat flour, ½ cup at a time, beating well after each addition. Knead about 5 minutes.
5. Lightly oil a large bowl and place the dough in the bowl and turn to coat with oil. Cover with a damp kitchen towel and let rise in a warm place until doubled in volume, about 1 hour.
6. Punch the dough down and turn it out onto a lightly floured surface. Divide the dough into 2 equal pieces and form into loaves. Place the loaves into 2 lightly greased 9" x 5" loaf pans for a more square shape or shape dough as desired and place directly onto an oiled cookie sheet or baking stone. Cover with damp towel and let rise again until doubled.
7. Preheat oven to 375°F. If using a baking stone, place it in the oven to preheat.
8. Bake for 40-45 minutes or until the top is golden brown and the bottom of the loaf sounds hollow when tapped. Remove loaves from pans, cool on a cooling rack, and brush the tops of the loaves with 2 Tablespoons of agave and sprinkle with oats.

Makes about 2 loaves

Spelt Herb Bread

INGREDIENTS:
- 1 cup warm water
- 2 teaspoons dry active yeast
- 1 teaspoon agave nectar
- ⅔ cup cottage cheese
- 2 eggs
- 2 Tablespoons neutral-tasting oil (grapeseed, untoasted sesame oil, coconut oil, **or** ghee)
- 1 ½ teaspoon high-quality salt
- 1 teaspoon fresh parsley, chopped
- 1 teaspoon fresh dill, chopped
- 1 teaspoon fresh chives, chopped
- 2 cups spelt flour
- 2 cups white spelt flour
- Extra flour and neutral-tasting oil for kneading and greasing pan

DIRECTIONS:
1. In a large bowl, combine warm water and yeast.
2. Add agave and dissolve in the yeast mixture. Stir until yeast is dissolved and allow yeast to foam for 10 minutes.
3. Add the following to the yeast water: cottage cheese, eggs, grapeseed oil, salt, and chopped herbs. Stir well.
4. Add spelt flour and stir vigorously for 3 minutes. Gradually begin to add the white spelt flour and keep stirring, making a firm dough.
5. Knead the dough on a lightly floured surface (spelt flour works well). Sprinkle oil over the top or add more flour if necessary. Knead until the dough is no longer sticky, about 10 minutes.
6. Place the dough in an oiled bowl, cover with a damp kitchen towel, and put in a warm place. Allow dough to rise until doubled, about 1 hour.
7. Preheat oven to 350°F. If using a baking stone, place it in the oven to preheat.
8. Punch the dough down and turn it out onto a lightly floured surface. Divide the dough into 2 equal pieces and form into loaves. Place the loaves into 2 lightly greased 9" x 5" loaf pans for a more square shape or shape dough as desired and place directly onto an oiled cookie sheet or baking stone. Cover with damp towel and let rise again until doubled.
9. Bake for 35-40 minutes or until the top is golden brown and the bottom of the loaf sounds hollow when tapped. If you are making breadsticks, reduce baking time to 15 minutes or until golden brown.
10. With a butter knife, loosen the sides, then gently remove from pans and cool on a cooling rack.

Makes about 2 loaves

Dill Bread

INGREDIENTS:
- ½ cup warm water
- 1 ½ teaspoons dry active yeast
- 2 Tablespoons agave nectar
- 1 ½ cups kamut flour
- ¼ cup tapioca flour
- ¾ cup rye flour
- 1 teaspoon dill seeds
- 1 teaspoon dill weed
- 1 teaspoon caraway seeds
- 1 teaspoon high-quality salt
- ¾ cup yogurt
- 2 Tablespoons neutral-tasting oil (grapeseed, untoasted sesame oil, coconut oil, **or** ghee)
- Extra flour and neutral-tasting oil for kneading and greasing pan

DIRECTIONS:
1. In a large bowl, combine warm water and yeast.
2. Add agave and dissolve in the yeast mixture. Stir until yeast is dissolved and allow yeast to foam for 10 minutes.
3. In a separate bowl, sift together kamut, tapioca, and rye flours. Add dill seeds, dill weed, caraway seeds, and salt. Mix.
4. Add dry ingredients to the yeast mixture, then add yogurt and oil. Stir until a sticky dough forms.
5. Cover the bowl with a damp kitchen towel and let the dough rise in a warm area for about 30 minutes or until doubled in size.
6. Punch the dough down and turn it out onto a lightly floured surface. Divide the dough into 2 equal pieces and form into loaves. Place the loaves into 2 lightly greased 9" x 5" loaf pans for a more square shape or shape dough as desired and place dough directly onto an oiled cookie sheet or baking stone. For bread sticks, roll out down into roll dough into 8" ropes. Cover with damp towel and let rise again until doubled.
7. Preheat oven to 375°F. If using a baking stone, place it in the oven to preheat.
8. Bake for 35-40 minutes or until the top is golden brown and the bottom of the loaf sounds hollow when tapped. If you are making breadsticks, reduce baking time to 15 minutes or until golden brown.
9. With a butter knife, loosen the sides, then gently remove from pans and cool on a cooling rack.

Makes 2 loaves or 6-10 bread sticks

Pumpernickel Bread

INGREDIENTS:

- 3 medium potatoes
- 4 cups water
- 1 Tablespoon of dry active yeast
- ½ cup warm water, if necessary
- ¼ cup molasses
- ⅛ cup agave nectar
- 1 ½ teaspoons high-quality salt
- 2 Tablespoons melted butter

- 1 ½ Tablespoons caraway seeds (optional)
- 3 cups rye flour
- 3 cups spelt flour
- 2 cups oat flour
- Extra flour and neutral-tasting oil (grapeseed, untoasted sesame oil, coconut oil, **or** ghee) for kneading and greasing pan

DIRECTIONS:

1. Quarter the potatoes and boil in 4 cups of water until soft. Remove the potatoes from the water and reserve the water. The potatoes can be used in another recipe but aren't needed for the bread.
2. Allow potato water to cool to just warm. Measure 2 ½ cups of warm potato water and set it aside.
3. In a separate bowl, sprinkle yeast over ½ cup of warm potato water, stir once and let foam for 10 minutes.
4. In a medium bowl, mix the reserved 2 ½ cups of potato water with the molasses, agave, salt, butter and optional caraway seeds. At this point you can freeze leftover potato water in ice-cube trays and then transfer to zip lock bags for future use.
5. Add the foaming yeast to the liquid mixture.
6. Stir in the rye flour and stir with vigor for about 2 minutes. Add the spelt flour and stir for another minute. Stir in the oat flour. The dough should be fairly stiff.
7. Scrape the dough off the sides of the bowl and cover with a damp towel. Let the dough rest for 30 minutes.
8. Drop dough onto a well-oiled surface and knead the dough for about 10 minutes. Add more flour if necessary until dough no longer sticks to your hands.
9. Wash the bowl, dry, and oil with grapeseed oil. Place dough back in the bowl, cover with a damp kitchen towel, and allow it to rise in a warm place for about an hour or until doubled.
10. Punch dough down, cover again, and let rise another 45 minutes or until doubled again.
11. Preheat oven to 375°F. If using a baking stone, place it in the oven to preheat.
12. Punch down the dough and let it rise another 10 minutes. Cut the dough in half. Shape the halves into two tapered ovals and place on a baking sheet that has been covered generously with cornmeal.
13. Cover again with the damp kitchen towel, place in a warm area, and let it rise for 30 minutes or until doubled. Cut diagonal slices across the top of the loaves with a sharp knife. Gently transfer the loaves onto the baking stone or to a baking sheet.
14. Bake loaves for 40 minutes.
15. Remove from the oven and place on cooling rack.

Makes about 3 loaves

Oat Bran Bread

INGREDIENTS:
- ¼ cup warm water
- 1 Tablespoon dry active yeast
- 2 Tablespoons agave nectar
- 1 cup warm milk (cow, goat, almond, rice, coconut, oat, etc.)
- 1 egg
- 2 Tablespoons neutral-tasting oil (grapeseed, untoasted sesame oil, coconut oil, **or** ghee)
- 1 teaspoon high-quality salt
- 1 cup oat flour
- 2 cups oat bran
- 1 cup graham flour
- Extra flour and neutral-tasting oil for kneading and greasing pan

DIRECTIONS:
1. In a large bowl, combine warm water and yeast.
2. Add agave and dissolve in the yeast mixture. Stir until yeast is dissolved and allow yeast to foam for 10 minutes.
3. Add the warm milk, egg, oil, and salt to the yeast mixture and stir until well combined.
4. Add oat flour, oat bran, and graham flour to the wet mixture and stir vigorously until well combined.
5. Knead dough on lightly floured surface. Add more graham flour if necessary until dough no longer sticks to your hands. Knead the dough until elastic.
6. Place dough into lightly greased 8" loaf pan or shape dough as desired and place dough directly onto an oiled cookie sheet. Cover with a damp kitchen towel, set in a warm place, and let it rise until doubled, about 45 minutes.
7. Preheat oven to 375°F. If using a baking stone, place it in the oven to preheat.
8. Bake for 40 minutes or until the top is golden brown and the bottom of the loaf sounds hollow when tapped.
9. Scrape sides with a butter knife, remove loaf from pan, and cool on a cooling rack.

Makes 1 loaf

Kamut Buttermilk Bread

INGREDIENTS:

- 2 cups warm water
- 2 ¼ teaspoons dry active yeast
- ⅓ cup agave nectar
- 1 ½ teaspoons high-quality salt
- 2 cups kamut flour
- 1 cup whole spelt flour
- 1 cup oat flour
- ½ cup oat bran
- ½ cup buttermilk powder
- Extra flour and neutral-tasting oil (grapeseed, untoasted sesame oil, coconut oil, **or** ghee) for kneading and greasing pan

DIRECTIONS:

1. In a large bowl, combine warm water and yeast.
2. Add agave and salt and dissolve in the yeast mixture. Stir until yeast is dissolved and allow yeast to foam for 10 minutes.
3. Add kamut, spelt, and oat flour to the wet mixture and stir vigorously. Add oat bran and buttermilk powder and mix until well combined.
4. Knead dough on lightly floured surface, adding more kamut flour if necessary until dough no longer sticks to your hands, about 10 minutes.
5. Place the dough back in an oiled bowl, cover with a damp kitchen towel, and place in a warm area. Allow dough to rise until doubled, about 1 hour.
6. Preheat oven to 375°F. If using a baking stone, place it in the oven to preheat.
7. Punch the dough down and turn it out onto a lightly floured surface. Divide the dough into 2 equal pieces and form into loaves. Place the loaves into 2 lightly greased 9" x 5" loaf pans for a more square shape or shape dough as desired and place directly onto an oiled cookie sheet or baking stone. Cover with damp towel and let rise again until doubled.
8. To make pizza with the dough, roll out the dough to about 1/2" thick. Top with pizza sauce and desired toppings. Bake pizza crust for about 15-18 minutes.
9. Bake loaves for 35-40 minutes or until the top is golden brown and the bottom of the loaf sounds hollow when tapped.
10. With a butter knife, loosen the sides, then gently remove from pan and cool on a cooling rack.

Makes about 2 loaves

Dark Rye Bread

INGREDIENTS:

- 1 cup water
- ½ cup molasses
- 5-6 orange peels, grated
- 2 Tablespoons caraway seeds
- 2 Tablespoons fennel seeds, crushed
- 1 Tablespoon butter
- 1 ½ teaspoons high-quality salt
- 2 cups buttermilk **or** ¼ cup buttermilk powder mixed with 1 ¾ cups water
- ½ teaspoon baking soda
- 2 Tablespoons dry active yeast
- 1 teaspoon agave nectar
- ¼ cup warm water
- 4 cups rye flour
- 3 cups kamut flour
- Extra flour and neutral-tasting oil (grapeseed, untoasted sesame oil, coconut oil, **or** ghee) for kneading and greasing pan

TOPPING:

- ⅛ cup molasses
- ⅛ cup water

DIRECTIONS:

1. In a saucepan, gently heat water, molasses, orange peel, caraway seeds, fennel seeds, butter, and salt. When butter is melted, set aside to cool until warm.
2. In a separate bowl, mix buttermilk and baking soda and stir into spiced liquid mixture.
3. Dissolve yeast and agave in ¼ cup warm water and let foam for about 10 minutes.
4. Add yeast liquid to spiced liquid mixture and begin to add rye flour. Mix thoroughly. Slowly add the kamut flour, making sure the dough remains soft yet firm.
5. Knead dough on lightly floured surface. Sprinkle dough with oil or add more kamut flour, as necessary, until dough no longer sticks to your hands. Knead the dough for about 10 minutes.
6. Place the dough in an oiled bowl, cover with a damp kitchen towel, and place in a warm area. Allow dough to rise until doubled, about 1 hour.
7. Preheat oven to 375°F. If using a baking stone, place it in the oven to preheat.
8. Punch the dough down and turn it out onto a lightly floured surface. Divide the dough into 2 equal pieces and form into loaves. Place the loaves into 2 lightly greased 9" x 5" loaf pans for a more square shape or shape dough as desired and place directly onto an oiled cookie sheet or baking stone. Cover with damp towel and let rise again until doubled.
9. Bake for 35-40 minutes or until the top is golden brown and the bottom of the loaf sounds hollow when tapped.
10. With a butter knife, loosen the sides and gently remove from pan and place on cooling rack.
11. Combine molasses and water and brush the molasses mixture over the bread.

Makes about 2 loaves

Orange Rye Bread

INGREDIENTS:
- ½ cup warm orange juice **or** water
- 2 teaspoons caraway seeds
- 1 teaspoon high-quality salt
- ¼ cup agave nectar
- 1 ½ teaspoons dry active yeast
- ¼ cup apple cider vinegar
- ½ cup rye flour
- ¾ cup white spelt flour
- ½ cup spelt flour
- Additional ½ cup spelt flour for kneading
- 1 teaspoon grated orange peel (optional)
- Extra flour and neutral-tasting oil (grapeseed, untoasted sesame oil, coconut oil, **or** ghee) for kneading and greasing pan

DIRECTIONS:
1. In a saucepan, gently warm the orange juice with caraway seeds, salt, and agave. Remove from heat and pour into a large bowl. If the mixture is too hot, allow it to cool or it will kill the yeast. Sprinkle the yeast over top. Gently stir and let foam for about 10 minutes.
2. Pour in vinegar and stir.
3. Mix in rye flour, white spelt flour, and spelt flour. Mix vigorously for about 3 minutes.
4. Lightly flour a surface with ¼ cup of the spelt flour. Knead for about 5 minutes. Slowly knead in the remaining ¼ cup of spelt flour. Slam dough about 10 times onto the counter. Divide the dough into 2 equal pieces and form into loaves. Place the loaves into 2 lightly greased 9" x 5" loaf pans for a more square shape or shape dough as desired and place dough directly onto an oiled cookie sheet or baking stone. Cover with damp towel and let rise again until doubled.
5. Preheat oven to 350°F. If using a baking stone, place it in the oven to preheat.
6. Bake for 30 minutes. Remove from oven, brush with oil, and top with optional orange peel. Place bread back in the oven and bake for another 20 -25 minutes.
7. With a butter knife, loosen the sides and gently remove from pan and place on cooling rack.

Makes about 2 loaves

Corn Bread
. . . .

INGREDIENTS:
- ¼ cup warm water
- 1 Tablespoon dry active yeast
- 1 teaspoon agave nectar
- 1 cup milk (cow, goat, almond, rice, coconut, oat, etc.)
- ¼ cup butter
- 1 teaspoon high-quality salt
- 2 Tablespoons agave nectar
- 1 cup cornmeal
- 2 eggs
- 2 cups kamut **or** spelt flour
- 2 cups oat **or** brown rice flour
- Cornmeal for baking sheet
- Extra flour and neutral-tasting oil (grapeseed, untoasted sesame oil, coconut oil, **or** ghee) for kneading and greasing pan

DIRECTIONS:
1. In a large bowl, combine warm water and yeast.
2. Add 1 teaspoon agave and dissolve in the yeast mixture. Stir until yeast is dissolved and allow yeast to foam for 10 minutes.
3. In a medium saucepan, gently heat the milk, butter, salt, and 2 Tablespoons of agave until all ingredients are dissolved.
4. Whisk the cornmeal into the melted milk mixture. When warm, whisk in the eggs. If the mixture is too hot, it will cook the egg.
5. Add the yeast liquid to the mixture, then the remaining flour. Stir vigorously for 3 minutes. Cover the bowl with a damp kitchen towel, place in a warm area, and let rise for 30 minutes.
6. Punch down dough and knead on a well-floured surface until it is elastic. Add flour as needed, until dough no longer sticks to your hands.
7. Divide the dough into 2 equal pieces. Shape the halves into 2 tapered ovals or about 16 rolls and place on a baking sheet that has been covered generously with cornmeal. Cover again with the kitchen cloth.
8. Preheat oven to 375°F. If using a baking stone, place it in the oven to preheat.
9. Bake for 35 minutes or until the top is golden brown and the bottom of the loaf sounds hollow when tapped. For rolls, bake for about 15 minutes.
10. Scrape sides with a butter knife, remove loaf from pan, and cool on a cooling rack.

Makes about 2 loaves or 16 rolls

Carob Bread

INGREDIENTS:
- 1 ¾ cup warm water
- 2 teaspoons dry active yeast
- ¼ cup agave nectar
- ½ teaspoon high-quality salt
- 3 Tablespoons buttermilk powder
- 3 Tablespoons carob powder
- ½ teaspoon clove powder
- ½ cup dried cherries, currants, dried papaya, **or** any other dried fruit
- 2 cups kamut flour
- 2 cups oat flour
- 1 cup tapioca flour
- 2 Tablespoons neutral-tasting oil (grapeseed, untoasted sesame oil, coconut oil, **or** ghee)
- 2 teaspoons pure vanilla extract
- Extra flour and neutral-tasting oil for kneading and greasing pan

DIRECTIONS:
1. In a large bowl, combine warm water and yeast.
2. Add agave and dissolve in the yeast mixture. Stir until yeast is dissolved and allow yeast to foam for 10 minutes.
3. In a large bowl, add salt, buttermilk powder, carob powder, clove powder, dried fruit, kamut flour, and oat flour. Stir well, about 3 minutes. Add tapioca flour and stir well.
4. Add oil, vanilla extract, and yeast mixture, and stir until well combined.
5. Flour a surface with kamut flour. Knead for about 5-10 minutes, adding more kamut flour until the dough no longer sticks to your hands. Place in a warm area and let rise until doubled.
6. Preheat oven to 325°F. If using a baking stone, place it in the oven to preheat.
7. Punch the dough down and turn it out onto a lightly floured surface. Divide the dough into 2 equal pieces and form into loaves. Place the loaves into 2 lightly greased 9" x 5" loaf pans for a more square shape or shape dough as desired and place dough directly onto an oiled cookie sheet or baking stone.
8. Bake for 50-60 minutes. Brush with water after 30 minutes to prevent over-baking the top of the bread. Continue baking for the remaining 20-30 minutes. Remove from oven and cool on a cooling rack.

Makes 1 large loaf or 2 small loaves

Peasant Bread

INGREDIENTS:

- ½ cup warm water
- 5 teaspoons dry active yeast
- 1 Tablespoon agave nectar
- 2 cups water
- ¼ cup apple cider vinegar
- ¼ cup molasses
- ¼ cup butter
- 4 cups rye flour
- 2 cups oat bran
- 2 Tablespoons caraway seeds, crushed
- 3 Tablespoons carob powder

- 2 teaspoons natural coffee substitute (like Cafix or Teecino)
- 2 teaspoons dried chives
- ½ teaspoon fennel, crushed
- 1 Tablespoon high-quality salt
- Extra flour and neutral-tasting oil (grapeseed, untoasted sesame oil, coconut oil, **or** ghee) for kneading and greasing pan

TOPPING:

- 1 egg yolk
- 1 Tablespoon water

DIRECTIONS:

1. In a large bowl, combine warm water and yeast.
2. Add agave and dissolve in the yeast mixture. Stir until yeast is dissolved and allow yeast to foam for 10 minutes.
3. In a small saucepan, gently heat water, vinegar, molasses, and butter. When butter is melted, set aside and allow to cool.
4. Add the following to the yeast mixture: rye flour, oat bran, caraway seeds, carob powder, coffee substitute, chives, fennel, and salt. Stir well.
5. Add cooled molasses mixture to the dough mixture and stir vigorously until the dough is stiff.
6. Knead dough on well-floured surface. Sprinkle oil over the top or add more flour as necessary so the dough no longer sticks to your hands. Knead for about 10 minutes.
7. Place the dough in an oiled bowl, cover with a damp kitchen towel, and set in a warm area. Allow dough to rise until doubled, about 1 hour.
8. Preheat oven to 375°F. If using a baking stone, place it in the oven to preheat.
9. Punch the dough down and turn it out onto a lightly floured surface. Divide the dough into 2 equal pieces and form into loaves. Place the loaves into 2 lightly greased 9" x 5" loaf pans for a more square shape or shape dough as desired and place dough directly onto an oiled cookie sheet or baking stone.
10. Cover with a towel and let rise again until doubled.
11. Mix egg yolk and water. Brush over the bread for a shiny crust. For simplicity, this step can be omitted.
12. Bake for 35-40 minutes.
13. With a butter knife, loosen the sides, then gently remove from pan and place on cooling rack.

Makes 2 loaves

Challah Bread

INGREDIENTS:
- 1 ⅓ warm milk (cow, goat, almond, rice, coconut, oat, etc.)
- 1 Tablespoon agave nectar
- 2 Tablespoons yeast
- 1 teaspoon high-quality salt
- ¼ cup agave nectar
- ¼ cup melted butter
- 3 eggs, beaten
- 4 cups kamut flour
- 1 ½ cups oat flour
- Extra flour and neutral-tasting oil (grapeseed, untoasted sesame oil, coconut oil, **or** ghee) for kneading and greasing pan

DIRECTIONS:
1. In a small saucepan, gently heat milk until warm.
2. Pour warm milk into a large bowl, add 1 Tablespoon of agave, and stir. Sprinkle yeast on top and stir until dissolved. Let sit and foam for about 10 minutes.
3. Next, whisk in the salt, ¼ cup of agave, butter, and eggs.
4. Stir in the kamut and oat flour and stir vigorously until well mixed.
5. Cover the bowl with a damp kitchen towel, set in a warm area, and allow the dough to rise for 1 hour, or until doubled in size.
6. When the dough has risen, cut it into 6 sections. Roll each section into a thick rope, about 8" long. Add more kamut so dough rolls easily and doesn't stick to your hands. Braid 3 ropes per loaf. You will have enough to make 2 loaves. Place the braids on oiled cookie sheets, cover with the damp towel, and rise again until doubled.
7. Preheat oven to 375°F. If using a baking stone, place it in the oven to preheat.
8. Bake loaves for 35 minutes or until golden. Remove from cookie sheets immediately and cool on wire racks.

OPTIONAL VARIATION:
Weave dyed Easter eggs into the braid to make a colorful egg-filled Challah bread for Easter!

Makes about 2 loaves

English Muffins

INGREDIENTS:
- ½ cup warm water
- 1 Tablespoon dry active yeast
- 1 cup hot water
- 2 teaspoons agave nectar
- 3 Tablespoons butter
- 1 teaspoon high-quality salt
- 1 cup kamut flour
- 1 cup oat flour
- ¼ cup buttermilk powder **or** whey powder
- 2 Tablespoons butter, melted
- 1¾ cup kamut flour
- ½ cup cornmeal for dusting
- Extra flour and neutral-tasting oil (grapeseed, untoasted sesame oil, coconut oil, **or** ghee) for kneading and greasing griddle

DIRECTIONS:
1. In a large bowl, combine warm water and yeast and allow yeast to foam for 10 minutes.
2. In a small saucepan, heat 1 cup water. Remove from heat and add agave, butter, and salt. The water should be hot enough to melt the butter. After butter is melted, allow mixture to cool slightly.
3. Meanwhile, combine kamut flour, oat flour, and buttermilk or whey powder in a large bowl.
4. Add the yeast solution to the butter mixture.
5. In a large bowl combine all the liquids with the flour mixture. Stir vigorously for 3 minutes. Cover with a clean, damp kitchen cloth and let rise in a warm area until the dough has doubled, about 1 hour.
6. Stir in 2 Tablespoons of melted butter and 1 ¾ cup of kamut flour. The dough should be stiff. If not add another ¼ cup oat flour.
7. Cover again and let rest another 30 minutes.
8. Knead dough on lightly floured surface (oat or kamut flour work well) and knead for 10 minutes. Try to add the least possible amount of flour to work the dough.
9. Roll the dough into ½" thick sheet and cut out circles with either a sharp pastry cutter or round cookie cutter. Make a clean, straight cut; if the edges are pinched, muffins won't rise properly.
10. Place the muffins on a cookie sheet that has been dusted with cornmeal. Dust the tops with cornmeal. Let rise for 30 minutes on the sheet.
11. Heat a greased griddle and cook muffins on griddle for 6 minutes on the first side on medium heat. Then flip and cook 4 minutes more. Cool the muffins on a wire rack. Store in glass containers or freeze for later use. To serve, split muffin in half and toast.

Makes about a dozen muffins

Stollen

INGREDIENTS:

- ½ cup warm water
- 1 teaspoon agave nectar
- 2 Tablespoon dry active yeast
- 1 cup water
- ½ cup melted butter
- ½ cup agave nectar
- 1 teaspoon high-quality salt
- ⅓ cup buttermilk powder
- 2 eggs
- 1 Tablespoon lemon zest
- 2 cups kamut flour

- 2 cups spelt flour
- 1 cup oat flour
- ¾ cup sliced almonds
- ½ cup raisins
- 1 cup cubed, honeyed papaya
- Extra flour and neutral-tasting oil (grapeseed, untoasted sesame oil, coconut oil, **or** ghee) for kneading and oiling bowl
- Butter for greasing pan

TOPPING:
- 3 Tablespoons melted butter

DIRECTIONS:

1. In a large bowl, combine warm water, 1 teaspoon agave, and yeast and allow yeast to foam for 10 minutes.
2. In a medium saucepan, gently heat 1 cup of water, butter, 1/2 cup agave, salt, and buttermilk powder until just dissolved. Then set aside to cool slightly.
3. In a small bowl, beat the eggs. Add to the yeast mixture.
4. Add lemon zest to yeast mixture.
5. Add yeast mixture to the warm butter mixture. Stir.
6. In a large bowl, combine kamut, spelt, and oat flours and mix well. Make a well in the center and add the liquids. Stir the mixture in singular strokes until all ingredients are thoroughly combined. Add almonds, raisins, and papaya and stir until all are evenly distributed.
7. Cover and place in a warm area for 30-40 minutes. After 30 minutes, punch down the dough and let it rise again for 30 minutes.
8. Knead dough on lightly floured surface for about 3-5 minutes, adding as little flour as possible. Place dough in a well-oiled bowl and let rise another 45 minutes.
9. Knead dough again on lightly floured surface. Cut the dough in half with a serrated knife and cut each half into five pieces. You will be making 2 braids.
10. Roll each piece into 16-inch strands. Join three strands of dough together at the beginning, and braid the three coils. Join them at the bottom as well to seal off the braid. Then twist two additional coils and place on top of the braid. Pinch the ends of the coils together and pinch the top coil twist into the braid at intervals.
11. Repeat for the second loaf.
12. Transfer loaves to a buttered cookie sheet. Cover with a clean towel and let rise until they double, about 30-40 minutes.
13. Preheat oven to 350°F. If using a baking stone, place it in the oven to preheat.
14. Brush each braid with melted butter and bake for 35 minutes.
15. For a softer crust, you can also brush the loaves with butter when they are removed from the oven and then sprinkle date sugar, coconut sugar, or maple sugar on top.
16. Cool on a wire rack before cutting into thin slices.

Makes 2 loaves

Pizza Crust

*Many bread recipes can also be used for making pizza crusts.
This one in particular is light and closely resembles a traditional
pizza dough.*

INGREDIENTS:
- 2 cups warm water
- 1 Tablespoon dry active yeast
- ⅓ cup agave nectar
- 2 teaspoons high-quality salt
- 2 cups kamut flour
- 1 cup spelt flour
- 1 cup white spelt flour
- 1 cup oat flour
- ¼ cup oat bran
- ¾ cup buttermilk powder
- 1 Tablespoon olive oil **or** grapeseed oil plus extra for greasing pan

DIRECTIONS:
1. In a large bowl, combine warm water and yeast and allow yeast to foam for 10 minutes.
2. Next, add agave and salt and dissolve in the yeast mixture. Let sit and foam for 10 minutes.
3. In a separate bowl, combine the kamut, spelt, white spelt, and oat flours. Add oat bran and buttermilk powder. Mix well.
4. Add dry ingredients to the yeast mixture and stir until a sticky dough forms. Cover the bowl with a damp towel and let the dough rise in a warm area for about 30 minutes or until doubled.
5. Preheat oven to 375°F. If using a baking stone, place it in the oven to preheat.
6. Turn the dough out onto a floured surface (any flour will be fine) and knead with your hands about 5-10 times. Add flour until dough no longer sticks to your hands.
7. Roll the dough to about 1/2" thick. Spread evenly into a well-oiled deep-dish pizza pan or spread onto a baking stone. Spread about 1 Tablespoon of oil over the dough with your hands.
8. For a thicker crust, prebake the crust at 350°F for 10 minutes, then increase the temperature to 375°F. Add toppings and bake another 10 minutes.
9. For a thinner crust, top the uncooked dough with pizza sauce and desired toppings. Bake at 375°F for 12-15 minutes.

Makes 2-3 thin crust or 1-2 deep-dish pizzas, depending on pan size.

Pretzels

. . . .

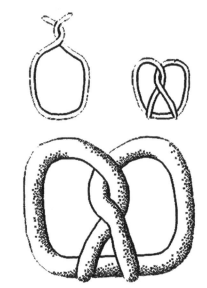

INGREDIENTS:
- 1 ¼ cup warm water
- 1 teaspoon agave nectar
- 1 teaspoon dry active yeast
- 4 ½ cups spelt **or** kamut flour
- 1 egg yolk
- 2 Tablespoons water
- Course sea salt to coat
- Neutral-tasting oil (grapeseed,
  untoasted sesame oil, coconut oil,
  or ghee) for greasing pan

DIRECTIONS:
1. In a large bowl, combine warm water, agave, and yeast and allow yeast to foam for
   10 minutes.
2. Gradually add flour and stir vigorously. Continue adding flour and keep stirring for about
   3 minutes to make a firm dough.
3. Knead dough on lightly floured surface about 5-10 times. Add flour as necessary, until dough
   no longer sticks to your hands.
4. Place the dough in a buttered bowl, cover with a damp cloth, and place in a warm area.
   Allow dough to rise until doubled, about 1 hour.
5. Preheat oven to 475°F.
6. Roll the dough into ¼" thick and 8" long ropes. Twist two ends and then fold back into
   a pretzel shape, indenting the dough with your thumb on the bottom left and right (see
   diagram above). Place onto a well-oiled cookie sheet.
7. Beat the egg yolk and water together and brush over pretzels. Sprinkle with coarse sea salt.
   Let rise until doubled in size.
8. Bake at 475°F for 8-10 minutes or until golden.

Makes about 3 dozen pretzels

Cinnamon Rolls

INGREDIENTS:

For the rolls:

- 1 cup warm milk (cow, goat, almond, rice, coconut, oat, etc.)
- ½ cup agave nectar
- 2 ½ teaspoons dry active yeast
- 1 teaspoon high-quality salt
- 2 ½ Tablespoons butter, melted
- 2 eggs, room temperature
- 2 cups oat flour
- 1 ½ cups kamut flour
- ½ cup millet flour
- ¾ cup date sugar, packed
- 2 ½ Tablespoons ground cinnamon

- ⅓ cup butter, softened
- Neutral-tasting oil (grapeseed, untoasted sesame oil, coconut oil, **or** ghee) for greasing pan
- More agave to drizzle

Topping:

- 1 (3-ounce) package cream cheese, softened
- ¼ cup butter, softened
- 1 cup agave nectar
- ½ teaspoon pure vanilla extract
- ⅛ teaspoon high-quality salt

DIRECTIONS:

1. Allow eggs and butter to warm to room temperature.
2. In a small saucepan, gently warm the milk—do not overheat.
3. In a large bowl mix together the warm milk, agave, yeast, and salt and let foam for about 10 minutes.
4. Mix in the butter and eggs.
5. Add oat, kamut, and millet flour and mix well. Stir rigorously for 5 minutes. Cover and let rise in a warm area for about 1 hour or until doubled in size.
6. After the dough has doubled in size, turn it out onto a floured surface, cover, and let rest for 10 more minutes.
7. Meanwhile, combine date sugar and cinnamon in a small bowl.
8. Sprinkle some flour on top of the dough and roll out to 16" x 21". Sprinkle with flour as necessary until dough rolls out smoothly.
9. Preheat oven to 400°F.
10. Spread ⅓ cup softened butter over the dough and sprinkle evenly with date sugar and cinnamon mixture. Drizzle agave lightly over sugar and cinnamon.
11. Roll dough into a log shape. Cut log into 12 rolls. Place rolls in a lightly greased 9" x 13" baking pan. Cover and let rise until nearly doubled, about 30 minutes.
12. Bake for about 15 minutes.

FOR THE TOPPING:

1. While rolls are baking, beat together cream cheese, ¼ cup softened butter, agave, vanilla and salt.
2. Spread frosting on warm rolls before serving.

Makes 12 rolls

Yeast-Free Breads

Banana Bread
. . . .

The flavor of this classic bread deepens with time.

INGREDIENTS:
- ½ cup butter
- 1 cup agave nectar
- 2 eggs
- 1 cup mashed bananas
- 1 teaspoon lemon juice
- 1 cup whole wheat pastry flour, kamut, **or** spelt flour
- 1 cup oat flour
- 1 Tablespoon baking soda
- ¾ teaspoon high-quality salt
- Neutral-tasting oil (grapeseed, untoasted sesame oil, coconut oil, **or** ghee) for greasing pan

DIRECTIONS:
1. Preheat oven to 375°F.
2. In a mixer, cream the butter and drizzle in the agave.
3. Add eggs, bananas, lemon juice, whole wheat pastry flour, oat flour, baking soda, and salt.
4. Pour batter into a greased 8" loaf pan.
5. Bake for 30 minutes or until a wooden pick inserted near center comes out clean.
6. With a butter knife, loosen the sides and gently remove from pan and place on cooling rack.

OPTIONAL ADDITIONS:
- Add 1 cup of chopped nuts of your choice at step 3.
- Add ½ teaspoon of ginger powder, ½ teaspoon cinnamon, and/or ¼ teaspoon cardamom powder.

Makes 1 loaf

Apricot Bread

INGREDIENTS:
- 1 ½ cups kamut flour
- 1 cup barley flour
- ½ cup brown rice flour
- 3 teaspoons baking powder
- 1 teaspoon ground cinnamon
- ½ teaspoon high-quality salt
- ¼ teaspoon ground nutmeg
- 1 cup milk (cow, goat, almond, rice, coconut, oat, etc.)
- ¾ cup agave nectar
- 1 egg, slightly beaten
- 2 Tablespoons grapeseed oil
- 1 cup chopped dried apricots
- ½ cup sunflower seeds, chopped walnuts, **or** chopped almonds
- ½ cup raisins
- Neutral-tasting oil (grapeseed, untoasted sesame oil, coconut oil, **or** ghee) for greasing pan

DIRECTIONS:
1. Preheat oven to 350°F.
2. Combine kamut flour, barley flour, brown rice flour, baking powder, cinnamon, salt, and nutmeg in a large bowl.
3. Combine milk, agave, egg, and grapeseed oil in a small bowl.
4. Pour liquid mixture over dry ingredients and stir until just moistened.
5. Add apricots, sunflower seeds, and raisins.
6. Pour into greased 9" x 5" x 13" loaf pan.
7. Bake for 55-60 minutes or until a wooden pick inserted near center comes out clean.
8. With a butter knife, loosen the sides and gently remove from pan and place on cooling rack.

Makes 1 loaf

Carrot Bread

INGREDIENTS:
- 1¼ cup oat flour
- ¾ cup brown rice flour
- ¼ cup amaranth flour
- 1 Tablespoon baking soda
- 2 teaspoons cinnamon powder
- ¾ teaspoon high-quality salt
- 1 cup neutral-tasting oil (grapeseed, untoasted sesame oil, coconut oil, **or** ghee)
- 1 cup agave nectar
- 3 eggs
- 2 cups grated carrot
- 1 teaspoon lemon juice
- 2 teaspoons pure vanilla extract
- Neutral-tasting oil for greasing pan

DIRECTIONS:
1. Preheat oven to 350°F.
2. In a mixer, add oat flour, brown rice flour, amaranth flour, baking soda, cinnamon, and salt and mix until well combined.
3. Add oil, agave, eggs, carrot, lemon juice, and vanilla. Mix until smooth.
4. Pour batter into a greased 8" loaf pan.
5. Bake for 45 minutes or until a wooden pick inserted near center comes out clean.
6. With a butter knife, loosen the sides and gently remove from pan and place on cooling rack.

Makes 1 loaf

Corn Bread with Whole Corn and Green Chili

INGREDIENTS:
- 2 Tablespoons butter, melted
- 1 cup cornmeal
- ¾ cup kamut flour
- ¼ cup oat bran **or** oat flour
- 4 teaspoons baking powder
- ¾ teaspoon high-quality salt
- 1 cup whole kernel corn, cut off the cob **or** frozen
- 1 cup milk (cow, goat, almond, rice, coconut, oat, etc,)
- ¼ cup agave nectar
- 2 large eggs
- ½ cup (4-ounce can) of green chilis, diced
- Neutral-tasting oil (grapeseed, untoasted sesame oil, coconut oil, **or** ghee) for greasing pan

DIRECTIONS:
1. Preheat oven to 350°.
2. Lightly oil 11" x 7" rectangular pan or large cast iron pot.
3. Gently melt butter in a double boiler or metal bowl resting over pot of boiling water.
4. Combine cornmeal, kamut flour, oat bran, baking powder, and salt in a large bowl.
5. In a separate bowl, combine corn kernels, milk, agave, melted butter, eggs, and green chili. (Green chili can be omitted, if desired.) Mix well, then add dry mixture.
6. Pour batter into greased dish.
7. Bake for 20-25 minutes or until a wooden pick inserted in the center comes out clean.
8. With a butter knife, loosen the sides and gently remove from pan and place on cooling rack.

Serves 8-12

Amaranth Cornbread

INGREDIENTS:
- ½ cup amaranth grain
- 1 ¼ cup water

- ½ cup cornmeal
- 1 cup barley flour
- ½ cup brown rice flour
- 1 ½ teaspoons baking powder
- ¾ teaspoon baking soda
- ¾ teaspoon high-quality salt
- 1 – 2 teaspoons cumin (optional)
- 1 cup milk (cow, goat, almond, rice, coconut, oat, etc.)
- 4 Tablespoons neutral-tasting oil (grapeseed, untoasted sesame oil, coconut oil, **or** ghee)
- 3 Tablespoons apple cider vinegar
- 2 Tablespoons agave nectar
- ½ cup corn kernels (optional)
- Neutral-tasting oil for greasing pan

DIRECTIONS:
1. In medium saucepan, combine amaranth and water. Bring to a boil, then reduce to a simmer. Cook for 20-30 minutes. Set aside. This can be done in advance.
2. Preheat oven to 350°F.
3. Oil a medium 9" x 16" pan.
4. In a large mixing bowl, combine cornmeal, barley flour, brown rice flour, baking powder, baking soda, salt, and cumin. Mix well.
5. Make a well in the center of the dry ingredients and add cooked amaranth, milk, oil, vinegar, agave, and corn kernels. Stir until well combined. Pour into greased baking dish.
6. Bake for 20-30 minutes or until a wooden pick inserted in the center comes out clean.
7. With a butter knife, loosen the sides and gently remove from pan and place on cooling rack.

Serves 6-8

Gluten-Free Breads

Potato Millet Bread (yeasted)

INGREDIENTS:

- 2 cups warm milk (cow, goat, almond, rice, coconut, oat, etc.)
- 2 Tablespoons agave nectar
- 1 ½ teaspoons dry active yeast
- 1 Tablespoon neutral-tasting oil (grapeseed, untoasted sesame oil, coconut oil, **or** ghee)
- 1 teaspoon high-quality salt
- 1 cup millet flour **or** ½ cup millet flour and ½ cup brown rice flour
- 1 cup potato flour
- ¼ cup brown rice flour

- 1 teaspoon xanthan gum **or** guar gum **or** a 50:50 combination of both
- 1 teaspoon kelp powder (optional mineral boost)
- 1 cup tapioca flour
- Extra flour and oil for kneading

Bread wash:

- 3 Tablespoons agave nectar
- 3 Tablespoons water

DIRECTIONS:

1. In a small saucepan, gently heat the milk until just warm.
2. In a small bowl, mix together the warm milk, agave, yeast, oil, and salt and allow yeast to foam for about 10 minutes.
3. In a large bowl, add millet flour, potato flour, brown rice flour, and gum. Add kelp powder if desired. Mix well, then add tapioca flour. Continue stirring until all dry ingredients are integrated.
4. Add the liquid mixture and mix the dough vigorously for 5 minutes. Knead dough with your hands in the bowl. If the mixture is too dry, add water 1 Tablespoon at a time until you get the desired consistency.
5. Cover the bowl with a damp kitchen towel and let the dough rise in a warm area for about 30 minutes or until doubled.
6. Knead dough on a surface lightly floured with brown rice flour. Sprinkle oil over dough or add more flour if necessary so that the dough no longer sticks to your hands. Knead for about 10 minutes.

7. Shape dough into a loaf and place in lightly greased 9" x 5" loaf pan for a more square shape or shape as desired and place directly onto an oiled cookie sheet or baking stone.
8. Cover with the towel and let rise again until doubled.
9. Preheat oven to 375°F. If using a baking stone, place it in the oven to preheat.

FOR THE BREAD WASH:

1. Brush a mixture of 3 Tablespoons agave and 3 Tablespoons of water over the bread.
2. Bake for 40-45 minutes or until golden.
3. With a butter knife, loosen the sides and gently remove from pan and place on cooling rack.

Makes about 1 loaf

Brown Rice Bread (yeasted)

INGREDIENTS:

- 3 cups warm water or as needed
- ¼ cup agave nectar
- 1 Tablespoon dry active yeast
- 6 cups brown rice flour
- ¼ cup neutral-tasting oil (grapeseed, untoasted sesame oil, coconut oil, **or** ghee)
- 1 Tablespoon high-quality salt
- 1 teaspoon xanthan gum **or** guar gum **or** a 50:50 combination of both
- Neutral-tasting oil for greasing pan

DIRECTIONS:

1. In a large bowl, combine warm water, agave, and yeast and allow yeast to foam for 10 minutes.
2. Add the following to the bowl of yeast water: brown rice flour, oil, salt, gum, and more warm water if necessary to make a soft dough. Cover the bowl with a damp kitchen towel and let the dough rise in a warm area for about 30 minutes.
3. Divide the dough into 2 equal pieces and form into loaves. Place the loaves into 2 lightly greased 9" x 5" loaf pans for a more square shape or onto an oiled cookie sheet.
4. Cover again with towel and let rise again until doubled.
5. Preheat oven to 350°F.
6. Bake for 20 minutes or until golden.
7. With a butter knife, loosen the sides and gently remove from pan and place on cooling rack.

Makes about 2 loaves

Gluten-Free Pizza Crust (yeasted)

INGREDIENTS:
- 1 ¾ cup warm water
- ¼ cup agave nectar
- 1 Tablespoon dry active yeast
- 2 teaspoons high-quality salt
- 1 ¼ cup tapioca flour
- 1 cup brown rice flour
- 1 cup sorghum flour
- 1 ½ cups millet flour
- 1 teaspoon xanthan gum **or** guar gum **or** a 50:50 combination of both
- 1 teaspoon apple cider vinegar
- ⅓ cup olive oil **or** grapeseed oil plus extra for topping and greasing pan
- 2 eggs

DIRECTIONS:
1. In a large bowl, combine warm water, agave, and yeast. Stir and allow yeast to foam for 10 minutes.
2. In a separate bowl, combine salt, tapioca flour, brown rice flour, sorghum flour, millet flour, and gum. Mix well.
3. Make a well in the dry ingredients and add yeast mixture to center.
4. Next, add vinegar, oil, and eggs, and stir all ingredients well.
5. Cover bowl with a damp towel and allow to sit in a warm area for 40 minutes or until dough has doubled.
6. Preheat oven to 375°F. If using a baking stone, place it in the oven to preheat.
7. Knead dough on lightly floured surface about 5-10 times. If the dough is sticky, keep sprinkling with flour until it no longer sticks to your hands.
8. Roll the dough to about ½" thick. Place dough onto baking stone or into a well-oiled, deep-dish pizza pan and spread evenly. Drizzle about 1 Tablespoon of oil on top of dough and spread with your hands.
9. For a thicker style crust, prebake at 350°F for 10 minutes. Increase temperature to 375°F and add toppings and bake another 10 minutes.
10. For a thinner crust, top the uncooked dough with pizza sauce and desired toppings. Bake at 375°F for 12-15 minutes.

Makes 2-3 thin crust or 1-2 deep-dish pizzas, depending on pan size.

Gluten-Free Pretzels (yeasted)

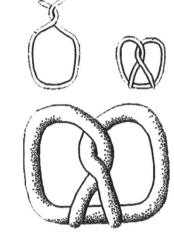

INGREDIENTS:

- 1 ¼ cup warm water
- 1 teaspoon agave nectar
- 1 teaspoon dry active yeast
- 2 cups tapioca flour
- 1 cup brown rice flour
- 1 ½ cups sorghum flour
- 1 teaspoon high-quality salt
- 1 ½ teaspoons xanthan gum
  or guar gum **or** a 50:50
  combination of both
- 1 egg yolk
- 2 Tablespoons water
- Course sea salt to coat
- Neutral-tasting oil (grapeseed, untoasted sesame oil, coconut oil, **or** ghee) for greasing pan

DIRECTIONS:

1. In a large bowl, combine warm water, agave, and yeast and allow yeast to foam for 10 minutes.
2. In a medium bowl, combine tapioca flour, brown rice flour, sorghum flour, salt, and gum. Mix well. Gradually add flour and stir vigorously. Continue adding flour and keep stirring for about 3 minutes to make a firm dough.
3. Knead dough on lightly floured surface about 5-10 times. If the dough is sticky, keep sprinkling with flour until the dough no longer sticks to your hands.
4. Place the dough in a buttered bowl. Cover with a damp cloth and set in a warm area. Allow dough to rise until doubled, about 1 hour.
5. Preheat oven to 475°F. If using a baking stone, place it in to the oven to preheat.
6. Roll the dough into ¼" thick and 8" long ropes. Twist two ends and then fold back into a pretzel shape, indenting the dough with your thumb on the bottom left and right sides (see diagram above). Place onto a well-oiled cookie sheet.
7. Beat the egg yolk and water together and brush over pretzels. Sprinkle with coarse sea salt. Let rise until doubled in size.
8. Bake for 8-10 minutes or until golden.

Makes about 3 dozen pretzels

Banana Chocolate Chip Bread

INGREDIENTS:
- Neutral-tasting oil (grapeseed, untoasted sesame oil, coconut oil, **or** ghee) for greasing pan
- 3 ripe bananas, mashed (about 1 cup of banana purée)
- ⅓ cup coconut oil
- ½ cup agave nectar
- 2 teaspoons pure vanilla extract
- ¾ cup brown rice flour
- ¾ cup white rice flour
- 1 teaspoon baking soda
- 2 ½ teaspoons baking powder
- ¼ teaspoon high-quality salt
- 1 Tablespoon arrowroot powder
- ½ teaspoon xanthan gum **or** guar gum **or** 50:50 combination of both
- 1 rounded teaspoon ground cinnamon
- ½ cup grain-sweetened chocolate chips

DIRECTIONS:
1. Preheat oven to 350°F. Lightly oil all sides of a standard bread loaf pan.
2. Peel the bananas and put on a plate. Use the back of a fork to mash the bananas. Measure 1 cup. Place in a large bowl.
3. Add coconut oil, agave, and vanilla to the bananas. Mix until smooth.
4. Add the dry ingredients to the bowl: brown rice flour, white rice flour, baking soda, baking powder, salt, arrowroot, gum, and cinnamon. Stir until smooth.
5. Stir in chocolate chips.
6. Pour batter into the prepared loaf pan and bake in the center of oven for 1 hour or until the loaf is firm, a bit crusty, and a wooden pick inserted into the center emerges clean.
7. Cool the loaf on a wire rack.

OPTIONAL ADDITIONS:
- Try adding ¼ cup of shredded coconut or chopped nuts for added protein.

Makes 1 loaf

My Bread Creations:

Use this section to write down some of your
favorite customized bread recipes from this chapter.

Recipe:
· ·

INGREDIENTS:

· ·

· ·

· ·

· ·

· ·

· ·

· ·

DIRECTIONS:

· ·

· ·

· ·

· ·

· ·

· ·

Serves _____

CHAPTER 11

MUFFINS

**Top Tips for Making
Great Muffins** 160

Muffins

Crumb Topping for Muffins 160

Muffin Base Recipe 161

Amaranth Oat Bran Muffins. 162

Barley Apple Muffins. 163

Blueberry Muffins. 164

Bran Muffins 165

Peanut Butter Muffins. 166

Spice Muffins. 167

Golden Yogurt Raisin Muffins . . 168

Kamut Oat Ricotta Muffins 169

Pastry Muffins

Pastry Muffin Base Recipe. 170

Date Nut Pastry Muffins. 171

Maple Pecan Pastry Muffins 172

Gluten-Free Muffins

Gluten-Free Muffin
Base Recipe. 173

Rice Bran Muffins 175

Nutty Rice Bran Muffins 176

Banana Rice Bran Muffins 177

Carrot Rice Muffins 178

Corn Muffins 179

Cranberry Muffins 180

Banana Coconut Muffins 181

Buckwheat Muffins. 182

Top Tips for Making Great Muffins

Preheat the Oven:

To get your batter to dome at the top, preheat the oven to 425°F. As soon as you put the muffin batter in the oven, reduce the heat to the temperature called for in the recipe. The initial high heat causes the batter to rise rapidly during the first few minutes of baking.

Cool the muffins:

Let your muffins cool on their sides; this will prevent soggy bottoms.

Avoid peaking:

Don't open the oven door until the last 15 minutes of baking to prevent muffins from collapsing.

Crumb Topping for Muffins

Crumb toppings transform ordinary muffins into a fancy affair. Sprinkle crumb topping over the batter in each muffin cup immediately before putting in the oven. The crumbs will appear to sink but they will rise to the top of the muffin while baking. For this trick to work it is very important that the oven is properly preheated and that you put the muffins into the oven right after adding the topping.

INGREDIENTS:
- ½ cup rolled oats
- ½ cup oat flour
- 3 Tablespoons shredded coconut
- 2 Tablespoons butter
- 1 ½ Tablespoons agave nectar

DIRECTIONS:
1. In a small bowl, combine the rolled oats, oat flour, and coconut.
2. Melt butter in small pot over gentle heat and add agave. Stir until dissolved.
3. Pour butter mixture evenly over the dry ingredients. Stir with a fork until you have crumbs.
4. Sprinkle over muffin tops and place in oven immediately and bake according to muffin recipe.

Makes topping for a dozen muffins

Muffin Base Recipe

This is a guide to making your own muffin creations. The base recipe allows you to explore your personal preferences, allowing you to try out your own delicious combinations. If you are feeling less adventurous I have included some of my favorite combinations to try.

INGREDIENTS:
- Neutral-tasting oil (grapeseed, untoasted sesame oil, coconut oil, **or** ghee) for greasing pan
- 2 cups flour (Try combining flours, including amaranth, oat, kamut, barley, whole wheat, brown rice, quinoa, graham, tapioca, **or** sorghum flours. You can also substitute ½-¾ cup bran for ½-¾ cup flour for a more fibrous muffin.)
- ½ teaspoon high-quality salt
- ½ teaspoon baking soda **or** 1 ½ teaspoons baking powder
- 1 teaspoon baking powder
- ⅓ cup buttermilk powder **or** whey powder
- 2 eggs
- ¾ cup agave nectar
- 1 cup water
- ¼ cup neutral-tasting oil (grapeseed, untoasted sesame oil, coconut oil, **or** ghee)

DIRECTIONS:
1. Preheat oven to 400°F.
2. Lightly oil a muffin pan or line with muffin cups.
3. In a medium bowl, combine dry ingredients: flour, salt, baking soda, baking powder, and buttermilk or whey powder.
4. In a small bowl, whisk together the wet ingredients: eggs, agave, water, and oil. If you are adding fruit, add it here.
5. Pour the blended liquid ingredients into the dry mixture and stir quickly, being sure to moisten all of the dry ingredients.
6. Fill each muffin cup ½ - ⅔ full with batter.
7. Bake for 15-20 minutes or until lightly browned. Try not to peak in on the muffins until at least 15 minutes have passed. Checking early may cause them to collapse.
8. Cool muffins for about 5 minutes, then transfer to a plate or wire racks to cool completely.
9. Serve with butter, nut butter, or jam.

OPTIONAL ADDITIONS:
- ½ – 1 cup frozen, fresh, or dried blueberries (reduce water by ¼ cup)
- 1 banana, mashed (reduce water by ¼ cup)
- ½ – 1 cup cranberries (dried, apple-juice sweetened, or fresh for a more tart flavor)
- ½ cup applesauce (reduce agave by ¼ cup)
- ½ teaspoon of spices like cinnamon, allspice, or ginger
- ½ cup dried fruit or nuts

Makes about a dozen muffins

Amaranth Oat Bran Muffins

INGREDIENTS:
- Neutral-tasting oil for greasing pan
- ¾ cup amaranth flour
- ¾ cup oat bran
- ½ cup oat flour
- ¼ teaspoon high-quality salt
- ½ teaspoon baking soda
- ⅓ cup buttermilk powder **or** whey powder
- 1 teaspoon baking powder
- 2 eggs
- 4 ½ Tablespoons agave nectar
- 1 cup water
- ¼ cup neutral-tasting oil (grapeseed, untoasted sesame oil, coconut oil, **or** ghee)

DIRECTIONS:
1. Preheat oven to 400°F.
2. Lightly oil a muffin pan or line with muffin cups.
3. In a medium bowl, combine dry ingredients: amaranth flour, oat bran, oat flour, salt, baking soda, buttermilk or whey powder, and baking powder.
4. In a small bowl, whisk together the wet ingredients: eggs, agave, water, and oil.
5. Pour the blended liquid ingredients into the dry mixture and stir quickly, being sure to moisten all of the dry ingredients.
6. Fill each muffin cup ½ - ⅔ full with batter.
7. Bake for 15-20 minutes or until lightly browned.
8. Allow muffins to cool in pan about 5 minutes, then transfer to a plate or wire racks to cool completely.
9. Serve with butter, nut butter, or jam.

Makes about a dozen muffins

Barley Apple Muffins

INGREDIENTS:
- Neutral-tasting oil for greasing pan
- 1 ½ cups barley flour
- ½ cup oat flour
- ½ teaspoon high-quality salt
- ½ teaspoon baking soda **or** 1 ½ teaspoons baking powder
- 1 teaspoon baking powder
- ½ teaspoon cinnamon (optional)
- ⅓ cup buttermilk powder **or** whey powder
- 2 eggs
- ½ cup agave nectar
- ¾ cup water
- ¼ cup melted butter **or** ¼ cup neutral-tasting oil (grapeseed, untoasted sesame oil, coconut oil**, or** ghee)
- ½ cup applesauce

DIRECTIONS:
1. Preheat oven to 400°F.
2. Lightly oil a muffin pan or line with muffin cups.
3. In a medium bowl, combine dry ingredients: barley flour, oat flour, salt, baking soda, baking powder, buttermilk or whey powder, and cinnamon.
4. In a small bowl, whisk together the wet ingredients: eggs, agave, water, melted butter or oil, and applesauce.
5. Pour the blended liquid ingredients into the dry mixture and stir quickly, being sure to moisten all of the dry ingredients.
6. Fill each muffin cup ½ - ⅔ full with batter.
7. Bake for 15-20 minutes or until lightly browned.
8. Allow muffins to cool in pans for about 5 minutes, then transfer to a plate or wire racks to cool completely.
9. Serve with butter, nut butter, or jam.

Makes about a dozen muffins

Blueberry Muffins

INGREDIENTS:
- Neutral-tasting oil for greasing pan
- 1 cup oat flour
- ¾ cup oat bran
- ¼ cup amaranth flour
- ¼ teaspoon high-quality salt
- ½ teaspoon baking soda
- ⅓ cup buttermilk powder **or** whey powder
- 1 teaspoon baking powder
- 2 eggs
- 4 ½ Tablespoons agave nectar
- ¾ cup water
- ¼ cup neutral-tasting oil (grapeseed, untoasted sesame oil, coconut oil, **or** ghee)
- ½ cup blueberries (frozen, fresh, or dried)

DIRECTIONS:
1. Preheat oven to 400°F.
2. Lightly oil a muffin pan or line with muffin cups.
3. In a medium bowl, combine dry ingredients: oat flour, oat bran, amaranth flour, salt, baking soda, buttermilk or whey powder, and baking powder.
4. In a small bowl, whisk together wet ingredients: eggs, agave, water, oil, and blueberries.
5. Pour the blended liquid ingredients into the dry mixture and stir quickly, being sure to moisten all of the dry ingredients.
6. Fill each muffin cup ½ - ⅔ full with batter.
7. Bake for 15-20 minutes or until lightly browned.
8. Allow muffins to cool in pans for about 5 minutes, then transfer to a plate or wire racks to cool completely.
9. Serve with butter, nut butter, or jam.

Makes about a dozen muffins

Bran Muffins

INGREDIENTS:
- Neutral-tasting oil for greasing pan
- 1 cup oat bran
- ¾ cup oat flour
- ¼ cup brown rice flour
- 1 teaspoon xanthan gum **or** guar gum **or** a 50:50 combination of both
- ¼ teaspoon high-quality salt
- ½ teaspoon baking soda
- ⅓ cup buttermilk powder **or** whey powder
- 1 teaspoon baking powder
- 2 eggs
- ½ cup agave nectar
- ¾ cup water
- ¼ cup neutral-tasting oil (grapeseed, untoasted sesame oil, coconut oil, **or** ghee)

DIRECTIONS:
1. Preheat oven to 400°F.
2. Lightly oil a muffin pan or line with muffin cups.
3. In a medium bowl, combine dry ingredients: oat bran, oat flour, brown rice flour, gum, salt, baking soda, buttermilk or whey powder, and baking powder.
4. In a small bowl, whisk together wet ingredients: eggs, agave, water, and oil.
5. Pour the blended liquid ingredients into the dry mixture and stir quickly, being sure to moisten all of the dry ingredients.
6. Fill each muffin cup ½ - ⅔ full with batter.
7. Bake for 15-20 minutes or until lightly browned.
8. Allow muffins to cool in pans for about 5 minutes, then transfer to a plate or wire racks to cool completely.
9. Serve with butter, nut butter, or jam.

Makes about a dozen muffins

Peanut Butter Muffins

INGREDIENTS:
- Neutral-tasting oil (grapeseed, untoasted sesame oil, coconut oil, **or** ghee) for greasing pan
- 1 cup brown rice flour
- 1 cup oat flour
- ½ cup oat bran
- ½ teaspoon high-quality salt
- ½ teaspoon baking soda **or** 1 ½ teaspoons baking powder
- 1 teaspoon baking powder
- ⅓ cup buttermilk powder **or** whey powder
- 2 eggs
- ¾ cup agave nectar
- 1 cup peanut butter
- 1 cup water
- 2 Tablespoons melted butter

DIRECTIONS:
1. Preheat oven to 400°F.
2. Lightly oil a muffin pan or line with muffin cups.
3. In a medium bowl, combine dry ingredients: brown rice flour, oat flour, oat bran, salt, baking soda, baking powder, and buttermilk or whey powder.
4. In a small bowl, whisk together wet ingredients: eggs, agave, peanut butter, water, and melted butter.
5. Pour the blended liquid ingredients into the dry mixture and stir quickly, being sure to moisten all of the dry ingredients.
6. Fill each muffin cup ½ - ⅔ full with batter.
7. Bake for 15-20 minutes or until lightly browned.
8. Allow muffins to cool in pans for about 5 minutes, then transfer to a plate or wire racks to cool completely.
9. Serve with butter, nut butter, or jam.

Makes about a dozen muffins

Spice Muffins

INGREDIENTS:
- Neutral-tasting oil for greasing pan
- 1 cup barley flour
- 1 cup oat flour
- ½ teaspoon high-quality salt
- 1 teaspoon cinnamon
- ¼ teaspoon allspice
- ¼ teaspoon ginger
- ½ teaspoon baking soda **or** 1 ½ teaspoons baking powder
- 1 teaspoon baking powder
- ⅓ cup buttermilk powder **or** whey powder
- 2 eggs
- ¾ cup agave nectar
- 1 cup water
- ¼ cup melted butter **or** neutral-tasting oil (grapeseed, untoasted sesame oil, coconut oil, **or** ghee)
- ½ cup raisins
- ½ cup snuts of your choice (optional)

DIRECTIONS:
1. Preheat oven to 400°F.
2. Lightly oil a muffin pan or line with muffin cups.
3. In a medium bowl, combine dry ingredients: barley flour, oat flour, salt, cinnamon, allspice, ginger, baking soda, baking powder, and buttermilk or whey powder.
4. In a small bowl, whisk together the wet ingredients: eggs, agave, water, and melted butter or oil.
5. Pour the blended liquid ingredients into the dry mixture and stir quickly, being sure to moisten all of the dry ingredients. Add raisins and optional nuts.
6. Fill each muffin cup ½ - ⅔ full with batter.
7. Bake for 15-20 minutes or until lightly browned.
8. Allow muffins to cool in pans for about 5 minutes, then transfer to a plate or wire racks to cool completely.
9. Serve with butter, nut butter, or jam.

Makes about a dozen muffins

Golden Yogurt Raisin Muffins

INGREDIENTS:
- Neutral-tasting oil for greasing pan
- 1 cup brown rice flour
- 1 cup oat flour
- ½ cup tapioca flour
- 1 teaspoon xanthan gum **or** guar gum **or** a 50:50 combination of both
- ½ teaspoon high-quality salt
- ½ teaspoon baking soda **or** 1 ½ teaspoons baking powder
- 1 teaspoon baking powder
- ½ cup golden raisins
- 2 eggs
- ½ cup agave nectar
- 1 cup yogurt
- ¼ cup melted butter **or** neutral-tasting oil (grapeseed, untoasted sesame oil, coconut oil or ghee)

DIRECTIONS:
1. Preheat oven to 400°F.
2. Lightly oil a muffin pan or line with muffin cups.
3. In a medium bowl, combine dry ingredients: brown rice flour, oat flour, tapioca flour, gum, salt, baking soda, baking powder, and raisins.
4. In a small bowl, whisk together wet ingredients: eggs, agave, yogurt, and melted butter or oil.
5. Pour the blended liquid ingredients into the dry mixture and stir quickly, being sure to moisten all of the dry ingredients.
6. Fill each muffin cup ½ - ⅔ full with batter.
7. Bake for 15-20 minutes or until lightly browned.
8. Allow muffins to cool in pans for about 5 minutes, then transfer to a plate or wire racks to cool completely.
9. Serve with butter, nut butter, or jam.

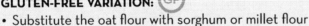

GLUTEN-FREE VARIATION: (GF)
- Substitute the oat flour with sorghum or millet flour

Makes about a dozen muffins

Kamut Oat Ricotta Muffins

INGREDIENTS

- Extra flour and neutral-tasting oil (grapeseed, untoasted sesame oil, coconut oil, **or** ghee) for greasing and flouring pan
- 2 large eggs
- 2 cups whole milk ricotta cheese
- ¾ cup agave nectar
- ⅔ cup butter, softened
- 2 ½ cups rolled oats
- 4 Tablespoons grated orange peel
- 1 teaspoon baking soda
- 2 cups kamut flour

DIRECTIONS

1. Preheat oven to 375°F.
2. Grease and flour a giant muffin tin.
3. In a medium bowl, whisk together wet ingredients: eggs, ricotta cheese, agave, and butter. Blend until smooth.
4. Mix in 2 cups of rolled oats (reserve the other ½ cup), orange peel, and baking soda. Slowly add kamut flour.
5. Fill each muffin cup ½ - ⅔ full with batter.
6. Sprinkle remaining ½ cup of rolled oats on each muffin.
7. Bake for 25 minutes or until wooden pick inserted near center comes out clean.
8. Remove from pan and cool slightly on wire racks. Serve warm.

Makes about 6 giant muffins

Pastry Muffins

Pastry Muffin Base Recipe
· ·

Pastry muffins are a close relative to the cupcake and more of a dessert than a breakfast food.

INGREDIENTS:
- Neutral-tasting oil (grapeseed, untoasted sesame oil, coconut oil, **or** ghee) for greasing pan
- 2 cups whole wheat pastry flour
- ½ teaspoon high-quality salt
- ½ teaspoon baking soda **or** 1 ½ teaspoons baking powder
- 1 teaspoon baking powder
- ⅓ cup buttermilk powder **or** whey powder
- 2 eggs
- ¾ cup agave nectar
- ¾ cup water
- ½ cup melted butter

DIRECTIONS:
1. Preheat oven to 400°F.
2. Lightly oil a muffin pan or line with muffin cups.
3. In a medium bowl, combine dry ingredients: whole wheat pastry flour, salt, baking soda, baking powder, and buttermilk or whey powder.
4. In a small bowl, whisk together the wet ingredients: eggs, agave, water, and butter. If you are adding fruit, add it here.
5. Pour the blended liquid ingredients into the dry mixture and stir quickly, being sure to moisten all of the dry ingredients.
6. Fill each muffin cup ½ - ⅔ full with batter.
7. Bake for 15-20 minutes or until lightly browned.
8. Allow muffins to cool in pans for about 5 minutes, then transfer to a plate or wire racks to cool completely.
9. Serve with butter, nut butter, or jam.

OPTIONAL ADDITIONS:
- ½ – 1 cup frozen, fresh, or dried blueberries (reduce water by ¼ cup)
- 1 banana, mashed (reduce water by ¼ cup)
- ½ – 1 cup cranberries (dried, apple-juice sweetened, or fresh for a more tart flavor)
- ½ cup applesauce (reduce agave by ¼ cup)
- ½ teaspoon spices like cinnamon, allspice, or ginger
- ½ cup dried fruit or nuts
- ½ teaspoon extract, such as vanilla, banana, chocolate, almond, or rum

Makes about a dozen muffins

Date Nut Pastry Muffins

INGREDIENTS:
- Neutral-tasting oil (grapeseed, untoasted sesame oil, coconut oil, **or** ghee) for greasing pan
- 2 cups whole wheat pastry flour
- ½ teaspoon high-quality salt
- ½ teaspoon baking soda **or** 1 ½ teaspoons baking powder
- 1 teaspoon baking powder
- ⅓ cup buttermilk powder **or** whey powder
- ½ teaspoon ground cinnamon
- 2 eggs
- ¾ cup agave nectar
- ¾ cup water
- ¼ cup melted butter
- ½ cup pecans **or** walnuts
- ½ cup chopped and pitted dates

DIRECTIONS:
1. Preheat oven to 400°F.
2. Lightly oil a muffin pan or line with muffin cups.
3. In a medium bowl, combine dry ingredients: whole wheat pastry flour, salt, baking soda, baking powder, buttermilk or whey powder, and cinnamon.
4. In a small bowl, whisk together wet ingredients: eggs, agave, water, and butter.
5. Pour the blended liquid ingredients into the dry mixture and stir quickly, being sure to moisten all of the dry ingredients. Add nuts and dates.
6. Fill each muffin cup ½ - ⅔ full with batter.
7. Bake for 15-20 minutes or until lightly browned.
8. Allow muffins to cool in pans for about 5 minutes, then transfer to a plate or wire racks to cool completely.
9. Serve with butter, nut butter, or jam.

Makes about a dozen muffins

Maple Pecan Pastry Muffins

INGREDIENTS:
- Neutral-tasting oil (grapeseed, untoasted sesame oil, coconut oil, **or** ghee) for greasing pan
- 2 cups whole wheat pastry flour
- ½ teaspoon high-quality salt
- ½ teaspoon baking soda **or** 1 ½ teaspoons baking powder
- 1 teaspoon baking powder
- ⅓ cup buttermilk powder **or** whey powder
- ½ cup chopped pecans
- 2 eggs
- ¼ cup maple syrup
- ½ cup agave nectar
- 1 cup water
- ¼ cup melted butter
- ½ teaspoon pure vanilla extract

DIRECTIONS:
1. Preheat oven to 400°F.
2. Lightly oil a muffin pan or line with muffin cups.
3. In a medium bowl, combine dry ingredients: whole wheat pastry flour, salt, baking soda, baking powder, buttermilk or whey powder, and chopped pecans.
4. In a small bowl, whisk together wet ingredients: eggs, maple syrup, agave, water, butter, and vanilla.
5. Pour the blended liquid ingredients into the dry mixture and stir quickly, being sure to moisten all of the dry ingredients.
6. Fill each muffin cup ½ - ⅔ full with batter.
7. Bake for 15-20 minutes or until lightly browned.
8. Allow muffins to cool in pans for about 5 minutes, then transfer to a plate or wire racks to cool completely.
9. Serve with butter, nut butter, or jam.

Makes about a dozen muffins

Gluten-Free Muffins

Gluten-Free Muffin Base Recipe

This is a guide to making your own gluten-free muffin creations.

INGREDIENTS:

- 1 cup gluten-free flour
  Make your own flour combinations or use the guide below. If your recipe calls for 1 cup of regular flour, try dividing the cup into parts so you can combine different gluten-free flours. For example, if you choose 3 flours, then 1 part = ⅓ cup. If you choose four flours, then 1 part = ¼ cup, etc.

> **GLUTEN-FREE FLOUR COMBINATIONS**
> - 1 part amaranth flour, 1 part brown rice flour, 1 part rice bran
> - 2 parts brown rice flour, 1 part rice bran
> - 1 part coconut flour, 1 part amaranth flour, 1 part sorghum flour
> - 1 part potato flour, 1 part brown rice flour, 1 part chickpea flour
>
> *(See chapter 3 for a complete list of gluten-free flours.)*

- Neutral-tasting oil for greasing pan
- 1 cup tapioca flour
- 1 ½ teaspoons xanthan gum **or** guar gum **or** a 50:50 combination of both (adds a binding quality that gluten normally gives)
- ½ teaspoon high-quality salt
- ½ teaspoon baking soda **or** 1 ½ teaspoons baking powder
- 1 teaspoon baking powder
- ⅓ cup buttermilk powder **or** whey powder
- 2 eggs
- ¾ cup agave nectar
- ¾ cup water
- ¼ cup melted butter **or** neutral-tasting oil (grapeseed, untoasted sesame oil, coconut oil, **or** ghee)

DIRECTIONS:

1. Preheat oven to 400°F.
2. Lightly oil a muffin pan or line with muffin cups.
3. In a medium bowl, combine dry ingredients: gluten-free flour, tapioca flour, gum, salt, baking soda, baking powder, and buttermilk or whey powder.
4. In a small bowl, whisk together the wet ingredients: eggs, agave, water, and butter or oil.
5. Pour the blended liquid ingredients into the dry mixture and stir quickly, being sure to moisten all of the dry ingredients.
6. Fill each muffin cup ½ - ⅔ full with batter.

7. Bake for 15-20 minutes or until lightly browned.
8. Allow muffins to cool in pans for about 5 minutes, then transfer to a plate or wire racks to cool completely.
9. Serve with butter, nut butter, or jam.

OPTIONAL ADDITIONS:
- ½ – 1 cup frozen, fresh, or dried blueberries (reduce water by ¼ cup)
- 1 banana, mashed (reduce water by ¼ cup)
- ½ – 1 cup cranberries (dried, apple-juice sweetened, or fresh for a more tart flavor)
- ½ cup applesauce (reduce agave by ¼ cup)
- ½ teaspoon spices like cinnamon, allspice, or ginger
- ½ cup dried fruit or nuts

Makes about a dozen muffins

Rice Bran Muffins

INGREDIENTS:
- Neutral-tasting oil for greasing pan
- 1 ½ cups brown rice flour
- 1 cup tapioca flour
- ½ cup rice bran
- 1 teaspoon xanthan gum **or** guar gum **or** a 50:50 combination of both
- ¼ teaspoon high-quality salt
- ½ teaspoon baking soda **or** 1 ½ teaspoons baking powder
- 1 teaspoon baking powder
- ⅓ cup buttermilk powder **or** whey powder
- 2 eggs
- ¾ cup agave nectar
- ¾ cup water
- ¼ cup neutral-tasting oil (grapeseed, untoasted sesame oil, coconut oil, **or** ghee)

DIRECTIONS:
1. Preheat oven to 400°F.
2. Lightly oil a muffin pan or line with muffin cups.
3. In a medium bowl, combine dry ingredients: brown rice flour, tapioca flour, rice bran, gum, salt, baking soda, baking powder, and buttermilk or whey powder.
4. In a small bowl, whisk together wet ingredients: eggs, agave, water, and oil.
5. Pour the blended liquid ingredients into the dry mixture and stir quickly, being sure to moisten all of the dry ingredients.
6. Fill each muffin cup ½ - ⅔ full with batter.
7. Bake for 15-20 minutes or until lightly browned.
8. Allow muffins to cool in pans for about 5 minutes, then transfer to a plate or wire racks to cool completely.
9. Serve with butter, nut butter, or jam.

Makes about a dozen muffins

Nutty Rice Bran Muffins

INGREDIENTS:
- Neutral-tasting oil for greasing pan
- 1 cup brown rice flour
- 1 cup tapioca flour
- ½ cup rice bran
- 1 teaspoon xanthan gum **or** guar gum **or** a 50:50 combination of both
- ½ teaspoon high-quality salt
- ½ teaspoon baking soda **or** 1 ½ teaspoons baking powder
- 1 teaspoon baking powder
- ⅓ cup buttermilk powder **or** whey powder
- 2 eggs
- ¾ cup agave nectar
- ¾ cup water
- ¼ cup neutral-tasting oil (grapeseed, untoasted sesame oil, coconut oil, **or** ghee)
- ½ cup peanut, almond, **or** any other nut butter of your choice

DIRECTIONS:
1. Preheat oven to 400°F.
2. Lightly oil a muffin pan or line with muffin cups.
3. In a medium bowl, combine dry ingredients: brown rice flour, tapioca flour, rice bran, gum, salt, baking powder, and buttermilk or whey powder.
4. In a small bowl, whisk together wet ingredients: eggs, agave, water, and oil, and nut butter.
5. Pour the blended liquid ingredients into the dry mixture and stir quickly, being sure to moisten all of the dry ingredients.
6. Fill each muffin cup ½ - ⅔ full with batter.
7. Bake for 15-20 minutes or until lightly browned.
8. Allow muffins to cool in pans for about 5 minutes, then transfer to a plate or wire racks to cool completely.
9. Serve with butter, nut butter, or jam.

Makes about a dozen muffins

Banana Rice Bran Muffins

INGREDIENTS:
- Neutral-tasting oil for greasing pan
- 1 cup brown rice flour
- 1 cup tapioca flour
- ½ cup rice bran
- 1 teaspoon xanthan gum **or** guar gum **or** a 50:50 combination of both
- ½ teaspoon high-quality salt
- ½ teaspoon baking soda **or** 1 ½ teaspoons baking powder
- 1 teaspoon baking powder
- ⅓ cup buttermilk powder **or** whey powder
- 2 eggs
- ½ cup agave nectar
- ¾ cup water
- ¼ cup neutral-tasting oil (grapeseed, untoasted sesame oil, coconut oil, **or** ghee)
- 1 cup mashed banana

DIRECTIONS:
1. Preheat oven to 400°F.
2. Lightly oil a muffin pan or line with muffin cups.
3. In a medium bowl, combine dry ingredients: brown rice flour, tapioca flour, rice bran, gum, salt, baking soda, baking powder, and buttermilk or whey powder.
4. In a small bowl, whisk together wet ingredients: eggs, agave, water, oil, and banana.
5. Pour the blended liquid ingredients into the dry mixture and stir quickly, being sure to moisten all of the dry ingredients.
6. Fill each muffin cup ½ - ⅔ full with batter.
7. Bake for 15-20 minutes or until lightly browned.
8. Allow muffins to cool in pans for about 5 minutes, then transfer to a plate or wire racks to cool completely.
9. Serve with butter, nut butter, or jam.

Makes about a dozen muffins

Carrot Rice Muffins

INGREDIENTS:
- Neutral-tasting oil for greasing pan
- 1 cup brown rice flour
- 1 cup tapioca flour
- 1 ½ teaspoons xanthan gum **or** guar gum **or** a 50:50 combination of both
- ½ teaspoon high-quality salt
- ½ teaspoon baking soda **or** 1 ½ teaspoons baking powder
- 1 teaspoon baking powder
- ⅓ cup buttermilk powder **or** whey powder
- 2 eggs
- ¾ cup agave nectar
- ¾ cup water
- ¼ cup neutral-tasting oil (grapeseed, untoasted sesame oil, coconut oil, **or** ghee)
- 1 cup grated carrot

DIRECTIONS:
1. Preheat oven to 400°F.
2. Lightly oil or line muffin pans with baking cups.
3. In a medium bowl, combine dry ingredients: brown rice flour, tapioca flour, gum, salt, baking soda, baking powder, and buttermilk or whey powder.
4. In a small bowl, whisk together wet ingredients: eggs, agave, water, oil, and carrot.
5. Pour the blended liquid ingredients into the dry mixture and stir quickly, being sure to moisten all of the dry ingredients.
6. Fill each muffin cup ½ - ⅔ full with batter.
7. Bake for 15-20 minutes or until lightly browned.
8. Allow muffins to cool in pans for about 5 minutes, then transfer to a plate or wire racks to cool completely.
9. Serve with butter, nut butter, or jam.

OPTIONAL VARIATION:
- Use ¾ cup carrot juice instead of water and reduce agave to ½ cup

Makes about a dozen muffins

Corn Muffins

INGREDIENTS:
- Neutral-tasting oil for greasing pan
- 1 ½ cups corn flour
- ½ cup tapioca flour
- 1 ½ teaspoons xanthan gum **or** guar gum **or** a 50:50 combination of both
- ½ teaspoon high-quality salt
- ½ teaspoon baking soda **or** 1 ½ teaspoons baking powder
- 1 teaspoon baking powder
- ⅓ cup buttermilk powder **or** whey powder
- 2 eggs
- ¾ cup agave nectar
- ¾ cup water
- ¼ cup neutral-tasting oil (grapeseed, untoasted sesame oil, coconut oil, **or** ghee)

DIRECTIONS:
1. Preheat oven to 400°F.
2. Lightly oil a muffin pan or line with muffin cups.
3. In a medium bowl, combine dry ingredients: corn flour, tapioca flour, gum, salt, baking soda, baking powder, and buttermilk or whey powder.
4. In a small bowl, whisk together wet ingredients: eggs, agave, water, and oil.
5. Pour the blended liquid ingredients into the dry mixture and stir quickly, being sure to moisten all of the dry ingredients and any optional additions.
6. Fill each muffin cup ½ - ⅔ full with batter.
7. Bake for 15-20 minutes or until lightly browned.
8. Allow muffins to cool in pans for about 5 minutes, then transfer to a plate or wire racks to cool completely.
9. Serve with butter, nut butter, or jam.

OPTIONAL ADDITIONS:
- ½ cup corn kernels
- ½ teaspoon cayenne pepper and black pepper
- ½ cup cheddar cheese.

Makes about a dozen muffins

Cranberry Muffins

INGREDIENTS:

- Neutral-tasting oil for greasing pan
- ½ cup brown rice flour
- ½ cup sorghum flour
- 1 cup tapioca flour
- 1 ½ teaspoons xanthan gum **or** guar gum **or** a 50:50 combination of both
- ½ teaspoon high-quality salt
- ½ teaspoon baking soda **or** 1 ½ teaspoons baking powder
- 1 teaspoon baking powder
- ⅓ cup buttermilk powder **or** whey powder
- 2 eggs
- ¾ cup agave nectar
- ¾ cup water
- ¼ cup melted butter **or** neutral-tasting oil (grapeseed, untoasted sesame oil, coconut oil, **or** ghee)
- ¾ cup fresh cranberries **or** ½ cup dried cranberries

DIRECTIONS:

1. Preheat oven to 400°F.
2. Lightly oil a muffin pan or line with muffin cups.
3. In a medium bowl, combine dry ingredients: brown rice flour, sorghum flour, tapioca flour, gum, salt, baking soda, baking powder, and buttermilk or whey powder.
4. In a small bowl, whisk together wet ingredients: eggs, agave, water, butter, or oil, and cranberries.
5. Pour the blended liquid ingredients into the dry mixture and stir quickly, being sure to moisten all of the dry ingredients.
6. Fill each muffin cup ½ - ⅔ full with batter.
7. Bake for 15-20 minutes.
8. Allow muffins to cool in pans for about 5 minutes, then transfer to a plate or wire racks to cool completely.
9. Serve with butter, nut butter, or jam.

Makes about a dozen muffins

Banana Coconut Muffins

INGREDIENTS:

- Neutral-tasting oil (grapeseed, untoasted sesame oil, coconut oil, **or** ghee) for greasing pan
- 1 cup coconut flour
- 1 teaspoon baking powder
- ¼ teaspoon high-quality salt
- 6 eggs
- 2 Tablespoons coconut milk **or** milk of choice
- 2 ¼ Tablespoons agave nectar
- 2 Tablespoons coconut oil
- 2 Tablespoons melted butter **or** melted coconut oil
- ½ teaspoon pure vanilla extract
- 2 ripe bananas, mashed

DIRECTIONS:

1. Preheat oven at 350°F.
2. Lightly oil a muffin pan or line with muffin cups.
3. In a medium bowl, combine dry ingredients: coconut flour, baking powder, and salt.
4. In a small bowl, whisk together wet ingredients: eggs, coconut milk, agave, coconut oil, melted butter or melted coconut oil, and vanilla.
5. Pour the blended liquid ingredients into the dry mixture and stir quickly, being sure to moisten all of the dry ingredients. Add the mashed bananas.
6. Fill each muffin cup ½ - ⅔ full with batter.
7. Allow muffins to cool in pans for about 5 minutes, then transfer to a plate or wire racks to cool completely.
8. Serve with butter, nut butter, or jam.

Makes about a dozen muffins

Buckwheat Muffins

INGREDIENTS:
- Neutral-tasting oil for greasing pan
- 1 ½ cups buckwheat flour
- ½ cup tapioca flour
- 1 ½ teaspoons xanthan gum **or** guar gum **or** a 50:50 combination of both
- ½ teaspoon high-quality salt
- ½ teaspoon baking soda **or** 1 ½ teaspoons baking powder
- 1 teaspoon baking powder
- ⅓ cup buttermilk powder **or** whey powder
- 2 eggs
- ¾ cup agave nectar
- ¾ cup water
- ¼ cup melted butter **or** neutral-tasting oil (grapeseed, untoasted sesame oil, coconut oil, **or** ghee)

DIRECTIONS:
1. Preheat oven to 400°F.
2. Lightly oil a muffin pan or line with muffin cups.
3. In a medium bowl, combine dry ingredients: buckwheat flour, tapioca flour, gum, salt, baking soda, baking powder, and buttermilk or whey powder.
4. In a small bowl, whisk together wet ingredients: eggs, agave, water, and melted butter or oil.
5. Pour the blended liquid ingredients into the dry mixture and stir quickly, being sure to moisten all of the dry ingredients.
6. Fill each muffin cup ½ - ⅔ full with batter.
7. Bake for 15-20 minutes.
8. Allow muffins to cool in pans for about 5 minutes, then transfer to a plate or wire racks to cool completely.
9. Serve with butter, nut butter, or jam.

Makes about a dozen muffins

My Muffin Creations:

Use this section to write down some of your favorite customized muffin recipes from this chapter.

Recipe:
· ·

INGREDIENTS:

· ·

· ·

· ·

· ·

· ·

· ·

· ·

DIRECTIONS:

· ·

· ·

· ·

· ·

· ·

· ·

Serves _____

My Muffin Creations:

Use this section to write down some of your favorite customized muffin recipes from this chapter.

Recipe:
· ·

INGREDIENTS:

DIRECTIONS:

Serves _____

CHAPTER 12

CAKES, BIRTHDAY CAKES, CUPCAKES, AND CHEESECAKES

Top Tips for Making Great Cakes.................. 186

Cakes and Birthday Cakes

Base Recipes

White Cake Base Recipe 193

White Birthday Cake Base Recipe................ 194

Chocolate Birthday Cake Base Recipe................ 195

German Chocolate Cake...... 196

Chocolate Chip Bundt Cake....197

Hazelnut Chocolate Chip Bundt Cake 198

Chocolate Ginger Cake 199

Pazorro 200

Irish Boiled Cake 201

Dark Chocolate Cake with Orange Ganache 202

Chocolate Raspberry Layer Cake....................204

Red Velvet Cake.............. 205

Carrot Cake.................. 206

Cheesecakes

New York Cheesecake 207

Ricotta Cheesecake 208

Gluten-Free Cakes

White Cake Base Recipe 209

Chocolate Zucchini Cake...... 210

Almond Orange Cake......... 211

Angel Food Cake 212

Chocolate Bundt Cake........213

Top Tips for Making Great Cakes

Start with the Right Tools:

- Cake pans and bakeware
- Electric mixer or hand mixer
- Wooden spoons
- Pastry brush
- Mixing bowls
- Measuring cups and spoons
- Parchment paper
- Whisk
- Sifter
- Offset spatula
- Rubber spatula
- Cake stand
- Cupcake tins
- Cupcake papers
- Cake decorating accessories

Grease and Flour Pans:

Grease pans generously with about 1 Tablespoon of fat per pan. Butter or organic shortening work best to grease pans. This is especially critical with bundt pans.

Use a paper towel, pastry brush, piece of waxed paper, or a butter wrapper to smear the fat into the pan. Sprinkle greased pan with flour or cocoa powder. Shake pan to evenly coat all sides and tap out any excess.

Preheating the Oven:

Turn on oven 10-15 minutes before you plan to use it to allow time for it to heat to baking temperature. Also, make sure that the oven racks are in the center.

Ingredients:

Always start with the best ingredients — you will be able to tell the difference. Choose quality chocolate, nuts, dried fruit, etc. Make sure that flours and spices aren't more than 1 year old. Butter provides the best flavor for cakes. You can also enhance the flavor by using milk or orange juice in place of water and melted butter in place of oil. To improve the cake's texture, try substituting buttermilk for regular milk. (For each cup of buttermilk used, add ½ teaspoon of baking soda to the dry ingredients.) Be sure to measure all ingredients carefully and accurately. For best results have all your ingredients at room temperature before beginning.

Eggs:

Eggs build structure in cakes and are used as a tenderizer (yolks contain lecithin, which is an emulsifier). Eggs also add nutrients, color, flavor, and moisture. Eggs separate best when cold, but egg whites whip up best at room temperature. If the recipe doesn't require you to separate the eggs, then leave them out to get to room temperature before baking or let them rest in a bowl of warm water for 10 minutes before beginning. Always use large, fresh eggs.

Butter:

Butter is best at room temperature. Leave it out on a plate for an hour before baking. If you forgot to do this, then grate or thinly slice the butter and let stand for about 10 minutes over a bowl of warm water.

Mixing:

Mixing cake batter hydrates, disperses, and aerates the ingredients. Be sure to have all ingredients prepared before you start mixing. Sift flour, baking soda, baking powder, and spices to avoid lumps. Cream butter and agave until light and fluffy. A hand mixer or mixer works great, but you can also cream by hand. Frequently scrape the batter down the sides of the bowl while mixing. Add in nuts, raisins, and fruits last to avoid color bleeding. Extracts should be added at the very end, and the batter should be at about 70°F - 75°F for best results.

Cake Enhancers:

Add a teaspoon of lemon juice to the butter and agave mixture before mixing the rest of the ingredients. This helps make the cake lighter. Beat the butter for at least 5 minutes to add air and make it fluffy. Add agave nectar and beat well again to add more air, which will make your cake lighter.

Separate eggs before adding them to recipes. Beat yolks until golden and creamy, then add them to the butter/agave mixture. Beat the egg whites until light and frothy before folding them into the butter mixture.

Moisture:

To increase moisture and lower the fat content, try substituting half of the oil in the recipe with either unsweetened yogurt or applesauce. Use sour cream in place of water — you won't taste the sour cream.

For chocolate cakes, add baking soda to your dry ingredients and mix with a teaspoon of vinegar to increase moisture and aid in rising. For fruit and dense cakes, keep a pan full of water in the oven when baking the cake.

Cake Pans:

Ideally, use the size pans called for in a recipe. To calculate the width of the pan measure across the top from inside edge to inside edge. You can substitute 8" square pans for round or use two 8" x 4" loaf pans. The baking time will be less, so begin checking about 15 minutes before the time suggested. See page 60 for cake pan conversions.

Shiny pans reflect the heat and are your best choice for cake baking. Glass and dark colored pans absorb the heat more quickly. To keep the cake from burning, reduce the oven temperature 25°F lower than recipe specifies. Spread batter evenly in pans so your cake bakes uniformly.

Baking:

Cake Baking Timetable

Cake Type	Baking Time
Sponge cake	45 minutes
Pound cake	1 hour
Layer cake	20-25 minutes
Fruit cake	3-4 hours, depending on size
Loaf cake	35-50 minutes
Cupcakes	30 minutes
Bundt cake	1-2 hours

- Bake cakes at 325°F to 360°F in a regular oven.
- Bake cakes at 330°F to 335°F in a convection oven.
- If your oven temperature is not reliably consistent, invest in an oven thermometer. Some ovens can be off by as much as 75°F. If your oven is too hot, your cake will rise too much in the middle.
- Optimum baking conditions are determined by the following factors: the richness or leanness of the formula, the liquidity and density of the batter, size of the pan, altitude, etc. Cakes that are larger in size and/or richer (lots of butter and cream) are generally baked at lower oven temperatures for longer periods of time. Cakes that have leaner ingredients and/or are smaller in size will bake for less time.
- For more information on baking at altitude, see page 55.
- Once your pans are filled with batter, tap the bottoms of the pans onto the counter to help release any bubbles in the batter.
- If your oven bakes unevenly on one side, do not pick up the pan, but rotate it about ⅔ into the baking time.
- Check on the cake 8 minutes before the recipe directions for doneness.
  - Use a toothpick, wood skewer, or piece of spaghetti to prick the center of the cake.
  - If the toothpick comes out clean, the cake is done.
  - If the toothpick is wet, continue to bake, and check at 2 minute intervals.
  - Cake is done when it springs back when lightly pressed, the sides shrink slightly away from the pan, and a cake tester or toothpick inserted in center comes out clean.
- Baking time varies depending on variables such as humidity, altitude, type of oven, the amount of batter, pan size, etc. A good indication that the cake is done is when its sweet smell permeates the air.
- Cupcakes: To create perfectly domed cupcakes, preheat your oven to 400°F and right before you place your pans inside to bake, lower the temperature to 350°F.

Cooling the Cake:

Cool the cake in pan for 10-15 minutes before loosening the edge and turning it out onto a wired rack to cool. Don't cool on stove top where there's heat, but instead on a rack on the counter. Gently insert a butter knife between the outside of the cake and the inside of the pan.

Run it along the pan to loosen the sides before turning over. To remove cake easily from pan, place two layers of paper towel over wire rack. The towel prevents the wire bars from breaking the crust or leaving imprints on top of cake. Place the covered rack over top of cake. Gently invert cake and let cool at least one hour before decorating with frosting.

Frosting the Cake:

- Chill the cake for about 15-20 minutes to make frosting easier. Lightly dust crumbs from the cake with a pastry brush, frost with a thin layer of frosting, then refrigerate until set. This will seal in the crumbs. Frost the cake with a final, heavier layer of frosting for a clean appearance.

- If your frosting is too thin or runny, lightly dust the top of the cake with flour or cocoa powder and then spread the frosting on top. This will help the frosting bind to the cake.

- To make ripples in the sides of the frosting with a cake comb, gently sweep the comb against the sides of the cake.

- Professionally decorated cakes have a silky, molten look. Frost your cake as usual, then use a hair dryer to blow-dry the surface until the frosting slightly melts.

- Try using colored, shredded coconut for a nice decorative touch. To color dried coconut, place it in a clean mason jar and don't fill it more than halfway. Add a few drops of natural food coloring, then close the jar and shake it until all the coconut is evenly tinted. Sprinkle coconut over frosting.

- Sprinkle chopped nuts onto the sides of frosted cakes. Walnuts, pecans, and almonds provide excellent decoration while adding flavor and nutrients.

Layering the Cake:

To split one solid cake in half: Loop a long strand of unflavored dental floss around the center of the cake horizontally. Cross the ends and slowly and firmly pull on each end to cut cleanly through the cake.

To connect two or more layers of cake: Lay the first layer on a cake plate and place waxed paper strips under the edges of the cake. This keeps the cake plate clean of frosting drippings if you are concerned about presentation. Place the layer's flattest side face-up on the platter. If the layer is too rounded to sit well, use a serrated bread knife to cut off the center bump of the cake. Place a dollop of frosting on top of the first cake layer and spread the frosting evenly with a frosting spatula. Next, set the top layer firmly in place with its rounder side up. It will not need to be leveled. Use the spatula to carefully spread the frosting around the top and side of the cake. When finished, slip waxed paper strips from under the cake.

Freezing the Cake:

Place frosted cakes unwrapped on a foil-lined cookie sheet. Freeze until hard and then tightly wrap cake. Unfrosted cakes will last up to 6 months in the freezer; frosted cakes will keep for up to 9 months. To thaw: unwrap cake and defrost in the refrigerator.

Gluten-Free Cake Tips:

- Add xanthan gum, guar gum, or a 50:50 combination of gums to your gluten-free flour. Gums give the batter some of the sticky gluten effect needed to create form in the baked good. You don't need more than ⅛ to ¼ teaspoon of gum per cup of flour.

- Add some protein when you use gluten-free flour. Since gluten is a protein, it can help to add some protein when you're substituting gluten-free flours for regular cake flour. Try replacing half a cup of water in your recipe with whole egg or egg whites.

- Gluten-free flours may require more baking powder or baking soda to compensate for their lack of elasticity. If you convert a recipe to gluten-free, it's a good idea to add about 25% more baking soda or baking powder than what is called for in the original gluten containing recipe.

Cake Troubleshooting:

Did you have a cake disaster? Check out this chart to help troubleshoot what happened and figure out what to do differently next time for a better outcome.

What Happened?	Potential Causes
The crust is too dark	- The oven temperature was too hot. - There was too much heat in the top of the oven.
The cake is too small	- The oven temperature was too hot. - The batter temperature was too high. - The batter temperature was too low. - An incorrect amount of water or liquids was used.
The cake burned on top	- The oven temperature was too hot. - The heat was all at the top of the oven (broil). - An incorrect amount of water or liquid was used.
The crust is shiny and sticky	- The oven temperature was too low. - The cake wasn't baked long enough. - There was too much sweetener in the recipe.
The crust is too thick	- The cake was baked too long.
The cake fell during baking	- There was too much movement during the baking process. - The oven door was opened prematurely. - The oven temperature was too low. - The batter was mixed excessively.
The top of the cake peaked and cracked	- The oven temperature was too hot, forming a crust too quickly. As the batter in the center continued to cook and rise, it erupted through the top of the cake. - The cake wasn't baked on the center rack of the oven.

What Happened?	Potential Causes
The cake shrunk	- The oven temperature was too hot. - Too much liquid was used. - The batter was too cool. - Mixing wasn't done properly or according to instruction. - The cake was baked for too long.
The cake rose unevenly	- The oven temperature was too hot. - The flour was not blended sufficiently into the batter. - The temperature inside the oven was uneven.
The cake stuck to the pan	- Pans were not adequately greased and floured. - If you are at high altitude, you need to add an additional layer of greased parchment paper to the pan. - The cake was cooled too long in the pan before trying to remove.
The cake overflowed into the oven	- The wrong size pan was used. - If at altitude, the batter expanded and you need to use a larger pan next time. - The pan was filled more than $2/3$ full of batter.
The cake is too dense and heavy	- The oven temperature was too low. - The eggs used were too small (always use large eggs). - The batter was not mixed and aerated enough. - The flour was not folded in gently (mix the cake batter on the lowest speed of the mixer). - The melted butter was too hot when it was added, which caused it to sink down through the whisked foam and effect aeration. - Too much flour was used.
The cake has poor flavor	- Low quality ingredients used. - Mixing wasn't done properly or according to instruction. - Pans were not properly cleaned or greased. - If you are at high altitude, you may need to add more fat and moisture.
The cake is tough	- The batter was mixed excessively. - There was insufficient liquid added. - There was too much liquid added.

What Happened?	Potential Causes
The cake lacks structure	- The batter was mixed excessively. - There was insufficient liquid added.
The cake dried out too soon	- It was baked for too long. - There was insufficient liquid added. - Mixing wasn't done properly or according to instruction. - The cake was cooled in a drafty location. - The cake was not properly sealed and airtight during storage.
The batter curdled and separated	- The ingredients used were not at room temperature. - The butter and agave were not creamed together well enough before the eggs were added. - The eggs were added too quickly.

Cakes, Birthday Cakes, and Cupcakes

Base Recipes

White Cake Base Recipe

INGREDIENTS:
- Organic vegetable shortening (coconut or palm) **or** butter and extra flour for greasing and flouring pan
- ½ cup butter, softened
- ⅔ cup agave nectar
- 2 eggs
- 2 teaspoons pure vanilla extract
- ½ cup milk (cow, goat, almond, rice, coconut, oat, etc.)
- 1 ½ cups whole wheat pastry flour
- 1 ¾ teaspoon baking powder
- ⅛ teaspoon high-quality salt

DIRECTIONS:
1. Preheat oven to 350°F.
2. Lightly oil and flour a 9" round cake pan or springform pan.
3. Cut 1" chunks of butter into a small bowl and add agave. Using a mixer, mix until well blended, about 3 minutes. Add eggs one at a time, then add vanilla and milk. Set aside.
4. In a large bowl, sift together the whole wheat pastry flour, baking powder, and salt. Add the wet ingredients and mix until smooth. Be careful not to overmix.
5. Pour batter into the prepared pan.
6. Bake on center rack for 30-40 minutes or until a wooden pick inserted in center comes out clean and the cake springs back to the touch.
7. For cupcakes, line muffin tins with cupcake paper liners, fill cups ½-¾ full with batter, and bake for 20-25 minutes.
8. Cool cake for 10 minutes. Loosen cake from pan by running a butter knife along the edges of the pan and gently invert the cake onto a cooling rack.
9. Cool completely and frost as desired. See Chapter 8 for recipes.

Makes one 9" cake or 12 cupcakes

White Birthday Cake Base Recipe

INGREDIENTS:
- Organic vegetable shortening (coconut or palm) **or** butter and extra flour for greasing and flouring pan
- 8 egg whites
- 1 cup butter
- 2 cups agave nectar
- Zest of 1 lemon
- 1 cup oat flour
- 1 ½ cups barley flour
- ½ cup brown rice flour
- 1 ½ teaspoons baking powder
- ¼ teaspoon cream of tartar

DIRECTIONS:
1. Preheat oven to at 350°F.
2. Lightly oil and flour a 9" round cake pan or springform pan.
3. In a mixer, beat egg whites until stiff. Place in a small bowl and set aside.
4. Cut 1" chunks of butter into a small bowl and add agave. Using a mixer, mix until well blended, about 3 minutes. Add grated lemon zest.
5. In a medium bowl, sift together dry ingredients: oat flour, barley flour, brown rice flour, baking powder, and cream of tartar. Add to the mixer with butter and agave, then fold in the egg mixture. Mix until smooth. Be careful not to overmix.
6. Pour the batter into the prepared pan.
7. Bake on center rack for 35-45 minutes or until a wooden pick inserted in center comes out clean and the cake springs back to the touch.
8. For cupcakes, grease or line muffin tins with cupcake paper liners, fill cups ½ -¾ full, and bake for 20-25 minutes.
9. Cool cake for 10 minutes. Loosen cake from pan by running a butter knife along the edges of the pan and gently invert the cake onto a cooling rack.
10. Cool completely and frost as desired. See Chapter 8 for recipes.

Makes one 9" cake or 12 cupcakes

Chocolate Birthday Cake Base Recipe

INGREDIENTS:
- Organic vegetable shortening (coconut or palm) **or** butter and extra flour for greasing and flouring pan
- 1 cup grain-sweetened chocolate chips
- 8 egg whites
- 1 cup butter
- 2 cups agave nectar
- Zest of 1 lemon
- 1 cup oat flour
- 1 ½ cups barley flour
- ½ cup brown rice flour
- 1 ½ teaspoons baking powder
- ¼ teaspoon cream of tartar

DIRECTIONS:
1. Preheat oven to at 350°F.
2. Lightly oil and flour a 9" round cake pan or springform pan.
3. In a double boiler or in a metal bowl placed over a saucepan of boiling water, melt chocolate.
4. In a mixer, beat egg whites until stiff. Place in a small bowl and set aside.
5. Cut 1" chunks of butter into a small bowl and add agave. Using a mixer, mix until well blended, about 3 minutes.
6. Fold in the melted chocolate. Add grated lemon zest.
7. In a medium bowl, sift together oat flour, barley flour, brown rice flour, baking powder, and cream of tartar. Add to the mixer with butter and agave, then fold in the egg mixture. Mix until smooth. Be careful not to overmix.
8. Pour the batter into the prepared pan.
9. Bake on center rack for 40-50 minutes or until wooden pick inserted in center comes out clean and the cake springs back to the touch.
10. For cupcakes, grease or line muffin cups with paper liners, fill cups ½-⅔ full, bake for 25-30 minutes.
11. Cool cake for 10 minutes. Loosen cake from pan by running a butter knife along the edges of the pan and gently invert the cake onto a cooling rack.
12. When the cake is completely cooled, frost as desired. See Chapter 8 for recipes.

Makes one 9" cake or 12 cupcakes

German Chocolate Cake

INGREDIENTS:

Cake:

- Organic vegetable shortening (coconut or palm) **or** butter and extra flour for greasing and flouring pan
- 4 ounces baker's chocolate, unsweetened
- ½ cup milk (cow, goat, almond, rice, coconut, oat, etc.)
- 1 cup oat flour
- 1 ½ cups kamut flour **or** whole wheat pastry flour
- ½ cup brown rice flour
- 1 ½ teaspoons baking soda
- ½ teaspoon xanthan gum **or** guar gum **or** a 50:50 combination of both
- ¼ teaspoon high-quality salt

- 1 cup butter, softened
- 1 ⅓ cups agave nectar
- 4 large eggs
- 1 teaspoon pure vanilla extract
- 1 cup water
- ⅛ cup buttermilk powder

Frosting:

- 6 egg yolks
- 1 cup agave nectar
- 1 cup butter, cut into small pieces
- ½ cup milk powder
- 2 teaspoons pure vanilla extract
- 4 cups sweetened, shredded coconut

DIRECTIONS:

For the cake:

1. Preheat oven to 350°F.
2. Lightly oil and flour two 9" round cake pans or springform pan.
3. In a small saucepan melt chocolate in milk over low heat, stirring constantly. Set mixture aside to cool for 10 minutes.
4. In a medium bowl, sift together dry ingredients: kamut flour, brown rice flour, baking soda, gum, and salt. Set aside.
5. In a large bowl, cream the butter and agave in a mixer on medium, about 3 minutes. Add eggs one at a time. Add the chocolate mixture and the vanilla extract. Blend until smooth.
6. Dissolve ⅛ cup buttermilk powder into 1 cup of water.
7. Alternately sprinkle flour and buttermilk liquid into butter and agave mixture, beat until smooth.
8. Divide the batter between the two prepared pans.
9. Bake on center rack for 25-30 minutes or until a wooden pick inserted in center comes out clean and the cake springs back to the touch.
10. Cool for 10 minutes. Loosen cake from pan by running a butter knife along the edges of the pan and gently invert the cake onto a cooling rack.

For the frosting:

1. In a large saucepan, beat together the egg yolks and agave. Stir in the butter, goat milk powder, and vanilla.
2. Stir constantly and cook for about 15-18 minutes or until thickened, bubbly, and golden in color. Remove from heat. Stir in the coconut. Transfer to a large bowl and cool until the frosting is room temperature and of good spreading consistency (about 2 hours). Once cake has cooled, spread frosting between the two layers and over top of the cake.

Makes one 2-layer, 9" cake

Chocolate Chip Bundt Cake

INGREDIENTS:
- Organic vegetable shortening (coconut or palm) **or** butter and extra flour for greasing and flouring pan
- 1 cup milk (cow, goat, almond, rice, coconut, oat, etc.)
- 1 cup agave nectar
- 6 Tablespoons butter, softened
- 2 large eggs
- 2 large egg whites
- 2 teaspoons pure vanilla extract
- 1 cup sorghum flour
- 1 cup oat flour
- 1 cup barley flour
- ¼ teaspoon xanthan gum **or** guar gum **or** a 50:50 combination of both
- ½ cup cocoa powder
- 1 teaspoon baking powder
- ½ teaspoon baking soda
- ½ teaspoon high-quality salt
- ⅔ cup grain-sweetened chocolate chips

DIRECTIONS:
1. Preheat oven to 350°.
2. Lightly oil and flour a 12-cup bundt pan.
3. In a large bowl, combine milk, agave, and butter and beat with a mixer on low, about 3 minutes. Add eggs and egg whites one at a time on medium speed. Add vanilla.
4. In a medium bowl, sift together dry ingredients: sorghum flour, oat flour, barley flour, gum, cocoa powder, baking powder, baking soda, and salt. Once mixed well, add to wet mixture and mix for about 2 minutes or until well blended. Fold in chips.
5. Spoon batter into prepared pan. Swirl batter using a knife. Bake on center rack for 45 minutes or until a wooden pick inserted in center comes out clean and the cake springs back to the touch.
6. Cool cake in the pan on a wire rack for 30 minutes. Loosen cake by running a knife along the edges of the pan and gently invert the cake onto a cooling rack. Serve warm, dusted with cocoa powder, or cool completely and glaze with *Cocoa Glaze* (see page 104).

Makes one bundt cake

Hazelnut Chocolate Chip Bundt Cake

INGREDIENTS:

- Organic vegetable shortening (coconut or palm) **or** butter and extra flour for greasing and flouring pan
- ½ cup hazelnuts
- 1 cup whole wheat pastry flour **or** oat flour
- 1 ½ teaspoons baking powder
- ½ cup butter, softened
- ¾ cup agave nectar
- 2 eggs
- ¼ teaspoon almond extract
- ¼ cup grain-sweetened chocolate chips

DIRECTIONS:

1. Preheat oven to 350°F.
2. Lightly oil and flour a 6-cup bundt pan.
3. In a blender or food processor blend hazelnuts into a fine powder.
4. In a medium bowl, sift together dry ingredients: whole wheat pastry flour and baking powder. Stir in ground hazelnuts.
5. In a large bowl, on the medium speed of an electric mixer, beat together the butter and agave, about 3 minutes. Add 2 eggs and ¼ teaspoon of almond extract. Stir in chocolate chips.
6. Pour into prepared pan.
7. Bake for 30-35 minutes or until a wooden pick inserted in center comes out clean and the cake springs back to the touch.
8. Cool cake in the pan on a wire rack for 30 minutes. Loosen cake by running a knife along the edges of the pan and gently invert the cake onto a cooling rack. Serve warm, dusted with cocoa powder, or cool completely and glaze with *Cocoa Glaze* (see page 104).

Makes one bundt cake

Chocolate Ginger Cake

INGREDIENTS:

Cake:

- Organic vegetable shortening (coconut or palm) **or** butter and extra flour for greasing and flouring pan
- 1/2 cup butter
- 9 ounces unsweetened chocolate **or** grain-sweetened chocolate chips
- 1 cup sorghum flour
- 1 cup oat flour
- ½ cup tapioca flour
- 1/2 cup cocoa powder, plus extra for dusting cake pan
- 1/2 cup unsweetened, shredded coconut
- ¼ teaspoon high-quality salt
- 3 teaspoons baking powder
- 3 teaspoons powdered ginger
- 1 teaspoon ground cinnamon

- ½ cup agave nectar
- 1 teaspoon vinegar (apple cider **or** brown rice vinegar)
- 1 teaspoon pure vanilla extract
- 1 cup coconut milk **or** milk of your choice
- 1 egg

OPTIONAL VARIATION:
- For an added ginger kick, add 1 Tablespoon of fresh pressed ginger juice to the cake batter.

CHOCOLATE GLAZE:
- ¼ cup milk (cow, goat, almond, rice, coconut, oat, etc.)
- 1 Tablespoon agave nectar
- 1 cup grain-sweetened, non-dairy chocolate chips

DIRECTIONS:

For the Cake:

1. Preheat oven to 350°F.
2. Lightly oil and flour a 12-cup bundt pan.
3. In a double boiler or a metal bowl placed over a saucepan of boiling water, melt butter and chocolate chips.
4. In a medium bowl, sift together dry ingredients: sorghum flour, oat flour, tapioca flour, cocoa powder, coconut, salt, baking powder, ginger, and cinnamon.
5. In a large bowl with a mixer, blend agave, vinegar, vanilla, coconut milk, egg, and optional fresh ginger juice, about 3 minutes. Slowly add in the flour mixture, stirring to combine. Add in melted chocolate and butter. Blend until smooth and batter can easily be spooned out, about 3 minutes.
6. Spoon evenly into the prepared pan.

7. Bake on center rack for 35-40 minutes or until a wooden pick inserted in center comes out clean and the cake springs back to the touch.
8. Cool cake for 10 minutes. Loosen cake from pan by running a butter knife along the edges of the pan and gently invert the cake onto a cooling rack.
9. Cool completely before glazing.

For the Chocolate Glaze:

1. Boil the milk and agave in a saucepan. Remove from heat and add chocolate chips. Stir until chocolate is totally melted.
2. Spoon a thin glaze over cake, allowing it to run down the sides. Place the cake in the refrigerator to help set the glaze. Repeat layering glaze as desired.

Makes one bundt cake

Parozzo (Chocolate-Covered Almond Cake)

This is a healthy twist to a traditional recipe from my home region of Abruzzo, Italy. Serve this as an elegant winter dessert.

INGREDIENTS:

Cake:

- Butter for greasing pan
- 1 cup almonds, blanched*
- 6 large eggs, separated into yolks and whites
- 1 ⅓ cups agave nectar
- ¾ cup semolina flour
- 2 Tablespoons tapioca flour
- 1 lemon, zest and juice

Chocolate topping:

- ½ cup grain-sweetened chocolate chips
- 1 Tablespoon butter, unsalted
- 1 teaspoon instant espresso coffee powder
- ⅔ cup grain-sweetened chocolate chips, chopped finely

DIRECTIONS:

For the Cake:

1. Preheat oven to 350°F.
2. Butter an 8½" pudding basin. If you don't have a pudding basin, use a regular 8" round cake pan and coat with flour, turning on its side to evenly coat.
3. In a hot skillet, pan toast the blanched almonds, stirring constantly, about 5 minutes.
4. In a blender, pulse almonds on low speed to make a fine flour, about 1 minute.
5. In a small bowl, beat the egg yolks and agave on medium for 3 minutes. Stir in almond flour, semolina flour, and tapioca flour. The texture should be stiff. Mix in the grated lemon zest and juice. Spoon into a large bowl.
6. Clean the mixer bowl, then whisk the egg whites until stiff and fold into the rest of the mixture.
7. Pour into the prepared pudding basin.
8. Bake on center rack for 45 minutes - 1 hour or until a wooden pick inserted in center comes out clean and the cake springs back to the touch.
9. Cool cake for 10 minutes. Loosen cake from pan by running a butter knife along the edges of the pan and gently invert the cake onto a cooling rack.

For the Chocolate Topping:

1. In a double boiler or a metal bowl placed over a saucepan of boiling water, melt chocolate and butter. Stir in espresso powder and mix well.
2. Pour glaze over cake and spread with a spatula. Let the frosting cool slightly, then add ⅔ cup of finely chopped chocolate to top.
3. The cake tastes best after sitting for a day, so make it a day ahead of serving if possible.

Makes one 8" cake

* Blanched means skins removed.

Irish Boiled Cake

INGREDIENTS:
- Organic vegetable shortening (coconut or palm) **or** butter for greasing pan
- ½ cup raisins
- ½ cup golden raisins
- ½ cup dried currants
- ¾ cup agave nectar
- ½ cup butter
- 1 cup water
- 1 ¼ cups oat flour
- ½ cup amaranth flour
- ½ cup brown rice flour
- 1 ½ teaspoons baking powder
- ½ teaspoon xanthan gum **or** guar gum **or** a 50:50 combination of both
- ⅛ teaspoon high-quality salt
- 1 teaspoon ground cinnamon
- ¼ cup dry sherry

DIRECTIONS:
1. In a medium saucepan, combine the raisins, golden raisins, currants, agave, butter, and water. Cook over medium heat, stirring occasionally, until boiling. Boil for 20 minutes, then remove from heat and set aside to cool.
2. Preheat oven to 350°F. Grease a 4 ½" x 8 ½" loaf pan.
3. In a medium bowl, mix dry ingredients: oat flour, amaranth flour, brown rice flour, baking powder, gum, salt, and cinnamon. Add the boiled ingredients along with the sherry and mix until well blended. Pour the batter into the prepared pan.
4. Bake for 45 minutes, then reduce oven to 325°F and bake 15 minutes more or until a wooden pick inserted in center comes out clean and the cake springs back to the touch.
5. Cool cake for 10 minutes. Loosen cake from pan by running a butter knife along the edges of the pan and gently invert the cake onto a cooling rack.

Makes one 8" loaf

Dark Chocolate Cake with Orange Ganache

· ·

This cake takes a little more work but is well worth it for special occasions.

INGREDIENTS:

Cake:

- Organic vegetable shortening (coconut or palm) **or** butter and extra flour for greasing and flouring pan
- 1 ¾ cups boiling water
- 1 ¾ cups cocoa powder
- 2 ounces high-quality dark chocolate, unsweetened and chopped
- ½ cup sour cream
- 1 Tablespoon pure vanilla extract
- 1 cup kamut flour
- ½ cup sorghum flour
- 1 ½ teaspoons baking soda
- ½ teaspoon high-quality salt
- ½ teaspoon xanthan gum **or** guar gum **or** a 50:50 combination of both
- 1 cup unsalted butter, softened
- ½ cup agave nectar
- 3 large eggs
- 3 Tablespoons orange zest

Ganache:

- 1 cup heavy cream
- 8 ounces high-quality dark chocolate, unsweetened, chopped
- 3 Tablespoons agave nectar
- 2 Tablespoons unsalted butter, softened
- 2 teaspoons orange zest
- 1 teaspoon orange essential oil

DIRECTIONS:

For the Cake:

1. Preheat oven to 350°F.
2. Lightly oil and flour a 9" round cake pan or springform pan.
3. In a medium bowl, pour boiling water over cocoa powder in an even stream, whisking until smooth. Stir in chopped chocolate and let stand 5 minutes.
4. Stir until blended and allow mixture to cool. Once cool, whisk in sour cream and vanilla.
5. In a another medium bowl, sift together kamut flour, sorghum flour, baking soda, salt, and gum. Set aside.

... together butter (cut into 1" pieces) and agave on medium
... e, beating well after each addition and scraping down
... w and add flour mixture and cocoa mixture in alternating
... mixture, beating until batter is well combined, about
..., and fold in.
... n, spreading batter evenly with a spatula.
... tes or until wooden pick inserted in center comes out
... the touch.
... ke from pan by running a butter knife along the edges of
... nto a cooling rack. Cool completely before icing.

... anache icing.
... to a boil. Cut up the chocolate finely while the cream is

... hen cream has come to a boil, add it to the bowl of
... colate to melt. Meanwhile, grate the orange zest finely.
... ange essential oil. Let ganache stand 3 minutes and
... d.
... minutes. Remove from the refrigerator and beat with
... t overbeat or it will become grainy).
... spatula, and serve.

recipe

Daikon *Radish Salad*

*Daikon Radish: Long white radish.
known for its crisp and sweet taste.
Popular ways to prepare are
to use in slaw, in stir frys, or pickle.
It is high in vitamin C, calcium, & phosphorus.
It can also aid in digestion,
& strengthen the immune system.*

INGREDIENTS: 1 daikon (~1 lb), ½ tsp salt,
2 tbs rice vinegar, 1 tbs olive oil,
Pinch of black pepper to taste,
Drizzle of honey for sweetness

DIRECTIONS:
Wash and peel daikon radish.
Grate radish or chop into thin spears and put into a bowl.
Toss radish with salt, vinegar, oil
and let marinate for 15 minutes
and enjoy as a refreshing side dish!
Drizzle with honey and enjoy as a refreshing side dish!
Optional: *if you don't like it too salty, toss the radish with salt first,
set aside for 15 minutes, and rinse radish or simply drain out
excess salty brine. Then toss with remaining ingredients.*
Optional additions: *add carrots, garlic, chile flakes, green onion,
cabbage, greens, sesame seeds, etc.*

www.farmcollaborative.org

Makes one 9" cake

204 | SWEETEN IT WITH AGAVE

Chocolate Raspberry Layer Cake

Delicious and rich, this cake is wonderful for special occasions.

INGREDIENTS:
- Organic vegetable shortening (coconut or palm) **or** butter and extra flour for greasing and flouring pan
- ½ cup butter
- ½ cup grain-sweetened chocolate chips
- 3 cups oat flour
- 1 cup brown rice flour
- ¾ cup cocoa powder
- 1 Tablespoon arrowroot flour
- 4 teaspoons baking powder
- ¾ cup brown rice syrup
- 1 cup agave nectar
- ½ cup cream (raw is ideal)
- ⅛ cup framboise liqueur **or** crème de cacao liqueur
- 5 eggs
- 1 jar of raspberry jelly (fruit-juice sweetened)

DIRECTIONS:
1. Preheat oven to 325°F.
2. Lightly oil and flour two 9" round cake pans or springform pan.
3. In a double boiler or metal bowl placed over a saucepan of boiling water, melt together butter and chocolate chips.
4. In a medium bowl, sift together dry ingredients: oat flour, brown rice flour, cocoa powder, arrowroot flour, and baking powder. Mix well.
5. In a large bowl with a mixer, beat together brown rice syrup, agave, cream, framboise, and eggs on medium, about 2 minutes.
6. Continue blending and add melted chocolate and butter. Slowly add flour. Mix the batter well, about 3 minutes more.
7. Bake on center rack for 25-30 minutes or until a wooden pick inserted in center comes out clean and the cake springs back to the touch. If you are using larger pans and not making layers, increase baking time by about 20 minutes.
8. Cool cake for 10 minutes. Loosen cake from pan by running a butter knife along the edges of the pan and gently invert the cake onto a cooling rack. Cool completely before icing.
9. Carefully place the first cake layer onto a cake platter. Evenly spread the raspberry jelly across the layer. Add the second cake layer on top.
10. Top with frosting or whipped cream.

Makes one 2-layer, 9" cake

Red Velvet Cake (Chocolate Beet Cake)

INGREDIENTS:
- Organic vegetable shortening (coconut or palm) **or** butter for greasing pan
- 1 cup kamut flour
- ¾ cup sweet rice flour
- ½ cup unsweetened cocoa powder (not Dutch process!)
- 2 teaspoons baking powder
- ½ teaspoon baking soda
- 1 teaspoon xanthan gum **or** guar gum **or** a 50:50 combination of both
- 2 cups red beets (about 2 large beets)
- ½ cup butter, softened
- 1 cup agave nectar
- 1 ⅓ cups buttermilk
- 3 eggs
- 2 teaspoons pure vanilla extract
- ¼ teaspoon organic natural red food coloring

DIRECTIONS:
1. Preheat oven to 350°F.
2. Lightly oil or butter 9" x 13" cake pan.
3. In a medium bowl, sift together dry ingredients: kamut flour, sweet rice flour, cocoa powder, baking powder, baking soda, and gum.
4. Wash and peel the beets. Finely grate beets into a bowl until you reach 2 cups and set aside.
5. In a large bowl, on the medium speed of an electric mixer, beat together the butter and agave until creamy, about 2 minutes. Slowly add buttermilk. Add eggs, one at a time and mix well.
6. Add grated beets, vanilla, and organic food coloring. Add flour mixture.
7. Pour into prepared cake pan.
8. Bake on center rack for 45 minutes or until a wooden pick inserted in center comes out clean and the cake springs back to the touch.
9. Cool cake for 10 minutes. Loosen cake from pan by running a butter knife along the edges of the pan and gently invert the cake onto a cooling rack.
10. Cool cake completely, then frost with the *Cream Cheese Frosting* (see page 110).

Makes one 9" x 13" sheet cake

Carrot Cake
· · · · · · · · · · · · · · · · ·

INGREDIENTS:
- Organic vegetable shortening (coconut or palm) **or** butter for greasing pan
- 1 ½ cups oat flour
- ½ cup brown rice flour
- ½ cup quinoa flour
- 2 teaspoons ground cinnamon
- 2 teaspoons baking soda
- 1 teaspoon high-quality salt
- 1 ⅓ cups agave nectar
- 1 ½ cups neutral-tasting oil (grapeseed, untoasted sesame oil, coconut oil, **or** ghee)
- 3 eggs
- 2 teaspoons pure vanilla extract
- 2 cups coconut flakes
- 2 cups carrots, shredded
- 1 can (8 ounces) crushed pineapple in juice (use a no-sugar-added product)
- ½ cup sunflower seeds (optional)
- ¼ cup currants (optional)

DIRECTIONS:
1. Preheat oven to 350°F.
2. Lightly oil or butter 9" x 13" cake pan.
3. In a large bowl, sift together dry ingredients: oat flour, brown rice flour, quinoa flour, baking soda, and salt. Mix with a spoon.
4. Make a deep well in the center of the dry ingredients. Add agave, oil, eggs, vanilla, coconut flakes, carrots, pineapple, and optional sunflower seeds and/or currants. Stir until all ingredients are well combined and batter is smooth.
5. Pour into prepared pan.
6. Bake on center rack for 50 minutes or until a wooden pick inserted in center comes out clean.
7. For cupcakes, line muffin pan with baking cups and fill each cup ½ full. Bake for 20-25 minutes.
8. Leave to cool for 10 minutes, then run a butter knife along the edges of the pan and gently invert the cake onto a cooling rack.
9. Once completely cool, frost with the *Cream Cheese Frosting* (see page 110).

OPTIONAL VARIATION:
Add ½ cup of shredded coconut to the cream cheese frosting.

Makes one 9" x 13" cake

Cheesecakes

New York Cheesecake

INGREDIENTS:

Graham Crust:

- Organic vegetable shortening (coconut or palm) **or** butter for greasing pan
- 1 cup graham flour **or** oat flour
- 2 Tablespoons butter, melted
- ⅓ cup water
- ½ teaspoon high-quality salt

Cheesecake:

- 4 (8 ounce) packages cream cheese
- 1 cup agave nectar
- ½ cup milk (cow, goat, almond, rice, coconut, oat, etc.)
- 4 eggs
- 1 cup sour cream
- 1 Tablespoon pure vanilla extract
- ¼ cup tapioca flour

DIRECTIONS:

For the crust:

1. Preheat oven to 350°F. Grease a 9" round pie pan. In a medium bowl, mix graham flour, melted butter, water, and salt. Press into pie pan. You can either place crust only on the bottom of the pan, or you can press it around the sides as well.
2. Prebake the crust at 350°F for 15 minutes. Remove from oven and cool completely.

For the cheesecake:

1. In a medium bowl, on the medium speed of an electric mixer, beat cream cheese with agave until smooth.
2. Blend in milk, then add in the eggs one at a time, mixing just enough to incorporate. Add sour cream, vanilla, and tapioca flour and beat until smooth. Pour filling into prepared crust.
3. Bake on center rack for 1 hour.
4. Turn the oven off and let cake cool in oven with the door closed for 5-6 hours to prevent cracking.
5. Chill in the refrigerator and serve when fully chilled. Top with fruit syrup.

Makes one 9" cheesecake

Ricotta Cheesecake

The extract or flavoring you choose will determine the overall flavor of this versatile cheesecake.

INGREDIENTS:

Crust:

- Organic vegetable shortening (coconut or palm) **or** butter for greasing pan
- 1 cup graham flour
- 2 Tablespoons butter, melted
- ⅓ cup water
- ½ teaspoon high-quality salt

GLUTEN-FREE VARIATION:
- Substitute the graham flour with ½ cup sorghum flour + ½ cup tapioca flour

Cheesecake:
- 1 ½ pounds ricotta cheese
- 16 ounces cream cheese
- ⅔ cup agave nectar
- 6 eggs
- ½ cup tapioca flour
- 1 cup sour cream
- 2 Tablespoons flavored liqueur (Kahlua, Framboise, Amaretto, **or** Crème de Cacao) **or** 1 Tablespoon pure vanilla or almond extract

DIRECTIONS:

For the crust:

1. Preheat oven to 325°F. Grease a 9" pie pan.
2. In a medium bowl, mix graham flour, melted butter, water, and salt. Press into pie pan, covering just the bottom of the pan or the bottom and the sides.
3. Prebake the crust for 15 minutes. Remove from the oven to cool.

For the cheesecake:

1. In medium bowl on the medium speed of a mixer, cream together ricotta cheese, cream cheese, and agave until smooth. Add in the eggs one at a time. Sprinkle in the flour, mixing well. Stir in the sour cream and liqueur or extract. Mix until blended, being careful not to overmix. Pour mixture into a prebaked pie crust.
2. Bake at 325°F on center rack for 1 ½ hours. Then turn the oven off and let cake cool in oven with the door closed for another hour to prevent cracking.
3. Cool on counter for another hour then chill thoroughly. Top with fruit syrup.

Makes one 9" cheesecake

Gluten-Free Cakes

White Cake Base Recipe (Gluten-Free)
. . . .

Makes a great birthday cake for gluten-free individuals!

INGREDIENTS:
- Organic vegetable shortening (coconut or palm) **or** butter and extra flour for greasing and flouring pan
- ⅔ cup brown rice flour
- ⅓ cup tapioca flour
- ½ cup sweet white rice flour
- ½ teaspoon baking powder
- ½ teaspoon xanthan gum **or** guar gum **or** a 50:50 combination of both
- ¼ teaspoon high-quality salt
- ½ cup butter (1 stick)
- ½ cup agave nectar
- 1 teaspoon pure vanilla extract
- 2 eggs
- ½ cup milk of your choice
- Zest of ½ lemon

DIRECTIONS:
Preheat oven to 350°F.
4. Lightly oil and flour 8" round cake pan.
5. In a medium bowl, sift together dry ingredients: brown rice flour, tapioca flour, sweet rice flour, baking powder, gum, and salt.
6. In a large bowl combine butter, agave, and vanilla. Beat on medium for 1 minute. Add the eggs one at a time and beat 2 minutes more. Slowly add the dry ingredients, milk, and grated lemon zest. Beat until smooth, about 3 minutes more.
7. Pour into prepared pan.
8. Bake on center rack for 15-20 minutes or until a wooden pick inserted in center comes out clean and the cake springs back to the touch.
9. Leave to cool for 10 minutes, then run a butter knife along the edges of the pan and gently invert the cake onto a cooling rack.
10. See chapter 8 for frosting recipes.

Makes one 8" cake

Chocolate Zucchini Cake

INGREDIENTS:
- Organic vegetable shortening (coconut or palm) **or** butter and extra flour for greasing and flouring pan
- 1 cup sorghum flour
- 1 cup millet flour
- ½ cup tapioca flour
- 4 Tablespoons cocoa powder
- 2 teaspoons buttermilk powder
- ½ teaspoon baking powder
- 1 teaspoon baking soda
- ½ teaspoon ground cinnamon
- ½ teaspoon clove powder
- ½ cup butter, cut into 1" slices
- ¼ cup neutral-tasting oil (grapeseed, untoasted sesame oil, coconut oil, **or** ghee)
- ½ cup agave nectar
- 2 eggs
- 1 teaspoon pure vanilla extract
- ⅓ cup milk (cow, goat, almond, rice, coconut, oat, etc.)
- 2 cups grated zucchini

DIRECTIONS:
1. Preheat oven to 350°F.
2. Lightly oil or butter 8" square cake pan.
3. In a medium bowl, sift together dry ingredients: sorghum flour, millet flour, tapioca flour, cocoa powder, buttermilk powder, baking powder, baking soda, cinnamon, and clove powder.
4. In a large bowl, on the medium speed of an electric mixer, beat together the butter, oil, and agave. Add eggs, vanilla, and milk. Beat for 3 minutes, being careful not to overmix.
5. Stir in grated zucchini and dry mixture.
6. Pour into prepared cake pan.
7. Bake on center rack for 30 minutes or until a wooden pick inserted in center comes out clean and the cake springs back to the touch.
8. Leave to cool for 10 minutes, then run a butter knife along the edges of the pan and gently invert the cake onto a cooling rack.

Makes one 8" square cake

Almond Orange Cake

INGREDIENTS:
- Organic vegetable shortening (coconut or palm) **or** butter and extra flour for greasing and flouring pan
- ½ cup almonds, blanched*
- 1 cup brown rice flour
- 1 teaspoon baking powder
- ⅓ cup neutral-tasting oil (grapeseed, untoasted sesame oil, coconut oil, **or** ghee)
- ⅓ cup agave nectar
- 6 drops pure vanilla extract
- 3 eggs
- 2 Tablespoons orange zest
- 1 drop of orange essential oil (optional)

DIRECTIONS:
1. Preheat oven to 400°F.
2. Lightly oil and flour an 8" round cake pan.
3. In a blender, pulse almonds on low speed to make a fine flour, about 1 minute.
4. In a medium bowl, combine dry ingredients: almond flour, brown rice flour, and baking powder.
5. In a large bowl, combine oil, agave, and vanilla. Beat with a mixer on low, about 1 minute. Add the eggs one at a time and beat about 2 minutes more.
6. Slowly add dry ingredients and mix. Fold in grated orange zest and optional orange essential oil. Beat until smooth, about 2 minutes more.
7. Pour into prepared cake pan.
8. Bake on center rack for 10 minutes, then increase temperature to 425°F and bake for 15 minutes more or until a wooden pick inserted in center comes out clean.
9. Cool cake for 10 minutes. Loosen cake from pan by running a butter knife along the edges of the pan and gently invert the cake onto a cooling rack.
10. Cool completely and frost as desired. See Chapter 8 for frosting recipes.

Makes one 8" cake

* Blanched means skins removed.

Angel Food Cake

INGREDIENTS:
- 12 egg whites, room temperature
- ½ cup sweet white rice flour **or** white rice flour
- ¾ cup tapioca flour
- 1 Tablespoon arrowroot flour
- ½ teaspoon xanthan gum **or** guar gum **or** a 50:50 combination of both
- ½ teaspoon high-quality salt
- 1 ½ teaspoons cream of tartar
- 1 teaspoon to 1 Tablespoon pure vanilla extract as desired to taste
- 1 teaspoon almond extract (optional)
- 1 cup agave nectar

DIRECTIONS:
1. Preheat oven to 325°F.
2. Separate egg whites and allow them to warm to room temperature.
3. In a medium bowl, sift together dry ingredients: sweet white rice flour, tapioca flour, arrowroot flour, and gum. Mix well and set aside.
4. In a small bowl, combine egg whites, salt, cream of tartar, vanilla, and almond extract.
5. Beat on high until stiff peaks form, about 2 minutes. Be careful not to overbeat.
6. Turn mixer off and drizzle in agave.
7. Sprinkle in dry ingredients and gently fold the batter until smooth.
8. Using a rubber spatula, carefully pour mixture into an ungreased 10" angel food cake pan.
9. Bake on center rack for 55 minutes. The cake should be golden on top and pull away from the sides of the pan. It is better to overbake than to underbake this type of cake.
10. When the cake has finished baking, take it directly from the oven and place it upside down on the neck of a bottle to help prevent it from falling as it cools. Once it has cooled, after about 30 minutes, turn it over and then remove it from the pan.
11. Serve with whipped cream and fruit syrup.

Makes one 10" cake

Chocolate Bundt Cake

INGREDIENTS:
- Organic vegetable shortening (coconut or palm) **or** butter and extra flour for greasing and flouring pan
- ¼ cup coconut flour
- ¼ cup sorghum flour
- ½ cup cocoa powder
- ½ teaspoon xanthan gum **or** guar gum **or** a 50:50 combination of both
- ½ teaspoon baking soda
- ½ cup milk (cow, goat, rice, almond, coconut, oat, etc.)
- ½ cup agave nectar
- 7 eggs
- ½ cup neutral-tasting oil (grapeseed, untoasted sesame oil, coconut oil, **or** ghee)

DIRECTIONS:
1. Preheat oven to 325°F.
2. Lightly oil and flour a 12-cup bundt pan.
3. In a medium bowl, sift together dry ingredients: coconut flour, sorghum flour, cocoa powder, gum, and baking soda.
4. In a large bowl, on the medium speed of an electric mixer, beat milk, agave, eggs, and oil on low.
5. Slowly add the dry ingredients and beat until smooth, about 3 minutes.
6. Pour the batter into the prepared pan. Tap pan lightly to even out batter and release air bubbles.
7. Bake on center rack for 25-30 minutes or until a wooden pick inserted in center comes clean and the cake springs back to the touch.
8. Cool cake for 10 minutes. Loosen cake from pan by running a butter knife along the edges of the pan and gently invert the cake onto a cooling rack.
9. Cool cake completely and dust with cocoa powder or glaze with *Cocoa Glaze* (see page 104). Refrigerate until 30 minutes before serving.

Makes one bundt cake

My Cake Creations:

*Use this section to write down some of your favorite
customized cake recipes from this chapter.*

Recipe:

. . . .

INGREDIENTS:

. . . .

. . . .

. . . .

. . . .

. . . .

. . . .

. . . .

DIRECTIONS:

. . . .

. . . .

. . . .

. . . .

. . . .

. . . .

Serves _____

CHAPTER 13

COOKIES AND BARS

Top Tips for Making Great Cookies and Bars............216

Cookies

Chocolate Chip Cookies 218

Eggless Chocolate Chip Cookies.................... 219

Oat Raspberry Thumbprint Cookies....................220

Oatmeal Raisin Cookies.......221

Chia Raisin Cookies.......... 222

Coco-Cocoa Cookies 223

Peanut Butter Cookies........224

Butter Cookies 225

Gingerbread Men & Women... 226

Pizzelles 227

Madeleine Cookies 228

Taralli....................... 229

Bars and Brownies

Lemon Bars 230

Cocoa Brownies..............231

Rich Chocolate Brownies...... 232

Gluten-Free Cookies and Brownies

KC's Chocolate Chip Coconut Cookies............. 233

Flourless Almond Cookies..... 234

Brownies..................... 235

Macaroons................... 235

Vegan Almond Macaroons..... 236

Top Tips For Making Great Cookies & Bars

Start with the Right Tools:

- Good measuring spoons that give you a multitude of measurements
- Large, medium, and small mixing bowls
- Liquid measuring cup
- Adjust-A-Cup measuring cup for easy agave nectar measuring
- Dry measuring cups
- Spatula
- Wooden spoons
- Mixer or hand mixer
- 4 Cookie sheets if you make batches
- Parchment paper
- Cookie cutters
- Wire cooling racks
- Metal pancake turner or spatula
- Timer
- Oven thermometer

Preheat the Oven:

Preheat the oven as soon as you begin your cookie project so there is enough time for the oven to get up to temperature.

Measure Carefully:

Be sure to measure your ingredients carefully. Don't be sloppy.

Use Butter:

Butter is what gives cookies their yummy flavor and crisp texture. Other fats such as grapeseed oil or coconut oil will give your cookies a different effect—which you may love. Let butter stand at room temperature for 30-45 minutes to allow it to soften. If it stands too long, butter will be mushy and melted. You can also measure butter and then cut into 1" chunks. Using a mixer, beat the butter into your chosen sweetener. Don't overbeat the butter and sweetener or your cookies will be flat. If you think you have overbeaten the butter, place the butter and sweetener mixture in the fridge for 10 minutes to help it set back up. Don't use whipped butter, which can ruin a recipe.

Cookie Sheets:

Place cookie sheets in the freezer while you are making the dough. This technique helps the cookies rise nicely. It's not necessary but try it out and see how it changes your cookies. If you are making multiple batches, it helps to have 4 cookie sheets. Also, if you need to reuse your cookie sheets for the next batch, be sure to fully clean them and rinse with cold water so they aren't hot when you put the next batch of cookie dough on them. That will help the cookies keep a nice shape. Avoid using nonstick bakeware; studies have documented the toxicity of this type of cookware. To be safe, oil a metal baking sheet well with grapeseed oil or lay parchment paper down on any kind of cookie sheet. Use cookie sheets that are at least 2 inches smaller than your oven for proper circulation of hot air. For this same reason, it's best to bake cookies one sheet at a time unless you have a convection oven. One more thing to note about your cookie sheet is that if you are having a problem with a cookie going flat, putting cookies on parchment instead of an oiled cookie sheet will help. The oil can contribute to cookies flattening.

Chill the Cookie Dough:

Chill cookie dough in the refrigerator for 30 minutes before baking. This is an easy fix for cookie dough that has been sitting out too long or lost its form. It is generally a good idea to let recipes with grain flours sit in the refrigerator for 30 minutes before baking, which allows the flour's flavor to blossom.

Use a Spatula:

Carefully remove cookies from cookie sheets with a spatula or pancake turner. This will prevent warm cookies from breaking and tearing.

Cooling the Cookies:

Cool cookies on wire racks. This prevents your cookies from getting soggy and allows the steam to evaporate.

Be Aware of Time:

Set a timer so you don't forget about the cookies. Work on your ability to smell when cookies are done; baking times may vary from one climate to another. Keep a close eye on the cookies, always checking in at the minimum baking time. You'll determine the appropriate time with the first batch.

Know Your Oven:

Know your oven temperature. Many ovens are not accurately calibrated. Purchase an oven thermometer to help you identify the exact temperature of your oven and prevent baking disasters.

Cookies

Chocolate Chip Cookies

INGREDIENTS:
- ½ cup butter **or** organic vegetable shortening (coconut or palm)
- ½ cup agave nectar
- 1 teaspoon pure vanilla extract
- 1 egg
- ¾ cup kamut flour
- 2 Tablespoons oat flour
- 1 teaspoon high-quality salt
- ⅛ teaspoon baking powder
- ¾ cup grain-sweetened chocolate chips

DIRECTIONS:
1. Preheat oven to 350°F.
2. In a large bowl, on the medium speed of an electric mixer, beat butter and agave until light and creamy.
3. Beat in vanilla and egg and mix for 2 minutes.
4. Add dry ingredients: kamut flour, oat flour, salt, and baking powder. Stir until batter is smooth.
5. Stir in chocolate chips.
6. Cover and chill the dough for 30 minutes or bake the cookies immediately.
7. Using a spoon or cookie-dough scooper, arrange uniform balls of cookie dough 3 inches apart on an ungreased baking sheet.
8. With your fingers or a fork flatten each cookie to ½" thickness.
9. Bake for 10-15 minutes or until lightly browned at the edges.
10. Remove cookies from cookie sheet and let cool on a wire rack.

OPTIONAL VARIATION:
Try adding 1 Tablespoon of chia seeds or ground flax seed to the flour for a nutritional boost!

Makes about a dozen cookies

Eggless Chocolate Chip Cookies

INGREDIENTS:
- ½ cup butter **or** organic vegetable shortening (coconut or palm)
- ½ cup agave nectar
- 1 teaspoon pure vanilla extract
- ¾ cup kamut flour
- 1 Tablespoon oat flour
- ½ teaspoon high-quality salt
- ⅛ teaspoon baking powder
- ½ cup grain-sweetened chocolate chips

DIRECTIONS:
1. Preheat oven to 300°F.
2. In a large bowl, on the medium speed of an electric mixer, beat butter and agave until light and creamy.
3. Add dry ingredients: kamut flour, oat flour, salt, and baking powder. Mix until batter is smooth.
4. Stir in chocolate chips.
5. Cover and chill the dough for 30 minutes or bake the cookies immediately.
6. Using a spoon or cookie-dough scooper, arrange uniform balls of cookie dough 3 inches apart on an ungreased baking sheet.
7. With your fingers or a fork flatten each cookie to ½" thickness.
8. Bake for 15 minutes or until lightly browned at the edges.
9. Remove cookies from cookie sheet and let cool on a wire rack.

Makes about a dozen cookies

Oat Raspberry Thumbprint Cookies

INGREDIENTS:
- ½ cup butter **or** organic vegetable shortening (coconut or palm)
- ½ cup neutral-tasting oil (grapeseed, untoasted sesame oil, coconut oil, **or** ghee)
- ¾ cup agave nectar
- 2 teaspoons pure vanilla extract
- 1 egg
- 2 cups oat flour
- 1 cup rolled oats
- 1 teaspoon ground cinnamon
- 1 teaspoon high-quality salt
- 1 teaspoon baking powder

- 1 jar of fruit-sweetened raspberry jelly

DIRECTIONS:
1. Grease cookie pans.
2. In a large bowl, on the medium speed of an electric mixer, beat butter, oil, and agave until light and creamy.
3. Beat in vanilla and egg and mix for 2 minutes.
4. Add dry ingredients: oat flour, rolled oats, cinnamon, salt, and baking powder. Stir until batter is smooth.
5. Chill dough for 30 minutes.
6. Preheat oven to 350°F.
7. Spoon uniform balls of batter onto cookie sheets, and make an indent in the center with your thumb. Add a dollop of raspberry jelly into the middle.
8. Bake for 15-20 minutes or until lightly browned at the edges.
9. Remove cookies from cookie sheet and let cool on wire rack.

Makes about a dozen cookies

Oatmeal Raisin Cookies

INGREDIENTS:
- ½ cup butter
- ⅓ cup agave nectar
- 1 egg
- 2 Tablespoons milk (cow, goat, almond, rice, coconut, oat, etc.)
- ½ teaspoon high-quality salt
- ½ teaspoon baking soda
- ½ cup oat flour
- ¼ cup brown rice flour
- ¼ cup barley flour
- 1 cup rolled oats
- ½ cup raisins **or** a combination nuts and raisins

DIRECTIONS:
1. In a large bowl, on the medium speed of an electric mixer, beat butter and agave nectar until light and creamy.
2. Add egg and milk and mix until smooth, about 3 minutes.
3. Stir in the salt, baking soda, oat flour, brown rice flour, and barley flour, then stir in the oats and raisins and/or nuts. Stir until batter is smooth.
4. Chill dough for 30 minutes.
5. Preheat oven to 350°F.
6. Using a spoon or cookie-dough scooper, arrange uniform balls of cookie dough 3 inches apart on an ungreased baking sheet.
7. Bake for 10-15 minutes or until lightly browned at the edges.
8. Remove cookies from cookie sheet and let cool on wire rack.

OPTIONAL VARIATIONS:
- Substitute raisins with chocolate chips for a chocolate chip oatmeal cookie.
- Add up to 1 cup of chopped nuts in addition to raisins or chocolate chips. You might want to make the cookies slightly larger in this case.

Makes about a dozen cookies

Chia Raisin Cookies

INGREDIENTS:
- 1 ¾ cups oat flour
- ½ cup amaranth flour
- ¾ teaspoon baking soda
- 1 ½ teaspoons high-quality salt
- ¼ cup chia seeds
- ⅓ cup butter **or** organic vegetable shortening (coconut or palm)
- ½ cup agave nectar
- ¼ cup milk (cow, goat, almond, rice, coconut, oat, etc.)
- 1 teaspoon pure vanilla extract
- ¾ cup raisins

DIRECTIONS:
1. Preheat oven to 350°F.
2. In a medium bowl, sift together dry ingredients: oat flour, amaranth flour, baking soda, and salt. Next, add chia seeds and mix well.
3. In a large bowl, on the medium speed of an electric mixer, beat butter and agave until light and creamy.
4. Add milk and vanilla and blend until smooth, about 2 minutes.
5. Add dry ingredients and mix until completely integrated. Fold in raisins.
6. Using a spoon or cookie-dough scooper, arrange uniform balls of cookie dough 3 inches apart on an ungreased baking sheet.
7. Bake for 8-10 minutes or until lightly browned at the edges.
8. Remove cookies from cookie sheet and let cool on a wire rack.

Makes about a dozen cookies

Coco-Cocoa Cookies

INGREDIENTS:
- ½ cup butter (1 stick), softened
- ½ cup agave nectar
- 1 egg
- 1 teaspoon pure vanilla extract
- 1 cup light coconut milk
- 1 teaspoon baking soda
- ½ teaspoon baking powder
- 1 teaspoon high-quality salt
- 1 cup unsweetened shredded coconut
- ¼ cup buttermilk powder **or** whey powder
- ½ cup cocoa powder
- ½ cup coconut flour
- ¼ cup tapioca flour
- ¼ cup sorghum flour
- ½ cup buckwheat flour
- 1 cup grain-sweetened chocolate chips

DIRECTIONS:
1. Preheat oven to 350°F.
2. In a large bowl, on the medium speed of an electric mixer, beat butter and agave until light and creamy.
3. Add egg, vanilla, and coconut milk and beat until smooth, about 1 minute.
4. Add dry ingredients: baking soda, baking powder, salt, shredded coconut, buttermilk or whey powder, cocoa powder, coconut flour, tapioca flour, sorghum flour, and buckwheat flour. Mix until batter is smooth.
5. Stir in the chocolate chips.
6. Using a spoon or cookie-dough scooper, arrange uniform balls of cookie dough 3 inches apart on an ungreased baking sheet.
7. Bake for 10-15 minutes or until lightly browned at the edges.
8. Remove cookies from cookie sheet and let cool on a wire rack.

Makes about 2 dozen cookies

Peanut Butter Cookies

INGREDIENTS:
- ½ cup butter
- 1 cup peanut butter
- 1 cup agave nectar
- 2 eggs
- 1 teaspoon pure vanilla extract
- 1 cup sorghum flour **or** oat flour
- 1 cup oat flour (substitute with millet flour for gluten free)
- ½ cup tapioca flour
- 1 teaspoon baking powder
- 1 teaspoon baking soda
- 1 teaspoon xanthan gum **or** guar gum **or** a 50:50 combination of both
- 1 teaspoon high-quality salt

DIRECTIONS:
1. In a large bowl, on the slow speed of an electric mixer, beat butter cut into 1" chunks and peanut butter for about 3 minutes. Little chunks may be present.
2. Add agave and continue beating until the mixture is smooth.
3. Add eggs one at a time, then add vanilla.
4. Add dry ingredients: sorghum flour (or oat flour), tapioca flour, baking powder, baking soda, gum, and salt and beat until smooth, about 3 minutes.
5. Chill dough thoroughly, about 30 minutes.
6. Preheat oven to 350°F.
7. Using a spoon or cookie-dough scooper, arrange uniform balls of cookie dough 3 inches apart on an ungreased baking sheet. Using the back of a fork, press a crisscross pattern into the cookies.
8. Bake for 8-10 minutes for chewy cookies, 10-12 minutes for crispy-chewy cookies, and up to 14 minutes for crispy cookies.
9. Remove cookies from cookie sheet and let cool on wire rack.

Makes about 2 dozen cookies

Yummy Tip:
You can make peanut butter cookie sandwiches by mixing equal parts peanut butter and agave nectar and sandwiching between two cookies!

Butter Cookies

INGREDIENTS:
- 2 ½ cups oat flour
- 1 cup brown rice flour
- ¼ teaspoon high-quality salt
- 2 teaspoons arrowroot flour
- 1 teaspoon baking powder
- 1 cup butter, softened
- ½ cup agave nectar
- 2 eggs
- 1 teaspoon pure vanilla extract

DIRECTIONS:
1. In a medium bowl, sift together dry ingredients: oat flour, brown rice flour, salt, arrowroot flour, and baking powder. Set aside.
2. In a large bowl, on the medium speed of an electric mixer, beat butter and agave until light and creamy.
3. Add the eggs and vanilla. Beat until smooth.
4. Slowly add the dry mixture. Mix until well combined. Do not overmix.
5. When the batter is smooth, divide batter in half and put in two covered bowls. Chill dough for about 30 minutes to an hour or until the dough is firm enough to roll.
6. Preheat oven to 375°F.
7. Line two cookie sheets with parchment paper.
8. Remove one half of the chilled dough from the refrigerator. On a floured surface with a floured rolling pin, roll out the dough to ⅛" thick. If you need to use more flour to prevent stickiness, use oat flour. Keep turning the dough as you roll, making sure it does not stick to the counter.
9. Cut out desired shapes using a lightly floured cookie cutter and transfer to the prepared baking sheets. Place the baking sheets with the unbaked cookies in the refrigerator for 10 -15 minutes to chill the dough. This prevents the cookies from spreading and losing their shape while baking.
10. Repeat for second half of chilled dough. Bake for 11-14 minutes or until they begin to brown around the edges. Since these cookies are fragile when hot, cool the cookies on the cookie sheet positioned on a wire rack for a few minutes before transferring to a wire rack to cool.

Makes about 2 dozen cookies

Gingerbread Men and Women

INGREDIENTS:
- ½ cup butter
- ½ cup agave nectar
- 1 teaspoon allspice powder
- ½ teaspoon nutmeg powder
- ½ teaspoon ground cinnamon
- 3 Tablespoons grated fresh ginger
- 1 egg
- 2 Tablespoons organic molasses
- 2 cups oat flour
- 2 cups barley flour
- 1 cup tapioca flour
- 1 teaspoon baking powder
- ½ cup buttermilk powder **or** whey powder
- 1 teaspoon high-quality salt
- ¾ cup date sugar

DIRECTIONS:
1. Preheat oven to 350°F.
2. In a large bowl, on the medium speed of an electric mixer, beat butter and agave until light and creamy.
3. Add allspice, nutmeg, cinnamon, and fresh ginger.
4. Beat in egg and molasses and mix for 2 minutes.
5. Add dry ingredients: oat flour, barley flour, tapioca flour, baking powder, buttermilk or whey powder, salt, and date sugar. Beat until smooth, about 3 minutes.
6. Chill dough for 30 minutes.
7. On a lightly floured surface, roll dough to about ⅛" thick. Cut cookies with lightly floured gingerbread people cookie cutters or desired cutter shapes. If you are working with small children, have them roll out heads and bodies and feet and make their own gingerbread people. They'll love it!
8. Bake for 15-20 minutes or until lightly browned at the edges.
9. Remove cookies from cookie sheet and let cool on wire rack.

Makes about 2 dozen cookies

Pizzelles

This is more healthful version of the traditional Italian cookie often served at Christmas. Shape these into waffle cups and fill with fruit salad or ice cream in the summer.

ADDITIONAL TOOLS NEEDED:
Pizzelle Iron

INGREDIENTS:
- 2 Tablespoons ground anise seeds (optional)
- 1 ½ cups oat flour
- 1 cup barley flour
- ½ cup tapioca flour
- ½ cup brown rice flour
- ¼ teaspoon baking soda
- 1 teaspoon baking powder
- 4 eggs
- 1 ⅓ cup agave nectar
- 1 cup butter, softened
- ¼ cup grapeseed oil **or** other neutral-tasting oil
- 1 teaspoon pure vanilla extract
- 3 Tablespoons anise flavoring (**or** 3 drops of anise essential oil)
- Zest of one lemon

OPTIONAL VARIATION:
If you want to change the anise flavor, try orange extract or orange essential oil. You can also substitute orange zest for the lemon zest.

DIRECTIONS:
1. In a medium bowl, combine the ground anise, oat flour, barley flour, brown rice flour, baking soda, and baking powder. Mix well and set aside.
2. In a large bowl, on the medium speed of an electric mixer, beat eggs until thick and lemony colored, about 1 minute.
3. Keep beating and add the agave, then beat in the butter, oil, vanilla, and anise flavoring and continue beating.
4. Slowly add in the flour mixture. Fold in the grated lemon zest.
5. Cover and chill dough for at least 30 minutes or, preferably, overnight.
6. Plug in the electric pizzelle iron and follow manufacturer's instructions.
7. When the pizzelle iron is ready, drop 1 Tablespoon of the batter onto the well-greased iron and bake until golden light brown in color. Remove the pizzelle with a fork or spatula and cool on wire rack.
8. For waffle cups, take the pizzelle fresh off the iron and lay over an upside-down cup. Cool completely and fill with ice cream, fruit salad, or whatever your heart desires. You can also use a pizzelle cone roller to make ice cream cones.
9. Place cooled cookies into tins for storage.

Pizzelle Tip:
If you are using anise oil, use a little less, since essential oils have much stronger flavors than extracts.

To determine your desired amount of flavoring, make one round of pizzelles in the iron, let cool, and taste. Increase anise flavoring if desired. For a crisper cookie add 2-3 Tablespoons of cornstarch in place of some of the flour.

Makes about 3 dozen pizzelles

Madeleine Cookies

This is a delicious and soft French cookie that makes a lovely accompaniment at tea time.

ADDITIONAL TOOLS NEEDED:
Madeleine pans

INGREDIENTS:
- Neutral-tasting oil (grapeseed, untoasted sesame oil, coconut oil, **or** ghee) **or** melted butter for greasing pan
- ½ cup tapioca flour plus extra for dusting
- ½ cup oat flour (substitute with white rice flour for gluten free)
- ½ teaspoon xanthan gum **or** guar gum **or** a 50:50 combination of both
- ½ teaspoon high-quality salt
- 10 Tablespoons unsalted butter, melted, cooled slightly
- ½ cup agave nectar
- 2 large eggs
- 1 teaspoon pure vanilla extract
- ½ teaspoon lemon zest

DIRECTIONS:
1. Preheat oven to 375°F.
2. Oil the Madeleine pans and dust them with tapioca flour.
3. In a medium bowl, sift together dry ingredients: tapioca flour, oat flour, gum, and salt. Set aside.
4. In a large bowl, on the medium speed of an electric mixer, beat butter and agave until just blended.
5. Add in the eggs, vanilla, and grated lemon zest.
6. Sprinkle in flour mixture and beat just until blended. Gradually add cooled melted butter in a steady stream, beating until just blended. Do not overmix.
7. Spoon 1 Tablespoon of batter into each Madeleine shell shape.
8. Bake for about 10-16 minutes or until puffed and slightly brown.
9. Let sit in the pan for 5 minutes, then gently remove from pan to cool on wire racks.
10. Repeat process for the second batch, being sure to clean the Madeleine pan, and then butter and flour pan again. Cool pans in freezer for 5 minutes before filling with batter. Repeat.

Makes about a dozen cookies

Taralli

· · · · · · · ·

A delightful, crispy Italian cookie.

INGREDIENTS:

- 2 cups oat flour
- 1 ½ cups sorghum flour
- 1 cup tapioca flour
- 1 cup white rice flour
- 1 ½ Tablespoons baking powder
- 1 Tablespoon anise seeds
- 6 large eggs
- ⅔ cup agave nectar
- ¾ cup (1 ½ sticks) unsalted butter, melted and cooled
- 1 ½ Tablespoons pure vanilla extract

DIRECTIONS:

1. Position racks in the upper and lower thirds of the oven.
2. Preheat to 350°F.
3. Line 3 baking sheets with parchment paper.
4. In a large bowl, sift together dry ingredients: oat flour, sorghum flour, tapioca flour, white rice flour, and baking powder. Add anise seeds. Mix well and set aside.
5. In a large bowl, on the medium speed of an electric mixer, beat the eggs for 1 minute. In the following order mix in: agave, butter, and vanilla. Fold in the flour mixture.
6. Plop the dough onto a lightly floured surface and knead 3-5 times to mix. Separate dough into 16 equal pieces. Roll each to an 8" thick rope, then press the ends together to form a circle (see picture). Place 5 or 6 on each baking sheet.
7. Place the baking sheets on the upper and lower racks and bake for 15 minutes.
8. Rotate pans top to bottom. Bake for another 15 minutes or until the taralli are slightly puffed and deep golden.
9. Transfer to wire racks to cool completely.

Makes about a dozen cookies

Bars And Brownies

Lemon Bars

INGREDIENTS:

Crust:

- ½ pound unsalted butter, at room temperature
- ⅓ cup agave nectar
- 1 cup oat flour
- ½ cup brown rice flour
- ½ cup barley flour
- ¼ teaspoon high-quality salt

Filling:

- 6 eggs at room temperature
- 2 cups agave nectar
- 2 Tablespoons lemon zest (4-6 lemons)
- 1 cup freshly squeezed lemon juice
- ½ cup oat flour
- ½ cup tapioca flour

DIRECTIONS:

For the crust:

1. Preheat oven to 350°F.
2. In a medium bowl, on the medium speed of an electric mixer, beat the butter and agave until smooth, about 2 minutes.
3. Add oat flour, brown rice flour, barley flour, and salt and beat until just mixed.
4. Plop the dough onto a well-floured surface and roll out to make a ball.
5. Flour hands and press the dough into a 9" x 13" x 2" baking sheet, building up a ½" edge on all sides. Chill for 15 minutes.
6. Bake the crust for 15-20 minutes or until lightly browned. Let crust cool but leave the oven on.

For the filling:

1. In a medium bowl, on the high speed of an electric mixer, beat the eggs for 3 minutes. Turn the speed down to medium and add the agave, grated lemon zest, and lemon juice. Slowly add the oat flour and tapioca flour and mix until smooth.
2. Pour the lemon filling over the crust.
3. Bake on center rack for 30-35 minutes or until the filling is set. Let cool to room temperature.
4. Cut into squares and serve.

Makes about 15-20 squares

Cocoa Brownies
· ·

INGREDIENTS:
- Neutral-tasting oil (grapeseed, untoasted sesame oil, coconut oil, **or** ghee) for greasing pan
- ½ cup butter (1 stick)
- ½ cup grain-sweetened chocolate chips
- 1 cup oat flour
- ½ cup brown rice flour
- ¼ teaspoon baking powder
- ¼ teaspoon high-quality salt
- 1 cup cocoa powder
- 1 cup agave nectar
- 3 eggs

DIRECTIONS:
1. Preheat oven to 350°F. Grease an 8" square baking pan.
2. In a double boiler or a metal bowl placed over a saucepan of boiling water, melt the butter. At this point you can add in and melt the chocolate chips for a blended chocolate brownie or you can add in the chips later for chocolate chip brownies.
3. In a large mixing bowl, mix together dry ingredients: oat flour, brown rice flour, baking powder, salt, and cocoa powder.
4. Stir butter (or butter and chocolate) into the flour mixture, then add the agave and eggs. Stir well, until there are no lumps and the batter is smooth.
5. Pour batter into prepared pan.
6. Bake for 13 -17 minutes. For gooey brownies, slightly underbake them.

Makes about a dozen brownies

Rich Chocolate Brownies

This rich brownie is free of cocoa powder and gets its flavor from melted chocolate.

INGREDIENTS:

- Neutral-tasting oil (grapeseed, untoasted sesame oil, coconut oil, **or** ghee) for greasing pan
- 10 Tablespoons butter
- 6 ounces unsweetened chocolate
- 1 cup oat flour
- 1 cup brown rice flour
- ½ cup tapioca flour
- ½ teaspoon baking powder
- ½ teaspoon high-quality salt
- 4 large eggs
- 1 ⅓ cups agave nectar
- 1 teaspoon pure vanilla extract

DIRECTIONS:

1. Preheat oven to 325°F. Grease an 8" square baking pan.
2. In a double boiler or a metal bowl placed over a saucepan of boiling water, melt the butter. Add chocolate and heat until melted. Remove from heat and let cool.
3. In a large mixing bowl, mix together dry ingredients: oat flour, brown rice flour, tapioca flour, baking powder, and salt.
4. Add the cooled chocolate/butter mixture to the flour mixture, then add eggs, agave, and vanilla. Stir well, until there are no lumps and the batter is smooth.
5. Pour batter into prepared pan.
6. Bake for 40 minutes. For gooey brownies, slightly underbake them.

Makes about a dozen brownies

Gluten-Free Cookies and Brownies

KC's Chocolate Chip Coconut Cookies

INGREDIENTS:

- Neutral-tasting oil (grapeseed, untoasted sesame oil, coconut oil, **or** ghee) for greasing pan
- 2 ¼ cups brown rice flour
- 1 teaspoon baking soda
- ¼ teaspoon high-quality salt
- Two 4-ounce sticks goat butter, softened
- ¾ cup agave nectar
- 1 teaspoon pure vanilla extract
- 2 eggs
- 9-ounce bag of grain-sweetened chocolate chips
- 1 cup coconut flakes

DIRECTIONS:

1. Preheat oven to 375°F. Grease a baking sheet.
2. In a medium bowl, mix together dry ingredients: brown rice flour, baking soda, and salt. Set aside.
3. In a large bowl, on the medium speed of an electric mixer, beat the butter, agave, and vanilla until smooth, about 2 minutes.
4. Beat in eggs and mix for 2 minutes more.
5. Slowly add in flour mixture and mix until the batter is smooth.
6. Fold in the chocolate chips and coconut flakes.
7. Using a spoon or cookie-dough scooper, arrange uniform balls of cookie dough 3 inches apart on a greased baking sheet.
8. Bake for 9-12 minutes or until lightly browned at the edges.
9. Remove cookies from cookie sheet and let cool on a wire rack.

Makes about a dozen cookies

Flourless Almond Cookies

INGREDIENTS:
- 1 cup almonds or more if necessary for a firm batter
- ¾ cup agave nectar
- 1 - 1 ½ egg whites
- ½ teaspoon pure vanilla extract

DIRECTIONS:
1. Preheat oven to 400°F. Cover two baking sheets with parchment paper.
2. In a blender or food processor, grind almonds and agave to make a fine meal.
3. Immediately add the egg whites before the almonds lose their oil. Pulse about 8-12 times.
4. Add the vanilla and pulse 3 times more.
5. Shape the batter into walnut-sized balls. Add more almonds as needed to make dough workable. Arrange balls on the parchment covered baking sheets. Use a pastry brush to brush each with a bit of water.
6. If desired, drizzle agave on top of each cookie and/or press an almond into each cookie.
7. Bake for 15-20 minutes or until lightly brown. Remove the cookie sheets from the oven and cool on the parchment trays positioned on wire cooling racks.
8. Cool completely. Dip in melted chocolate, if desired. Store in a glass storage container up to one week or freeze up to 3 months.

Makes about 16 cookies

Brownies

INGREDIENTS:

- Neutral-tasting oil (grapeseed, untoasted sesame oil, coconut oil, **or** ghee) for greasing pan
- 1 stick butter
- ½ cup grain-sweetened chocolate chips
- ½ cup brown rice flour
- ¼ cup tapioca flour
- ½ cup cocoa powder
- ½ teaspoon xanthan gum **or** guar gum **or** a 50:50 combination of both
- ¼ teaspoon high-quality salt
- 1 cup agave nectar
- 3 eggs
- 1 teaspoon pure vanilla extract

DIRECTIONS:

1. Preheat oven to 350°F. Grease an 8" square baking pan.
2. In a double boiler or a metal bowl over a saucepan of boiling water, melt the butter and chocolate. At this point you can melt the chocolate chips with the butter for a blended chocolate effect, or add the chips into the batter later for chocolate chip brownies.
3. In a large mixing bowl, mix together dry ingredients: brown rice flour, tapioca flour, cocoa powder, gum, and salt.
4. When the butter or butter/chocolate mixture is melted, add to flour, and add the agave, eggs, and vanilla. Stir well, until there are no lumps and the flour is completely mixed.
5. Pour batter into prepared pan.
6. Bake for 20-25 minutes. For gooey brownies, slightly underbake them.

Makes about a dozen brownies

Macaroons

INGREDIENTS:

- Coconut oil for greasing pan
- 2 egg whites
- 1 teaspoon pure vanilla extract
- ½ teaspoon high-quality salt
- ¾ cup agave nectar
- 2 ¼ cups shredded or flaked coconut
- ¼ cup coconut flour

DIRECTIONS:

1. Preheat oven to 350°F. Grease a baking sheet with coconut oil.
2. In a medium bowl, on the medium speed of an electric mixer, beat egg whites until stiff.
3. Beat in vanilla and salt. Gradually beat in agave, about 1 Tablespoon at a time.
4. Fold in coconut and coconut flour. Mix well and let sit in the refrigerator for 20 minutes to stiffen batter. Shape the batter into walnut-sized balls and place on the greased baking sheet, about 1" apart.
5. Bake for 20 minutes. The outside of the cookie should be golden brown and the inside should be soft.

Makes about 2 dozen macaroons

Vegan Almond Macaroons

INGREDIENTS:
- Coconut oil for greasing pan
- ½ cup agave nectar
- 2 Tablespoons coconut oil
- ½ cup almonds (**or** ½ cup shredded coconut)
- 1 cup unsweetened shredded coconut
- 1 teaspoon ground cinnamon
- 1 teaspoon pure vanilla extract
- ¼ teaspoon high-quality salt

DIRECTIONS:
1. Preheat oven to 400°F. Grease a baking sheet with coconut oil.
2. In a medium saucepan, heat the agave and coconut oil gently over low heat. Remove from heat and cool slightly.
3. In a blender or food processor, grind almonds to make a fine meal.
4. In a large bowl, combine the almond meal, coconut, melted coconut/agave mixture, cinnamon, vanilla, and salt. Mix well.
5. The consistency should be firm enough to shape into balls. If the mixture is runny, let it sit for a few minutes so the coconut can rehydrate. If it is still runny, add ½ cup more coconut.
6. Form into balls and place on the greased baking sheet, about 1" apart.
7. Bake 12-15 minutes. The outside of the cookie should be golden brown and the inside should be soft.

Makes about a dozen macaroons

My Cookie and Bar Creations:

Use this section to write down some of your favorite cookie and bar recipes from this chapter.

Recipe:

INGREDIENTS:

DIRECTIONS:

Serves _____

My Cookie and Bar Creations:

Use this section to write down some of your favorite cookie and bar recipes from this chapter.

Recipe:

INGREDIENTS:

....

....

....

....

....

....

....

DIRECTIONS:

....

....

....

....

....

....

Serves _____

CHAPTER 14

PUDDINGS AND CUSTARDS

Understanding the Differences................240

Top Tips for Making Great Puddings and Custards.....240

Puddings and Custards

Pudding Base Recipe 242

Simple Vanilla Pudding........243

Chocolate Pudding 244

Earl Grey Pudding 245

Rose Delight 245

Maple Pumpkin Custard 246

Strawberries and Cream Parfait 247

Creamy Rice Pudding 248

Coconut Brown Rice Pudding. .248

Tapioca Pudding..............249

Chai Tapioca 249

Barley Pudding 250

Banana Cream Pudding 250

Torta de Banana 251

Coconut Pudding.............252

Vanilla Amasake Pudding......252

Mocha Amasake Pudding......253

Chia Chocolate Pudding 254

Mocha Chia Pudding..........255

Chia Banana Coconut Pudding .255

Rhubarb Yogurt Swirl 256

Understanding The Differences

What is the difference between a custard and a pudding? The answer literally depends on what country you're in. The strict definition of *custard* is a dessert with eggs and milk that is either baked (with or without a hot bath) or stirred over gentle heat until thickened. Sometimes thickeners such as flour, tapioca flour, arrowroot flour, gelatin, and cornstarch are added. In North America, *puddings* are referred to as sweet milk-based desserts similar to custards but can also include other types of desserts, like bread pudding and rice pudding. In Great Britain, these categories also include savory dishes like Yorkshire pudding and blood pudding.

Top Tips for Making Great Puddings and Custards

Start with the Right Tools:

• Small bowl
• Saucepan
• Whisk
• Silicon spatula
• Ramekins (for individual servings)

Know Your Ingredients:

Milk:

The milk you choose will add a distinct flavor to your pudding or custard. Try using creamier milks, such as coconut, cow, goat, or almond milk. For even more decadence, substitute ½ - 1 cup of cream for milk in the recipe. Coconut cream, made by placing a can of coconut milk in the refrigerator and scooping the coconut cream off the top, will also add depth and richness. If you use dairy milk, try to use raw, unpasteurized milk whenever possible.

Eggs:

Eggs add thickness to the consistency of puddings and custards. Heat kills enzymes in raw egg yolks, which will otherwise break down the starch bonds and thin the pudding. Also make sure to bring your mixture to just under a simmer (208°F) after adding egg yolks to prevent curdling.

Starch and Thickeners:

There are many different thickeners you can use, including arrowroot flour, tapioca flour, cornstarch, xanthan gum, guar gum, agar-agar seaweed, and kudzu powder. You can also use oat bran or ground flax seed, but these will give a more grainy texture to your pudding or custard.

Agave Nectar:

Agave nectar works perfectly in puddings, adding a gentle, low-glycemic sweetness.

Extracts and Flavoring:

Flavors like vanilla, almond, orange, lemon, mint, chocolate, or hazelnut will add body and flavor to puddings.

Cooking Tips:

To avoid the pudding skin that forms on the top of chilled pudding, cover pudding with PVC-free plastic wrap or cover with a plate to keep the air out. Let the pudding or custard chill for about 2 hours to set.

Don't worry if you don't have all the ingredients for a recipe — improvise, substitute, be creative, and have fun!

Puddings and Custards

Pudding Base Recipe

INGREDIENTS:
- 3 large eggs
- 2 cups milk (cow, goat, almond, rice, coconut, oat, etc.)
- ⅓ cup agave nectar
- 2 Tablespoons cornstarch **or** 4 teaspoons arrowroot flour **or** tapioca flour
- ⅛ teaspoon high-quality salt
- 2 Tablespoons butter
- 1 teaspoon pure vanilla extract

DIRECTIONS:
1. Separate the egg yolks from the egg whites. Whisk the egg yolks for 2 minutes.
2. In a medium saucepan, combine milk and eggs and beat for 2 minutes. Add agave, cornstarch, and salt.
3. Cook, whisking constantly, over medium heat until mixture comes to a gentle simmer. Be careful not to overcook.
4. Whisk in the butter and vanilla just until the butter is completely incorporated, about 30 seconds. Turn heat down low and simmer to evaporate off the extract's alcohol.
5. Pour into a bowl or individual containers.
6. Chill until set, about 2 hours.

OPTIONAL VARIATIONS:
- For lemon pudding, add 1 teaspoon lemon extract and the zest of 1 lemon.
- For chocolate pudding, melt 1 cup of chocolate into the pudding, or stir 5 Tablespoons of cocoa powder into the cold milk mixture.

Serves 4

Simple Vanilla Pudding

INGREDIENTS:
- 3 large eggs
- 2 cups milk (cow, goat, almond, rice, coconut, oat, etc.)
- ⅓ cup agave nectar
- 2 Tablespoons cornstarch **or** 4 teaspoons arrowroot flour **or** tapioca flour
- ⅛ teaspoon high-quality salt
- 2 Tablespoons butter
- 1 Tablespoon pure vanilla extract

DIRECTIONS:
1. Separate the egg yolks from the egg whites. Whisk the egg yolks for 2 minutes.
2. In a medium saucepan, combine milk and eggs and beat for 2 minutes. Add agave, cornstarch, and salt.
3. Cook, whisking constantly, over medium heat until mixture comes to a gentle simmer. Be careful not to overcook.
4. Whisk in the butter and vanilla just until the butter is completely incorporated, about 30 seconds. Turn heat down low and simmer to evaporate off the extract's alcohol.
5. Pour into a bowl or individual containers.
6. Chill until set, about 2 hours.

Serves 4

Chocolate Pudding

INGREDIENTS:
- 3 large eggs
- 3 Tablespoons cornstarch
- 3 Tablespoons unsweetened cocoa powder
- 3 cups cold milk (cow, goat, almond, rice, coconut, oat, etc.)
- ⅓ cup agave nectar
- 3 ounces high-quality chocolate **or** ½ cup grain-sweetened chocolate chips, chopped
- 1 teaspoon pure vanilla extract
- ¼ teaspoon high-quality salt

DIRECTIONS:
1. Separate the egg yolks from the egg whites. Whisk the egg yolks for 2 minutes in a medium bowl. Set aside.
2. In a 4-quart saucepan, mix the cornstarch and cocoa. Slowly whisk in the cold milk, a little at a time to ensure no lumps form. Add agave. Scrape the bottom and sides of the saucepan with a spatula.
3. Over medium-low heat, continue stirring the pudding until it thickens to the point that it lightly coats the back of the spatula or spoon, about 5 minutes.
4. Continue cooking and stirring constantly as the pudding comes to a gentle simmer, about 2 minutes more. Reduce the heat to low.
5. Ladle ½ cup of the hot pudding into the egg yolks and whisk rapidly. Repeat two times.
6. Add the egg yolk mixture back to the saucepan, stirring constantly.
7. Heat mixture to just under a simmer, stirring continuously. Remove from the heat.
8. Add the chopped chocolate and continue stirring for about 1 minute, until the chocolate is melted and well combined with the other ingredients.
9. Stir in vanilla and salt.
10. If the pudding is lumpy, pour it through a single mesh strainer, using a plastic spatula to press it through. Immediately pour the pudding into a medium-sized bowl.
11. Cover with a plate or PVC-free plastic wrap.
12. Let cool, then refrigerate until completely cool, about 2 hours.
13. Spoon pudding into 6 glasses, ramekins, or cups to serve.

Serves 4-6

Earl Grey Pudding

INGREDIENTS:

Pudding:

- 2 cups milk (cow, goat, almond, rice, coconut, oat, etc.)
- 3 Tablespoons earl grey tea leaves
- ⅓ cup agave nectar
- 2 eggs
- 4 egg yolks

Caramel sauce:

- ½ cup dark agave nectar

DIRECTIONS:

1. Preheat oven to 300°F.
2. Make a milk tea by combining 1 cup of milk and tea leaves in a small saucepan. Boil over medium heat for about 5 minutes.
3. Strain tea and add agave and remaining 1 cup of milk.
4. Separate the egg yolks from 4 of the eggs. Whisk 2 whole eggs and 4 egg yolks for 2 minutes in a large bowl. Add milk tea. Divide evenly among 6 ramekins or oven-proof tea cups. Boil water for water bath.
5. Place pudding cups in a deep square cake pan or Pyrex dish. Fill dish with boiling water until the water almost reaches the same level as the pudding liquid. Bake for about 30 minutes.
6. While pudding is baking, make caramel sauce. Place agave in saucepan and stir constantly over medium heat for 15-20 minutes. Pour over pudding.
7. Chill pudding until firm, about 1 hour.

Serves 4

Rose Delight

This makes a lovely dessert to serve on Valentine's Day—or any day.

INGREDIENTS:

- 2 cups milk (cow, goat, almond, rice, coconut, oat, etc.)
- ¼ cup and 1 Tablespoon agave nectar
- ¼ cup cornstarch
- 2 Tablespoons rosewater

DIRECTIONS:

1. In a medium saucepan, bring 1 ½ cups of milk to a gentle boil, then add agave and stir.
2. In a small bowl, mix remaining ½ cup cold milk with cornstarch and stir.
3. Blend ⅓ cup of hot milk into the cold milk, then return all of it to the hot milk in the saucepan.
4. Boil while stirring constantly, about 10 minutes.
5. Add rosewater right before the end.
6. Serve hot or chilled. Top with rose petals for an elegant touch.

OPTIONAL VARIATION:
Try adding a teaspoon of cardamom powder in step one.

Serves 3-4

Maple Pumpkin Custard

INGREDIENTS:
- Neutral-tasting oil (grapeseed, untoasted sesame oil, coconut oil, **or** ghee) for greasing pan
- ¾ cup pumpkin **or** squash purée (fresh or from a can)
- 1 ½ cups milk (cow, goat, almond, rice, coconut, oat, etc.)
- 4 large eggs
- ½ cup maple syrup
- ¼ cup agave nectar
- 1 teaspoon ground cinnamon
- ½ teaspoon ground nutmeg
- ¼ teaspoon high-quality salt

DIRECTIONS:
1. If you are using fresh pumpkin cut it into quarters, position on baking sheet with 2 Tablespoons of water sprinkled on top, and bake on a greased baking sheet at 350°F for 45 minutes or until soft and cooked. Scoop out the soft flesh, measure ¾ cup, and purée. Skip this step if you are using canned pumpkin.
2. Turn down oven to 325°F.
3. In a medium saucepan, boil 4 cups of water for a water bath.
4. In a small saucepan, scald the milk over low heat, so that it steams but does not boil. Stir constantly.
5. In a large bowl, whisk the eggs, maple syrup, and agave until smooth.
6. Gently and gradually whisk warm milk into the egg mixture (go slowly so the egg doesn't cook). Add the pumpkin purée, spices, and salt. Whisk until totally blended.
7. Fill 6 ramekins with custard and place in a deep baking dish. Pour boiling water into the pan so that it comes up halfway on the custard cups.
8. Place the pan in the oven and bake uncovered for 45-50 minutes. The custards are done when they are set on the edges but the centers move when shaken.
9. Transfer the cups to a wire rack and let cool for 45 minutes.
10. Cover and refrigerate for 1 hour before serving.

Serves 6

Strawberries and Cream Parfait

INGREDIENTS:
- 3 Tablespoons tapioca flour
- 3 cups milk (cow, goat, almond, rice, coconut, oat, etc.)
- ⅓ cup agave nectar
- 1 large egg
- 1 teaspoon orange zest
- 2 Tablespoons orange liqueur
- 1 teaspoon pure vanilla extract
- 2 pints strawberries, sliced
- 2 Tablespoons agave nectar

DIRECTIONS:
1. In a blender, combine tapioca flour, milk, agave, egg, and grated orange zest. Blend until smooth.
2. Pour into a heavy, medium-sized saucepan and bring to a boil, stirring constantly, over medium heat. Remove from heat and stir in 1 Tablespoon orange liqueur and vanilla. Let pudding cool for 20 minutes, stirring occasionally to prevent a skin from forming.
3. In a large bowl, toss berries with 2 Tablespoons agave and remaining 1 Tablespoon orange liqueur. Let stand for 10 minutes.
4. Layer strawberries and pudding in six 8-ounce parfait glasses or wine glasses. Layer berries at the bottom of each glass, cover with a layer of pudding, and repeat. Top puddings with the remaining strawberries.
5. Cover and chill for several hours before serving.

Serves 6

Creamy Rice Pudding

INGREDIENTS:

- 1 ½ cups water
- ¾ cup uncooked white rice
- 2 cups milk (cow, goat, almond, rice, coconut, oat, etc.)
- ¼ cup agave nectar
- ¼ teaspoon high-quality salt
- 1 egg, beaten
- ⅔ cup cup golden raisins
- 1 Tablespoon butter
- ½ teaspoon pure vanilla extract

DIRECTIONS:

1. In a small saucepan, bring 1 ½ cups of water to a boil. Add rice and stir. Reduce heat, cover, and simmer for 20 minutes.
2. In a medium saucepan, combine 1 ½ cups cooked rice, 1 ½ cups milk, agave, and salt. Cook over medium heat until thick and creamy, 15-20 minutes.
3. Stir in remaining ½ cup milk, beaten egg, and raisins. Cook 2 minutes more, stirring constantly.
4. Remove from heat, and stir in butter and vanilla. Serve warm.

Serves 4

Coconut Brown Rice Pudding

INGREDIENTS:

- 2 13-ounce cans coconut milk
- 3 ¼ cups milk (cow, goat, almond, rice, coconut, oat, etc.)
- ¾ cup sweet brown rice **or** short-grain brown rice
- ¼ teaspoon high-quality salt
- ½ cup agave nectar
- ½ cup raisins

DIRECTIONS

1. In a medium saucepan, combine all ingredients. Bring to a boil over medium-high heat.
2. Reduce the heat so the liquid simmers very gently. Cook uncovered, stirring occasionally, until rice is tender but chewy and absorbs most of the liquid, about 1 ½ hours.
3. Remove the pudding from the heat and transfer to a bowl or divide among 4-6 individual bowls. Cover and chill in the refrigerator, about 1 hour.

Serves 4-6

Tapioca Pudding

INGREDIENTS:

- 1 cup medium or small tapioca pearls
- 4 cups milk (cow, goat, almond, rice, coconut, oat, etc.)
- 3 large eggs
- ½ teaspoon high-quality salt
- ¾ cup agave nectar
- Zest of one lemon

DIRECTIONS:

1. Soak tapioca in milk overnight in the refrigerator.
2. Cook tapioca and milk in a double boiler or a metal bowl placed over a saucepan of boiling water for 45 minutes, stirring frequently. Stir in optional spices.
3. Separate the egg yolks from the egg whites. Whisk the egg yolks for 2 minutes in a small bowl. Add salt, agave, and grated lemon zest.
4. When tapioca is fully cooked, add a spoonful of cooked tapioca to the egg mixture, then add warmed egg/tapioca mixture back to the rest of the tapioca. This brings the eggs up to temperature and prevents them from cooking in the pudding.
5. Cook another 5 minutes. Serve warm or chilled.

OPTIONAL VARIATIONS:
- Stir in 1 star anise, 1 stick of cinnamon, or 3 cardamom pods.
- For a more elegant touch, reserve the egg whites, add a pinch of salt, and whip them until softly stiff, then fold back into the tapioca at the end.

Serves 4

Chai Tapioca Pudding

INGREDIENTS:

- 1 cup small tapioca pearls
- 4 cups milk (cow, goat, almond, rice, coconut, oat, etc.)
- 2 cups water
- 8 Tablespoons chai tea
- 1 cup cream
- ½ cup agave nectar

DIRECTIONS:

1. Soak tapioca pearls in 1 cup of milk overnight.
2. Make chai tea first. Boil 2 cups of water and add 8 Tablespoons of chai tea of your choice, either herbal or black tea chai. Steep for 15-20 minutes. Strain.
3. In a large saucepan, over medium heat, heat remaining 3 cups of milk, cream, strained chai, and tapioca. Stir continuously for 20 minutes.
4. Add agave and continue to stir for 5 more minutes.
5. Serve warm or chilled.

Serves 4

Barley Pudding

INGREDIENTS
- 2 cups barley, washed
- 5 cups water
- Pinch high-quality salt
- 4 eggs
- ⅔ cup agave nectar
- 1 teaspoon lemon extract
- 1 cup milk (cow, goat, almond, rice, coconut, oat, etc.)

DIRECTIONS
1. In a medium saucepan, boil the barley in the water with salt for about 40 minutes. Set aside to cool.
2. Preheat oven to 350°F.
3. In a medium bowl, beat eggs, agave, and lemon extract on medium with a mixer for 3 minutes.
4. Gradually add milk and mix well. Beat for 1 minute more.
5. Add barley and stir.
6. Pour into a baking dish positioned within a larger pan of boiling water.
7. Bake for about 30-45 minutes.
8. Serve warm or chilled.

Serves 4-6

Banana Cream Pudding

INGREDIENTS:
- 2 large bananas
- ½ teaspoon ground cinnamon
- 2 Tablespoons agave nectar
- 1 teaspoon lemon juice
- ½ teaspoon pure vanilla extract
- 1 cup cream (**or** coconut cream)

DIRECTIONS:
1. In a blender or with an immersion blender, purée bananas, cinnamon, agave, lemon juice, and vanilla.
2. In a mixer, whip cream until stiff. If you use coconut cream, it won't act exactly the same as cream, but whip it until fluffy.
3. Fold the banana mixture into the whipped cream, and serve immediately in small parfait glasses, topped with thinly sliced bananas.

Serves 3-4

Torta de Banana

This is an adaption from a traditional Brazilian dessert.

INGREDIENTS:

Cream Pudding:

- 3 cups cream (**or** coconut cream)
- 1 cup coconut milk
- ½ cup agave nectar
- 5 Tablespoons cornstarch
- 3 eggs, separated into yolks and whites
- ½ teaspoon ground cinnamon
- 12 bananas split in half (preferably green)
- ½ teaspoon baking powder

Topping:

- 3 Tablespoons date sugar
- Pinch ground cinnamon

Meringue Frosting:

- Reserved egg whites from pudding
- 1/2 teaspoon baking powder

DIRECTIONS:

For Cream Pudding:

1. Preheat oven to 325°F.
2. In a medium saucepan, heat cream over medium heat. Pour 1 cup coconut milk into a measuring cup and stir in cornstarch until dissolved. Slowly add the coconut milk mixture to the saucepan. Set aside and allow to cool until the mixture is warm.
3. Separate the eggs. Set the egg whites aside. In a small bowl, beat the egg yolks. Ladle a cup of the warm cream mixture into the egg yolks. Stir.
4. Add agave to egg yolk and cream mixture. Gradually add back to cream mixture and bring to a boil. Stir constantly. Simmer for 20 minutes.
5. Meanwhile, mix date sugar and cinnamon in a small bowl for the topping. Set aside.
6. Split the bananas in half. In a rectangular baking dish, add half of the cream pudding. Place one layer of bananas on top of the pudding. Sprinkle half of the date sugar topping on top, then add the second half of the cream pudding. Top with remaining topping.

For Meringue Frosting:

1. Using an electric hand mixer, beat the reserved egg whites with ½ teaspoon of baking powder until stiff peaks form. Cover the pudding with the meringue.
2. Bake for 5 minutes or until the meringue turns golden brown.
3. Serve warm.

Serves 4

Coconut Pudding

INGREDIENTS:
- 2 cups coconut milk
- 4 Tablespoons agave nectar
- 4 Tablespoons arrowroot flour **or** 6 Tablespoons cornstarch
- 1 cup milk (cow, goat, almond, rice, coconut, oat, etc.)
- ½ teaspoon pure vanilla extract (optional)

DIRECTIONS:
1. In a medium saucepan, combine 1 cup coconut milk, agave, and arrowroot. Stir well.
2. Heat the mixture over low, stirring often, until thick.
3. Add remainder of coconut milk and milk and continue to heat until thickened. Add optional vanilla. Pour into parfait glasses or a bowl, cover, and chill until firm.
4. Top with shaved coconut or dried coconut.

Serves 4

Vanilla Amasake Pudding

This pudding is a dairy-free, egg-free Japanese dessert. Many of the ingredients are unusual, but can be found in a health food stores or online.

INGREDIENTS:
- 1 cup plain amasake
- 1 ½ cups almond milk **or** milk of your choice
- ½ cup agave nectar
- Pinch high-quality salt
- 1 ½ Tablespoons agar-agar (kanten)
- 1 ½ Tablespoons crushed kudzu **or** ¾ teaspoon tapioca **or** arrowroot flour
- 1 Tablespoon pure vanilla extract

DIRECTIONS:
1. In a blender, combine amasake, almond milk, agave, and salt. Blend until smooth.
2. Pour mixture into medium-sized saucepan. Sprinkle agar-agar flakes on top and simmer over medium heat without stirring. After 2 minutes, gently stir until agar-agar is dissolved.
3. In a small cup, dissolve kudzu in 2 Tablespoons of cold water. Add to pudding, whisking quickly. Simmer 2 minutes more, stirring constantly until pudding thickens.
4. Remove from heat and stir in vanilla. Pour into custard cups or small bowls.
5. Cover and chill until firm before serving, about 1 hour.

Serves 4

Mocha Amasake Pudding

INGREDIENTS:
- 1 cup water
- 2 teaspoons cocoa powder
- 2 Tablespoons instant grain coffee, like Kaffix or Roma
- 1 cup plain amasake
- 1 ½ cups almond milk **or** milk of your choice
- ½ cup agave nectar
- Pinch high-quality salt
- 1 ½ Tablespoons agar-agar flakes (kanten)
- 1 ½ Tablespoons crushed kudzu **or** ¾ teaspoon tapioca or arrowroot flour
- 1 teaspoon pure vanilla extract

DIRECTIONS:
1. In a medium saucepan, bring 1 cup of water to boil, then dissolve cocoa powder and grain coffee into it.
2. Add the cocoa mixture to a blender with amasake, almond milk, agave, and salt. Blend until smooth.
3. Add contents of the blender back into the saucepan.
4. Sprinkle agar-agar flakes on top and simmer over medium heat without stirring. After 2 minutes, gently stir until agar-agar is dissolved.
5. In a small cup, dissolve kudzu in 2 Tablespoons of cold water, then add to pudding, whisking quickly. Simmer 2 minutes more, stirring constantly until pudding thickens.
6. Remove from heat and stir in vanilla. Pour into custard cups or small bowls.
7. Cover and chill until firm before serving, about 1 hour.

Serves 4

Chia Chocolate Pudding

The chia seeds provide the thickening agent for this lovely pudding. Chia seeds are high in essential fatty acids.

INGREDIENTS:

- 1 cup grain-sweetened chocolate chips
- ¼ cup almonds
- 2 bananas
- ¾ cup coconut milk
- 1 Tablespoon agave nectar
- 2 Tablespoons chia seeds
- 1 teaspoon pure vanilla extract
- 1 teaspoon pure almond extract
- ½ teaspoon ground nutmeg
- ½ teaspoon high-quality salt

DIRECTIONS:

1. In a double boiler or metal bowl placed over a saucepan of boiling water, melt chocolate chips.
2. Dry blend almonds in a blender and pulse until you have a fine powder. Be careful not to blend too long, making almond butter.
3. Add bananas, coconut milk, agave, chia seeds, vanilla, almond extract, nutmeg, and salt to the blender. Add chocolate and blend until smooth.
4. Pour into custard cups or small bowls.
5. Cover and chill until firm before serving, about 1 hour.

Serves 6

Mocha Chia Pudding

INGREDIENTS:
- 1 ½ cups grain coffee, brewed and cooled
- ¾ cup chia seeds
- 1 ½ cups orange juice (preferably fresh)
- 4 Tablespoons raw cacao powder **or** carob powder **or** cocoa powder
- 1 Tablespoon orange blossom water (available in Middle Eastern markets and online)
- 4 Tablespoons agave nectar or to taste
- 1 teaspoon pure vanilla extract

DIRECTIONS:
1. Prepare the grain coffee according to package instructions and allow to cool.
2. Combine grain coffee, chia seeds, orange juice, cacao powder, orange blossom water, agave, and vanilla in a blender and purée until smooth.
3. Pour into custard cups or small bowls.
4. Cover and chill until firm before serving, about 1 hour.

Serves 6

Chia Banana Coconut Pudding

INGREDIENTS:
- ¾ cup coconut milk
- 1 banana
- 3 Tablespoons chia seeds
- 1-2 Tablespoons agave nectar or to taste

DIRECTIONS:
1. Combine all ingredients in a blender or food processor and purée until smooth.
2. Pour into custard cups or small bowls.
3. Cover and chill until firm before serving, about 1 hour.

Serves 2

Rhubarb Yogurt Swirl

INGREDIENTS:
- 1 cinnamon stick
- 3 whole cloves
- 1 star anise
- 1 2" long strip lemon zest
- 2 ¼ pounds rhubarb, trimmed and cut into ½" pieces (8 cups)
- 1¼ cups agave nectar
- 2 cups plain yogurt
- ½ cup whipping cream

DIRECTIONS:
1. Combine cinnamon stick, cloves, star anise, and lemon zest in a cheesecloth bag and tie firmly with string.
2. In a large saucepan, combine rhubarb, agave, and the spice bag. Bring to a boil over medium-high heat. Cook, stirring occasionally, until the mixture has the consistency of applesauce, about 6-8 minutes. Discard the spice bag.
3. Chill rhubarb mixture in the refrigerator for about 1 hour.
4. Meanwhile, line a colander with cheesecloth and set over a bowl. Spoon in yogurt and let it drain in the refrigerator until it measures 1 ½ cups, about 45 minutes - 1 hour.
5. In a chilled bowl, whip the cream until stiff, about 10 minutes.
6. Place the drained yogurt in a medium-sized bowl. Add the rhubarb mixture and gently fold in, leaving some swirls.
7. Swirl in the whipped cream.
8. Spoon into individual dishes.
9. Cover and refrigerate for at least 1 hour or up to 6 hours.

Serves 4

My Pudding and Custard Creations:

Use this section to write down some of your favorite customized pudding and custard recipes from this chapter.

Recipe:

· ·

INGREDIENTS:

DIRECTIONS:

Serves _____

My Pudding and Custard Creations:

Use this section to write down some of your favorite customized pudding and custard recipes from this chapter.

Recipe:

. . . .

INGREDIENTS:

....

....

....

....

....

....

....

DIRECTIONS:

....

....

....

....

....

....

Serves _____

CHAPTER 15

PIES AND TARTS

Top Tips for Baking Great Pies and Tarts 260

Pie Crust Base Recipes

3 Ways to Make Whole Grain Pie Crusts 263

Filling and Baking the Pie 267

Oil Crust 268

Butter Crust 268

Organic Vegetable Shortening Crust 269

Combo Crust: Half Shortening, Half Butter 269

Egg Crust 269

Cheese Crust 269

Whole Grain Pie Crust Recipes

Whole Wheat and Barley Oil Crust . . 270

Oat Butter Oil Crust 270

Oat Brown Rice Butter Oil Crust 271

Kamut Oil Crust 271

Millet Corn Kamut Oil Crust 271

Kamut Oat Butter Crust 272

Whole Wheat Buttermilk Shortening Crust 272

Barley Combo Crust 272

Gluten-Free Pie Crust Recipes

Tapioca Rice Crust 273

Millet Sorghum Corn Crust 274

Sweet Amaranth Crust 274

Coconut Crust 275

Pocket Pies and Toaster Pastries 276

Pie Fillings

Fresh Fruit Pie Base Recipe 278

Apple Pie 279

Strawberry Pie 280

Blueberry Pie 280

Cherry Pie 281

Banana Cream Pie 282

Coconut Cream Pie 283

Lemon Meringue Pie 284

Orange Meringue Pie 285

Mango Key Lime Pie 286

Pecan Pie 287

Pumpkin Pie 288

Sweet Potato Pie 289

Empanadas 290

Raw Pie Crusts

Simple Raw Macadamia Crust 291

Simple Brazil Nut Crust 291

Raw Pecan Pie Crust 292

Raw Pistachio Crust 292

Raw Date Nut Pie Crust 293

Raw Walnut Crust 294

Raw Pecan Almond Date Crust 294

Raw Pie Fillings

Raw Coconut Lime Pie Filling 295

Raw Key Lime Filling 295

Raw Lemon Filling 296

Raw Meringue Pie Topping 296

Raw Banana Cream Pie Filling 297

Raw Chocolate Cream Pie Filling 298

Raw Chocolate Banana Pie Filling 298

Raw Strawberry Pie Cups 299

Raw Chocolate Rose Pie Cups 300

Top Tips for Making Great Pies and Tarts

Plan Ahead:

Be sure to begin pie preparation ahead of time so that ingredients may chill and a prebaked crust may cool.

Start with the Right Tools:

- Bowl
- Measuring cups and spoons
- Waxed paper or parchment paper
- PVC-free natural plastic wrap
- Tin foil
- Rolling pin
- Knife, fork
- Pie weight chain (great for weighing down prebaked crusts; beans and foil will work, too)
- Pie dish (preferably glass or ceramic)
- Cooling rack
- Cookie sheet
- Pie server

OPTIONAL GADGETS:
- Pastry cutter
- Pie crust shield
- Pie stands and pie racks
- Pie marker to cut even slices of pie
- Pie top cutter to make pretty designs in the top crust
- Food processor

Keep Ingredients Cold:

For best results, refrigerate all ingredients prior to making the crust — even the flour. All liquids should be ice-cold.

Choose Quality Ingredients:

Flour:

Generally it is best to choose flours that are low in protein so the crust stays tender. If you are not sensitive to wheat, then whole wheat pastry flour works well. If you are following a wheat-free diet, the best pie crust flours are barley, kamut, and oat flour. If you are following a gluten-free diet, then tapioca, brown rice flour, sorghum, sweet white rice, and corn work nicely. You will find that all whole grain flours impart their own unique flavors and textures, so be sure to explore a variety of flours to discover your preferences.

Salt:

As always, I recommend using high-quality salts with color, such as grayish or pink varieties, which are higher in vitamins and minerals.

Sweetener (Agave nectar):

Adding a little agave to a pie crust is certainly not traditional, but it adds a gentle sweetness that makes the crust pleasant and delicious.

Baking Powder:

Some recipes call for baking powder. Baking powder lifts and aerates the dough slightly without weakening it and makes the dough tender. If you choose not to use baking powder, double the salt.

Vinegar:

Vinegar relaxes the dough without losing flakiness, makes it easier to roll, makes it shrink less, and acts as a tenderizer. To try this, add 1 ½ teaspoons of apple cider vinegar to the ice water in a recipe.

Eggs:

Some pie crusts include eggs and some do not. Experiment to discover your preference. To give your crust a golden sheen, lightly beat an egg, add about a Tablespoon of water to thin it, and brush over the crust. Bake as usual. You can also coat the bottom of your pie crust with the egg wash and prebake the crust to prevent soggy-bottomed pies.

Fat:

Fats that are solid at room temperature work well in crusts. These include unsalted butter, organic vegetable shortening (coconut or palm), or coconut oil. Fats should be chilled prior to use to make the crust flakey. If it is too warm, the flour will absorb too much of the fat and will produce a tough crust. If you are using butter, cut into small pieces prior to adding to the flour. The type of fat you choose will add its own distinct flavor and flakiness. You get a great flakey crust when little pieces of broken-up butter are in the dough. For a buttery flavor without the quantity of butter, mix half organic shortening and half butter. Neutral-tasting oils, such as grapeseed oil and toasted sesame oil can be used in pie crust recipes, but they do not produce a flakey crust. If you are looking for a traditional pie crust, oils are not your best option; however, they work fabulously for quick crusts that can be simply pressed into the pan. Avoid using vegetable shortenings made from partially hydrogenated oils, which contain harmful transfats. Seek out shortening made with palm oil or coconut oil instead.

Liquid:

For a tender crust, use just enough liquid to moisten the flour without getting it too wet. If too much liquid is added, you will need to add more flour, which could lead to a tough dough; too little liquid will make a dry dough that won't hold together. Add liquid to the flour mixture gradually, and mix the dough by hand with a fork or a pastry blender. Always remember to use liquids that are ice-cold, unless the recipe specifies otherwise.

Choose the Right Pie Pan:

Choose a glass or dull metal pie plate over shiny metals that tend to keep the crust from browning properly. When using a glass pie plate, reduce the oven temperature by 25°F. It is not necessary to oil a pie pan since the fat in the crust prevents it from sticking to the dish.

Pie Crust Making Tips:

Rolling and Shaping the Pie Crust:

Try using a silicone baking mat, which will show you the measurement of the circle you are rolling. For crusts that require rolling, chill the dough for 30 minutes first. You can roll out the pie dough between two pieces of waxed paper or parchment paper, which saves on cleanup. To keep the waxed paper from slipping, sprinkle a few drops of water on the countertop before arranging the paper.

For Tender Crusts:

Use butter or organic palm or coconut shortening for the most tender crust. Adding baking powder or vinegar can also produce a more tender dough.

For Flakey Crusts:

Substitute ice-cold sour cream or heavy cream for water. Butter and shortening create the flakiest crusts. You can also substitute vodka for half of the liquid called for in a recipe.

Preventing Soggy Crusts:

Try refrigerating the pie crust for 15 minutes before filling it. Prebake the crust for 10 minutes, then remove and seal the bottom by brushing it with a lightly beaten egg white, then refrigerate for 15 minutes. This keeps berries and other fruits from making the pie bottoms mushy. Another trick to prevent soggy pie bottoms is to set the pie pan on a metal cookie sheet while baking. This will also help to catch any bubbling over of the filling. It is also helpful to cool baked pies on a wire cooling rack set on the counter or a pie rack. The rack allows air to circulate under the pie, preventing the steam from making the bottom soggy. None of the above steps are necessary but all are helpful in preventing soggy-bottomed pies.

Top Crusts:

Be sure to make deep slits in top crusts or the filling will turn out soggy. If the top is getting too dark, reduce oven temperature and cover with foil or a pie protector.

Preventing Burnt Crusts:

Keep crusts from getting too dark by using a pie rim (available at cooking supply stores or online) or cover edges with foil. Whole grains tend to brown more quickly than white flour, so it's a good idea to have one.

3 Ways to Make Whole Grain Pie Crusts

If you are accustomed to making pie crusts with white flour, you will notice that working with whole grain flours is different. You will find that whole grains add a distinctive flavor to crusts that you don't encounter with white flour. One thing to note is that whole grains inevitably soak up more moisture than white flour, so try to work with the dough as little as possible with your hands, as this can dry out the dough.

There are three methods here for making pie crust dough: *Easy Press-In, Traditional By Hand,* and *Traditional by Food Processor.*

The recipes that can be used in conjunction with these three styles of pie crust are found in the following section. Breaking the formulas apart allows you to mix and match recipe ingredients with style of crust.

If you prefer to follow a recipe, skip ahead to *Whole Grain Pie Crust Recipes* on page 270.

Easy Press-in Oil Crust — By Hand or Food Processor

(No chilling necessary)

This method is best for easy and quick preparation and works wonderfully with oil crusts. If you choose to use butter, simply melt it. For recipes that call for top and bottom crusts, press the bottom pie shell in the pie pan, and crumble the remaining dough on top.

DIRECTIONS:
1. Preheat oven to 350°F or according to recipe.
2. Combine dry ingredients: flours, baking powder, and salt and mix well.
3. Add oil or melted butter and agave and mix well.
4. Start adding water slowly and mixing until you get a firm dough. Stop when the mixture is cohesive but not crumbly and not sticky.
5. Press the crust into the pie pan with your hands—this is a great project for kids.
6. Prebake the crust for 15 minutes at 350°F or according to recipe.
7. Add filling and follow filling instructions for baking times. You may also choose not to prebake your crust for a more moist crust.

Traditional Pie Crust — Made by Hand

(Chilling necessary)

DIRECTIONS:
1. Measure and combine dry ingredients: flour, salt, and baking soda in a large bowl and stir with a fork. Chill in the freezer for at least 30 minutes.
2. Remove from freezer and mix in butter, organic vegetable shortening, coconut oil, or oil. Coat each piece of fat with flour. Using your fingers, two knives, or a pastry blender, cut the fat into the flour. Work gently and quickly, forcing the flour into the fat and creating a moist and sandy texture.
3. Add agave nectar.
4. Add cold water a tablespoon or 2 at a time, using it to bring together all the crumbs into a dough. Add water gradually as needed. The dough should hold together without being too crumbly and dry or too sticky.
5. Divide the dough in half, and form into a flattened disc, about 4" across and a couple inches thick.
6. Wrap each disc in a piece of PVC-free plastic wrap and seal tightly so it is airtight. Chill in the refrigerator for at least an hour. If you are going to keep them on hand for later use, keep them wrapped in plastic wrap and keep in a freezer bag . They will last in the freezer for about a month. Defrost in the refrigerator when you are ready to use them.
7. Roll a disc between 2 pieces of plastic wrap, waxed paper, or parchment paper to prevent dough from sticking to the rolling pin. You may need to sprinkle some flour on it if the dough is too sticky, but do so sparingly or the dough can become too tough. Working from the inside out, roll the dough into a large circle until it is uniformly 1" thick and the appropriate size. You want it to be slightly larger than your pie dish. Repeat for second disc.
8. Carefully lay the crust into your pie dish and pinch sides. If you still need to make your filling, you can let the crust sit on the counter for a little while until you're ready to bake, but if you are going to take more than 45 minutes, stick it back in the fridge until you are ready to assemble the pie.
9. Depending on the recipe, you will either prebake the crust or go straight to filling and baking the pie. See *Filling and Baking the Pie* on page 267.

Traditional Pie Crust — Made with Food Processor

(Chilling necessary)

If you have a food processor, it will definitely be a quicker route than making the crust by hand. Because pie crusts are temperature sensitive, food processors have an advantage over hand mixing, so use one if you have it. The dough will come together in seconds, while working with the dough by hand can warm it up.

DIRECTIONS:

1. Measure and combine dry ingredients: flour, salt, and baking soda in a bowl and stir with a fork. Chill in the freezer for at least 30 minutes.
2. Remove dry ingredients from the freezer and place in a food processor and add the fat. You can use ½" chunks of cold butter or organic vegetable shortening, coconut oil, etc.
3. Pulse several times to combine or until the mixture starts to look like small beads.
4. Add agave nectar.
5. If you are using vinegar, add it to the cold liquid. Add a few tablespoons of the cold liquid to the dry ingredients and pulse again. Continue adding cold liquid gradually as needed. The dough should hold together without being too crumbly and dry or too sticky.
6. Stop pulsing the food processor and touch the dough. Ideally you want it to be soft but not sticky or crumbly, which is achieved by getting the liquid amount right. If it turns out sticky, then add a little more flour. If the dough comes out very hard, then you probably mixed it too much and may need to start over. If it comes out too crumbly, then add a little more water. Just be careful and move slowly until you have the hang of it.
7. Divide the dough in half and form into a flattened disc, about 4" across and a couple inches thick.
8. Wrap each disc in a piece of PVC-free plastic wrap and seal tightly so it is airtight. Chill in the refrigerator for at least an hour. If you are going to keep them on hand for later use, keep them wrapped in plastic wrap and keep in a freezer bag. They will last for in the freezer for about a month. Defrost in the refrigerator when you are ready to use them.
9. Roll a disc between 2 pieces of plastic wrap, waxed paper, or parchment paper to prevent dough from sticking to the rolling pin. You may need to sprinkle some flour on it if the dough is too sticky, but do so sparingly or the dough can become too tough. Working from the inside out, roll the dough into a large circle until it is uniformly 1 inch thick and the appropriate size. You want it to be slightly larger than your pie dish. Repeat for second disc.
10. Carefully lay the crust into your pie dish and pinch sides. If you still need to make your filling, you can let the crust sit on the counter for a little while until you're ready to bake, but if you are going to take more than 45 minutes, stick it back in the fridge until you are ready to assemble the pie.
11. Depending on the recipe, you will either prebake the crust, or go straight to filling and baking the pie. See *Filling and Baking the Pie* on page 267.

OPTIONAL ADDITIONS FOR PIE CRUSTS:

- **Nuts:** Sprinkle toasted ground nuts such as almond, cashew, or Brazil nuts over the dough and gently press them in before filling and baking. Sesame seeds also add a nice nutty flavor.
- **Spice:** Spice up your crusts with nutmeg, cardamom, ginger, or cinnamon. Try adding ¼ - 1 teaspoon of spice, according to your taste.
- **Chocolate crust:** Add 2 Tablespoons of cocoa powder to your dry ingredients.
- **Egg wash:** Add a glossy shine to the top of your crust. Lightly beat an egg, add a small amount of water, and brush onto the top crust with a pastry brush or a clean paper towel.
- **Sweet sprinkle:** If you want a crunchy sweet finish, try sprinkling low-glycemic date sugar over the top of the pie instead of white sugar and bake.
- **Crumb topping:** To make a crumble topping for 1 pie, mix 2 Tablespoons agave, ½ cup butter, and ½ cup flour. Stir well and crumble over the top of the pie. Bake according to the recipe you're using.
- **Decorate the pie:** If you want to add designs to your pie, you can either use a pie top cutter or you can roll out excess dough and cut out shapes with a cookie cutter and attach to the top of the pie crust with milk. Finish with an egg wash. You can also cut out strips of dough and form a lattice on top of the pie.

Filling and Baking the Pie

Prebake — Then Fill

In some cases you will need to prebake your crust, especially with delicate pie fillings such as custard, egg-based, or no-bake pies. Prebaking helps to prevent a soggy bottom and creates a flakey crust.

DIRECTIONS:
1. Preheat oven to 350°F.
2. Roll out the pie crust. Gently fold the crust in half and then in quarter. Place dough in the pie dish and gently unfold.
3. Prick the bottom of the crust with a fork, which will prevent the dough from puffing up or shrinking.
4. Press the edges of the crust down with a fork or press the dough with your fingers around the top edge. Remove excess dough if needed.
5. Prebake crust for 10-15 minutes. If you notice air bubbles forming on the base of the crust, remove the pie from the oven and place a pie weight chain on top or add a large piece of foil filled with 1 cup of beans. If the recipe calls for a fully baked pie shell then bake it for 20 minutes with weights, then for an additional 5-10 minutes without the weights.
6. Add filling and put the crust back in the oven according to the time specified in recipe. The pie should be removed when the top edges are a golden brown and the bottom is cooked. If you notice that the edges of the crust are getting too brown and the rest of the pie still needs to bake, add a pie crust shield on top or place foil around the edges.
7. Remove the crust from the oven and let cool completely. The baked crust will keep uncovered for a day or two, but use quickly to prevent it from going stale.
8. Fill crust with filling and follow filling instructions.

Fill - No Prebake

DIRECTIONS:
1. Preheat oven to 350°F.
2. Roll out the pie crust. Gently fold the crust in half and then in quarter. Place dough in the pie dish and gently unfold.
3. Prick the bottom of the crust with a fork, which will prevent the dough from puffing up or shrinking.
4. Press the edges of the crust down with a fork or press the dough with your fingers around the top edge. Remove excess dough.
5. Add your pie filling.
6. Add top crust if desired. Carefully lay the top crust over the filling and pinch the edges into the bottom crust. Remove excess dough from the edges. With a sharp knife, carefully cut some slashes into the top of the crust to help steam escape as the pie bakes. You can also use pie top cutters to make designs in the top crust. For a glossy sheen, brush pie crust with egg wash.
7. Bake according to your recipe's instructions.

Pie Crust Base Recipes

If you choose to experiment with making your own pie crust recipe, this section will help give you base recipes to work off of. If you don't want to experiment, simply refer to the section with actual recipes instead.

There are many different types of pie crusts to make. Here you will find base recipes for an oil crust (which requires no rolling pin and can be easily pressed into your pie pan), butter crust (a traditional pie crust that is mixed by hand or a food processor and rolled out with a rolling pin), an organic shortening crust (which is a dairy-free version of the butter crust and is also mixed by hand or with a food processor and rolled with a rolling pin), a butter/shortening combo crust (mixed by hand or food processor and rolled out with a rolling pin), and an egg crust (a more eggy crust that is mixed by hand or food processor and rolled out with a rolling pin).

These pie crust recipes work best with whole wheat pastry flour, kamut, spelt, barley, and oat flours. Other grain flours can supplement the recipe, but it's best if you include one of these flours if you are experimenting with your own grain flour combinations.

If you are experimenting with gluten-free flours, refer to the gluten-free pie crust recipes below; the proportions don't always convert exactly from gluten-containing grains such as spelt and whole wheat to gluten-free grains.

All recipes fit two 8" or 9" pie pans, so you can either top the pie with a top crust or make two pies. You can also divide the recipe in half to make one crust.

Oil Crust

Use Easy Press-In Method

- 2 cups flour
- ¼ teaspoon baking powder
- 1 teaspoon high-quality salt
- ¼ - ½ cup oil (grapeseed, sesame, coconut, olive for savory pie)
- ½ cup ice water **or** milk
- 1 Tablespoon agave nectar

Butter Crust

Use either Traditional by Hand or Traditional with a Food Processor Method

- 2 ¼ cups flour
- 1 teaspoon high-quality salt
- ¼ teaspoon baking powder
- 14 Tablespoons unsalted butter, cold
- 5-7 Tablespoons ice water
- 1 Tablespoon cider vinegar (optional)
- 1 Tablespoon agave nectar

Organic Vegetable Shortening Crust

Use either Traditional by Hand or Traditional with a Food Processor Method

- 3 cups flour
- 1 ¼ teaspoons high-quality salt
- 2 teaspoons baking powder
- 6 Tablespoons ice water **or** milk
- 1 Tablespoon cider vinegar (optional)
- 1 Tablespoon agave nectar
- 1 cup organic vegetable shortening (coconut or palm) **or** coconut oil

Combo Crust: Half Shortening, Half Butter

Use either Traditional by Hand or Traditional with a Food Processor Method

- 3 cups flour
- 1 ¼ teaspoons high-quality salt
- 2 teaspoons baking powder
- 6 Tablespoons ice water **or** milk
- 1 Tablespoon cider vinegar (optional)
- 1 Tablespoon agave nectar
- ½ cup organic vegetable shortening (coconut or palm) **or** coconut oil
- ½ cup butter

Egg Crust

Use either Traditional by Hand or Traditional with a Food Processor Method

- 3 cups flour
- 1 well-beaten egg
- ½ cup ice water
- 1 teaspoon apple cider vinegar (optional)
- ½ cup butter **or** organic vegetable shortening (coconut or palm) **or** coconut oil
- ½ teaspoon high-quality salt

Cheese Crust

To make a cheese crust, substitute 1 cup grated cheese for 2 Tablespoons of fat. Use cheddar, Monterey jack, pepper jack, or mozzarella.

Whole Grain Pie Crust Recipes

The following recipes can be followed exactly or improvised upon. Once you've selected your pie crust of choice, pick the method you will use to make it:

- Easy Press-in
- By Hand
- With a Food Processor

The directions for the pie crust recipes are linked to the corresponding pie crust styles. The purpose is for you to come up with your own custom pie creations. Feel free to experiment with the different styles, types of crusts, and fillings.

Once you have made your crust, you can fill it using one of the recipes in the following section. When you discover a combination you like, make notes in the back of this section, so you'll have it for next time!

All recipes work for two 8" or 9" pie pans. If you have extra dough, roll it into shapes and decorate the top of your pie, or make mini tarts.

Whole Wheat and Barley Oil Crust

INGREDIENTS:

- 1 cup whole wheat pastry flour
- 1 cup barley flour
- ½ cup grapeseed oil
- ½ cup ice water **or** milk
- 1 Tablespoon vinegar
- 1 Tablespoon agave nectar

For preparation directions, see *Easy Press-in Oil Crust* on page 263.

Oat Butter Oil Crust

INGREDIENTS:

- 2 cups oat flour
- ¼ teaspoon baking powder
- 1 teaspoon high-quality salt
- ½ cup melted butter
- ½ cup ice water **or** milk
- 1 Tablespoon agave nectar

For preparation directions, see *Easy Press-in Oil Crust* on page 263.

Oat Brown Rice Butter Oil Crust

INGREDIENTS:

- 2 cups oat flour
- ½ cup brown rice flour
- 1 ¼ cups tapioca flour
- ½ teaspoon high-quality salt
- 1 cup butter, melted
- 2 Tablespoons agave nectar

For preparation directions, see *Easy Press-in Oil Crust* on page 263.

Kamut Oil Crust

INGREDIENTS:

- 1 cup kamut flour **or** whole wheat **or** spelt flour
- 1 cup millet flour
- ⅔ cup cornmeal
- ½ teaspoon baking powder
- 1 teaspoon high-quality salt
- ½ cup grapeseed oil
- ½ cup ice water
- 1 Tablespoon agave nectar

For preparation directions, see *Easy Press-in Oil Crust* on page 263.

Millet Corn Kamut Oil Crust

INGREDIENTS:

- ¾ cup millet flour
- ¾ cup kamut flour **or** whole wheat **or** spelt flour
- ⅓ cup cornmeal
- ¼ teaspoon baking powder
- ¼ teaspoon high-quality salt
- 3 Tablespoons grapeseed oil
- ½ -⅔ cup water

For preparation directions, see *Easy Press-in Oil Crust* on page 263.

Kamut Oat Butter Crust

INGREDIENTS:

- 1 ½ cups kamut flour
- 1 cup oat flour
- 1 ½ Tablespoons agave nectar
- 1 teaspoon high-quality salt
- ⅔ cup unsalted butter, cold
- 4 - 6 Tablespoons ice water

For preparation directions, see *Traditional Pie Crust* (by hand or food processor) on pages 264 and 265.

Whole Wheat Buttermilk Shortening Crust

INGREDIENTS:

- 2 cups whole wheat flour
- 2 Tablespoons buttermilk powder
- ½ teaspoon baking powder
- 1 teaspoon high-quality salt
- 2 Tablespoons agave nectar
- ½ cup organic vegetable shortening (coconut or palm)
- 2 Tablespoons orange juice
- ½ cup ice water

For preparation directions, see *Traditional Pie Crust* (by hand or food processor) on pages 264 and 265.

Barley Combo Crust

INGREDIENTS:

- 3 cups barley flour
- 1 ¼ teaspoons high-quality salt
- 2 teaspoons baking powder
- 6 Tablespoons ice water **or** milk
- 1 Tablespoon cider vinegar (optional)
- 1 Tablespoon agave nectar
- ½ cup organic vegetable shortening (coconut or palm) **or** coconut oil
- ½ cup butter

For preparation directions, see *Traditional Pie Crust* (by hand or food processor) on pages 264 and 265.

Gluten-Free Pie Crust Recipes

Working with gluten-free flours is a little different, so refer to the recipes below for some variations. All recipes make two 8" or 9" pie crusts, or one pie with one top crust.

Time Saving Tip:
Double or triple the recipe and freeze balls of dough that you can you pull out at a future date for an impromptu pie!

Tapioca Rice Crust

INGREDIENTS:

- 1 cup white rice flour
- ¾ cup tapioca flour
- ¾ cup cornstarch **or** arrowroot flour
- 1 teaspoon xanthan gum **or** guar gum **or** a 50:50 combination of both
- 1 teaspoon high-quality salt
- ¾ cup butter **or** organic vegetable shortening (coconut or palm) **or** coconut oil, plus extra for greasing pan
- 2 Tablespoons agave nectar
- 1 egg
- 1 Tablespoon vinegar
- 2-3 Tablespoons ice water

DIRECTIONS:

1. Preheat oven to 450°F if you are prebaking the crust. If you are not prebaking set oven temperature to what the pie recipe calls for.
2. In a medium bowl, combine white rice flour, tapioca flour, cornstarch or arrowroot, gum, and salt.
3. Cut in butter, shortening, or oil with a pastry blender or a mixer until crumbs the size of peas form.
4. In a separate bowl, mix together the agave, egg, and vinegar and beat lightly. Add to the crumb mixture.
5. Next, sprinkle in about 2-3 Tablespoons of ice water, 1 Tablespoon at a time. Use more or less water as needed. Dough should hold together when gathered into a ball in your hands and shouldn't be too wet or crumbly.
6. Divide the dough into two halves and place in 2 covered containers. Refrigerate for 30 minutes.
7. Roll each ball out between two pieces of waxed paper dusted with gluten-free flour. Roll to desired thickness and shape to fit the pie pan.
8. Oil your pie pan with oil or butter.
9. Next, peel off the top sheet of waxed paper and lay your oiled pie pan on the rolled dough. Place it upside down and centered, then put your hand underneath the dough and flip it over so the dough is centered in the pie pan.
10. Peel off the bottom waxed paper and press the dough into the pie pan. Shape the edge.
11. Prebake for 10-12 minutes.
12. Add filling and follow baking instructions for filling. Top pie with second crust if desired.

Millet Sorghum Corn Crust

INGREDIENTS:

- 1 ½ cups millet flour
- 1 ½ cups sorghum flour
- ⅔ cup cornmeal
- ¼ teaspoon baking powder
- ¼ teaspoon high-quality salt
- 3 Tablespoons neutral-tasting oil (grapeseed, untoasted sesame oil, coconut oil, **or** ghee), plus extra for greasing pan
- 1 Tablespoon agave nectar
- ½ cup ice water **or** milk of choice

DIRECTIONS:

1. Preheat oven to 350°F.
2. In a mixer or large bowl, combine dry ingredients: millet flour, sorghum flour, cornmeal, baking powder, and salt.
3. Add oil and agave and mix well.
4. Start adding 1 Tablespoon of ice water slowly and mixing until you have a firm dough.
5. Oil a pie pan and press the crust into it or chill the dough in the refrigerator for 30 minutes, then roll it out with a rolling pin between 2 sheets of waxed paper and place in pie pan.
6. Prebake the crust for 15 minutes.
7. Cool crust and pour in filling and follow filling instructions for pie baking times. For a moister crust, don't prebake.

Sweet Amaranth Crust

INGREDIENTS:

- 1 cup amaranth flour
- 1 cup tapioca flour
- ½ cup millet flour
- ½ cup cornstarch **or** arrowroot flour
- 1 ½ cups date sugar
- 1 ½ cups butter **or** organic vegetable shortening (coconut or palm) **or** coconut oil
- ½ cup agave nectar

DIRECTIONS:

1. Preheat oven to 400°F.
2. In a mixer or large bowl, combine dry ingredients: amaranth flour, tapioca flour, millet flour, arrowroot or cornstarch, and date sugar.
3. Add butter in pieces to the mixer, or work in with a pastry blender. Do this until small crumbs form. Add agave.
4. Split dough in half.
5. Press half of the crumbles into the pie dish.
6. Use the second half to crumble on top of your filling or roll dough using a rolling pin dusted with gluten-free flour, and lay carefully on top of filling-stuffed pie, then press sides closed. Or, you can cut the rolled dough into strips and criss-cross on top, especially if it's hard to handle.
7. Alternately, you can use the second half of dough for another pie instead of as a top.
8. If you want to preheat your crust, do so for 5 minutes at 400°F.

Coconut Crust

INGREDIENTS:
- 1 cup coconut milk
- ¼ cup flax meal, ground
- 1 cup coconut flour
- 1 cup almond flour **or** meal
- 1 teaspoon high-quality salt
- ½ cup coconut oil **or** organic vegetable shortening (coconut or palm)
- ¼ cup agave nectar

DIRECTIONS:
1. Mix coconut milk and flax meal in a small bowl. Set aside.
2. In a large mixing bowl, combine coconut flour, almond flour, and salt.
3. Using a mixer or hand mixer, cut in coconut oil and agave until a crumbly mixture forms.
4. Slowly add the coconut milk mixture until a firm dough forms, not too sticky, not too crumbly. Turn the dough out onto lightly floured board. Dust with coconut flour.
5. Put dough between two sheets of waxed paper and roll to a size that is slightly larger than that of your pie dish.
6. Very carefully, move the dough to your pie dish. This dough is fragile but will mend easily.
7. Fill pie and bake according to pie recipe instructions.

Pocket Pies and Toaster Pastries

You can pick your favorite crust, your favorite filling, and make a little pocket pie instead of a regular pie. Kids love them.

ADDITIONAL TOOLS NEEDED:
- *Rolling pin*
- *2" cookie cutter*
- *Pastry brush*

INGREDIENTS:
- 1 ½ cups kamut flour
- ½ cup tapioca flour
- 2 teaspoons baking powder
- ¾ teaspoon high-quality salt
- 6 Tablespoons organic vegetable shortening (coconut or palm)
- ¾ cup milk (cow, goat, almond, rice, coconut, oat, etc.)
- 2 Tablespoons agave nectar
- 1 egg mixed with 1-2 teaspoons water (egg wash)
- Neutral-tasting oil (grapeseed, untoasted sesame oil, coconut oil, **or** ghee)
- Pie filling **or** pudding of your choice

DIRECTIONS FOR POCKET PIES:
1. In a large bowl, combine kamut flour, tapioca flour, baking powder, and salt.
2. Add shortening and knead it into the flour with your hands until crumbly.
3. Add milk and agave and mix in with a spatula until dough begins to come together.
4. Knead dough on a surface lightly floured with kamut flour, about 10-20 times.
5. Dust a rolling pin well with flour and roll the dough to ⅓" -½" thick, then cut into rounds using a 2 ¼" cookie cutter.
6. Roll each little round as thinly as possible, about 5-6" in diameter. Spoon 1-2 Tablespoons of your filling onto the dough, brush the edges of the bottom half of the dough lightly with the egg wash, fold over and seal the edges together with the back of a fork, dipping it into flour as needed. Gently press down to flatten and evenly distribute the filling inside the pocket pie.

To pan-fry pies:

1. Place a medium sauté pan or cast iron skillet over medium low heat.
2. Add 1-2 Tablespoons oil.
3. Once heated, place 2-3 pies at a time into pan and sauté until golden brown on both sides, about 3-4 minutes per side. Allow to cool 4-5 minutes before serving.

To bake pies:

1. Preheat the oven to 350°F.
2. Place finished pies onto an ungreased cookie sheet and bake for 25-30 minutes or until golden brown.

Makes about 20 pocket pies

DIRECTIONS FOR TOASTER PASTRIES:

1. Preheat oven to 350°F.
2. Divide the dough in half.
3. On a lightly floured surface, roll out dough to less than ⅛" thick.
4. Cut into 4" x 5" rectangles with a sharp knife.
5. Place 3-5 Tablespoons of filling onto center of one 4" x 5" piece of dough. Brush around the edges with egg wash and top with second piece of dough. Seal edges by pressing together with tines of fork.
6. Gently press down to flatten and evenly distribute the filling and dock the top of the pie by poking holes in it with a fork.
7. Repeat with second half of the dough.
8. Bake on an ungreased cookie sheet for 20 minutes.
9. Remove from the oven, cool completely, and place into re-sealable bags or in rectangular glass storage containers until ready to toast. The pies will not be brown until toasted.

Makes about 10 pastries

Pie Fillings

Fresh Fruit Pie Base Recipe

This is a simple, tasty, and healthful pie that is guaranteed to impress.

INGREDIENTS:
- 1 cup apple juice, apple cider, juice, **or** water
- 2 Tablespoons agar-agar flakes
- ½ cup agave nectar
- 3 ½ cups fresh fruit, such as peaches, apples, cherries, apricots, blueberries, strawberries, **or** pears
- ½ teaspoon tapioca flour **or** arrowroot flour
- 1 teaspoon pure vanilla extract
- ½ teaspoon high-quality salt
- 1 Tablespoon lemon juice

- 2 pie crusts

DIRECTIONS:
1. Preheat oven to 350°F. Prepare your pie crust and add to pie pan. Seal with an egg wash if you want a crisp bottom. Prebake the crust for 15 minutes. Remove from oven and set aside.
2. In a saucepan, gently heat apple juice and agar-agar. Let simmer as you go to the next step.
3. Drizzle ¼ cup of agave as a layer on the bottom of the prebaked crust.
4. Slice fresh fruit and assemble into the pie crust. Drizzle with the remainder of the agave.
5. After 5 minutes of cooking the apple juice mixture, add tapioca or arrowroot flour and stir until thickened. Add vanilla, salt, and lemon juice.
6. Pour mixture over fruit.
7. Add top crust to the pie, if desired. Pinch crust around the edges and create slits from the center down.
8. Put the pie back in the oven and bake for another 25 minutes.
9. Remove from oven and cool on a cooling rack.

Makes filling for one 8" or 9" pie

Apple Pie

INGREDIENTS:
- 5-6 organic apples
- 1 ½ Tablespoons cornstarch **or** 1 Tablespoon arrowroot flour **or** tapioca flour
- ¼ teaspoon high-quality salt
- ¼ teaspoon cinnamon
- ¼ teaspoon nutmeg
- 2 Tablespoons lemon juice
- ½ cup agave nectar
- 2 Tablespoons butter

- 2 pie crusts, unbaked

DIRECTIONS:
1. Preheat oven to 350°F.
2. Peel, core, and thinly slice apples. Place in a medium-sized bowl and set aside.
3. Combine cornstarch, salt, cinnamon, and nutmeg. Sprinkle over apples and toss evenly.
4. Sprinkle in lemon juice and agave and toss once more.
5. Add to unbaked pie shell. Dot with butter. Place second crust on top and seal around the edges.
6. Bake for 40 minutes.

OPTIONAL VARIATION:
You can also add lemon zest with the juice.

Makes filling for one 8" or 9" pie

Strawberry Pie

INGREDIENTS:

- 6 Tablespoons cornstarch **or** 4 Tablespoons arrowroot flour **or** tapioca flour
- ½ cup water
- 1 cup fresh strawberries, cut in slices or chunks
- Zest from ½ lemon
- ¾ cup agave nectar

- 2 pie crusts, unbaked

DIRECTIONS:

1. Preheat oven to 350°F.
2. Mix cornstarch in a medium saucepan. Add water gradually and stir.
3. Bring to a boil. Add strawberries and grated lemon zest and cook 3 minutes, until clear and thickened. Stir constantly and gently.
4. Add agave and stir for 1 minute.
5. Remove saucepan from heat and add contents to 2 unbaked pie crusts.
6. Bake for 45 minutes - 1 hour. For a crisper crust, prebake the crust for 10-15 minutes, add filling, then bake for 45 minutes.
7. Remove from oven and let cool on a cooling rack. Let cool completely to set, about 2-3 hours.

Makes filling for one 8" or 9" pie

Blueberry Pie

INGREDIENTS:

- 6 Tablespoons cornstarch **or** 4 Tablespoons of arrowroot flour **or** tapioca flour
- 6 cups fresh or frozen blueberries
- 2 cups agave nectar
- Zest from 1 lemon
- 1 cup water
- 2 Tablespoons lemon juice

- 2 unbaked pie crusts

DIRECTIONS:

1. Preheat oven to 350°F.
2. Mix cornstarch in a medium saucepan. Add water gradually and stir.
3. Bring to a boil. Add blueberries and grated lemon zest and cook 3 minutes, until clear and thickened. Stir constantly but carefully to prevent berries from crushing.
4. Remove saucepan from heat and add lemon juice.
5. Add contents to 2 unbaked pie crusts.
6. Bake at 350°F for 45 minutes – 1 hour. For a crisper crust, prebake the crust for 10-15 minutes, add filling, then bake for 45 minutes.
7. Remove from oven and let cool on a cooling rack. Let cool completely to set, about 2-3 hours.

Makes filling for one 8" or 9" pie

Cherry Pie

INGREDIENTS:

- 6 cups pitted cherries
- 2 cups cherry juice (**or** blend ¼ cup cherries in 1 cup water in the blender for 1 minute)
- ½ cup agave nectar
- 4 Tablespoons agar-agar flakes
- 2 Tablespoons butter
- 2 Tablespoons kudzu dissolved in ⅛ cup cold water **or** 2 teaspoons arrowroot flour **or** tapioca flour
- ½ teaspoon pure almond extract

- 2 prebaked pie crusts

DIRECTIONS:

1. Preheat oven to 350°F.
2. Cook down cherries in cherry juice, about 5-10 minutes. Add agave and stir until dissolved. Add agar-agar and stir well.
3. Mix in butter.
4. Stir kudzu into a ⅛ cup of water. When totally dissolved, add to cherry mixture and stir well. If you are using tapioca or arrowroot, simply add it to the mixture and stir. Add almond extract. Make sure all ingredients are dissolved and the mixture is thickened.
5. Prebake the crust for 10-15 minutes, add filling, then bake for 30-45 minutes.
6. Remove from oven and let cool on a cooling rack. Let cool completely to set, about 2-3 hours.

Makes filling for one 8" or 9" pie

Banana Cream Pie

INGREDIENTS:
• 1 cup milk (cow, goat, almond, rice, coconut, oat, etc.)
• 1 banana
• 1 Tablespoon arrowroot flour
• ⅓ cup tapioca flour
• ¼ teaspoon high-quality salt
• ½ cup agave nectar
• 3 egg yolks, beaten
• 2 Tablespoons butter
• 1 cup coconut cream (place two 14-ounce cans in the refrigerator and remove cream)
• 1 ¼ teaspoons pure vanilla extract
• 4 bananas, sliced

• 1 pie crust

DIRECTIONS:
1. Preheat oven to 350°F. Prebake pie crust for 10-15 minutes. Remove from oven and let cool on a cooling rack.
2. Add milk to a blender and blend with 1 banana and arrowroot flour. Set aside.
3. In a saucepan, combine the tapioca flour and salt. Add banana milk gradually while stirring gently. Add agave. Cook over medium heat, stirring constantly, until the mixture is bubbly. Keep stirring and cook for about 2 more minutes, then remove from heat.
4. Beat 3 egg yolks. Stir a small quantity of the hot mixture into the beaten egg yolks to warm them, then immediately add egg yolk mixture to the rest of the hot mixture. Cook for 2 more minutes, stirring constantly.
5. Remove the mixture from the stove, and add butter, coconut cream, and vanilla. Stir until the mixture has a smooth consistency.
6. Slice bananas and arrange into your prebaked and cooled pie crust. Top with pudding mixture.
7. Bake at 350°F for 12-15 minutes. Chill for an hour before serving.

Makes filling for one 8" or 9" pie

Coconut Cream Pie

INGREDIENTS:
- 1 cup milk (cow, goat, almond, rice, coconut, oat, etc.)
- 1 cup coconut milk (unsweetened)
- 2 Tablespoons unsalted butter
- 1 Tablespoon virgin coconut oil
- ⅓ cup tapioca flour
- 1 Tablespoon arrowroot flour
- 3 egg yolks, beaten
- ½ teaspoon high-quality salt
- ⅓ cup agave nectar
- 1 cup coconut cream (place two 14-ounce cans in the refrigerator and remove cream)
- 1 cup unsweetened coconut flakes
- 1 teaspoon pure vanilla extract
- 2 Tablespoons lime juice
- ⅓ cup unsweetened shredded coconut (for topping)

- 1 prebaked and cooled *Coconut Crust* (see page 275).

DIRECTIONS:
1. In a small saucepan, heat the milk and coconut milk gently. Simmer on low heat for five minutes. Remove from heat, set aside, and let cool.
2. In a medium saucepan on low heat, gently melt butter and coconut oil. Sprinkle in the tapioca flour and arrowroot flour. Stir until it thickens into a light paste and cook on low heat until a light golden color is achieved, roughly 5 minutes.
3. Add the milk infusion to the medium saucepan a little bit at a time.
4. Beat 3 egg yolks. Stir a small quantity of the hot mixture into the beaten egg yolks to warm them, then immediately add the egg yolk mixture to the rest of the hot mixture. Cook for 2 more minutes, stirring constantly.
5. Add the salt and agave and stir. When thoroughly mixed, raise heat to medium-low. Stir continuously and cook until first signs of thickening begin and then remove from heat.
6. Add coconut cream, coconut flakes, vanilla, and lime juice. Mix until smooth. Cool for about 5 minutes, then pour into the prebaked and cooled coconut pie crust.
7. Cover with waxed paper and place in the refrigerator for 2-3 hours to allow to set.
8. In a dry skillet, toast the shredded coconut for 3 minutes, stirring occasionally. Set aside.
9. Top pie with toasted coconut shreds.

OPTIONAL VARIATION:
For a creamier and dairy-free pie, use an additional 1 cup of coconut cream in place of milk.

Makes filling for one 8" or 9" pie

Lemon Meringue Pie

INGREDIENTS:

Lemon Custard:

- 3 large eggs, separated into yolks and whites
- 5 Tablespoons cornstarch **or** 3 Tablespoons arrowroot flour **or** tapioca flour
- 1 cup agave nectar
- 1 cup water
- ½ cup lemon juice
- 1-2 Tablespoons lemon zest
- 3 Tablespoons butter

- 1 prebaked and cooled crust of your choice

Meringue:

- 3 egg whites (from separated eggs above)
- ½ teaspoon pure vanilla extract
- ⅓ cup agave nectar

DIRECTIONS:

For the Lemon Custard:

1. Preheat oven to 350°F.
2. Separate eggs into yolks and whites, beat yolks, and set aside. Whisk cornstarch, agave, and water in a medium saucepan. Finely grate the lemon zest. Add lemon juice, zest, and beaten egg yolks and cook over medium heat, stirring constantly, until the mixture begins to bubble and thicken, about 10 minutes.
3. Remove from heat, whisk in butter, and add to prepared crust.

For the Meringue:

1. In a large bowl, beat egg whites and vanilla with a mixer or hand mixer until foamy.
2. Gradually drizzle in agave, continuing to beat until stiff peaks form.
3. Dollop meringue over the filling, spreading it to the crust's edge to prevent shrinking.
4. Bake until meringue is golden brown, about 10-15 minutes. Cool on wire rack.

Makes filling for one 8" or 9" pie

Orange Meringue Pie

This recipe makes two pies. Cut the recipe in half for one pie.

INGREDIENTS:

Orange Custard:

- 10 egg yolks (reserve 6 whites for meringue)
- 1 cup agave nectar
- ¼ cup white rice flour
- ¼ cup tapioca flour
- ¾ cup butter, melted (1 ½ sticks)
- ¼ cup orange zest
- 4 cups orange juice — fresh squeezed or store bought, no sugar added

Meringue:

- 6 egg whites (from separated eggs above)
- 1 teaspoon pure vanilla extract
- ⅔ cup agave nectar

- 2 pie crusts

DIRECTIONS:

For the Orange Custard:

1. Preheat oven to 450°F.
2. Separate eggs, placing 10 yolks in one bowl and 6 whites in another bowl. In a medium bowl, beat together egg yolks and agave until the mixture is thick.
3. Add in white rice flour, tapioca flour, melted butter, orange zest, and orange juice. Mix until smooth.
4. Prebake pie crusts for 10 minutes. Remove from oven, add custard, and continue to bake for 10 minutes.
5. Reduce the oven temp to 350°F and bake for 25 additional minutes. Meanwhile, make the meringue.

For the Meringue:

1. In a large bowl, beat the reserved 6 egg whites and vanilla until foamy.
2. Gradually drizzle in agave, continuing to beat until stiff peaks form.
3. Dollop meringue over the filling, spreading it to the crust's edge to prevent shrinking.
4. Bake until meringue is golden brown, about 10-15 minutes. Cool on wire rack.

Makes filling for two 8" or 9" pies

Mango Key Lime Pie

This easy pie filling requires no baking.

INGREDIENTS:
- 1 ½ cups cold milk (cow, goat, almond, rice, coconut, oat, etc.)
- 2 Tablespoons agar-agar flakes
- 2 Tablespoons arrowroot flour
- ⅛ teaspoon high-quality salt
- 1 ripe medium mango, enough to make 1 cup of mango purée
- Water
- ⅓ cup freshly squeezed lime juice (5-7 key limes or 2-3 regular limes)
- ½ cup agave nectar

- 1 prebaked and cooled crust of your choice

DIRECTIONS:
1. Prebake a pie crust of your choice and allow to cool.
2. Place cold milk, agar-agar, arrowroot, and salt in a medium saucepan. Stir to submerge the agar-agar. Then bring the mixture up to a boil over medium heat. Stir constantly to prevent scorching. After 3 minutes, turn heat to low and simmer until the agar-agar dissolves, about 2 more minutes. Set aside.
3. In a blender, blend the mango until smooth. Add a little bit of water, but only the amount necessary to form a purée.
4. Add lime juice, agave, and milk mixture to the blender and blend for 10 seconds.
5. Transfer filling to prepared pie shell. Refrigerate until set, 45-60 minutes. It will also gel at room temperature in about 1 ½ hours.

Makes filling for one 8" or 9" pie

Pecan Pie

ADDITIONAL TOOLS NEEDED:

Pie crust shield

INGREDIENTS:
- 1 ½ cups pecans, broken
- 2 cups dark agave nectar
- 3 large eggs
- ⅓ cup butter, cut into chunks
- 1 teaspoon pure vanilla extract
- ¼ teaspoon high-quality salt

- 1 pie crust, unbaked

DIRECTIONS:
1. Preheat oven to 350°F.
2. In a dry skillet, roast the pecans over medium heat for 5 minutes. Set aside.
3. Cook dark agave in pan and gently boil for 10 minutes. Remove from heat.
4. Beat eggs lightly and pour into syrup mixture gradually and beat constantly to prevent eggs from becoming scrambled eggs in the syrup!
5. Cut the butter into small chunks and add to the mixture while beating the eggs. Stir in vanilla and salt. Mix until butter is melted.
6. Add roasted pecans to the uncooked pie crust. Pour liquid mixture over top.
7. Carefully place pie in the oven and bake for about 30 minutes. Remove pie from oven, place a pie-crust shield on it, and return to the oven for another 30 minutes (a total of 1 hour).
8. Pie is done when a knife inserted in the center comes out clean. If not done, bake for another 10 minutes.
9. Cool pie on a wire rack.

Makes filling for one 8" or 9" pie

Pumpkin Pie

INGREDIENTS:
- 1 small pumpkin for baking (**or** one 16-ounce can pumpkin purée)
- 2 eggs
- ⅔ cup agave nectar
- 2 Tablespoons arrowroot flour **or** tapioca flour
- 1 ½ teaspoons cinnamon
- ½ teaspoon ginger
- ½ teaspoon freshly grated nutmeg
- ¼ teaspoon allspice
- ¼ teaspoon cloves
- ½ teaspoon high-quality salt
- 1 cup coconut milk

- 1 pie crust, unbaked

DIRECTIONS:
1. Preheat oven to 350°F.
2. Cut pumpkin into quarters, remove the seeds, and place on a cookie sheet with ⅛ cup of water on the bottom. Bake for about 45 minutes or until pumpkin is soft. Remove from oven and let cool. Scoop out the flesh and measure 2 cups for the pie. Leave the oven on.
3. Place pumpkin in a food processor or blender and add all remaining ingredients: eggs, agave, arrowroot, cinnamon, ginger, nutmeg, allspice, cloves, salt, and coconut milk. Purée until smooth.
4. Pour mixture into the unbaked pie crust.
5. Bake for 40 minutes. A knife inserted in the center should come out nearly clean.
6. Cool pie on a wire rack.
7. Serve topped with whipped cream and a sprinkle of nutmeg.

Makes filling for one 8" or 9" pie

Sweet Potato Pie

INGREDIENTS:
- 2 large or 3 small yams **or** sweet potatoes
- ½ cup butter (1 stick)
- 1 cup agave nectar
- 1 Tablespoon arrowroot flour
- ½ Tablespoon baking powder
- 2 eggs
- ½ Tablespoon freshly grated nutmeg
- ½ teaspoon high-quality salt
- 1 Tablespoon pure lemon extract
- 1 cup coconut milk

- 1 pie crust, unbaked

DIRECTIONS:
1. Preheat oven to 350°F.
2. Wash, peel, and cut the sweet potatoes into large chunks. Place in a saucepan, cover with water, and boil for 40 minutes or until soft.
3. Place cooked sweet potatoes in a food processor or blender and add butter. Pulse.
4. Add agave, arrowroot, baking powder, eggs, nutmeg, salt, lemon extract, and coconut milk. Purée until smooth.
5. Pour the mixture into an uncooked pie crust.
6. Bake for 35-40 minutes. A knife inserted in the center should come out nearly clean.
7. Cool pie on a wire rack.
8. Serve topped with whipped cream and a sprinkle of nutmeg.

Makes filling for one 8" or 9" pie

Empanadas

INGREDIENTS:

Crust:

- 1 Tablespoon melted butter
- 4 cups flour (see combinations in box below)
- 1 teaspoon high-quality salt
- ¾ cup organic vegetable shortening (coconut or palm)
- 2 egg yolks, slightly beaten
- ¼ cup agave nectar
- Flour for dusting
- ¼ cup sesame oil, grapeseed oil, **or** coconut oil for pan-frying

Meat Filling:

- 1 Tablespoon sesame, olive, ghee, coconut, **or** grapeseed oil
- 2 cloves garlic, minced
- 1 large onion, chopped
- 1 tomato, chopped
- 1 cup ground pork
- 2 cups ground chicken **or** turkey
- Salt and pepper to taste
- 1 teaspoon cumin powder (optional)
- ½ teaspoon chili powder (optional)

DIRECTIONS:

Crust:

1. Begin melting butter over low heat. When melted, set aside in a bowl.
2. Add flour and salt to a food processor and pulse three times.
3. Add shortening and pulse for 10 seconds, or until crumbles form. Keeping the food processor on, add egg yolks and agave. Mix until a ball forms.
4. Turn the dough out onto a lightly floured board and flour hands and rolling pin. Sprinkle with more flour to prevent sticking, stretching dough out gradually while rolling. Roll until the dough is ½" thick uniformly.
5. Dip a pastry brush in the melted butter and brush over the top surface of the dough. Roll the dough up tight like a jellyroll. Cut into 1" thick pieces. Flatten each piece and roll into little rounds.
6. Place a Tablespoon or more of meat filling in each circle, dip your pastry brush in water and brush along bottom edge. Fold and press edges together with an empanada tool or fork.
7. Heat oil in a deep pan. Pan fry empanadas until golden brown.

Meat Filling:

1. Heat oil in a skillet and add garlic and onion. Sauté until lightly brown.
2. Add tomato and ground meat. If adding spices, do so here. Season with salt and pepper to taste. Set aside.

Makes about a dozen empanadas

Great flour combinations:

- 2 parts spelt flour and 2 parts oat flour
- 2 parts kamut flour, 1 part oat flour, and 1 part brown rice flour
- 2 parts sorghum flour, 1 part brown rice flour, 1 part corn flour, and 1 teaspoon guar gum
- 2 parts sorghum flour, 1 part corn flour, and 1 part tapioca flour

Raw Pie Crusts

Even if you aren't a raw foodie, you might still love making raw pies. They are flourless and alive and have a refreshing and nutty quality to them. They do require special gear, such as a food processor and, at times, a food dehydrator.

All recipes make one pie crust.

Simple Raw Macadamia Crust

ADDITIONAL TOOLS NEEDED:
Food processor

INGREDIENTS:
- Coconut oil to grease pan
- 3 cups macadamia nuts
- ¼ teaspoon high-quality salt
- ½ teaspoon pure vanilla extract

DIRECTIONS:
1. Oil a standard pie dish with and set aside.
2. In a clean, dry food processor, add the nuts and salt. Blend until a dough develops, about 10-15 seconds.
3. Add vanilla, and blend 5 more seconds.
4. Spoon mixture into pie dish and press evenly to make a uniform crust.
5. Fill pie crust as desired.

Simple Brazil Nut Crust

ADDITIONAL TOOLS NEEDED:
Food processor

INGREDIENTS:
- Coconut oil to grease pie pan
- ½ cup Brazil nuts
- ¼ teaspoon high-quality salt
- 1 Tablespoon agave nectar
- ½ cup dates

DIRECTIONS:
1. Oil a standard pie dish with and set aside.
2. In a clean, dry food processor, add the nuts, dates, and salt. Blend until a dough develops, about 10-15 seconds.
3. Add agave and blend 5 more seconds.
4. Spoon mixture into pie dish and press evenly to make a uniform crust.
5. Fill pie crust as desired.

Raw Pecan Pie Crust

ADDITIONAL TOOLS NEEDED:
- *Food processor*
- *Food dehydrator*

INGREDIENTS:
- Coconut oil to grease pan
- 2 ½ cups pecans, soaked for 3 hours and drained
- 1 Tablespoon coconut butter
- 3 Tablespoons agave nectar
- 1 teaspoon pure vanilla extract
- ¼ teaspoon high-quality salt

DIRECTIONS:
1. Oil a 9 ½" tart pan (with removable bottom) with coconut oil. Set aside.
2. Blend pecans, coconut butter, agave, vanilla extract, and salt in food processor until you get a bread-crumb consistency.
3. Spoon pie crust mixture into the tart pan and press it evenly to form a uniform crust.
4. Dehydrate at 110°F for 24 hours, or you can use an oven on the lowest setting with the door slightly ajar for 12-18 hours.
5. Fill pie crust as desired.

Raw Pistachio Crust

ADDITIONAL TOOLS NEEDED:
- *Food processor*
- *Food dehydrator*

INGREDIENTS:
- Coconut oil to grease pan
- 1 ½ cups pistachios
- 2 ½ Tablespoons agave nectar
- 1 Tablespoon water
- ½ teaspoon high-quality salt
- 1 teaspoon pure vanilla extract

DIRECTIONS:
1. Oil a 9 ½" tart pan (with removable bottom) with coconut oil. Set aside.
2. Blend pistachios, agave, water, salt, and vanilla in a food processor until you get a bread-crumb consistency.
3. Spoon pie crust mixture into the tart pan and press evenly to form a uniform crust.
4. Dehydrate at 110°F for 24 hours, or use an oven on the lowest setting with the door slightly ajar for 12-18 hours.
5. Fill pie crust as desired.

Raw Date Nut Pie Crust

ADDITIONAL TOOLS NEEDED:
Food processor

INGREDIENTS:
- Coconut oil to grease pie pan
- 1 cup almonds
- 2 cups macadamia nuts
- 1 cup pitted dates
- 1 Tablespoon orange juice
- ¼ teaspoon high-quality salt
- ½ teaspoon pure vanilla extract

DIRECTIONS:
1. Oil a standard pie dish with and set aside.
2. Grind the almonds in a dry food processor until you get a flour consistency. Do not overgrind. Remove from food processor and set aside. To avoid this step, use premade almond flour.
3. Add macadamia nuts to the food processor. Grind until you start to get an oily-nut-butter kind of consistency.
4. Add dates and let them run in the food processor until the mixture begins to ball up as the oils start to pull from the nuts.
5. While the processor is still running, add orange juice, salt, and vanilla. The clumps of mixture will suddenly ball up in one solid mass. Stop the food processor.
6. On a piece of waxed paper, sprinkle some of the almond mixture, then plop your wet mixture in the center and press down. Add more almond flour on top. Put another sheet of waxed paper on top and roll the dough to the desired shape. It should be a little bigger than the diameter of your pie pan. Remove top waxed paper.
7. Sprinkle more almond powder in pie tin, then gently flip the pie crust into the pan. Remove waxed paper, and gently press into the pie dish. You can also dust the top of the pie with the remaining almond flour.
8. Fill pie crust as desired.
9. If you have extra dough, roll it into little balls and keep in the fridge as a great raw treat.

Raw Walnut Crust

INGREDIENTS:

- Coconut oil to grease pie pan
- 2 cups walnuts, soaked overnight
- 1 ripe banana
- 1 cup raisins
- 1 Tablespoon orange juice
- ½ teaspoon ground cinnamon (optional)

DIRECTIONS:

1. Oil a standard pie dish with and set aside.
2. In a food processor, blend walnuts, banana, raisins, orange juice, and cinnamon until ingredients form into a big ball, then stop.
3. Spoon mixture into the pie pan and press evenly to form a uniform crust.
4. Fill pie crust as desired.

Raw Pecan Almond Date Crust

INGREDIENTS:

- Coconut oil to grease pie pan
- 1 cup pecans, soaked overnight
- ½ cup almonds, soaked overnight
- ½ cup dates, pitted
- ½ teaspoon spices (cinnamon, ginger, cardamom, allspice, etc.)
- ½ teaspoon tamari

DIRECTIONS:

1. Oil a standard pie dish with and set aside.
2. Drain and rinse pecans and almonds and add to a food processor. Add remaining ingredients (dates, spices, and tamari) and blend, leaving some crunchy consistency to crust.
3. Spoon mixture into the pie pan and press evenly to form a uniform crust.
4. Fill pie crust as desired.

Raw Pie Fillings

All recipes make one filling for an 8" or 9" pie.

Raw Coconut Lime Pie Filling

INGREDIENTS:

- 3 cups coconut meat (from approximately 5 young coconuts)
- ⅓ cup lime juice
- 3 Tablespoons agave nectar
- 1 teaspoon pure vanilla extract
- 1 Tablespoon coconut butter
- 1 teaspoon lecithin
- ¼ teaspoon high-quality salt
- ¼ cup unsweetened almond milk (see recipe on page 75 if you want to make it from scratch)

DIRECTIONS:

1. Blend coconut meat, lime juice, agave, vanilla, coconut butter, lecithin, and salt in a blender.
2. Add almond milk gradually until a thick, pudding-like consistency is achieved.
3. Pour the filling into a prepared raw pie crust and spread evenly.
4. Place in the refrigerator for at least 3 hours so that the filling sets.

Makes filling for one 8" or 9" pie

Raw Key Lime Pie Filling

INGREDIENTS:

- ⅔ cup lime juice
- 1 ripe avocado
- ½ cup coconut cream (place one 14-ounce can of coconut milk in the fridge overnight and scoop off cream)
- ½ cup agave nectar
- ½ teaspoon high-quality salt
- 1 teaspoon pure vanilla extract
- 1 drop lime essential oil (food-grade)
- ½ teaspoon spirulina (optional, for green color and added nutritional boost)
- 1 Tablespoon soy lecithin
- ¼ cup coconut butter

DIRECTIONS:

1. Blend lime juice, avocado, coconut cream, agave, salt, vanilla, lime essential oil and optional spirulina in a blender. Blend until smooth.
2. Add the soy lecithin and coconut butter, blending until incorporated.
3. Pour the filling into a prepared raw pie crust and spread evenly. Place in the refrigerator for at least 2 hours so that the filling sets.
4. Top with raw meringue (see recipe on page 296).

Makes filling for one 8" or 9" pie

Raw Lemon Pie Filling

You will need to prepare the Irish moss 24 hours ahead, so be sure to give yourself enough time.

INGREDIENTS:

- 2 ½ dry ounces Irish moss (see glossary for instructions)
- 1 ¾ cups lemon juice
- ⅛ teaspoon turmeric powder **or** ½ teaspoon fresh turmeric juice (press fresh turmeric in a garlic press to extract juice)
- ½ teaspoon pure vanilla extract
- ¼ teaspoon high-quality salt
- 1 ⅔ cups agave nectar
- 1 drop essential oil of lemon (food grade)

DIRECTIONS:

1. Prepare Irish moss 24 hours beforehand.
2. In a blender, add Irish moss, lemon juice, and turmeric and blend until smooth.
3. Add vanilla, salt, lemon essential oil, and agave and blend 10 seconds more.
4. Pour into prepared raw crust and let set in the refrigerator for about an hour.
5. Top with raw meringue to make a lemon meringue pie (see recipe below.)

Makes filling for one 8" or 9" pie

Raw Meringue Pie Topping

You will need to prepare the Irish moss and soak the cashews a day ahead, so be sure to give yourself enough time.

INGREDIENTS:

- ⅓ cup cashews, soaked overnight
- 1 dry ounce Irish moss (see glossary for instructions)
- ½ cup water
- 3 Tablespoons agave nectar
- 1 cup coconut milk, homemade (see pages 79-80) **or** from a can
- ½ cup raw young coconut meat
- ¼ teaspoon high-quality salt
- 1 teaspoon pure vanilla extract
- 1 ½ teaspoons lemon juice
- ½ cup coconut butter
- 1 teaspoon soy lecithin

DIRECTIONS:

1. Prepare Irish moss 24 hours beforehand.
2. Soak cashews overnight.
3. Add Irish moss and water to blender and blend until smooth.
4. Add soaked cashews, agave, coconut milk, coconut meat, salt, vanilla, and lemon juice. Blend until smooth.
5. Add coconut butter and soy lecithin and blend for another 30 seconds or until incorporated.
6. Pour into a glass pie pan or shallow wide bowl and let sit in the fridge for about 2-3 hours, or until set. When it is firm, top your raw pie with your delicious meringue!

Makes filling for one 8" or 9" pie

Raw Banana Cream Pie Filling

INGREDIENTS:

Banana custard:

- 4 bananas
- 1 ripe avocado, pitted
- 2 teaspoons pineapple juice
- ½ teaspoon pure vanilla extract
- 2 Tablespoons agave nectar

Cream topping:

- ½ cup pine nuts, soaked 6 hours
- ½ cup water
- 1 Tablespoon agave nectar
- ¼ teaspoon guar gum **or** xanthan gum **or** a 50:50 combination of both
- ¼ cup shredded coconut

DIRECTIONS:

For the Custard:

1. Add bananas, avocado, pineapple, vanilla, and agave to a blender and blend until smooth.
2. Pour into your prepared raw crust and clean the blender for the next step.

For the Topping:

1. Blend pine nuts, water, agave, and gum until smooth.
2. Swirl into pie.
3. Place in the refrigerator to set for 1-2 hours.
4. Top with shredded coconut and serve chilled.

Makes filling for one 8" or 9" pie

Raw Chocolate Cream Pie Filling

You will need to prepare the Irish moss 24 hours ahead, so be sure to give yourself enough time.

INGREDIENTS:

- ½ dry ounce Irish moss (see glossary for instructions)
- 1 cup nutmilk
- 1 small avocado
- 1 teaspoon pure vanilla extract
- ⅓ cup raw cacao powder **or** raw carob powder
- 3 Tablespoons agave nectar
- 2 Tablespoons coconut butter

DIRECTIONS:

1. Prepare Irish moss 24 hours beforehand.
2. In a blender, mix Irish moss and nutmilk and blend until smooth.
3. Add remaining ingredients (avocado, vanilla, raw cacao powder, agave, and coconut butter) and blend until smooth.
4. Pour into prepared raw crust and let set in the refrigerator for about an hour.

Makes filling for one 8" or 9" pie

Raw Chocolate Banana Pie Filling

INGREDIENTS:

- 2 large ripe avocados
- ½ cup raw cacao powder **or** raw carob powder
- ½ cup agave nectar
- 1 Tablespoon pure vanilla extract
- ¼ teaspoon high-quality salt

- 3 Bananas

DIRECTIONS:

1. In a blender, combine all ingredients except bananas until smooth.
2. Place a quarter of the filling into your prepared raw pie crust and spread evenly.
3. Slice the bananas. Place a layer of bananas on the filling, then put remaining filling on top of bananas and spread filling evenly.
4. Cover and chill 1-2 hours before serving.

Makes filling for one 8" or 9" pie

Raw Strawberry Pie Cups

INGREDIENTS:
- Raw pie crust dough of your choice
- 2 ½ cups fresh strawberries, cut into chunks (**or** use fruit of choice: blueberries, peaches, apricots, raspberries, mangoes, etc.)
- ¼ cup water
- 1 teaspoon agar-agar powder
- 3 Tablespoons agave nectar

DIRECTIONS:
1. Line a muffin pan or little bowls with muffin cups.
2. Add a heaping spoonful of raw pie crust dough and press evenly into the bottoms of the muffin cups.
3. Wash and cut fruit and add to the muffin cups.
4. In a saucepan, heat water until hot but not boiling. Add agar-agar powder. Stir until dissolved. Add agave, stir well, then pour over the fruit until cups are ¾ full.
5. Cover and chill in the refrigerator for 2-3 hours.

OPTIONAL VARIATION:
You can make this as a pie instead of as individual servings.

Makes 12 individual cups

Raw Chocolate Rose Pie Cups

INGREDIENTS:
- Raw pie crust dough of your choice
- 2 cups cashews
- 2 Tablespoons coconut butter
- ¾ cup water
- ½ cup raw cacao powder **or** raw carob powder
- ¼ cup agave nectar
- 1 Tablespoon soy lecithin
- ½ teaspoon xanthan gum **or** guar gum **or** a 50:50 combination of both
- 1 Tablespoon rose water (found in Indian and Middle Eastern markets or online)

DIRECTIONS:
1. Line a muffin pan or small bowls with muffin cups.
2. Add a heaping spoonful of raw pie crust dough and press evenly into the bottoms of the muffin cups.
3. Combine cashews, coconut butter, water, raw cacao powder, agave, lecithin, gum, and rose water in a blender and mix until smooth.
4. Pour filling into cups and let set for 2-3 hours in the refrigerator.
5. Top with rose petals and pomegranate seeds for a special touch.

OPTIONAL VARIATION:
You can make this as a pie instead of as individual servings.

Makes 12 individual cups

My Pie and Tart Creations:

Use this section to write down some of your favorite customized pie and tart recipes from this chapter.

Recipe:

INGREDIENTS:

....

....

....

....

....

....

....

DIRECTIONS:

....

....

....

....

....

....

Serves _____

My Pie and Tart Creations:

*Use this section to write down some of your favorite
customized pie and tart recipes from this chapter.*

Recipe:

. . . .

INGREDIENTS:

....

....

....

....

....

....

....

DIRECTIONS:

....

....

....

....

....

....

Serves _____

CHAPTER 16

COBBLERS, CRISPS, AND CRUMBLES

Understanding the Differences..................304

Cobblers

    Base Recipe..................304

    Peach Cobbler 306

Crisps

    Base Recipe..................307

    Apple Crisp 308

Crumbles

    Base Recipe..................309

    Berry Almond Crumble 310

Understanding the Differences

Cobblers are fruit stews that are dotted with a sweet dough before baking.

Crisps are deep-dish fruit desserts baked with a crumb or streusel topping. Crisp toppings often contain ingredients such as oats and nuts, which give them a coarser topping than cobblers or crumbles.

Crumbles are made from raw sliced fruit and are topped with a crumbly pastry mixture made from flour, sweetener, and butter and then baked.

Cobblers

Cobbler Base Recipe

INGREDIENTS:

Fruit:

- 6 cups fresh fruit (peaches, apples, apricots, etc)
- 1 ½ Tablespoons cornstarch
- ½ teaspoon cinnamon
- 1 ¼ teaspoon lemon juice
- ½ cup agave nectar

Topping:

- 1 cup oat flour
- ⅓ cup barley flour
- 2 teaspoons baking powder
- ½ teaspoon high-quality salt
- ¼ cup organic vegetable shortening (coconut or palm) **or** coconut oil
- ⅔ cup milk (cow, goat, almond, rice, coconut, oat, etc.)
- 2 Tablespoons agave nectar

Gluten-Free Variation:
 ⅔ cup brown rice flour + ⅓ cup sorghum flour

DIRECTIONS:

For the Fruit:

1. Wash, peel, and pit fruit as needed.
2. In a large saucepan, combine cornstarch and cinnamon. Add in fruit, lemon juice, and agave and stir the entire mixture until fruit is evenly coated.
3. Cook fruit over medium heat, stirring continually. Cook until the mixture boils and continue boiling for 1 more minute.
4. Pour fruit into a 9" square or 8" x 10" rectangle baking dish and begin to prepare the topping.

For the Topping:

1. Preheat the oven to 400°F.
2. In a large bowl, combine oat flour, barley flour, baking powder, and salt and stir thoroughly with a fork.
3. Cut in the shortening and stir until you have fine crumbs.
4. Pour in milk and agave and stir until all the ingredients are evenly mixed.
5. Add big spoonfuls of the topping to the hot fruit. There should be enough topping for 8-10 large spoonfuls.
6. Bake for 25-30 minutes or until the topping is golden brown.
7. Serve cobbler warm with ice cream.

Makes 8-10 servings

Peach Cobbler

INGREDIENTS:

Fruit:

- 6 cups sliced peaches (approximately 5 peaches)
- 1 ½ Tablespoons cornstarch
- ½ teaspoon cinnamon
- 1¼ teaspoons lemon juice
- ½ cup agave nectar
- 1 Tablespoon peach schnapps (optional)

Topping:

- ¾ cup oat flour
- ⅓ cup barley flour
- ¼ cup tapioca flour
- 2 teaspoons baking powder
- ½ teaspoon high-quality salt
- ¼ cup organic vegetable shortening (coconut or palm) **or** coconut oil
- ⅔ cup milk (cow, goat, almond, rice, coconut, oat, etc.)
- 2 Tablespoons agave nectar

DIRECTIONS

For the Fruit:

1. Wash, peel, and pit the peaches. Cut into cubes and measure 6 cups. Set aside.
2. In a large saucepan, combine the cornstarch and cinnamon. Add fruit, lemon juice, and agave and stir until the fruit is evenly coated.
3. Cook over medium heat, stirring continually. If using schnapps, add it here. Cook until the mixture boils and continue to boil for 1 more minute.
4. Pour the fruit into a 9" square or 8" x 10" rectangle baking dish and begin to prepare the topping.

For the Topping:

1. Preheat the oven to 400°F.
2. Combine oat flour, barley flour, tapioca flour, baking powder, and salt in a bowl and stir thoroughly with a fork.
3. Cut in the shortening and stir until you have fine crumbs.
4. Pour in the milk and agave and stir until all the ingredients are evenly mixed.
5. Add big spoonfuls of the topping to the hot fruit. There should be enough topping for 8-10 large spoonfuls.
6. Bake for 25-30 minutes or until the topping is golden brown.
7. Serve cobbler warm with ice cream.

Makes 8-10 servings

Crisps

Crisp Base Recipe:

INGREDIENTS:

Fruit:

- Butter for greasing baking dish
- 6 cups fresh fruit (apples, peaches, pears, blueberries, and rhubarb **or** a combo)
- ¼ cup agave nectar

Topping:

- ¾ cup oat **or** barley flour (use ¾ cup sorghum flour for gluten free)
- ¾ cup rolled oats
- 1 teaspoon ground nutmeg
- 1 ¼ teaspoons ground cinnamon
- ½ teaspoon high-quality salt
- ½ cup butter, softened
- 1 cup agave nectar

DIRECTIONS:

For the Fruit:

1. Preheat the oven to 375°F.
2. Butter the bottom and sides of a 9" x 11" baking dish.
3. Peel, core, and slice fruit. Spread fruit evenly in the bottom of the baking dish. Drizzle agave over the fruit.

For the Topping:

1. In a small bowl, combine flour, oats, nutmeg, cinnamon, and salt and mix until well blended.
2. Stir in the butter and agave.
3. The mixture should have a crumbly texture. Sprinkle evenly over fruit.
4. Bake 30 minutes or until golden brown and crispy.
5. Remove from the oven and serve warm with a scoop of ice cream.

Makes 8-10 servings

Apple Crisp

INGREDIENTS:

Fruit:

- 2 lbs apples, peeled and sliced
- ½ cup agave nectar
- 1 teaspoon ground cinnamon
- ½ teaspoon nutmeg

Topping:

- 1 cup oat flour
- 1 ¼ teaspoons ground cinnamon
- ½ teaspoon high-quality salt
- ¼ cup butter, softened
- ¼ cup agave nectar

DIRECTIONS:

For the Fruit:

1. Preheat oven to 375°F.
2. Prepare apples by coring, peeling, and slicing. You should have about 4½ cups. In a large bowl, toss apples with agave, cinnamon, and nutmeg.
3. Pour into a 2-quart baking dish.

For the Topping:

1. In a medium bowl, mix oat flour, cinnamon, and salt.
2. Stir in butter and agave. The mixture should have a crumbly texture. Sprinkle evenly over apples.
3. Bake 30 minutes or until golden brown and crispy.
4. Remove from the oven and serve warm with a scoop of ice cream.

Makes 8-10 servings

Crumbles

Crumble Base Recipe

INGREDIENTS:

Fruit:

- 6 cups fresh fruit (apples, blueberries, strawberries, peaches, rhubarb, cherry, plums, etc.)
- Neutral-tasting oil (grapeseed, untoasted sesame oil, coconut oil, **or** ghee) for greasing pan
- Juice of ½ lemon
- ⅓ cup agave nectar
- 1 Tablespoon arrowroot flour
- 1 teaspoon cinnamon (optional)
- ¼ teaspoon nutmeg (optional)

Topping:

- ¾ cup barley **or** oat flour (use ¾ cup sorghum flour for gluten free)
- ½ teaspoon cinnamon
- ½ cup agave nectar
- ½ cup butter, cold, cut into small pieces

DIRECTIONS:

For the Fruit:

1. Preheat the oven to 375°F.
2. Wash, peel, cut, and pit fruit as needed. If using apples, cut them into thick slices.
3. Place fruit in a 9" square or 9" round, greased baking dish. Top with lemon juice and agave.
4. Toss to coat fruit. Stir in arrowroot flour and optional spices.

For the Topping:

1. In a small bowl, mix flour, cinnamon, agave, and butter until the mixture has a crumbly texture. Sprinkle evenly over the fruit, then place the dish in the oven.
2. Bake covered 30-40 minutes or until fruit is tender and the topping is golden brown and crispy.
3. Remove from the oven and serve warm with a scoop of ice cream or a dollop of whipped cream.

Makes 8-10 servings

Berry Almond Crumble
· ·

INGREDIENTS:

Fruit:

- 1 ½ lbs sweet cherries (5 cups), rinsed and pitted
- 1 cup fresh raspberries, rinsed
- Neutral-tasting oil (grapeseed, untoasted sesame oil, coconut oil, **or** ghee) for greasing pan
- Juice of ½ lemon
- ⅓ cup agave nectar
- 1 Tablespoon arrowroot flour
- 1 Tablespoon kirsch **or** brandy (optional)

Topping:

- ¾ cup oat flour
- ¾ cup rolled oats
- ½ teaspoon ground cinnamon
- ⅛ teaspoon high quality salt
- ½ cup agave nectar
- ½ cup butter, cold, cut into small pieces
- 3 Tablespoons frozen orange juice from concentrate
- 1 Tablespoon slivered almonds

DIRECTIONS:

For the Fruit:

1. Preheat oven to 375°F.
2. Rinse and pit the cherries (or buy pitted cherries). Place cherries and raspberries in a 9" x 9" or 9" round, greased baking dish. Top with lemon juice and agave. Toss to coat fruit. Stir in arrowroot flour and optional liqueur.

For the Topping:

1. In a small bowl, combine oat flour, rolled oats, cinnamon, and salt and mix well.
2. Add agave, butter, and orange juice until the mixture has a crumbly texture. Stir in almonds. Sprinkle evenly over the fruit, then place the dish in the oven.
3. Cover and bake 20 minutes, then remove the cover and bake another 15 minutes or until topping is golden brown and crispy.
4. Remove from the oven and serve warm with a scoop of ice cream or a dollop of whipped cream.

Serves 8-10

My Cobbler, Crisp, and Crumble Creations:

*Use this section to write down some of your favorite
customized cobbler, crisp, and crumble recipes from this chapter.*

Recipe:

INGREDIENTS:

....

....

....

....

....

....

....

DIRECTIONS:

....

....

....

....

....

....

Serves _____

My Cobbler, Crisp, and Crumble Creations:

*Use this section to write down some of your favorite
customized cobbler, crisp, and crumble recipes from this chapter.*

Recipe:

INGREDIENTS:

DIRECTIONS:

Serves _____

ICE CREAM

Dairy Ice Cream

Ice Cream Base Recipe............314

    Peanut Butter Ice Cream............314

    Mint Chocolate Chip
    Ice Cream.........................314

    Espresso Chocolate Chip Ice Cream ..314

    Chocolate Ice Cream 314

    Fruit Ice Cream 314

    Banana Ice Cream 314

    Green Tea Ice Cream 315

    Maté Cocido Ice Cream.............315

Gelato Base Recipe...............316

    Strawberry Gelato..................316

    Raspberry Gelato...................316

    Chocolate Gelato 316

    Hazelnut Gelato 316

    Ricotta Gelato.....................317

    Avocado Gelato 317

Dairy-Free Ice Cream

**Coconut Milk Ice Cream
Base Recipe** 318

    Chai Chocolate Chip Coconut
    Ice Cream.........................318

    Coffee Coconut Ice Cream..........319

    Maté Coconut Ice Cream 319

    Ginger Mango Lime Ice Cream.......319

    Mango Coconut Sherbet 320

    Raspberry Coconut Milk Sherbet 320

    Strawberry Coconut Milk
    Ice Cream.........................320

    Mint Chocolate Chip Coconut
    Ice Cream.........................321

    Strawberry Cacao Chip
    Coconut Ice Cream.................321

**Cashew Milk Ice Cream
Base Recipe** 322

    Chia Seed Raw Ice Cream...........322

Dairy Ice Cream

Ice Cream Base Recipe

INGREDIENTS:
- 5 eggs
- 1 cup agave nectar
- 5 cups milk
- 2 ¼ cups heavy cream
- ½ teaspoon high-quality salt
- 4 ½ teaspoons pure vanilla extract
- 1 teaspoon xanthan gum **or** guar gum **or** a 50:50 combination of both (optional)*
- Grated or ground vanilla bean (optional)

DIRECTIONS:
1. Beat eggs and agave with a hand mixer, a mixer, or by hand. Continue to beat until the mixture starts to become frothy, about 5 minutes.
2. Add milk, cream, salt, vanilla extract, gum, and vanilla bean and mix thoroughly.
3. Pour mixture into an ice cream maker and follow manufacturer's instructions.

OPTIONAL ADDITIONS:
- **Peanut Butter Ice Cream:** After step 2, stir in ½ cup peanut butter, then proceed to step 3.
- **Mint Chocolate Chip Ice Cream:** After step 2, stir in ½ cup chocolate shavings, cacao nibs, or chopped grain-sweetened chocolate chips. Add 2-3 drops mint essential oil. Proceed to step 3.
- **Espresso Chocolate Chip:** After step 2, stir in ½ cup chocolate shavings or chopped grain-sweetened chocolate chips and ⅔ cup strongly brewed espresso. Proceed to step 3.
- **Chocolate Ice Cream:** After step 2, add 1 cup melted grain-sweetened chocolate or unsweetened chocolate plus ¼ cup agave nectar. You can also add ½ cup raw cacao or cocoa powder. Proceed to step 3.
- **Fruit Ice Cream:** In a blender, blend 1 cup fruit of your choice into 3 cups milk. Use this milk in step 2.
- **Banana Ice Cream:** Add 1-2 puréed bananas at the end of step 2. Proceed to step 3.

Feel free to experiment with your own ice cream creations.

Makes 8-10 servings

*The addition of gum to ice cream will make it smoother in texture and reduce iciness.

Green Tea Ice Cream

INGREDIENTS:

- 3 Tablespoons hot water
- 1 Tablespoon maccha (matcha) green tea powder
- 2 egg yolks
- 4 Tablespoons agave nectar
- ¾ cup milk
- ¾ cup heavy cream
- ½ teaspoon xanthan gum **or** guar gum **or** a 50:50 combination of both
- ¼ teaspoon high-quality salt

DIRECTIONS:

1. Mix hot water and green tea powder in a small bowl, then set aside to cool.
2. Beat the egg yolks and agave with a hand mixer, a mixer, or by hand.
3. Add green tea mixture. Continue to beat until the mixture starts to become stiff.
4. Add milk, cream, gum, and salt and mix thoroughly.
5. Pour mixture into an ice cream maker and follow manufacturer's instructions.

Makes 4-6 servings

Maté Cocido Ice Cream

I discovered maté ice cream in a quaint gourmet ice cream shop in Buenos Aires. I got hooked and had to create a version with agave nectar. Enjoy!

INGREDIENTS:

- ½ cup water
- ¾ cup maté leaf
- 2 egg yolks
- 4 Tablespoons agave nectar
- ¾ cup milk
- ¾ cup heavy cream
- 1/2 teaspoon xanthan gum **or** guar gum **or** a 50:50 combination of both
- ¼ teaspoon high-quality salt

DIRECTIONS:

1. Heat water until hot and steaming (not boiling), then pour into a cup with 1/2 cup maté leaf. Cover and set aside to cool.
2. Beat egg yolks and agave with a hand mixer, a mixer, or by hand.
3. Add 3 Tablespoons of the strong maté leaf tea from step 1. Continue to beat until the mixture becomes frothy, about 4 minutes.
4. Add milk, cream, gum, and salt and mix thoroughly.
5. Pour mixture into an ice cream maker and follow manufacturer's instructions.

Makes 4-6 servings

Gelato Base Recipe

Feel free to experiment with your own gelato creations.

INGREDIENTS:
- 6 cups milk
- 1 cup agave nectar
- 12 egg yolks, beaten
- 1 Tablespoon of grated lemon **or** orange peel

DIRECTIONS:
1. In large saucepan, combine 3 cups milk, agave, and egg yolks. Mix well and gently heat on medium until mixture just coats a metal spoon. Remove from heat.
2. Stir in remaining 3 cups milk and lemon or orange peel.
3. Remove from heat, place a plate on top of the saucepan, and allow to cool in the refrigerator. Refrigerate several hours or overnight.
4. Pour mixture into an ice cream maker and follow manufacturer's instructions.

OPTIONAL ADDITIONS:
- **Strawberry Gelato:** In a blender, blend 1 cup strawberries into 3 cups milk. Use this mixture in step 2.
- **Chocolate Gelato:** Add 1 cup melted grain-sweetened chocolate or unsweetened chocolate plus ¼ cup agave nectar.
- **Raspberry Gelato:** In a blender, blend 1 cup raspberries into 3 cups milk. Use this mixture in step 2.
- **Hazelnut Gelato:** Toast ½ cup hazelnuts, then rub off skins with a kitchen towel and allow to cool. Add to a good blender like a Vitamix and make into a course powder. In step 1, cook the ground hazelnuts in the milk for about 20 minutes. Let sit for an hour, strain, and return to pan. Add the egg yolks and proceed with recipe.

Makes 8-10 servings

Ricotta Gelato

INGREDIENTS:
- 1 ¼ cups half-and-half
- 1 ¼ cups milk
- 1 16-ounce container whole-milk ricotta
- ⅓ cup agave nectar
- 1 3" cinnamon stick

- 2" strip lemon rind removed with a vegetable peeler
- 2 Tablespoons agave nectar
- ½ teaspoon pure vanilla extract

DIRECTIONS:
1. In a medium saucepan, whisk together the half-and-half, milk, ricotta, and agave. Add cinnamon stick and bring just to a boil. Stir.
2. Remove from heat, add the lemon rind, and let the liquid rest with the lid on for 10 minutes.
3. Strain through a fine sieve set over a bowl. Stir in agave and vanilla.
4. Chill the mixture in the refrigerator with a lid on top for an hour or until chilled.
5. Pour mixture into an ice cream maker and follow manufacturer's instructions.
6. Top with a fruit sauce.

Makes 8-10 servings

Avocado Gelato

INGREDIENTS:
- 2 cups whole milk
- ½ cup agave nectar
- Orange rind from 1 orange
- Pinch high-quality salt
- 1 teaspoon pure vanilla extract

- 2 Tablespoons arrowroot flour
- 2 firm and ripe avocados (about 1 lb)
- 1 teaspoon vitamin C powder (to preserve the color)

DIRECTIONS:
1. In a heavy 2-quart saucepan, bring 1 ½ cups milk, agave, orange rind, and salt to a simmer over moderate heat.
2. In a small bowl, mix arrowroot and remaining ½ cup milk until arrowroot is dissolved. Whisk into the simmering milk. Bring to a boil, stirring constantly. Boil for 1 minute.
3. Remove orange rind and allow mixture to cool in the refrigerator.
4. Peel avocados and remove the pits. Purée in a blender with vitamin C and cooled milk mixture until smooth.
5. Pour mixture into an ice cream maker and follow manufacturer's instructions.

Makes 8-10 servings

Ice Cream

Coconut Milk Ice Cream Base Recipe

INGREDIENTS:

- 3 ½ cups unsweetened coconut milk (two 14-ounce cans)
- ⅔ cup agave nectar
- 1 teaspoon pure vanilla extract
- 1 teaspoon xanthan gum **or** guar gum **or** a 50:50 combination of both

DIRECTIONS:

1. Purée all ingredients in blender until smooth.
2. Pour mixture into an ice cream maker and follow manufacturer's instructions.

OPTIONAL ADDITIONS:
Try adding 1 ½ cups fresh fruit, dried cherries, cacao nibs, shaved chocolate, cookie dough, or nuts.

Makes 4-6 servings

Chai Chocolate Chip Coconut Ice Cream

INGREDIENTS:

- 3 ½ cups unsweetened coconut milk (two 14-ounce cans)
- ⅔ cup strongly brewed chai (spice tea)
- ⅔ cup agave nectar
- 1 teaspoon xanthan gum **or** guar gum **or** a 50:50 combination of both
- ⅔ cup grain-sweetened chocolate chips **or** raw cacao nibs

DIRECTIONS:

1. Purée all ingredients except chocolate chips in blender until smooth.
2. Add chocolate chips or cacao nibs and blend until the chocolate chips or nibs are broken up to the desired size.
3. Pour mixture into an ice cream maker and follow manufacturer's instructions.

Makes 4-6 servings

Coffee Coconut Ice Cream

INGREDIENTS:

- 3 ½ cups unsweetened coconut milk (two 14-ounce cans)
- ⅔ cup strongly brewed coffee
- ⅔ cup agave nectar
- 1 teaspoon pure vanilla extract
- 1 teaspoon xanthan gum **or** guar gum **or** a 50:50 combination of both

DIRECTIONS:

1. Purée all ingredients in blender until smooth.

2. Pour mixture into an ice cream maker and follow manufacturer's instructions.

Makes 4-6 servings

Maté Coconut Ice Cream

INGREDIENTS:

- 3 ½ cups unsweetened coconut milk (two 14-ounce cans)
- ⅔ cup strongly brewed maté
- ⅔ cup agave nectar
- 1 teaspoon pure vanilla extract
- 1 teaspoon xanthan gum **or** guar gum **or** a 50:50 combination of both

DIRECTIONS:

1. Purée all ingredients in blender until smooth.

2. Pour mixture into an ice cream maker and follow manufacturer's instructions.

Makes 4-6 servings

Ginger Mango Lime Coconut Ice Cream

INGREDIENTS:

- ⅓ cup finely grated fresh ginger
- 3 ½ cups unsweetened coconut milk (two 14-ounce cans)
- ⅔ cup agave nectar
- 5 Tablespoons fresh lime juice
- 1 Tablespoon grated lime peel
- Pinch high-quality salt
- 2 mangoes, peeled, pitted, and sliced
- 1 teaspoon xanthan gum **or** guar gum **or** a 50:50 combination of both

DIRECTIONS:

1. Finely grate the ginger and measure ⅓ cup, including the juices.
2. Purée ginger and all ingredients in blender until smooth.

3. Pour mixture into an ice cream maker and follow manufacturer's instructions.
4. Garnish with thinly sliced lime.

Makes 4-6 servings

Mango Coconut Sherbet

INGREDIENTS:
- 3 ½ cups unsweetened coconut milk (two 14-ounce cans)
- 1 ½ cups cubed mango, frozen **or** fresh
- ⅔ cup agave nectar
- 1 teaspoon pure vanilla extract
- 1 teaspoon xanthan gum **or** guar gum **or** a 50:50 combination of both

DIRECTIONS:
1. Purée all ingredients in blender until smooth.
2. Pour mixture into an ice cream maker and follow manufacturer's instructions.

Makes 4-6 servings

Raspberry Coconut Sherbet

INGREDIENTS:
- 3 ½ cups unsweetened coconut milk (two 14-ounce cans)
- 1 ½ heaping cups frozen **or** fresh raspberries (**or** other berries)
- ⅔ cup agave nectar
- 1 teaspoon pure vanilla extract
- ½ cup of Framboise liqueur (optional)
- 1 teaspoon xanthan gum **or** guar gum **or** a 50:50 combination of both

DIRECTIONS:
1. Purée all ingredients in blender until smooth.
2. Pour mixture into an ice cream maker and follow manufacturer's instructions.

Makes 4-6 servings

Strawberry Coconut Milk Ice Cream

INGREDIENTS:
- 3 ½ cups unsweetened coconut milk (two 14-ounce cans)
- 1 ½ heaping cups frozen **or** fresh strawberries
- ⅔ cup agave nectar
- 1 teaspoon pure vanilla extract
- 1 teaspoon xanthan gum **or** guar gum **or** a 50:50 combination of both

DIRECTIONS:
1. Purée all ingredients in blender until smooth.
2. Pour mixture into an ice cream maker and follow manufacturer's instructions.

Makes 4-6 servings

Mint Chocolate Chip Coconut Ice Cream

INGREDIENTS:
- ⅔ cup grain sweetened chocolate chunks **or** raw cacao nibs
- 3 ½ cups unsweetened coconut milk (two 14-ounce cans)
- 3 drops peppermint essential oil **or** 1 teaspoon mint extract
- ⅔ cup agave nectar
- 1 teaspoon xanthan gum **or** guar gum **or** a 50:50 combination of both

DIRECTIONS:
1. Grate chocolate until you have ⅔ cup of shavings. Set aside.
2. Purée all ingredients (except chocolate shavings) in a blender until smooth. If using cacao nibs, blend with the other ingredients in the blender until they are broken up to the desired size.
3. Stir in chocolate shavings.
4. Pour mixture into an ice cream maker and follow manufacturer's instructions.

Makes 4-6 servings

Strawberry Cacao Chip Coconut Milk Ice Cream

INGREDIENTS:
- ⅔ cup chocolate shavings **or** raw cacao nibs
- 3 ½ cups unsweetened coconut milk (two 14-ounce cans)
- 1 ½ heaping cups of frozen **or** fresh strawberries
- ⅔ cup grain-sweetened chocolate chips **or** raw cacao nibs
- ⅔ cup agave nectar
- 1 teaspoon pure vanilla extract
- 1 teaspoon xanthan gum **or** guar gum **or** a 50:50 combination of both

DIRECTIONS:
1. Grate chocolate until you have ⅔ cup of shavings. Set aside.
2. Purée all ingredients (except chocolate shavings) in a blender until smooth. If using cacao nibs, blend with other ingredients in the blender until they are broken up to the desired size.
3. Stir in chocolate shavings.
4. Pour mixture into an ice cream maker and follow manufacturer's instructions.

Makes 4-6 servings

Cashew Milk Ice Cream Base Recipe

INGREDIENTS:

- 2 cups cashews, soaked
- 4 cups water
- ½ cup dates
- ¼ teaspoon high-quality salt

- 1 teaspoon pure vanilla extract
- 1 teaspoon xanthan gum **or** guar gum **or** a 50:50 combination of both

DIRECTIONS:

1. Soak cashews overnight.
2. Drain cashews and purée in blender. Add 4 cups water. Blend until smooth.
3. Strain mixture using a nutmilk bag.
4. Rinse blender, then combine strained nutmilk, dates, salt, vanilla, and gum. Blend until smooth.
5. Pour mixture into ice cream maker and follow manufacturer's instructions.

OPTIONAL ADDITIONS:

- Add 1 ½ cups frozen or fresh fruit or raw cacao powder or grain-sweetened chocolate chips.
- Add food-grade essential oils or extracts.
- Add nuts or cookie dough.

Makes 6-8 servings

Chia Seed Raw Ice Cream

INGREDIENTS:

- 2 cups raw cashews, soaked for 2 hours or more
- 2 Tablespoons chia seeds
- 1 cup water
- 1 14-ounce can coconut milk **or** 1 fresh coconut (meat and milk)

- ⅔ cup agave nectar
- ¼ cup coconut butter
- 4 teaspoons pure vanilla extract
- ½ teaspoon high-quality salt

DIRECTIONS:

1. Measure cashews into a bowl, cover with water, and set aside for at least 2 hours.
2. Place chia seeds and 1 cup water in a glass jar and let sit for 1 hour.
3. Combine all ingredients in a blender and pureé until smooth.
4. Pour mixture into ice cream maker and follow manufacturer's instructions.

OPTIONAL VARIATION:

Try using seeds of ½ of a vanilla bean in place of 2 teaspoons of the extract for a stronger vanilla flavor.

Makes 6-8 servings

My Ice Cream Creations:

Use this section to write down some of your favorite customized ice cream recipes from this chapter.

Recipe:

INGREDIENTS:

DIRECTIONS:

Serves _____

My Ice Cream Creations:

Use this section to write down some of your favorite customized ice cream recipes from this chapter.

Recipe:

. . . .

INGREDIENTS:

....

....

....

....

....

....

....

DIRECTIONS:

....

....

....

....

....

....

Serves _____

CHAPTER 18

RAW FOOD TREATS

Raw Chocolate

Raw Chocolate Candy
Base Recipe 326

Raw Chocolate Syrup 327

Raw Chocolate Nut Drink 327

Superfood Balls

Dried Fruit Bon Bons
Base Recipe 328

Goji Chocolate Power Balls 329

Maca Balls 330

Chocolate Tahini Balls 331

Raw Candies and Treats

Coconut Haystacks 332

Hemp Chocolate Fudge Bars . . 333

Raw Chocolate Truffles 334

Raw Chocolate Walnut Truffles 335

Raw Almond Chocolates 335

Carob Balls 336

Lemon Cashew Cookies 336

Raw Chocolate

Raw Chocolate Candy Base Recipe

INGREDIENTS:
- ¼ cup raw coconut oil
- ½ cup unrefined raw cocoa butter
- ¼ teaspoon Himalayan salt
- ¼ cup raw coconut butter (or substitute with cocoa butter **or** mango butter)
- 1 cup raw cacao powder (**or** raw carob powder)
- ½ cup raw agave nectar

DIRECTIONS:
1. In a double boiler or by placing a metal bowl placed over a saucepan of boiling water, gently melt coconut oil, cocoa butter, coconut butter, and salt. Remove from heat.
2. Add cacao powder and agave and mix well by hand, hand mixer, or immersion blender. Mixture should be thin enough to pour. Add a little more melted coconut oil if it is too thick.
3. Pour into chocolate molds (or onto a cookie sheet if you don't have molds) and freeze or refrigerate for 30-45 minutes or until solid.
4. Unmold chocolate once it is solid. (Or cut into squares if using a cookie sheet.)
   Tip: If chocolate is soft at room temperature, add more cocoa butter next time.
5. Store in a glass container in a cool place or in the refrigerator or freezer.

OPTIONAL ADDITIONS:
Try adding one or more of the following:

- **Floral waters** like rosewater or orange blossom water
- **Dried fruit** like raspberries, blueberries, goji berries, or currants
- **Spices** like cardamom, cayenne, black pepper, lavender, or orange peel
- **Essential oils** like peppermint, lavender, orange, or bergamot
- **Nuts** like chopped almonds, hazelnuts, macadamia nuts, peanuts, or walnuts.

Makes 20-40 candies, depending on mold size

Raw Chocolate Syrup

This makes a great topping for raw ice cream.

INGREDIENTS:

- 1 cup raw agave nectar
- ½ cup raw cacao powder
  (**or** raw carob powder)
- ¼ teaspoon high-quality salt
- 1 teaspoon pure vanilla extract.

DIRECTIONS:

1. Combine all ingredients in a tall glass. Blend well with an immersion blender. For larger quantities, use a mixer.
2. Store in a mason jar and keep it in the fridge.

OPTIONAL ADDITIONS:
Try adding ¼ teaspoon cayenne pepper for a Mexican flare or 2 drops of peppermint essential oil.

Makes about 1 cup

Raw Chocolate Nut Drink

INGREDIENTS:

- 1 cup cashews, almonds, macadamia nuts, **or** Brazil nuts
- 3 ¼ cup water
- 4 Tablespoons raw cacao powder **or** raw carob powder
- ¼ teaspoon high-quality salt
- ¼ cup raw agave nectar
- 1 teaspoon pure vanilla extract
- 1 ¾ cup coconut milk (one 13.5-ounce can)

DIRECTIONS:

1. Measure nuts into a glass bowl, cover with water, and let sit overnight. If you don't get to them the next day, simply rinse with fresh water and try the next day. (Don't go more than 2-3 days.)
2. Drain and rinse nuts. Combine nuts and water in a blender and blend on high for about 2 minutes.
3. Pour liquid through a nutmilk bag or a cheesecloth-lined strainer. Squeeze the nutmilk into a clean bowl. Rinse the blender. Pour nutmilk back into blender.

(You can use the nut pulp in cookies or store in the freezer for later use.)

4. Add remaining ingredients: raw cacao powder, salt, agave, vanilla, and coconut milk and blend until smooth.
5. Store in the refrigerator.

OPTIONAL ADDITIONS:
Try adding a banana for a yummy banana-chocolate drink.

Makes about 4 cups

Superfood Balls

Dried Fruit Bon Bons Base Recipe

These make delicious and nourishing snacks for between meals or for a special treat.

INGREDIENTS:
- ⅛ cup raw coconut oil
- ⅛ cup unrefined raw cocoa butter (or substitute with coconut butter **or** mango butter)
- ½ cup raw cacao powder **or** raw carob powder
- ¼ cup raw agave nectar
- 4 Tablespoons hulled hemp seeds
- 2 teaspoons Spirulina powder
- ¼ teaspoon Himalayan salt **or** high-quality salt
- ¼ cup dried Bing cherries (**or** dried fruit of your choice)

DIRECTIONS:
1. Place a sheet of waxed paper on a plate.
2. In a double boiler or a metal bowl placed over a saucepan of boiling water, gently melt coconut oil and cocoa butter. Remove from heat.
3. Add cacao powder, agave, hemp seeds, spirulina, and salt. Stir well.
4. Fill 1 Tablespoon halfway with the mixture, add 1 dried Bing cherry, then fill the rest of the spoon with mixture. Pack tightly into a nice ball that will keep its form. Drop ball onto the waxed paper. Repeat.
5. Place the plate of candies in the freezer for about 30 minutes. Store in a glass container in a cool place or in the refrigerator.

OPTIONAL ADDITIONS:
Add in one of the following at step 3:

- ¼ cup goji berries, longan berries, mulberries, figs, apricots, or any other dried, chopped fruit
- 1 Tablespoon nuts, finely chopped (substitute for 1 Tablespoon of hemp seeds)
- 1 Drop orange, lemon, rose, mint, lavender, or other edible essential oil
- ½ teaspoon cinnamon, cardamom, allspice, or nutmeg

Makes about 25 candies

Goji Chocolate Power Balls

These are guaranteed to transform you into your favorite superhero.

INGREDIENTS:
- ¼ cup raw coconut oil
- ½ cup unrefined raw cocoa butter (or substitute with coconut butter **or** mango butter)
- 1 cup raw cacao powder **or** raw carob powder
- ½ cup raw agave nectar
- ¼ cup hulled hemp seeds
- 2 Tablespoons chia seeds
- 4 teaspoons spirulina powder
- 2 teaspoons immunity-boosting mushroom powder (reishi or cordyceps work well)
- 2 Tablespoons goji berries
- ¼ teaspoon Himalayan salt **or** high-quality salt

DIRECTIONS:
1. Place a sheet of waxed paper on a plate.
2. In a double boiler or a metal bowl placed over a saucepan of boiling water, gently melt coconut oil and cocoa butter. Remove from heat.
3. Add cacao powder, agave, hemp seeds, chia seeds, spirulina, mushroom powder, goji berries, and Himalayan salt. Stir well.
4. Pack mixture tightly into a Tablespoon and gently place on the waxed paper, ensuring that balls keeps their form. Repeat.
5. Place the plate of candies in the freezer for about 30 minutes.
6. Store in a glass container in a cool place or in the refrigerator or freezer.

Makes about 30 candies

Maca Balls

INGREDIENTS:
- ½ cup sesame seeds
- ½ cup young coconut meat (1 young coconut)
- ½ cup raisins
- 2 cups dried apricots, soaked overnight
- 1 cup Brazil nuts
- 1 teaspoon ginger powder
- ½ teaspoon cardamom powder
- 2 teaspoons maca powder
- 1 Tablespoon raw coconut butter
- ¼ teaspoon high-quality salt
- 2 Tablespoons raw agave nectar

DIRECTIONS:
1. Line a cookie sheet with waxed paper. Place another sheet of waxed paper on the counter and cover with sesame seeds.
2. Open the young coconut. Reserve the water and scrape out the meat. Measure ½ cup coconut meat.
3. In a food processor, combine raisins, apricots, coconut meat, Brazil nuts, ginger powder, cardamom powder, maca powder, coconut butter, salt, and agave.
4. Mix until ingredients form a ball in the food processor. If ball doesn't form, add coconut water from the young coconut, 1 Tablespoon at a time until the mixture pulls together into a ball.
5. Roll the mixture into small balls about the size of walnuts. Roll each ball in sesame seeds to coat, then place on the cookie sheet.
6. Freeze until hardened, about an hour.
7. Store in a glass container in a cool place or in the refrigerator or freezer.

Makes about 30 candies

Chocolate Tahini Balls

INGREDIENTS:
- 1 cup sesame seeds
- ½ cup raw coconut oil
- ½ cup raw coconut butter (or substitute with cocoa butter **or** mango butter)
- 1 cup raw cacao powder (**or** raw carob powder)
- ½ cup raw tahini (**or** nut butter of choice)
- 1 teaspoon pure vanilla extract
- ½ teaspoon high-quality salt (use less if nut butter is salty)
- ½ cup raw agave nectar

DIRECTIONS:
1. Line a cookie sheet with waxed paper. Place another sheet of waxed paper on the counter and cover with sesame seeds.
2. In a double boiler or a metal bowl placed over a saucepan of boiling water, gently melt coconut oil and cocoa butter. Remove from heat.
3. Add in raw cacao powder, tahini, vanilla, salt, and agave and stir well. If adding any additional ingredients, do so here.
4. Place the bowl in the refrigerator for 30 minutes.
5. Using a melon scooper or spoon, form the mixture into uniform balls. Roll each ball in sesame seeds to coat.
6. Place the coated sesame balls onto the cookie sheet lined with waxed paper, and place in the refrigerator for 15 more minutes.
7. Store in a glass container in a cool place or in the refrigerator or freezer.

OPTIONAL ADDITIONS:
- Add a pinch of cayenne for a spicy kick.
- Add coconut shreds, dried fruit, pumpkin or sunflower seeds, or chopped nuts.

Makes about 30 candies

Raw Candies And Treats

Coconut Haystacks

INGREDIENTS:
- ½ cup shredded coconut
- ¼ cup raw coconut oil
- ½ cup unrefined raw cocoa butter (or substitute with coconut butter **or** mango butter)
- 1 cup raw cacao powder (**or** raw carob powder)
- ⅓ cup raw agave nectar
- ¾ cup shredded coconut
- 2 Tablespoons goji berries (optional)
- ¼ cup nuts of your choice
- ¼ cup dried fruit of your choice
- ½ teaspoon Himalayan salt or high-quality salt
- 1 teaspoon pure vanilla extract

DIRECTIONS:
1. Line a cookie sheet with waxed paper. Place another sheet of waxed paper on the counter and cover with ½ cup shredded coconut.
2. In a double boiler or a metal bowl placed over a saucepan of boiling water, melt coconut oil and cocoa butter. Remove from heat.
3. Add in cacao powder, agave, ¾ cup shredded coconut, goji berries, nuts, fruit, salt, and stir well.
4. Using a melon scooper or spoon, form the mixture into uniform balls. Roll each ball in shredded coconut to coat. Place on the cookie sheet lined with waxed paper, then place in the freezer for about 10 minutes.
5. Store in a glass container in a cool place or in the refrigerator or freezer.

Makes about 30 candies

Hemp Chocolate Fudge Bars

INGREDIENTS:

- ¾ cup raw coconut oil
- ¼ cup unrefined raw cocoa butter (or substitute with coconut butter **or** mango butter)
- ½ cup raw coconut butter (or substitute with mango butter **or** cocoa butter)
- 2 cups raw cacao powder (**or** raw carob powder)
- ¾ cup raw agave nectar
- 1 ½ cups hulled hemp seeds
- 3 Tablespoons chia seeds
- 2 Tablespoons spirulina powder
- 2 Tablespoons maca powder
- 1 Tablespoon pure vanilla extract
- ½ teaspoon Himalayan salt or high-quality salt

DIRECTIONS:

1. In a double boiler or a metal bowl placed over a saucepan of boiling water, melt coconut oil, cocoa butter, and coconut butter. Remove from heat.
2. Add cacao powder, agave, hemp seeds, chia seeds, spirulina, maca, vanilla, and salt. Stir well.
3. Pour mixture onto a cookie sheet and evenly distribute. Place cookie sheet flat in the freezer for 1 hour, which helps firm the chocolate and makes it easy to cut.
4. Remove from freezer, cut into bars or squares, and store in a glass container.
5. Store in the refrigerator for a fudgy hemp bar or in the freezer for a harder candy.

Makes about 1 full cookie sheet of chocolate or about 50 squares

Raw Chocolate Truffles

INGREDIENTS:
- ¼ cup dried apricots, chopped
- ¼ cup medjool dates, chopped
- ⅔ cup raw tahini
- ½ cup raw cacao powder (**or** raw carob powder)
- ¼ cup goji berries
- 1 Tablespoon cacao nibs
- 2 Tablespoons agave nectar
- 1 teaspoon coconut oil
- ¼ teaspoon high-quality salt
- 1 teaspoon ginger powder (optional)
- 1 teaspoon maca powder (optional)

FOR DUSTING:
- ½ cup raw cacao power
- ½ cup raw cacao nibs

DIRECTIONS:
1. Finely chop the apricots and dates.
2. In a bowl, mix tahini with cacao powder, then add the chopped fruit, goji berries, cacao nibs, agave, coconut oil, and salt. If adding optional ginger and maca, do so here. Mix until smooth. Refrigerate for 30 minutes.
3. To dust the truffles, place cacao powder in one bowl and raw cacao nibs in another bowl. If the cacao nibs are big, try breaking them down first with a mortar and pestle.
4. Take the truffle mix out of the refrigerator. Using a melon scooper or spoon, scoop out the truffles and shape into uniform balls.
5. Roll in the cacao powder and then in raw cacao nibs.
6. Store in a glass container in a cool place or in the refrigerator or freezer.

Makes about 30 candies

Raw Chocolate Walnut Truffles

INGREDIENTS:
- 1 cup raw walnuts (**or** any other nut)
- ½ cup pitted dates
- 4 Tablespoons raw cacao powder (**or** raw carob powder)
- 1 Tablespoon agave nectar
- ¼ cup young coconut water (either fresh **or** canned, *not* coconut milk)

FOR DUSTING:
- ¼ cup raw cacao powder (**or** raw carob powder)

DIRECTIONS:
1. Blend walnuts and dates in a food processor until the mixture is smooth.
2. Add in cacao powder, agave, and coconut water. When the mixture forms a ball in the processor, stop blending.
3. Put the dusting cacao powder on a plate.
4. Using a melon scooper or spoon, scoop out the truffles and shape into uniform balls. Roll each ball in cacao powder.
5. Store in a glass container in a cool place or in the refrigerator or freezer.

Makes about a dozen candies

Raw Almond Chocolates

INGREDIENTS:
- ¼ cup raw agave nectar
- ½ cup raw almond butter
- 1 Tablespoon raw coconut oil
- ½ cup raw cacao powder (**or** raw carob powder)

DIRECTIONS:
1. Line a cookie sheet with waxed paper.
2. In a large mixing bowl, combine agave, almond butter, and coconut oil. Mix until smooth.
3. Mix in 4 Tablespoons raw cacao powder. Stir until completely smooth. Keep adding more cacao until the mixture has the consistency of dough.
4. Using a melon scooper or spoon, scoop out the truffles and shape into uniform balls and place on cookie sheet.
5. Freeze for about an hour or until the chocolate is firm.
6. Store in a glass container in the refrigerator or freezer.

Makes about a dozen candies

Carob Balls

INGREDIENTS:

- 1 cup raw agave nectar
- 1 cup raw almond butter
- 2 teaspoons pure vanilla extract
- 1 cup nuts, chopped
- ½ cup raw carob powder

- 1 cup sesame seeds
- 1 cup shredded coconut
- 1 cup chopped sunflower seeds

FOR DUSTING:

- ¼ cup sesame seeds **or** shredded coconut

DIRECTIONS:

1. Line a cookie sheet with waxed paper.
2. In a medium bowl, combine agave, almond butter, and vanilla. Mix until smooth and set aside.
3. In a separate bowl, add nuts, carob powder, sesame seeds, coconut, and sunflower seeds. Mix well.
4. Add dry ingredients to the agave mixture and mix until smooth.
5. Place sesame seeds or coconut on a plate.
6. Using a melon scooper or spoon, scoop out the mixture and shape into uniform balls.
7. Roll each ball in sesame seeds or shredded coconut.
8. Store in a glass container in the refrigerator or freezer.

Makes about 20 candies

Lemon Cashew Cookies

INGREDIENTS:

- 1 ½ cups raw cashews
- ½ cup shredded coconut
- 3 Tablespoons agave nectar

- 1 teaspoon pure vanilla extract
- 1 Tablespoon lemon zest (about 1 lemon)

DIRECTIONS:

1. Place cashews in blender and blend on low until you get a cashew powder.
2. In a medium bowl, combine cashew powder, coconut, agave, and vanilla.
3. Add lemon zest and stir well.
4. Using a melon scooper or spoon, scoop out the mixture and shape into uniform balls and place on Teflon dehydrator sheets.
5. Dehydrate the cookies at 105 °F overnight (about 10 hours).

Makes 12 cookies

My Raw Food Treat Creations:

*Use this section to write down some of your favorite
raw food treat recipes from this chapter.*

Recipe:

INGREDIENTS:

DIRECTIONS:

Serves _____

My Raw Food Treat Creations:

Use this section to write down some of your favorite raw food treat recipes from this chapter.

Recipe:

. . . .

INGREDIENTS:

. . . .

. . . .

. . . .

. . . .

. . . .

. . . .

. . . .

DIRECTIONS:

. . . .

. . . .

. . . .

. . . .

. . . .

. . . .

Serves _____

CHAPTER 19

CANDIES WITH A HEALTHY TWIST

Making Your Own Chocolate

Simple Chocolate Base Recipe 340

Chocolate Covered Cherries
and Strawberries 341

Truffles

Chocolate Framboise Rose Truffles...342

Pomegranate Chocolate Truffles 343

Chocolate Mint Truffles 344

Chocolate Lavender Truffles........345

Candies

Chocolate Peanut Butter Cups 346

Nougat Caramel Candy Bar 347

Peppermint Patties 348

Sesame Almond Candy 349

Sesame Crunch Candy..............350

Halvah 351

Chocolate Halvah.................. 351

Gluten-Free Halvah.................352

Tahini Candy 352

Easy Nutty Fudge...................353

Making Your Own Chocolate

Simple Chocolate Base Recipe

INGREDIENTS:
- ¼ cup coconut oil
- ½ cup unrefined cocoa butter
- ¼ cup coconut butter (or substitute with cocoa butter **or** mango butter)
- ¼ teaspoon high-quality salt
- 1 cup cocoa powder
- ½ cup agave nectar

DIRECTIONS:
1. In a double boiler or a metal bowl placed over a saucepan of boiling water, gently melt coconut oil, cocoa butter, coconut butter, and salt. Remove from heat.
2. Add cocoa powder and agave and mix well by hand, hand mixer, or immersion blender. Mixture should be thin enough to pour. Add a little more melted coconut oil if it is too thick.
3. Pour into chocolate molds (or onto a cookie sheet if you don't have molds) and freeze or refrigerate for 30-45 minutes or until solid.
4. Unmold chocolate once it is solid. (Or cut into squares if using a cookie sheet.)
   Tip: If the chocolate is soft at room temperature, add more cocoa butter next time.
5. Store in a glass container in a cool place or in the refrigerator or freezer.

OPTIONAL ADDITIONS:
Try adding one or more of the following:

- **Floral waters** like rosewater or orange blossom water
- **Dried fruit** like raspberries, blueberries, goji berries, or currants
- **Spices** like cardamom, cayenne, black pepper, lavender, or orange peel
- **Essential oils** like peppermint, lavender, orange, or bergamot
- **Nuts** like chopped almonds, hazelnuts, macadamia nuts, peanuts, or walnuts.

Makes 20-40 candies, depending on mold size

Chocolate Covered Cherries and Strawberries

Enjoy this wonderful summertime dessert either alone or with agave-sweetened whipped cream.

ADDITIONAL TOOLS NEEDED:
Cherry pitter

INGREDIENTS:
- 3 dozen of the best quality Bing cherries with stems **or** a large box of perfectly ripe strawberries
- 6 ounces unsweetened dark chocolate
- ½ cup agave nectar
- 1 Tablespoon coconut oil

DIRECTIONS:
1. Wash and blot dry cherries or strawberries.
2. Pit the cherries leaving the stem on. To do this press the cherry pitter into the side of the cherry until it meets the seed, then press quickly to expel the seed.
3. In a double boiler or a metal bowl placed over a saucepan of boiling water, melt chocolate. Add agave and stir until liquid. Mix in coconut oil.
4. Line a cookie sheet with waxed paper.
5. Dip the fruit, one at a time, into the melted chocolate-oil mixture, and place on the waxed paper.
6. Refrigerate for at least 1 hour to harden the coating on the fruit.

Makes about 3 dozen candies

Truffles

Truffles make an elegant addition to a tea party, gathering, wedding, or party.

Chocolate Framboise Rose Truffles

INGREDIENTS:
- 10 ounces unsweetened chocolate
- ⅓ cup agave nectar
- ⅔ cup coconut milk (do not use "lite" coconut milk)
- ¼ cup fine quality French Framboise liqueur
- Two dropperfuls of French Rose Absolute (see below)

FOR DUSTING:
- ½ cup cocoa powder

DIRECTIONS:
1. Line a cookie sheet with waxed paper. Place another sheet of waxed paper on the counter and cover with cocoa powder for dusting.
2. In a double boiler or a metal bowl placed over a saucepan of boiling water, melt chocolate. Add agave and stir until liquid.
3. Blend in coconut milk and mix until integrated and smooth.
4. Remove from heat and add Framboise and two dropperfuls of French Rose Absolute to the chocolate mixture and stir thoroughly.
5. Chill for 30 minutes or until hardened. Using a melon scooper or spoon, form the mixture into uniform balls. Roll each ball in cocoa powder. Add more as necessary.
6. Place truffles onto the cookie sheet and refrigerate for 15 minutes.
7. Store in a glass container in a cool place or in the refrigerator or freezer.
8. For an elegant touch, garnish with rose petals.

Makes about 20 truffles

How to make French Rose Absolute:

1. Fill a 1-ounce dropper bottle ¾ full with the strongest pure grain alcohol you can find. Use 151 proof vodka if you can't find anything stronger.
2. Add 5 drops of Rose Absolute essential oil to this mixture and shake vigorously to dissolve it completely.
3. Label your bottle and keep on hand for truffle making.

Pomegranate Chocolate Truffles

INGREDIENTS:
- 14 ounces unsweetened chocolate
- ½ cup agave nectar
- ⅔ cup pomegranate concentrate (available at Middle Eastern stores or online)
- ⅔ cup heavy whipping cream (preferably raw)
- 2 teaspoons pure vanilla extract

FOR DUSTING:
- ½ cup cocoa powder

DIRECTIONS:
1. In a double boiler or a metal bowl placed over a saucepan of boiling water, melt chocolate. Add agave and stir until liquid. Remove from heat.
2. Blend in pomegranate concentrate, cream, and vanilla and mix until smooth.
3. Chill in the refrigerator overnight or until it hardens.
4. Line a cookie sheet with waxed paper. Put another sheet of waxed paper on the counter and cover with ½ cup of cocoa powder for dusting. Add more as necessary.
5. Using a melon scooper or spoon, form the mixture into uniform balls. Roll each ball in cocoa powder. Place finished truffles on the cookie sheet.
6. Freeze until hardened, about 30 minutes.
7. Store in a glass container in a cool place or in the refrigerator or freezer.
8. For an elegant touch, garnish with fresh pomegranate seeds.

Makes about 30 truffles

Chocolate Mint Truffles

INGREDIENTS:
- 14 ounces of unsweetened chocolate
- ½ cup agave nectar
- ⅔ cup heavy whipping cream
- 5-6 drops food-grade peppermint **or** spearmint essential oil

FOR DUSTING:
- ½ cup cocoa powder

DIRECTIONS:
1. In a double boiler or a metal bowl placed over a saucepan of boiling water, melt chocolate. Add agave and stir until liquid. Remove from heat.
2. Blend in cream and stir well.
3. Add 5-6 drops of mint essential oil, according to taste. Stir well.
4. Chill in the refrigerator overnight or until it hardens.
5. Line a cookie sheet with waxed paper. Place another sheet of waxed paper on the counter and cover with ½ cup cocoa powder for dusting. Add more as necessary.
6. Using a melon scooper or spoon, form the mixture into uniform balls. Roll each ball in cocoa powder. Place finished truffles on the cookie sheet.
7. Freeze until hardened, about 30 minutes.
8. Store in a glass container in the refrigerator or freezer.
9. For an elegant touch, garnish with mint leaves.

Makes about 30 truffles

Chocolate Lavender Truffles

INGREDIENTS:
- 12 fresh lavender heads (**or** 6 Tablespoons dried flowers)
- ⅓ cup heavy whipping cream
- 10 ounces unsweetened chocolate, divided in half
- ½ cup agave nectar, divided in half
- 2 Tablespoons butter
- 1 drop food-grade lavender essential oil

DUSTING:
- ½ cup cocoa powder

DIRECTIONS:
For Lavender Cream:

1. If using fresh lavender, remove flowers from stems and measure 6 Tablespoons. If using dry, simply measure 6 Tablespoons.
2. Place cream in a metal bowl over a saucepan of simmering water. Add lavender and gently infuse in the cream, breaking the flowers into the cream. You should be able to taste the lavender in the cream.

For Chocolate:

1. While lavender infuses, melt half of the chocolate (5 ounces) in a double boiler or a metal bowl placed over a saucepan of boiling water. Mix in ¼ cup agave and stir well.
2. Strain the lavender cream into the chocolate mixture and stir well.
3. Chill in the refrigerator overnight or until it hardens.
4. Line a cookie sheet with waxed paper. Place another sheet of waxed paper on the counter and cover with ½ cup cocoa powder for dusting. Add more as necessary.
5. Using a melon scooper or spoon, form the mixture into uniform balls. Roll each ball in cocoa powder. Place finished truffles on the cookie sheet.
6. Freeze until hardened, about 30 minutes.
7. In a double boiler, melt remaining 5 ounces chocolate, ¼ cup agave, and butter. Stir until smooth. Remove from heat and add 1 drop lavender essential oil.
8. Remove the lavender balls from the freezer, and dip in melted chocolate. Return to cookie sheet and put in freezer for another 2 hours.
9. Store in a glass container in the refrigerator or freezer.
10. For an elegant touch, garnish with fresh lavender buds.

Makes about 20 truffles

Candies

Chocolate Peanut Butter Cups

INGREDIENTS:

Peanut Butter Filling:

- 1 cup freshly ground peanut butter (**or** almond butter)
- ¼ teaspoon high-quality salt
- ¼ cup agave nectar
- Water, as needed

Chocolate:

- 1 cup grain-sweetened chocolate chips
- 1 teaspoon coconut oil
- 1 teaspoon pure vanilla extract
- 1 teaspoon almond extract
- Miniature candy foil cups as molds

DIRECTIONS:

For Peanut Butter Filling:

1. In a small bowl, combine peanut butter, salt, and agave.
2. With a hand mixer or an immersion blender, cream ingredients, adding water as necessary.

For Chocolate Cups:

1. In a double boiler or a metal bowl placed over a saucepan of boiling water, melt chocolate and coconut oil. Add vanilla and almond extract.
2. Using a small pastry brush, paint melted chocolate over the entire interior surface of the mini foil cups. Place cups on a cookie sheet and freeze until chocolate has hardened.
3. Recoat with another layer of chocolate and freeze again. When set, carefully peel foil from chocolate cups. If chocolate softens, refreeze. Store molds in freezer until needed.
4. Gently spoon the peanut butter filling into chocolate cups so that the cups are ¾ full. Keep refrigerated until ready to serve. For an added touch, pipe the filling into the cups using a pastry tube fitted with a fluted edge.
5. Store in a glass container in the refrigerator or freezer.

Makes about 20 candies

Nougat Caramel Candy Bar

INGREDIENTS:

Caramel:

- 1 cup dates
- 1 cup water
- Juice of ½ lemon
- 1 Tablespoon coconut oil
- ¼ teaspoon high-quality salt
- ¼ cup agave nectar

Nougat Filling:

- 1 cup almonds (**or** peanuts)
- 1 cup cashews (**or** Brazil or macadamia nuts)
- 2 ¼ Tablespoons agave nectar
- 1 Tablespoon water or more if needed

Chocolate:

- 1 cup raw cacao powder (**or** cocoa powder)
- ¾ cup agave nectar
- ½ cup coconut butter
- ½ teaspoon pure vanilla extract **or** almond extract
- ¼ cup water

DIRECTIONS:

For the Caramel:

1. Soak the dates in 1 cup water and lemon juice for an hour. Remove the dates and reserve the soaking water.
2. In a blender, combine soaked dates, coconut oil, and sea salt. Blend, adding reserved soaking water 1 Tablespoon at a time until mixture is thick and creamy.

For the Nougat:

1. Line a cookie sheet with waxed paper.
2. In a coffee grinder or blender, grind almonds and cashews into a fine powder.
3. In a medium bowl, combine nut powders, agave, and water. Stir until mixture has a thick paste-like consistency. Form the nougat into 1" squares. Arrange on a cookie sheet. Freeze for 1 hour.
4. Once frozen, remove nougat from the freezer. Gently spread caramel over the top. Then return to the freezer while you make the chocolate.

For the Chocolate:

1. In a large bowl, combine cocoa powder, agave, coconut butter, vanilla or almond extract, and water and mix until smooth and creamy.
2. Remove candies from the freezer. Cut into bars, if desired. Dip each candy into the chocolate. Place on cookie sheet and freeze for an additional hour or until the chocolate hardens.
3. Store in a glass container in the refrigerator or freezer.

Makes about 30 candies

Peppermint Patties

INGREDIENTS:

Mint Layer:

- 3 cups shredded coconut
- ⅓ cup agave nectar
- ½ teaspoon mint extract **or** 3 drops food-grade peppermint essential oil

Chocolate:

- 3 cups shredded coconut
- ⅓ cup agave nectar
- ⅛ cup cocoa powder, raw cacao powder, **or** raw carob powder
- ½ teaspoon pure vanilla extract
- ⅛ teaspoon high-quality salt

DIRECTIONS:

For Mint Layer:

1. Blend 3 cups coconut in a Vita-mix on low speed. Use a spatula to scrape down sides and blend until the mixture becomes the consistency of butter. Do not overblend or the oil will separate from the butter. If you don't have a Vita-Mix, use an ordinary blender, but blend in two separate batches of 1 ½ cups of coconut at time.
2. In a medium bowl, combine coconut butter paste, agave, and mint extract. Use a spatula to mix well. Set aside.

For Chocolate:

1. Repeat the process of making coconut butter. Blend 3 cups of coconut in a Vita-mix on low speed with the lid off.
2. When it reaches the desired consistency, place in a separate bowl and mix in agave, cocoa powder, vanilla, and salt. Mix well and set aside.

Assemble the Chocolates:

1. Press half of the chocolate into the bottom a 4" square baking dish or other container.
2. Place in freezer for 5 minutes or until solid.
3. Remove from freezer and spread mint filling over the chocolate. Return to freezer for 5 more minutes.
4. Spread the second half of the chocolate mixture over the mint layer. Freeze until solid.
5. To remove chocolates from pan, gently pry out candies with a spatula and place on a cutting board. Cut your patties into the desired shape using a sharp, thin knife.
6. Store in a glass container in the refrigerator or freezer.

Makes about 30 candies

Sesame Almond Candy

INGREDIENTS:
- ½ cup almonds, soaked overnight
- 1 cup almond butter
- ⅓ cup agave nectar
- ¼ teaspoon high-quality salt
- ⅓ cup raisins
- 1 Tablespoon flaxseed oil
- 6 Tablespoons sesame seeds

DIRECTIONS:
1. In a glass bowl, cover almonds with water and soak overnight. If you do not get to them the next day, simply rinse with fresh water, and try again the next day. (Don't wait more than 3 days.)
2. Chop the soaked almonds into small pieces and place in a large bowl.
3. Add almond butter, agave, salt, raisins, flax oil, and 1 Tablespoon sesame seeds and mix well.
4. Cover a plate with about 5 Tablespoons sesame seeds (more if needed). Form the almond mixture into balls and roll in sesame seeds to coat.
5. Store in a glass container in the refrigerator.

Makes about 25 candies

Sesame Crunch Candy

INGREDIENTS:

- Neutral-tasting oil (grapeseed, untoasted sesame oil, coconut oil, **or** ghee) for greasing pan
- 2 cups sesame seeds
- 2 Tablespoons black sesame seeds (optional)
- ⅔ cup agave nectar
- ½ teaspoon high-quality salt

DIRECTIONS:

1. Grease a cookie sheet.
2. Tear off a piece of parchment paper that is a little bigger than the cookie sheet and set aside.
3. In a large skillet, toast regular and black sesame seeds over medium heat until golden and aromatic. Set aside a spoonful of untoasted seeds to compare the color. Stir often at the beginning, then continuously as the seeds begin to change color. Watch closely to prevent burning. Remove immediately from heat and transfer to a cool container so they don't continue to cook. Set aside.
4. Add optional additions to sesame seeds.
5. In the same skillet, add agave and salt. Bring to a boil on medium heat, stirring continuously, then let boil for 10 minutes, still stirring. Remove from heat.
6. Working quickly, stir seeds into the agave mixture. Transfer immediately to the baking sheet, spreading as best you can with a spatula. Place the parchment over the top to protect hands, then use the palm of your hand to press the seeds into an even and thin sheet. A rolling pin works well to create an even sheet. Remove the parchment paper.
7. Cut into squares of any size or allow to cool for 15 minutes, then break candy into pieces.
8. Store in layers separated by waxed paper in a glass container.

OPTIONAL ADDITIONS:

- Add ¼ teaspoon cayenne pepper
- Add ½ teaspoon ginger or cinnamon
- Add ¼ cup hijiki, arame, or sea palm seaweed
- Add 1 Tablespoon chia seeds

Makes about 30 candies

Halvah

INGREDIENTS:
- ½ cup agave nectar
- ½ cup butter
- 1 cup tahini (sesame seed butter)

- 1 teaspoon pure vanilla extract
- 1 ½ cups oat flour

DIRECTIONS:
1. In a small saucepan, boil agave on medium-high heat for 10 minutes to reduce volume.
2. In a double boiler or metal bowl placed over a saucepan of boiling water, melt butter. Remove from heat.
3. Add agave, tahini, and vanilla and mix until smooth.
4. Stir in oat flour and mix thoroughly. Let sit for an hour.
5. Preheat the oven to 325°F.
6. Spread mixture into an 8" square baking pan.
7. Bake for 10 minutes, cool, then cut into 2" squares and cover to store.

Makes about 30 pieces

Tip
Tahini separates in the jar, be sure to mix it well to reintegrate the oil before using.

Chocolate Halvah

INGREDIENTS:
- ½ cup agave nectar
- ½ cup butter
- 1 cup tahini (sesame seed butter)

- 1 teaspoon pure vanilla extract
- ¾ cup cocoa powder
- ¾ cup oat flour

DIRECTIONS:
1. In a small saucepan, boil agave on medium-high heat for 10 minutes to reduce volume.
2. In a double boiler or metal bowl placed over a saucepan of boiling water, melt butter. Remove from heat.
3. Add agave, tahini, and vanilla and mix until smooth.
4. Stir in the oat flour and cocoa powder and mix thoroughly. Let sit for an hour.
5. Preheat the oven to 325°F.
6. Spread mixture into an 8" square baking pan.
7. Bake for 10 minutes, cool, then cut into 2" squares and cover to store.

Makes about 30 pieces

Gluten-Free Halvah

INGREDIENTS:
- ½ cup agave nectar
- ½ cup butter
- 1 cup tahini (sesame seed paste)
- 1 teaspoon pure vanilla extract

- ½ cup millet flour (**or** cocoa powder)
- ½ cup sorghum flour
- ½ cup tapioca flour

DIRECTIONS:
1. In a small saucepan, boil agave on medium-high heat for 10 minutes to reduce volume.
2. In a double boiler or metal bowl placed over a saucepan of boiling water, melt butter. Remove from heat.
3. Add agave, tahini, and vanilla and mix until smooth.
4. Stir in the millet, sorghum, and tapioca flour and mix thoroughly. Let sit for an hour.
5. Preheat the oven to 325°F.
6. Spread mixture into an 8" square baking pan.
7. Bake for 10 minutes, cool, then cut into 2" squares and cover to store.

Makes about 30 pieces

Tahini Candy

INGREDIENTS:
- 1 cup tahini (sesame seed paste)
- ¼ cup nutritional yeast
- ½ cup hemp seeds
- 4 ½ Tablespoons agave nectar

- 2 Tablespoons coconut oil
- ½ cup raisins **or** any other dried fruit
- Sesame seeds

DIRECTIONS:
1. Line a cookie sheet with waxed paper. Place another sheet of waxed paper on the counter and cover with sesame seeds.
2. In a medium bowl, mix tahini, yeast, hemp seeds, agave, coconut oil, and raisins.
3. Roll the mixture into balls and coat with sesame seeds.
4. Store in a glass container, either in the refrigerator or in a cool place.

Makes about 30 candies

Easy Nutty Fudge

INGREDIENTS:
- ½ cup nut butter (such as tahini, almond, peanut, cashew, **or** sunflower)
- ¼ cup agave nectar
- 1 teaspoon pure hazelnut **or** vanilla extract

DIRECTIONS:
1. In a medium bowl, combine all ingredients until smooth.
2. Smooth candy in small square dish. Place in the refrigerator for 30 minutes.
3. Cut into squares.
4. Store in a glass container, either in the refrigerator or in a cool place.

OPTIONAL ADDITION:
Try adding cocoa powder, raw cacao powder, or carob powder for a chocolate fudge.

Makes about 30 pieces

My Healthy Candy Creations:

Use this section to write down some of your favorite healthy candy recipes from this chapter.

Recipe:

INGREDIENTS:

DIRECTIONS:

Serves _____

CHAPTER 20

SNACKS

Snack Bars and Energy Bars

Chocolate Chip Oat Bars. 356

Granola Bars .357

Homemade Protein Bar
Base Recipe. 358

Maca Energy Bar 359

Almond Flax Nut Bar. 359

Green Energy Bar 360

Spirulina Chia Energy Bar 360

Oat Bran Bars 361

Oat Prune Bars. 362

Other Snacks

Sesame Bars .363

Sweet Chipotle Cashew Crunch . . 364

Coconut Melon Snack 365

Banana Coconut Snack 365

Fried Bananas with
Chocolate Sauce 366

Chocolate Chip Oat Bars

These are great for snacking on the go! They can also be made ahead of time and frozen.

INGREDIENTS:
- Neutral-tasting oil (grapeseed, untoasted sesame oil, coconut oil, **or** ghee) **or** melted butter for greasing pan
- 1 cup butter, softened
- ⅓ cup agave nectar
- 1 teaspoon pure vanilla extract
- 1 ½ cups oat flour
- 1 ½ cups rolled oats
- 1 teaspoon high-quality salt
- 1 cup grain-sweetened chocolate chips

DIRECTIONS:
1. Preheat oven to 350°F. Grease a 9" x 13" pan.
2. In large bowl, mix butter, agave, and vanilla until smooth and creamy.
3. Add oat flour, rolled oats, and salt and mix well.
4. Stir in chocolate chips.
5. Press into pan.
6. Bake for 20-30 minutes or until light golden brown around the edges. Remove from oven and cool.
7. Cut into bars, then wrap in waxed paper, tape closed, label, and date. Freeze for future use, if desired.

Makes about 25 squares

Granola Bars

INGREDIENTS:
- Neutral-tasting oil **or** melted butter for greasing pan
- ½ cup agave nectar
- 1 cup neutral-tasting oil (grapeseed, untoasted sesame oil, coconut oil, **or** ghee)
- 2 eggs
- 2 cups rolled oats
- 1 ½ cups oat flour
- 1 teaspoon baking soda
- 1 cup raisins **or** diced dates
- 1 cup chopped nuts (optional)
- 1 ½ teaspoons ground cinnamon
- ¼ teaspoon high-quality salt

AGAVE GLAZE:
- ¼ cup agave nectar
- 2 Tablespoons organic butter

DIRECTIONS:
1. Preheat oven to 350°F. Grease a 15 ½" x 10 ½" jellyroll pan.
2. Whisk agave, oil, and eggs in a large bowl until smooth.
3. Add oats, oat flour, baking soda, raisins, nuts, spices, and salt. Mix well.
4. Spread mixture into the pan with spatula.
5. Bake for 17-22 minutes. Remove from oven and cool.
6. Heat ¼ cup agave and 2 Tablespoons butter in a 1-quart pan over medium heat. Stir constantly until butter is melted.
7. Cut the granola bars into 1-serving sizes and drizzle with agave glaze.
8. Wrap in waxed paper, tape closed, label, and date. Freeze for future use, if desired.

Makes about 20 bars

Homemade Protein Bar Base Recipe

Why spend 3 dollars for a protein bar when you can make your own with higher quality ingredients at a lower cost? Make ahead of time and freeze them, then pull one out to take on the go! These are also great (and nutritious) in a kid's lunch box.

INGREDIENTS:
- Neutral-tasting oil (grapeseed, untoasted sesame oil, coconut oil, **or** ghee) for greasing pan
- 1 cup nut butter of your choice
- ½ cup agave nectar
- ¼ teaspoon pure vanilla extract
- ⅓ cup sunflower seeds
- ⅔ cup dried fruit of choice
- 3 Tablespoons seeds of choice
- ⅓ cup shredded coconut, seeds, **or** chopped nuts
- 3 cups puffed whole grain cereal (kamut, brown rice, amaranth, **or** quinoa)

DIRECTIONS:
1. Grease an 8" square pan or jellyroll pan.
2. In a large bowl, combine nut butter, agave, and vanilla and mix until smooth.
3. Add sunflower seeds, dried fruit, seeds, and coconut and combine thoroughly with the nut butter mixture.
4. Add cereal and stir until all ingredients are well combined.
5. Wet hands slightly, then firmly press the mixture into the oiled pan.
6. Cut into bars, then wrap in waxed paper, tape closed, label, and date. Freeze for future use, if desired.

OPTIONAL VARIATIONS:
Try one or more of the following for a superfood boost:

- Add 1 Tablespoon spirulina, maca powder, chia seeds
- Add 1 Tablespoon mushroom powder, such as reishi
- Add 1 Tablespoon raw cacao powder

Makes about 20 bars

Maca Energy Bar

INGREDIENTS:

- Neutral-tasting oil (grapeseed, untoasted sesame oil, coconut oil, **or** ghee) for greasing pan
- 1 cup nut butter of your choice
- ½ cup agave nectar
- ¼ teaspoon pure vanilla extract
- ⅓ cup sunflower seeds
- ⅔ cup diced dried fruit of choice
- 3 Tablespoons sesame seeds
- 2 Tablespoons flax seeds
- ¼ cup maca powder
- 3 cups puffed whole grain cereal (kamut, brown rice, amaranth, **or** quinoa)

DIRECTIONS:

1. Grease an 8" square pan or jellyroll pan.
2. In a large bowl, combine nut butter, agave, and vanilla and mix until smooth.
3. Add the sunflower seeds, dried fruit, sesame seeds, flax seeds, and maca powder and combine thoroughly with the nut butter mixture.
4. Add cereal and stir until all ingredients are well combined.
5. Wet hands slightly, then firmly press the mixture into the oiled pan.
6. Cut into bars, then wrap in waxed paper, tape closed, label, and date. Freeze for future use, if desired.

Makes about 20 bars

Almond Flax Nut Bar

INGREDIENTS:

- Neutral-tasting oil (grapeseed, untoasted sesame oil, coconut oil, **or** ghee) for greasing pan
- 1 cup almond butter
- ½ cup agave nectar
- ¼ teaspoon pure vanilla extract
- ⅓ cup chopped nuts of choice
- ⅓ cup raisins
- 3 Tablespoons chia seeds
- ⅔ cup flax seeds
- 3 cups puffed millet **or** other puffed whole grain cereal

DIRECTIONS:

1. Grease an 8" square pan or jellyroll pan.
2. In a large bowl, combine the almond butter, agave, and vanilla and mix until smooth.
3. Add nuts, raisins, chia seeds, and flax seeds and mix thoroughly with the nut butter mixture.
4. Add puffed millet and stir until all ingredients are well combined.
5. Wet hands slightly, then firmly press the mixture into the oiled pan.
6. Cut into bars, then wrap in waxed paper, tape closed, label, and date. Freeze for future use, if desired.

Makes about 20 bars

Green Energy Bar

INGREDIENTS:
- Neutral-tasting oil (grapeseed, untoasted sesame oil, coconut oil, **or** ghee) for greasing pan
- 1 cup nut butter of your choice
- ½ cup agave nectar
- 1 teaspoon pure vanilla extract
- 1 cup hulled hemp seeds
- ⅔ cup dried fruit of choice
- 2 Tablespoons spirulina powder
- 3 cups puffed brown rice cereal (**or** other whole grain cereal)

DIRECTIONS:
1. Grease an 8" square pan or jellyroll pan.
2. In a large bowl, combine nut butter, agave, and vanilla and mix until smooth.
3. Add hemp seeds, dried fruit, and spirulina and mix thoroughly with the nut butter mixture.
4. Add cereal and stir until all ingredients are well combined.
5. Wet hands slightly, then firmly press the mixture into the oiled pan.
6. Cut into bars, then wrap in waxed paper, tape closed, label, and date. Freeze for future use, if desired.

Makes about 20 bars

Spirulina Chia Energy Bar

INGREDIENTS:
- Neutral-tasting oil (grapeseed, untoasted sesame oil, coconut oil, **or** ghee) for greasing pan
- 1 ½ Tablespoons spirulina powder
- 2 cups oat flour
- 1 ½ Tablespoons raw cacao powder
- 1 Tablespoon chia seeds
- 1 cup nut butter of choice
- ½ cup agave nectar

DIRECTIONS:
1. Grease a 9" x 16" pan or jellyroll pan.
2. In a large bowl, mix spirulina, oat flour, raw cacao powder, and chia seeds.
3. In another bowl, mix the nut butter and agave. Mix well and add to the dry mixture.
4. Using your hands, thoroughly mix all ingredients. If mixture is too sticky, add a little more flour. Knead it with your hands and make sure all the ingredients are well combined. If mixture is too dry, add a little more nut butter.
5. Wet hands slightly, then firmly press the mixture into the oiled pan.
6. Cut into bars, then wrap in waxed paper, tape closed, label, and date. Freeze for future use, if desired.

Makes about 20 bars

Oat Bran Bars

INGREDIENTS:
- Neutral-tasting oil for greasing pan
- 3 cups oat bran
- 1 ⅓ cups rolled oats
- ½ cup raisins
- ½ cup chopped nuts **or** sunflower seeds
- ½ cup agave nectar
- ⅓ cup neutral-tasting oil (grapeseed, untoasted sesame oil, coconut oil, **or** ghee)

DIRECTIONS:
1. Grease a 9" x 12" baking pan.
2. In large bowl, combine oat bran, rolled oats, raisins, and nuts and mix well.
3. In a saucepan, heat agave and bring to a light boil for 5 minutes. Add oil and remove from heat. Pour over oat-nut mixture and toss to coat.
4. Press evenly into prepared pan. Let stand 1 hour.
5. Cut into bars, then wrap in waxed paper, tape closed, label, and date. Freeze for future use, if desired.

Makes about 25 bars

Oat Prune Bars

INGREDIENTS:
- Neutral-tasting oil (grapeseed, untoasted sesame oil, coconut oil, **or** ghee) for greasing pan
- 1 ¼ cups pitted prunes
- ½ cup orange juice
- 1 cup oat flour
- 1 cup rolled oats
- ½ teaspoon baking soda
- ½ teaspoon high-quality salt
- ¼ teaspoon ground cinnamon
- ½ cup nuts, chopped (optional)
- 6 Tablespoons butter, softened
- ½ cup agave nectar
- 1 egg

DIRECTIONS:
1. Preheat oven to 350°F. Grease an 8" square baking pan.
2. Blend prunes and orange juice in a blender until almost smooth, being sure to scrape down the sides. Add to a small saucepan and gently boil over medium heat until thickened, stirring often. Set aside.
3. In a small bowl, combine oat flour, rolled oats, baking soda, and salt and stir until completely mixed.
4. In a large bowl, cream together butter and agave. Beat in egg. Add dry ingredients and mix until well combined.
5. Evenly spread half of the oat mixture on the bottom of your pan.
6. Cover with orange-prune-nut mixture to within ½" of edges.
7. Crumble the remaining oat mixture over top to cover the prune mixture. Pat down gently.
8. Bake for 30-35 minutes or until browned and springy to the touch.
9. Cut into bars, then wrap in waxed paper, tape closed, label, and date. Freeze for future use, if desired.

Makes about 20 bars

Sesame Bars

INGREDIENTS:
- Neutral-tasting oil (grapeseed, untoasted sesame oil, coconut oil, **or** ghee) for greasing pan
- 1 cup agave nectar
- 1 cup rolled oats (**or** other rolled whole grains)
- 1 teaspoon orange zest
- 2 cups sesame seeds
- 1 ½ cups shredded coconut
- 1 teaspoon pure vanilla extract
- 1 teaspoon high-quality salt
- 4 Tablespoons nut butter of your choice
- ½ cup chopped nuts (optional)

DIRECTIONS:
1. Preheat oven to 350°F. Grease an 8" square baking pan.
2. In a large bowl, mix all ingredients well.
3. Pat mixture into baking pan uniformly.
4. Bake for 45 minutes or until golden brown. Allow to cool.
5. Cut into bars, then wrap in waxed paper, tape closed, label, and date. Freeze for future use, if desired.

Makes about 20 bars

Sweet Chipotle Cashew Crunch

INGREDIENTS:
- Neutral-tasting oil (grapeseed, untoasted sesame oil, coconut oil, **or** ghee) for greasing foil
- 2 ½ cups roasted cashews
- ½ cup roasted sunflower seeds
- ¼ cup (half a stick) butter
- ½ cup agave nectar
- 1 teaspoon chipotle powder (**or** any other chili powder)
- ½ teaspoon high-quality salt
- 3 Tablespoons sesame seeds

DIRECTIONS:
1. Place a sheet of foil on a cookie sheet and grease with oil.
2. Roast cashews and sunflower seeds (if unroasted) in a dry skillet. Stir frequently and remove from heat once the nuts and seeds are roasted. Nuts are done when they are fragrant. Be careful not to burn. Set aside.
3. In a medium saucepan, over medium heat, add butter, agave, chipotle, and salt. Stir constantly and cook for about 10 minutes.
4. Add roasted cashews, roasted sunflower seeds, and sesame seeds. Turn heat to high and stir until mixture is very thick and the nuts and seeds begin to brown, 4-6 minutes.
5. Immediately pour mixture onto the greased foil, spreading as thinly as possible with the back of a spoon.
6. Cool until mixture is lukewarm, about 15 minutes.
7. With your hands, release brittle from foil, then pull or break it into bite-sized pieces. Once cool, immediately store in a glass airtight container.

Makes about 30 pieces

Coconut Melon Snack

INGREDIENTS:
- 1 cup coconut milk
- 2 Tablespoons agave nectar
- 1 teaspoon fresh lime juice
- ¼ cup shredded coconut
- 1 melon, scooped into balls or cubed

DIRECTIONS:
1. In a large bowl, combine coconut milk, agave, and lime juice. Mix well.
2. Scoop out melon with a melon scooper or cut into cubes and add to the bowl.
3. Add shredded coconut and stir gently to combine ingredients.
4. Serve in parfait glasses on a hot summer day.

Serves 6

Banana Coconut Snack

INGREDIENTS:
- 4 ripe bananas
- 2 cups coconut milk
- 2 teaspoons arrowroot flour
- 2 Tablespoons agave nectar
- ½ teaspoon ground cinnamon
- 2 Tablespoons coconut oil

DIRECTIONS:
1. Peel the bananas and cut longways into ¼" wide strips.
2. In a medium saucepan, combine coconut milk and arrowroot flour. Stir and bring to boil. Add agave and cinnamon and stir. Simmer for 5-10 minutes.
3. Heat coconut oil in a frying pan or cast iron skillet. When oil is hot, drop in the bananas. Cook for 3 minutes on each side, then remove and serve on plates.
4. Top with coconut sauce and serve hot.
5. For an added touch, top with shredded coconut or raw cacao nibs.

Serves 4

Fried Bananas with Chocolate Sauce

INGREDIENTS:

Chocolate Sauce:

- 2 Tablespoons coconut oil
- 1 Tablespoon coconut butter
- ¼ cup cocoa powder
- 3 Tablespoons agave nectar
- 2 teaspoons arrowroot flour
- ¼ cup almond milk

Bananas:

- 4 ripe bananas
- 2 Tablespoons coconut oil
- ½ teaspoon ground cinnamon **or** allspice

DIRECTIONS:

1. First, prepare the chocolate sauce. In a small saucepan, heat coconut oil, coconut butter, cocoa powder, and agave.
2. In a small bowl, dissolve the arrowroot flour in the almond milk. Add to saucepan and stir. Simmer for 10 minutes.
3. Cut bananas longways into ¼" thick strips.
4. Heat coconut oil in a frying pan or cast iron skillet and add spices. Let spices cook in the oil for 1 minute and then lay the bananas in the pan. Cook for 3 minutes on each side, then remove and serve on plates.
5. Top with chocolate sauce and serve hot.
6. For an added touch, top with shredded coconut or raw cacao nibs.

Serves 4

My Snack Creations:

Use this section to write down some of your favorite customized snack recipes from this chapter.

Recipe:
· ·

INGREDIENTS:

DIRECTIONS:

Serves _____

My Snack Creations:

Use this section to write down some of your favorite customized snack recipes from this chapter.

Recipe:

. . . .

INGREDIENTS:

....

....

....

....

....

....

....

DIRECTIONS:

....

....

....

....

....

....

Serves ....

CHAPTER 21

FUN FOODS FOR KIDS
(AND THE YOUNG AT HEART)

Fun Foods

Gelatin-Free Agar Jello 370

Digestive Biscuits for Toddlers 371

Brown Rice Crispy Treats. 372

Peanut Butter Rice Crispy Treats. 372

Caramel Corn 373

Sweet and Cheesy Popcorn 374

Popsicles

Fruit Juice Popsicles Base Recipe 375

Peach Blueberry Fruit Popsicles 376

Creamy Piña Colada Popsicles. 376

Creamy Mango Coconut Popsicles . . . 377

Creamy Apricot Popsicles. 377

Coco-Coconut Banana Popsicles 378

Banana Chocolate Crunch Popsicles 378

Herbal Popsicles Base Recipe 379

Mint Apple 380

Milky Lavender 380

Rose Pomegranate 380

Citrus Raspberry. 380

Elderberry Blueberry 380

Green Tea Popsicles 381

Sweet Red Bean Popsicles. 381

Lemonade Popsicles 382

Chocolate Fudge Popsicles. 382

Gelatin-Free Agar Jello

Instead of gelatin, this recipe calls for agar-agar, a tasteless seaweed that thickens and gelatinizes, making it an excellent option for vegetarians. Nutritionally, agar-agar contains iodine, calcium, iron, and phosphorous, and is a good source of natural fiber.

ADDITIONAL TOOLS NEEDED:
- *Jello molds*
- *Parfait glasses or medium bowl*

INGREDIENTS:
- 2 cups fruit juice (**or** sparkling wine for adults)
- 1 Tablespoon agar-agar flakes **or** 1 ½ teaspoons agar-agar powder
- 2 Tablespoons agave nectar
- Fresh sliced fruit of choice (avoid kiwi and pineapple which interfere with the gelatinizing process)

DIRECTIONS:
1. In a saucepan, gently heat the juice, then add agar-agar and agave. Stir well and bring to a boil. Reduce heat and simmer, stirring for about 5 minutes or until the agar-agar is dissolved.
2. Pour agar-agar mixture into mold, glasses, or bowl.
3. Gently layer fruit into each container.
4. Cover and chill about 2-4 hours or until soft set.

OPTIONAL VARIATIONS:
Instead of juice, try purée of peach or pear.

Makes about 2 cups

Digestive Biscuits for Toddlers

Make your own homemade biscuits for children using this simple, wholesome recipe made with quality ingredients.

INGREDIENTS:
- 1 cup kamut flour
- ½ cup tapioca flour
- ½ cup rolled oats
- ¼ cup ground flax seeds
- ¼ cup wheat germ
- ¼ cup sesame seeds
- ¼ cup shredded coconut
- ½ teaspoon high-quality salt
- ¼ teaspoon baking soda
- 2 Tablespoons buttermilk powder
- ¼ cup agave nectar
- ½ cup (1 stick) butter
- ⅓ cup cold water
- 1 teaspoon pure vanilla extract
- Neutral-tasting oil (grapeseed, untoasted sesame oil, coconut oil, **or** ghee) **or** melted butter for greasing pan

DIRECTIONS:
1. Combine dry ingredients: kamut flour, tapioca flour, rolled oats, flax seeds, wheat germ, sesame seeds, coconut, salt, baking soda, and buttermilk powder in large bowl.
2. Combine wet ingredients: agave, butter, water, and vanilla in another bowl.
3. Add just enough of the wet ingredients to the dry ingredients to mix it evenly, then continue adding slowly to avoid clumps. Blend until dough can be packed into a ball. Refrigerate for at least 30 minutes and up to 24 hours.
4. Preheat oven to 325°F.
5. Dust a surface with kamut flour. With a floured rolling pin. roll dough out ⅛" thick. Cut with cookie cutters in desired shapes.
6. Bake on greased cookie sheet for 20-25 minutes.

Makes about 2 dozen biscuits

Brown Rice Crispy Treats

INGREDIENTS:
- 3 Tablespoons butter
- ¾ cup agave nectar
- 4 cups puffed brown rice (**or** other puffed whole grain cereal, such as amaranth, kamut, etc.)
- Butter for greasing pan

DIRECTIONS:
1. Combine butter and agave in a large saucepan and boil for 5 minutes.
2. Remove from heat and add puffed grain.
3. Evenly spread the mixture into a buttered 8" square baking pan.
4. Let cool and cut into squares.

Makes about 16 squares

Peanut Butter Rice Crispy Treats

These are great for parties or for Halloween. Cut into squares and serve in decorative baking cups.

INGREDIENTS:
- 1 Tablespoon butter
- ¾ cup agave nectar
- 1 cup peanut butter
- 4 cups puffed brown rice (**or** other puffed whole grain, such as amaranth, kamut, millet, etc.)
- Butter for greasing pan

DIRECTIONS:
1. Combine butter and agave in a large saucepan and boil for 5 minutes.
2. Remove from heat and add peanut butter. Mix well. If the peanut butter is lumpy, try using an immersion blender to get all the ingredients smooth and well mixed.
3. Add puffed grain and combine all ingredients gently.
4. Evenly spread the mixture into a buttered 8" square baking pan.
5. Let cool and cut into squares.

Makes about 16 squares

Caramel Corn

INGREDIENTS:

Popcorn:

- ⅔ cup corn kernels
- 4 Tablespoons neutral-tasting oil (grapeseed, untoasted sesame oil, coconut oil, **or** ghee)

Caramel Sauce:

- 1 ⅔ cups dark amber agave nectar
- 1 cup (2 sticks) butter
- 1 Tablespoon molasses
- 1 teaspoon high-quality salt
- ½ teaspoon baking soda
- 2 cups salted chopped nuts (optional)

DIRECTIONS:

For the Popcorn:

1. Heat oil in a large saucepan.
2. Add popcorn kernels and cover pan with lid. Keep on low to medium heat.
3. When the corn starts to pop, keeping the lid on the pan, lift the pan off the burner or flame and swirl. Return to heat. When you no longer hear popcorn popping, remove from heat and uncover. You can avoid this step if you have a popcorn popper, which is a bit easier.

For the Caramel Sauce:

4. Preheat oven to 225°F. Place your popped popcorn in large roasting pan and set aside.
5. In a small saucepan, combine agave, butter, molasses, and salt. Cook over medium heat, stirring occasionally, until mixture comes to a full boil. Continue to cook, stirring occasionally, until candy thermometer reaches 250°F.
6. Remove from heat and stir in baking soda. The caramel will foam up a little and turn a lighter color when you add the baking soda.
7. Carefully pour the hot caramel mixture over the popcorn. Add nuts, if desired. Using a wooden spoon, stir until all popcorn is coated with caramel.
8. Bake for 20 minutes. Remove from oven, stir to evenly coat the popcorn with the caramel sauce, and return again to the oven. Bake for another 20 minutes, then remove from oven. Immediately spread caramel corn out onto waxed paper and let it cool completely.
9. Break the caramel corn into bite-sized pieces, and store in a tightly covered glass container.

Makes about 5 quarts

Sweet and Cheesy Popcorn

This is a fantastic after-school snack that kids will love.

INGREDIENTS:

- 3 Tablespoons neutral-tasting oil (grapeseed, untoasted sesame oil, coconut oil, **or** ghee)
- ½ cup popping corn kernels
- 2 Tablespoons agave nectar
- 4-5 Tablespoons nutritional yeast
- 1 Tablespoon butter, melted (use oil for dairy free)
- 2 teaspoons spirulina (optional for an added nutritional boost, will make the popcorn green)
- High-quality salt to taste

DIRECTIONS:

1. Heat oil in a large saucepan.
2. Add popcorn kernels and cover pan with lid. Keep on low to medium heat.
3. When the corn starts to pop, keeping the lid on the pan, lift the pan off the burner or flame and swirl. Return to heat. When you no longer hear popcorn popping, remove from heat and uncover. You can avoid this step if you have a popcorn popper, which is a bit easier.
4. Add remaining ingredients: agave, nutritional yeast, butter, spirulina, and salt and stir well. Add desired optional flavorings and additions here.

OPTIONAL VARIATIONS:
You can create various different flavors by adding: cayenne pepper, black pepper, cumin, cocoa powder, sesame seeds, powdered nettles, powdered seaweed, vanilla powder, nutmeg, raw cacao powder, cinnamon, or date sugar.

Makes 5 quarts

Popsicles

Fruit Juice Popsicles Base Recipe

ADDITIONAL TOOLS NEEDED:
- *Popsicle molds*
- *Wooden popsicle sticks*

INGREDIENTS:
- 1 Tablespoon agave nectar
- 2 cups fruit juice of your choice (apple, orange, grapefruit, blueberry, pineapple, cherry, carrot, pomegranate, etc.)
- Chunks of fruit (optional)

DIRECTIONS:
1. Stir agave into juice.
2. Add chunks of fruit, if you desire.
3. Pour into popsicle molds and freeze for about 30 minutes. Insert sticks and return to freezer.
4. Freeze the popsicles for at least 6 hours.

OPTIONAL VARIATIONS:
Try these with juice blends like cranberry-apple, blueberry-pomegranate, cherry-raspberry, pomegranate-cherry, carrot-ginger-apple, orange-banana, pineapple-orange, etc.

Makes about a dozen popsicles

Peach Blueberry Fruit Popsicles

ADDITIONAL TOOLS NEEDED:
- *Popsicle molds*
- *Wooden popsicle sticks*
- *Blender*

INGREDIENTS:
- 1 cup of fresh **or** frozen peaches
- ½ cup of fresh **or** frozen blueberries
- 2 Tablespoons agave nectar
- 1 cup water **or** milk (cow, goat, almond, rice, coconut, oat, etc.)

DIRECTIONS:
1. Purée peaches, blueberries, agave, and water or milk in a blender for 1 minute.
2. Pour into popsicle molds and freeze for about 30 minutes. Insert sticks and return to freezer.
3. Freeze the popsicles for at least 6 hours.

Makes about a dozen popsicles

Creamy Pinã Colada Popsicles

ADDITIONAL TOOLS NEEDED:
- *Popsicle molds*
- *Wooden popsicle sticks*
- *Blender*

INGREDIENTS:
- 2 cups fresh pineapple, cubed
- 1 cup coconut milk
- 3 Tablespoons agave nectar
- ½ teaspoon high-quality salt

DIRECTIONS:
1. Purée pineapple, coconut milk, agave, and salt in a blender for 1 minute.
2. Pour into popsicle molds and freeze for about 30 minutes. Insert sticks and return to freezer.
3. Freeze the popsicles for at least 6 hours.

Makes about a dozen popsicles

Creamy Mango Coconut Popsicles

ADDITIONAL TOOLS NEEDED:
- *Popsicle molds*
- *Wooden popsicle sticks*
- *Blender*

INGREDIENTS:
- 1 ½ cups cubed mango, fresh **or** frozen
- 1 can (14 ounces) coconut milk
- 2 Tablespoons agave nectar
- ¼ cup lime juice

DIRECTIONS:
1. Purée mango, coconut milk, agave, and lime juice in a blender for 1 minute.
2. Pour into popsicle molds and freeze for about 30 minutes. Insert sticks and return to freezer.
3. Freeze the popsicles for at least 6 hours.

Makes about a dozen popsicles

Creamy Apricot Popsicles

ADDITIONAL TOOLS NEEDED:
- *Popsicle molds*
- *Wooden popsicle sticks*
- *Blender*

INGREDIENTS:
- 2 cups apricot juice
- 1 fresh apricot (pit removed)
- ½ cup milk (cow, goat, almond, rice, coconut, oat, etc.)
- ½ teaspoon pure vanilla extract

DIRECTIONS:
1. Purée apricot juice, apricot, milk, and vanilla in blender for 1 minute.
2. Pour into popsicle molds and freeze for about 30 minutes. Insert sticks and return to freezer.
3. Freeze the popsicles for at least 6 hours.

Makes about a dozen popsicles

Coco-Coconut Banana Popsicles

ADDITIONAL TOOLS NEEDED:
Wooden popsicle sticks

INGREDIENTS:
- 2 Bananas
- ½ cup shredded coconut
- 1 Tablespoon cocoa powder **or** raw cacao powder
- Agave nectar

DIRECTIONS:
1. Line a cookie sheet with waxed paper.
2. Peel bananas. Cut them in half (not longwise) and push popsicle sticks into bottoms, so that tips are pointing upward.
3. Mix shredded coconut and cocoa powder on a plate.
4. On another plate, add agave. Roll bananas in agave, then in the coconut-cocoa mixture on the other plate.
5. Place the banana pops on the cookie sheet, and freeze. Banana pops will be ready to eat in 3 hours.

Makes 4 popsicles.

Banana Chocolate Crunch Popsicles

ADDITIONAL TOOLS NEEDED:
Wooden popsicle sticks

INGREDIENTS:

- 2 bananas
- Chocolate syrup (see page 108)

Crunch:

- Granola, chopped nuts **or** cacao nibs

DIRECTIONS:
1. Line a cookie sheet with waxed paper.
2. Peel bananas. Cut them in half (not longwise) and push popsicle sticks into bottoms, so that tips are pointing upward.
3. Dip banana in chocolate syrup and roll in granola, nuts, or cacao nibs.
4. Place the banana pops on the cookie sheet and freeze. Banana pops will be ready to eat in 3 hours.

Makes 4 popsicles

Herbal Popsicles Base Recipe

These can be a fun way to get the benefits of medicinal herbs into kids' little bodies. Try using a cough tea for sore throats or immune boosting teas for colds. For everyday, make these with juice from fresh herbs in your garden or your favorite tea.

ADDITIONAL TOOLS NEEDED:
- *Popsicle molds*
- *Wooden popsicle sticks*

INGREDIENTS:
- 3-4 tea bags of your favorite herbal tea (Traditional Medicinals tea blends are great and can be found in most health food stores)
- 1 ½ cups water
- 2-4 Tablespoons agave nectar

DIRECTIONS:
1. Steep 3 tea bags in 1 ½ cups hot water and add agave. Let sit until cool. You can let it sit overnight for the most potent infusion.
2. Add juice or milk, if you desire.
3. Pour into popsicle molds and freeze for about 30 minutes. Insert sticks and return to freezer.
4. Freeze the popsicles for at least 6 hours.

OPTIONAL ADDITIONS:
- Add ¾ cup juice of orange, pineapple, apple, blueberry, cherry, etc. Fresh is best if you have it.
- Add the fresh squeezed juice of two lemons or limes.
- Add ¾ cup coconut milk or milk of choice.

A Few Ideas for Herbal Popsicles:

Let your creative juices flow and feel free to experiment to find your favorite flavors.

Mint Apple

Brew a strong infusion of peppermint tea in 1 ½ cups of water. Add ¾ cup apple juice and 2-4 Tablespoons of agave. Pour into molds and freeze.

Milky Lavender

Brew a strong infusion of lavender flowers in 1 ½ cups of water. Add ¾ cup milk of your choice and 2-4 Tablespoons of agave. Pour into molds and freeze.

Rose Pomegranate

Brew a strong infusion of rosehips (high in Vitamin C) in 1 ½ cups of water. Add ¾ cup pomegranate juice, a splash of rosewater, and 2-4 Tablespoons of agave. Pour into molds and freeze.

Citrus Raspberry

Brew a strong infusion of raspberry leaf plus one clove in 1 ½ cups of water. Add the juice of one lemon and 2-4 Tablespoons of agave. Add in fresh strawberries, if desired. Pour into molds and freeze.

Lemon Balm and Lemon

Brew a strong infusion of lemon balm tea in 1 ½ cups of water. Add ¾ cup apple juice, the juice of one lemon, and 2-4 Tablespoons of agave. Pour into molds and freeze.

Elderberry Blueberry

Brew a strong infusion of elderberries in 1 ½ cups of water. Add ¾ cup blueberry juice and 2-4 Tablespoons of agave. Add in fresh blueberries, if desired. Pour into molds and freeze.

Makes about 6 popsicles

Green Tea Popsicles

ADDITIONAL TOOLS NEEDED:
- *Popsicle molds*
- *Wooden popsicle sticks*

INGREDIENTS:
- 2 cups strongly brewed green tea
- 2 Tablespoons agave nectar (or more to taste)

DIRECTIONS:
1. Brew green tea, strain, and add agave. If using orange juice or milk, make the green tea with 1 cup of water, then add 1 cup of juice or milk to the brewed tea.
2. Pour into popsicle molds and freeze for about 30 minutes. Insert sticks and return to freezer.
3. Freeze the popsicles for at least 6 hours.

OPTIONAL VARIATIONS:
Brew the tea in orange juice or milk.

Makes about a dozen popsicles

Sweet Red Bean Popsicles

This is a Korean dessert that is delicious and is very nourishing to the kidneys!

ADDITIONAL TOOLS NEEDED:
- *Popsicle molds*
- *Wooden popsicle sticks*
- *Blender*

INGREDIENTS:
- 1 cup red aduki beans
- 2 cups water
- 2 cups milk (coconut milk works well)
- 1 cup agave nectar

DIRECTIONS:
1. Soak the aduki beans in water overnight or for at least 5 hours. Discard any beans that rise to the top.
2. Drain beans and add to a saucepan. Add 2 cups of water and bring to a boil. Then turn down heat and simmer for an hour, stirring occasionally. When the beans are soft, remove from heat. (Alternate step: cook beans in a pressure cooker or a crock pot, which requires less of your attention.)
3. Allow beans to cool.
4. In a blender, purée beans, milk, and agave until smooth. For bean chunks in the popsicles, reserve ½ cup of the cooked beans and stir in at end.
5. Pour into popsicle molds and freeze for about 30 minutes. Insert sticks and return to freezer.
6. Freeze the popsicles for at least 6 hours.

Makes about a dozen popsicles

Lemonade Popsicles

ADDITIONAL TOOLS NEEDED:
• Popsicle molds
• Wooden popsicle sticks
• Blender

INGREDIENTS:
• ¾ cup agave nectar
• 1 cup lemon juice, freshly squeezed from 4-6 lemons
• 3 cups water
• 1 quarter of a lemon (optional)

DIRECTIONS:
1. Combine all ingredients in a blender and blend on high for 10 seconds. If you'd like some bits of lemon rind, add the quarter of a lemon and blend 20 seconds more.
2. Pour into popsicle molds and freeze for about 30 minutes. Insert sticks and return to freezer.
3. Freeze the popsicles for at least 6 hours.

OPTIONAL VARIATION:
Substitute limes for lemons and use this recipe to make Limeade Popsicles.

Makes about a dozen popsicles

Chocolate Fudge Popsicles

ADDITIONAL TOOLS NEEDED:
• Popsicle molds
• Wooden popsicle sticks
• Blender

INGREDIENTS:
• ⅓ cup agave nectar
• 2 Tablespoons cornstarch **or** 1 ½ Tablespoons arrowroot flour
• 1 Tablespoon coconut butter **or** coconut oil
• 2 Tablespoons cocoa powder **or** raw cacao powder
• 2 ½ cups milk (cow, goat, almond, rice, coconut, oat, etc.)
• 1 teaspoon pure vanilla extract

DIRECTIONS:
1. In small saucepan, combine agave, cornstarch, coconut butter, cocoa powder, and milk. Stir well.
2. Over medium heat, gently melt ingredients and stir occasionally until thickened.
3. Remove from heat and add vanilla.
4. Pour into popsicle molds and freeze for about 30 minutes. Insert sticks and return to freezer.
5. Freeze the popsicles for at least 6 hours.

OPTIONAL VARIATION:
For a creamier popsicle, substitute ¼ cup cream for milk.

Makes about a dozen popsicles

My Fun Food Creations:

Use this section to write down some of your favorite customized fun food recipes from this chapter.

Recipe:

INGREDIENTS:

DIRECTIONS:

Serves _____

384 | SWEETEN IT WITH AGAVE

My Fun Food Creations:

Use this section to write down some of your favorite customized fun food recipes from this chapter.

Recipe:

· ·

INGREDIENTS:

· ·

· ·

· ·

· ·

· ·

· ·

· ·

DIRECTIONS:

· ·

· ·

· ·

· ·

· ·

· ·

Serves _____

CHAPTER 22

BREAKFAST FOODS

Cold Cereal

Top Tips for Making a
Great Granola 386

Ideas to Inspire your
Granola Creation 387

Granola Base Recipe #1: Oil Free . . . 388

Granola Base Recipe #2: Bran Style . 388

Granola Base Recipe #3:
Combo Granola 389

Hot Cereal

Steel Cut Oatmeal 390

Blueberry Bran Oatmeal 391

Sweet Morning Grits 391

Cardamom Grits 392

Quick Rice Cereal 392

Hot Quinoa Breakfast 393

Oat Bran Cereal 393

Oat Bran Cereal with Slippery Elm . . 394

Hot Bran Cereal 394

French Toast

Simple French Toast 395

Pancakes

Whole Wheat Pancakes 396

Buckwheat Pancakes 397

Whole Grain Buttermilk Pancakes . . 398

Sweet Rice Pancakes 399

Ricotta Cheese Pancakes 399

Fermented Buckwheat Pancakes . . . 400

Waffles

Whole Wheat Apple Waffles 401

Amaranth Apple Waffles 402

Sesame Yogurt Waffles 403

Quinoa Waffles 404

Millet Waffles 405

Buttermilk Teff Waffles 405

Cold Cereal

Granola
· · · · · · · · · · · ·

Instead of buying boxed cereal with processed grains, questionable oils, and added sugar, you can easily make your own granola at home. The end result will be higher in quality and less expensive, too. Following are recipes for three different types of granola. Try them all and see which style suits you.

Top Tips for Making a Great Granola:

- When you are mixing agave and oil in a granola recipe, make sure you thoroughly mix them, so that they are completely combined. Do this before adding dry ingredients.
- When baking granola, keep a careful eye on it, stirring from time to time and watching as it browns.
- Never bake the dried fruit in a granola recipe. Add it at the end.
- Deep cookie sheets work well for making granola.
- Thoroughly cool your granola before putting it into airtight glass containers. Granola becomes more crisp as it cools. If put away hot, it will become soggy.
- Because of the oil, granola will not stay fresh for long, so it is best to use it within a couple of weeks. For a longer lasting granola, try the oil-free recipe.

Ideas to Inspire your Granola Creation:

DRIED FRUIT	NUTS	SEEDS	OILS	ROLLED GRAIN FLAKES
Apples	Almonds	Chia	Coconut	Barley
Apricots	Brazil nuts	Flax	Grapeseed	Kamut
Banana chips	Cashews	Pumpkin	Sesame	Oat
Blueberries	Macadamia nuts	Sesame		Rye
Cherries		Sunflower		Spelt
Cranberries	Peanuts			
Dates	Pecans			
Figs	Pistachios			
Goji berries	Walnuts			
Papaya				
Peaches				
Pears				
Pineapple				
Plantain chips				
Prunes				
Raisins				

Granola Base Recipe #1: Oil Free

INGREDIENTS:

- Oil for greasing pan (melted butter, ghee, **or** neutral-tasting oil)
- 3 cups rolled oats (**or** any other rolled grain)
- 1 cup shredded, unpeeled apple
- ½ cup wheat germ **or** oat bran

- ¼ cup agave nectar
- ¼ cup water
- 1 teaspoon ground cinnamon
- 1 teaspoon pure vanilla extract **or** almond extract

DIRECTIONS:

1. Preheat oven to 325°F. Oil a cookie sheet and spread a sheet of foil on the counter.
2. In a large bowl, combine oats, apple, and wheat germ. Mix well.
3. In a small saucepan, stir together agave, water, and cinnamon. Heat to boiling, then remove from heat.
4. Stir in vanilla or almond extract.
5. Pour wet ingredients over oat mixture and mix well.

6. Spread oat mixture evenly onto cookie sheet.
7. Bake for 45 minutes or until golden brown, stirring occasionally.
8. Remove from oven and spread granola onto foil to cool.
9. Store in an airtight container in the refrigerator up to 4 weeks.

Makes about 4 cups

Granola Base Recipe #2: Bran Style

INGREDIENTS:

- Oil for greasing pan (melted butter, ghee, **or** neutral-tasting oil)
- ¼ cup grapeseed, coconut, **or** sesame oil
- ⅓ cup agave nectar
- 4 cups rolled oats (**or** other rolled grain)

- ¼ cup wheat germ **or** oat bran
- ½ cup sliced almonds (**or** other nut)
- ¾ cup raisins (**or** other dried fruit)

DIRECTIONS:

1. Preheat oven to 300°F. Oil a cookie sheet and spread a sheet of foil on the counter.
2. Blend oil and agave in a large bowl. Add oats, wheat germ, and almonds and mix well to coat.
3. Spread oat mixture evenly onto cookie sheet.
4. Bake for 25 minutes or until golden brown,

stirring occasionally.
5. Remove from oven, stir in raisins, and spread granola onto foil to cool.
6. Store in an airtight container at room temperature for up to 2 weeks.

Makes about 5 cups

Granola Base Recipe #3: Combo Granola

INGREDIENTS:
- Oil for greasing pan (melted butter, ghee, **or** neutral-tasting oil)
- 4 cups mixed rolled grains (i.e., 2 cups oats and 2 cups rye)
- ½ cup sunflower seeds (**or** any other seed)
- ½-1 cup cashews (**or** any other nut)
- ½ teaspoon high-quality salt
- 1 Tablespoon ground cinnamon (optional)
- 1-2 cups dried cherries (**or** any other dried fruit)
- ½ cup agave nectar
- ⅓ cup grapeseed oil, coconut oil, ghee, **or** unroasted cold pressed sesame oil
- 1 teaspoon pure vanilla extract **or** almond extract

DIRECTIONS:
1. Preheat oven to 325°F. Oil a cookie sheet and spread a sheet of foil on the counter.
2. In a large bowl, mix together rolled grains, seeds, nuts, salt, and cinnamon. Measure and set the dried fruit aside.
3. In a small bowl, combine agave, oil, and vanilla or almond extract. Mix well.
4. Add liquid to dry ingredients and mix thoroughly. The liquids will be absorbed and the granola will become darker and more shiny.
5. Bake for 25-30 minutes or until golden brown, stirring occasionally.
6. Remove from oven, stir in the cherries, and spread granola onto foil to cool.
7. Store in an airtight container at room temperature for up to 2 weeks.

Makes about 5 cups

Hot Cereal

Steel Cut Oatmeal
. . . .

If you enjoy oatmeal and have never had steel cut, you are in for a treat. These oats are minimally processed, have a higher glycemic index, and provide a more hearty breakfast.

INGREDIENTS:
- 1 cup steel cut oats
- 1 Tablespoon butter **or** ghee
- 3 cups water
- ¼ teaspoon high-quality salt
- ½ cup milk (cow, goat, almond, rice, coconut, oat, etc.)
- 1 Tablespoon agave nectar
- ½ teaspoon ground cinnamon (optional)

Time Saving Tip:
Soak the oats overnight so they cook more quickly.

DIRECTIONS:
1. In a large saucepan, toast oats in butter for 2 minutes or until oats begin to smell roasted and start to brown.
2. Add water and salt and bring to a boil, then lower to a simmer.
3. Cook on low for 25 minutes, covered.
4. Add milk and cook for another 10 minutes.
5. Remove from heat, add agave and cinnamon, and let sit another 10 minutes with the lid on. Fluff with a fork.

OPTIONAL ADDITIONS:
Try adding in any of the following to enhance your oatmeal:

- Cinnamon, star anise, cardamom
- Dates, prunes, raisins, cranberries, apricots, banana chips, walnuts
- Sesame seeds, pumpkin seeds, sunflower seeds, tahini, peanut butter, fresh fruit

Makes 3-4 servings

Blueberry Bran Oatmeal

INGREDIENTS:

- 1 cup water
- ½ cup rolled oats
- ¼ cup oat bran
- 1 cup frozen blueberries
- ½ teaspoon ground cinnamon (optional)
- Milk of choice
- ¼ cup agave nectar
- 1 Tablespoon ground flax seed (optional)

DIRECTIONS:

1. In a medium saucepan, add water, rolled oats, oat bran, frozen blueberries, and cinnamon. Simmer for 10 minutes, stirring occasionally. Add milk as necessary for desired consistency.
2. Remove from heat and stir in agave and flax seed.
3. Serve hot.

Makes 3-4 servings

Sweet Morning Grits

INGREDIENTS:

- 3 Tablespoons unsalted butter
- 1 cup stone-ground white grits (not instant)
- 4 cups warm water
- ½ teaspoon high-quality salt
- 2 cups milk (cow, goat, almond, rice, coconut, oat, etc.)
- ¼ cup agave nectar

DIRECTIONS:

1. In a large saucepan, melt the butter. Add grits and lightly roast over high heat, stirring until heated through, about 5 minutes.
2. Gradually whisk in warm water and salt. Reduce heat to low and cook, using a wooden spoon to stir every 2 to 3 minutes or until the water has been absorbed and the grits are thickened, about 20 minutes.
3. Whisk in milk and agave until smooth. Cook, stirring often about 30 minutes longer.
4. Serve hot with fresh fruit.

Makes 3-4 servings

Time Saving Tip:
Make a large batch of grits to reheat during the week for breakfast.

Cardamom Grits

INGREDIENTS:

- 2 cups milk (cow, goat, almond, rice, coconut, oat, etc.)
- 4 cardamom pods, lightly crushed
- 1 cinnamon stick
- ½ cup agave nectar
- 3 Tablespoons unsalted butter
- 1 cup stone-ground white grits (not instant)
- 4 cups warm water
- ½ teaspoon high-quality salt
- 1 teaspoon pure vanilla extract

DIRECTIONS:

1. In a small saucepan, combine milk with cardamom pods, cinnamon stick, and agave. Simmer for about 10 minutes.
2. Remove from the heat and let stand for 45 minutes. Strain the infused milk into a bowl and discard the solids. (This step can be done the night before and left to sit overnight.)
3. In a large saucepan, melt butter. Add the grits and lightly roast over high heat, stirring until heated through, about 5 minutes.
4. Gradually whisk in warm water and salt. Reduce heat to low and cook, using a wooden spoon to stir every 2-3 minutes, until the water has been absorbed and the grits have thickened, about 20 minutes.
5. Whisk in the infused milk until smooth. Add vanilla. Cook, stirring often, about 30 minutes longer.
6. Serve hot with fresh fruit.

Makes 3-4 servings

Quick Rice Cereal

This is a great breakfast for whipping up in a hurry!

INGREDIENTS:

- 1 cup leftover brown rice
- 2 cups milk (cow, goat, almond, rice, coconut, oat, etc.)
- ¼ teaspoon high-quality salt
- Agave nectar to taste

DIRECTIONS:

1. In a medium saucepan, combine rice, milk, and salt and bring to a boil. Stir and serve once all ingredients are hot, about 5 minutes.
2. Drizzle agave over cereal as desired.

OPTIONAL ADDITIONS:

Add cinnamon, cardamom, dried fruit, fresh fruit, butter, or ghee.

Makes 1 serving

Hot Quinoa Breakfast

INGREDIENTS:

- ½ cup quinoa
- ½ cup raisins (**or** any other dried fruit)
- 1 cup water
- 1 peach, peeled, pitted, and cut in cubes (**or** any other seasonal fruit)
- Milk (cow, goat, almond, rice, coconut, oat, etc.)
- Agave nectar to taste

DIRECTIONS:

1. In a medium saucepan, heat quinoa and dried fruit in water. Cook for 15 minutes or until fluffy. Remove from heat and keep covered for 10 minutes. This allows the quinoa to fluff up even more.

2. Serve with fresh fruit and milk and drizzle with agave.

Makes 2 servings

Oat Bran Cereal

INGREDIENTS:

- 1 ⅓ cup water
- ¾ cup oat bran
- ¼ teaspoon high-quality salt
- 1 Tablespoon agave nectar

DIRECTIONS:

1. In a medium saucepan, bring water to a boil. Turn down the heat and add oat bran, salt, and agave and stir.
2. Continue stirring as the mixture will thicken quickly. Cook about 8 minutes.
3. Top with any combination of spices, fruits, and nuts.

OPTIONAL ADDITIONS:
Add milk of any kind, fresh fruit, dried fruit, nut butter, ghee, butter, spices, and nuts to your liking.

Makes 2 servings

Oat Bran Cereal with Slippery Elm

This is an especially helpful breakfast for digestion and promoting regular bowel movements.

INGREDIENTS:

- 1 ⅓ cup water
- ¾ cup oat bran
- ¼ teaspoon high-quality salt
- ½ teaspoon cinnamon
- 1 Tablespoon agave nectar
- 4 Tablespoons slippery elm

DIRECTIONS:

1. In a medium saucepan, bring water to a boil. Turn down the heat and add oat bran, salt, cinnamon, and agave.
2. Continue stirring as the mixture will thicken quickly. Cook about 8 minutes.
3. Add slippery elm and cook for 3 minutes more.

OPTIONAL ADDITIONS:
Add milk of any kind, fresh fruit, dried fruit, nut butter, ghee, butter, spices, and nuts to your liking.

Makes 2 servings

Hot Bran Cereal

This breakfast is high in fiber and is infinitely versatile — you can add fresh fruit, dried fruit, nut butter, agave nectar, and spices, like cinnamon, nutmeg, and allspice.

INGREDIENTS:

- ½ cup oat bran
- ½ cup rice bran (this offers variety, but you can use all oat bran instead)
- 2 cups water
- ½ teaspoon high-quality salt
- 1 pat of butter (to your liking)
- 1 Tablespoon agave nectar
- 1 Tablespoon date sugar (this offers variety, but agave works well, too)

DIRECTIONS:

1. In a small saucepan, combine oat bran, rice bran, and water. Put on high heat to bring up the temperature. Stir.
2. When bubbles start to form, lower heat. Stir occasionally. It will become thick in about 5 minutes.
3. Add butter, agave, and date sugar. Serve hot.

OPTIONAL ADDITIONS:
Top with any of the following combinations:

- Banana and dried Bing cherries
- Prunes and tahini
- Raisins and cinnamon
- Cooked apples and cinnamon.
- Bananas and raisins

Makes 2-3 servings

French Toast

Simple French Toast

INGREDIENTS:

- 2 eggs
- ⅔ cup milk (cow, goat, almond, rice, coconut, oat, etc.)
- ½ teaspoon high-quality salt
- 1 Tablespoon agave nectar
- ¼ teaspoon ground cinnamon (optional)
- ¼ teaspoon ground nutmeg (optional)
- 1 teaspoon vanilla extract (optional)
- 6 thick slices of 100% whole grain bread **or** gluten-free bread

FOR THE GRIDDLE:

Neutral-tasting oil (grapeseed, untoasted sesame oil, coconut oil, **or** ghee)

DIRECTIONS:

1. In a deep, rectangular baking dish, beat together the eggs, milk, salt, agave, desired spices, and vanilla, until smooth
2. Oil a griddle or skillet and place over medium-high heat.
3. Dip each slice of bread into the egg mixture, soaking both sides well. Place on the hot griddle. Cook both sides until golden in color.
4. Serve hot with fresh fruit and agave.

OPTIONAL VARIATION:
Use a cookie cutter to make the bread into shapes like hearts or stars.

Makes 3-4 servings

Pancakes

Whole Wheat Pancakes

INGREDIENTS:
- 1 ½ cups whole wheat flour
- ½ cup oat flour (**or** another ½ cup whole wheat flour)
- 1 teaspoon high-quality salt
- 1 Tablespoon baking powder
- 2 eggs, separated into egg yolks and egg whites
- ¼ cup neutral-tasting oil (grapeseed, untoasted sesame oil, coconut oil, **or** ghee)
- 2 cups milk (cow, goat, almond, rice, coconut, oat, etc.) **or** water
- 3 Tablespoons agave nectar

FOR THE GRIDDLE:
Neutral-tasting oil (grapeseed, untoasted sesame oil, coconut oil, **or** ghee)

DIRECTIONS:
1. In a medium bowl, mix together dry ingredients: whole wheat flour, oat flour, salt, and baking powder.
2. Separate the eggs into egg yolks and egg whites. Beat the egg yolks, and set the egg whites aside for later.
3. Stir the beaten yolks, oil, agave, and milk into the flour mixture. Use enough liquid (milk or water) to make a batter the consistency of thick, heavy cream.
4. Using an electric mixer, beat the egg whites until stiff. Fold gently into the batter.
5. Ladle the mixture onto a hot, oiled griddle. When holes appear on the surfaces of the pancakes, flip and cook until other sides are browned.
6. Serve hot with fresh fruit and agave.

Makes 5 servings

Buckwheat Pancakes

INGREDIENTS:
- ¾ cup buckwheat flour
- ¾ cup quinoa, millet, kamut, whole wheat, **or** tapioca flour (*Each flour has a distinct taste and texture, so experiment and discover your own preferences. Another option is to use all buckwheat flour, but it can be a bit dense.*)
- ⅛ teaspoon high-quality salt
- 2 teaspoons baking powder
- 1 egg, lightly beaten
- 3 Tablespoons neutral-tasting oil (grapeseed, untoasted sesame oil, coconut oil, **or** ghee)
- 3 Tablespoons agave nectar
- 1 cup milk (cow, goat, almond, rice, coconut, oat, etc.)

FOR THE GRIDDLE:
Neutral-tasting oil (grapeseed, untoasted sesame oil, coconut oil, **or** ghee)

DIRECTIONS:
1. In a medium bowl, mix together dry ingredients: flours, salt, and baking powder.
2. Stir in the egg, oil, agave, and milk. Use enough liquid (milk or water) to make a batter the consistency of thick, heavy cream.
3. Ladle the mixture onto a hot, oiled griddle. When holes appear on the surfaces of the pancakes, flip and cook until other sides are browned.
4. Serve hot with fresh fruit and agave.

Makes 3-4 servings

Whole Grain Buttermilk Pancakes

INGREDIENTS:
- 1 cup millet flour
- 1 cup brown rice flour (**or** ½ cup brown rice flour, ½ cup buckwheat flour)
- ¼ cup tapioca flour
- ¼ cup buttermilk powder
- ½ teaspoon high-quality salt
- 1 teaspoon baking powder
- 2 eggs, lightly beaten
- 3 Tablespoons neutral-tasting oil (grapeseed, untoasted sesame oil, coconut oil, **or** ghee)
- ¼ cup agave nectar
- 1 cup milk (cow, goat, almond, rice, coconut, oat, etc.)

FOR THE GRIDDLE:
Neutral-tasting oil (grapeseed, untoasted sesame oil, coconut oil, **or** ghee)

DIRECTIONS:
1. In a medium bowl, mix together the millet flour, brown rice flour, tapioca flour, buttermilk powder, salt, and baking powder.
2. Stir in the eggs, oil, agave, and milk. Use enough liquid (milk or water) to make a batter the consistency of thick, heavy cream.
3. Ladle the mixture onto a hot, oiled griddle. When holes appear on the surfaces of the pancakes, flip and cook until other sides are browned.
4. Serve hot with fresh fruit and agave.

OPTIONAL VARIATION:
For fluffier pancakes, separate the eggs into egg yolks and egg whites. Beat the egg yolks into the batter. Then beat the egg whites until stiff and fold gently into the batter.

Makes 4-5 servings

Sweet Rice Pancakes

INGREDIENTS:

- ½ cup brown rice flour
- ½ cup sweet rice flour (**or** white rice flour)
- ¾ cup tapioca flour
- ½ teaspoon high-quality salt
- 1 teaspoon baking powder
- 2 eggs, lightly beaten
- 3 Tablespoons neutral-tasting oil (grapeseed, untoasted sesame oil, coconut oil, **or** ghee)
- ¼ cup agave nectar
- 1 cup milk (cow, goat, almond, rice, coconut, oat, etc.)

FOR THE GRIDDLE:
Neutral-tasting oil (grapeseed, untoasted sesame oil, coconut oil, **or** ghee)

DIRECTIONS:

1. In a medium bowl, mix together the brown rice flour, sweet rice flour, tapioca flour, salt, and baking powder.
2. Stir in the eggs, oil, agave, and milk. Use enough liquid (milk or water) to make a batter the consistency of thick, heavy cream.
3. Ladle the mixture onto a hot, oiled griddle. When holes appear on the surfaces of the pancakes, flip and cook until other sides are browned.
4. Serve hot with fresh fruit and agave.

Makes 4-5 servings

Ricotta Cheese Pancakes

INGREDIENTS:

- 1 cup ricotta (**or** cottage cheese)
- 4 eggs, beaten
- ¼ cup agave nectar
- ½ cup butter, melted (**or** ½ cup of coconut oil, ghee, **or** grapeseed oil)
- ½ teaspoon pure vanilla extract
- ¼ cup brown rice flour
- ½ cup oat flour
- ½ teaspoon high-quality salt

FOR THE GRIDDLE:
Neutral-tasting oil (grapeseed, untoasted sesame oil, coconut oil, **or** ghee)

DIRECTIONS:

1. In a medium bowl, mix ricotta, eggs, agave, butter, and vanilla with a whisk or mixer.
2. Add brown rice flour, oat flour, and salt. Mix well.
3. Oil a cast iron griddle or frying pan and bring to high heat.
4. Spoon batter onto the hot surface, creating pancakes 3" in diameter.
5. Turn only once to cook both sides evenly.
6. Serve hot with fresh fruit and agave.

Makes 2-3 servings

Fermented Buckwheat Pancakes

This recipe takes a little more planning but offers a unique pancake experience.

INGREDIENTS:

Part I:

- 1 cup buckwheat flour
- 1 cup warm water
- 1 teaspoon dry active yeast (about half a package)
- 1 teaspoon agave nectar

Part II:

- 2 eggs (separated into egg whites and egg yolks)
- 2 Tablespoons butter, gently melted but not hot
- ½ teaspoon high-quality salt
- 2 Tablespoons agave nectar
- 2 Tablespoons tapioca flour

FOR THE GRIDDLE:

Neutral-tasting oil (grapeseed, untoasted sesame oil, coconut oil, **or** ghee)

DIRECTIONS:

Part I:

1. In a large bowl, combine buckwheat flour, warm water, yeast, and agave.
2. Cover the bowl with a damp, clean kitchen towel and put in a warm place to ferment overnight, about 6-10 hours.

Part II:

1. Separate the egg yolks and egg whites.
2. In a medium bowl, combine the egg yolks, butter, salt, agave, and tapioca flour and mix well.
3. Using an electric mixer or hand mixer, beat the egg whites until stiff. Fold into the wet mixture.
4. Add the fermented mixture and stir well.
5. Ladle the mixture onto a hot, oiled griddle. When holes appear on the surfaces of the pancakes, flip and cook until other sides are browned.
6. Serve hot with fresh fruit and agave.

Makes 2-3 servings

Waffles

Whole Wheat Apple Waffles
· ·

ADDITIONAL TOOLS NEEDED:
Waffle iron

INGREDIENTS:
- 2 eggs, beaten
- 1 ¾ cups milk (cow, goat, almond, rice, coconut, oat, etc.)
- ¼ cup neutral-tasting oil (grapeseed, untoasted sesame oil, coconut oil, **or** ghee), plus extra for greasing iron
- ¼ cup unsweetened applesauce
- 2 Tablespoons agave nectar
- 1 teaspoon pure vanilla extract
- 1 ¼ cups whole wheat pastry flour (**or** whole wheat flour)
- ½ cup ground flax seed
- ¼ cup oat bran
- 4 teaspoons baking powder
- ½ teaspoon high-quality salt

DIRECTIONS:
1. In a large bowl, whisk together the eggs, milk, oil, applesauce, agave, and vanilla.
2. Stir in the whole wheat pastry flour, ground flax seed, oat bran, baking powder, and salt. Mix until smooth.
3. Preheat a waffle iron and, using a pastry brush, coat it with oil.
4. Pour batter into waffle iron in batches and cook until crisp and golden brown.
5. Serve hot with fresh fruit and agave.

OPTIONAL VARIATIONS:
To make wheat-free waffles, use kamut flour instead of whole wheat flour.
To make gluten-free waffles, use millet flour instead of wheat flour.

Makes 3-4 servings

Amaranth Apple Waffles

ADDITIONAL TOOLS NEEDED:
Waffle iron

INGREDIENTS:
- 2 eggs, beaten
- 1 ¾ cups milk (cow, goat, almond, rice, coconut, oat, etc.)
- ¼ cup neutral-tasting oil (grapeseed, untoasted sesame oil, coconut oil, **or** ghee), plus extra for greasing iron
- ¼ cup unsweetened applesauce
- 2 Tablespoons agave nectar
- 1 teaspoon pure vanilla extract
- ⅔ cup amaranth flour
- ½ cup brown rice flour
- ⅓ cup tapioca flour
- ½ cup flax seed meal
- 4 teaspoons baking powder
- 1 teaspoon xanthan gum **or** guar gum **or** a 50.50 combination of both
- ½ teaspoon high-quality salt

DIRECTIONS:
1. In a large bowl, whisk together the eggs, milk, oil, applesauce, agave, and vanilla.
2. Stir in the amaranth flour, brown rice flour, tapioca flour, flax seed meal, baking powder, gum, and salt.
3. Mix until smooth.
4. Preheat a waffle iron and, using a pastry brush, coat it with oil.
5. Pour batter into waffle iron in batches and cook until crisp and golden brown.
6. Serve hot with fresh fruit and agave.

Makes 3-4 servings

Sesame Yogurt Waffles

ADDITIONAL TOOLS NEEDED:
Waffle iron

INGREDIENTS:
- 2 eggs, beaten
- 1 cup milk (almond, rice, cow, goat, etc.)
- 1 cup plain yogurt
- ¼ cup neutral-tasting oil (grapeseed, untoasted sesame oil, coconut oil, **or** ghee), plus extra for greasing iron
- ¼ cup agave nectar
- 1 teaspoon pure vanilla extract
- 1 cup kamut flour
- 1 cup oat flour
- ¼ cup sesame seeds
- 4 teaspoons baking powder
- ½ teaspoon xanthan gum **or** guar gum **or** a 50:50 combination of both
- ¼ cup buttermilk powder
- ½ teaspoon high-quality salt

DIRECTIONS:
1. In a large bowl, whisk together the eggs, milk, yogurt, oil, agave, and vanilla.
2. Stir in the kamut flour, oat flour, sesame seeds, baking powder, gum, buttermilk powder, and salt. Mix until the batter is smooth.
3. Preheat a waffle iron and, using a pastry brush, coat it with oil.
4. Pour batter into waffle iron in batches, and cook until crisp and golden brown.
5. Serve hot with fresh fruit and agave.

Makes 3-4 servings

Quinoa Waffles

ADDITIONAL TOOLS NEEDED:
Waffle iron

INGREDIENTS:
- 2 eggs, beaten
- 1 ¾ cups milk (cow, goat, almond, rice, coconut, oat, etc.)
- ¼ cup neutral-tasting oil (grapeseed, untoasted sesame oil, coconut oil, **or** ghee), plus extra for greasing iron
- 2 Tablespoons agave nectar
- 1 teaspoon pure vanilla extract
- 1 cup quinoa flour (**or** amaranth flour)
- ¾ cup brown rice flour
- ¼ cup tapioca flour
- ¼ cup cornstarch (**or** tapioca flour)
- 4 teaspoons baking powder
- ½ teaspoon xanthan gum **or** guar gum **or** a 50:50 combination of both
- ½ teaspoon high-quality salt

DIRECTIONS:
1. In a large bowl, whisk together the eggs, milk, oil, agave, and vanilla.
2. Stir in quinoa flour, brown rice flour, tapioca flour, cornstarch, baking powder, gum, and salt. Mix until the batter is smooth.
3. Preheat a waffle iron and, using a pastry brush, coat it with oil.
4. Pour batter into waffle iron in batches and cook until crisp and golden brown.
5. Serve hot with fresh fruit and agave.

Makes 3-4 servings

Millet Waffles

ADDITIONAL TOOLS NEEDED:
Waffle iron

INGREDIENTS:
- 2 eggs, beaten
- 1 ¾ cups milk (cow, goat, almond, rice, coconut, oat, etc.)
- ¼ cup neutral-tasting oil (grapeseed, untoasted sesame oil, coconut oil, **or** ghee), plus extra for greasing iron
- 2 Tablespoons agave nectar
- 1 teaspoon pure vanilla extract

- 1 cup millet flour
- ¾ cup brown rice flour
- ¼ cup tapioca flour
- ¼ cup cornstarch (**or** tapioca flour)
- 4 teaspoons baking powder
- ½ teaspoon xanthan gum **or** guar gum **or** a 50:50 combination of both
- ½ teaspoon high-quality salt

DIRECTIONS:
1. In a large bowl, whisk together the eggs, milk, oil, agave, and vanilla.
2. Stir in millet flour, brown rice flour, tapioca flour, cornstarch, baking powder, gum, and salt. Mix until the batter is smooth.

3. Preheat a waffle iron and, using a pastry brush, coat it with oil.
4. Pour batter into waffle iron in batches and cook until crisp and golden brown.
5. Serve hot with fresh fruit and agave.

Makes 3-4 servings

Buttermilk Teff Waffles

ADDITIONAL TOOLS NEEDED:
Waffle iron

INGREDIENTS:
- 2 eggs, beaten
- 2 cups milk (cow, goat, almond, rice, coconut, oat, etc.)
- ¼ cup neutral-tasting oil (grapeseed, untoasted sesame oil, coconut oil, **or** ghee), plus extra for greasing iron
- ¼ cup agave nectar
- 1 teaspoon pure vanilla extract
- ½ cup teff flour

- ½ cup brown rice flour
- ½ cup tapioca flour
- ½ cup cornstarch (**or** tapioca flour)
- ¼ cup buttermilk powder
- 4 teaspoons baking powder
- ½ teaspoon xanthan gum **or** guar gum **or** a 50:50 combination of both
- ½ teaspoon high-quality salt

DIRECTIONS:
1. In a large bowl, whisk together the eggs, milk, oil, agave, and vanilla.
2. Stir in the teff flour, brown rice flour, tapioca flour, cornstarch, buttermilk powder, baking powder, gum, and salt. Mix until the batter is smooth.

3. Preheat a waffle iron and, using a pastry brush, coat it with oil.
4. Pour batter into waffle iron in batches and cook until crisp and golden brown.
5. Serve hot with fresh fruit and agave.

Makes 3-4 servings

My Breakfast Creations:

*Use this section to write down some of your favorite
customized breakfast recipes from this chapter.*

Recipe:

INGREDIENTS:

DIRECTIONS:

Serves _____

GLOSSARY OF INGREDIENTS

The recipes in this book are packed with the highest quality and most nutritious ingredients. Some of these ingredients may be new to you, but they should all be commonly available at your natural food store or online. This glossary will help you understand more about these unique ingredients — their healing qualities, distinctive properties, and characteristics.

Açaí powder Brazilians call Açaí "The Tree of Life." Açaí fruit is one of the top superfoods for its antioxidant power. It is packed with amino acids and essential fatty acids. The fatty acid content in açaí resembles that of olive oil and is rich in monounsaturated oleic acid. Its flavor is a combination of berries and chocolate. Açaí is wonderful in smoothies, homemade raw chocolate, or ice cream.

Agar-agar Agar-agar is a tasteless seaweed that is used in desserts for its thickening ability. It is often used in place of animal-derived gelatin in puddings, aspics, pie fillings, and jellies. Add 2 Tablespoons of agar flakes per 1 cup of simmering liquid to be gelled. For 1 cup of a citrus juice, use 3 Tablespoons. Agar-agar is a quality source of iodine, calcium, iron, phosphorus, and vitamins.

Agave nectar Agave nectar is a natural sweetener made from the aguamiel juice of the agave plant, which grows in the high desert regions of Central Mexico. Highly versatile, it has a neutral, sweet taste, is an excellent substitute for sugar, and it has a low glycemic index.

Aloe vera juice Aloe vera juice is touted for many health benefits when ingested internally, including improved circulation, immunity strengthening, blood sugar regulation, and weight loss. Aloe vera juice is made from leaves that are picked, scrubbed, ground then cold-pressed. The aloin is then filtered out. Aloin, a stimulant laxative found in unprocessed aloe vera, has been banned from commercial aloe products, including aloe juice, since 2002. Today, all aloe vera juice purchased in the United States has been refined to eliminate aloin. Avoid "flavored," "re-constituted," or "from concentrate," products, and be sure to choose one with no added sweetener. Choose a product that uses organic aloe barbadensis miller, which is the most nutrient-dense species, and look for aloe vera juice that undergoes "whole leaf cold processing." Only purchase juice that is in a tinted bottle, because those sold in clear glass lose important nutrients through oxidization. Remember that good-quality options are likely not the cheapest ones.

Amaranth flour—*See flours*

Amasake A traditional, sweet Japanese drink made from fermented rice. No sugar is usually added, as it is naturally sweet.

Arrowroot flour—*See flours*

Baking powder Baking powder is a leavening agent; it is added to baked goods before cooking to produce carbon dioxide, which causes them to rise. Baking powder contains sodium bicarbonate (baking soda), as well as an acidifying agent (cream of tartar), and a drying agent (usually starch). Baking powder is available as single-acting baking powder and as double-acting baking powder. Single-acting powders are activated by moisture, so you need to bake those recipes which include this product immediately after mixing. Double-acting powders react in two phases and can stand for a while before baking. With double-acting powder, some gas is released at room temperature when the powder is added to dough, but the majority of the gas is released after the temperature of the dough increases in the oven. You can substitute baking powder in place of baking soda (you'll need more baking powder and it may affect the taste of the recipe), but you can't use baking soda when a recipe calls for baking powder. Baking soda by itself lacks the acidity to make a cake rise. However, you can make your own baking powder by mixing two parts cream of tartar with one part baking soda.

Baking soda Baking soda is pure sodium bicarbonate. When baking soda is combined with moisture and an acidic ingredient (for example: yogurt, chocolate, buttermilk, or honey), the resulting chemical reaction produces bubbles of carbon dioxide that expand under oven temperatures, causing baked goods to rise. The reaction begins immediately upon mixing the ingredients, so when you bake with recipes that call for baking soda, you'll need to put them in the oven immediately

Barley flour—*See flours*

Brown rice flour—*See flours*

Buckwheat (kasha) flour—*See flours*

Butter I highly recommend using organic butter that is free of hormones, steroids, and antibiotics. Ideally, use butter made from raw milk from cows that have been exclusively grass fed. Studies have shown raw milk butter from grass-fed cows to have increased nutrients and the perfect ratio of omega-3 to omega-6 fatty acids. If you can't find butter from a raw, grass-fed dairy, at the very least buy organic butter to avoid chemicals and hormones that are heavily concentrated in regular milk products. Cultured butter is one step above organic due to the addition of beneficial bacteria and enzymes, which promote healthy digestion. These enzymes and bacteria are normally lost during pasteurization. This butter has a slightly higher fat content and works well with baking.

Buttermilk powder Buttermilk is cultured skim milk. The milk is then pasteurized and concentrated with an evaporator and finally dried to produce buttermilk powder. Buttermilk powder adds a tang to recipes and acts as a natural leaving agent to help baked goods rise. It is often used in biscuits and pancakes, is low in fat, and provides an excellent source of protein. It is contains notable amounts of calcium, phosphorous, riboflavin, and vitamin B12.

Carob powder Carob offers a distinct flavor to recipes and has some worthy nutritional benefits. Carob is derived from the dried and roasted pod of a Mediterranean evergreen tree. The ground powder is dark brown in color, resembles cocoa powder, and is sometimes used as a substitute for cocoa. One Tablespoon of unsweetened carob powder has 25 calories, no fat, no saturated fat, no cholesterol, and about 6 grams of carbohydrate. On the other hand, one Tablespoon of unsweetened cocoa powder contains 12 calories, 1 gram of fat, no saturated fat, no cholesterol, and about 3 grams of carbohydrates. Unlike chocolate, carob does not contain caffeine.

Cacao nibs Raw, fermented cacao beans that have been chopped into small chunks, cacao nibs work great in ice cream and raw treats.

Chia seeds Most people know chia as the pet growing sprouts out of its back, "ch, ch, ch, chia!" Yes, these are the same seeds; but you may not know that chia is rich in omega-3 fatty acids — even more so than flax seeds. Unlike flax seeds, chia seeds won't deteriorate or go rancid during storage due to their high levels of antioxidants. They also don't have to be ground to make their nutrients available to the body. Eat chia seeds whole, throw them in smoothies, in your hot morning breakfast, puddings, or even yogurt. A unique quality of chia is that it forms a gel if left in water. Chia seeds soaked in lemon water or fruit juice is a common drink in Mexico known as *chia fresca*. Researchers suggest that this reaction also takes place in the stomach, which slows the process by which digestive enzymes break down carbohydrates and convert them into sugar. This may explain why Aztec warriors would be sustained for 24 hours from 1 Tablespoon of seeds. Ground chia seeds can be used in baked goods, including breads, cakes, and biscuits. Highly nutritious, they provide fiber, calcium, phosphorus, magnesium, manganese, copper, iron, molybdenum, niacin, and zinc.

Chickpea (garbanzo) flour—*See flours*

Cocoa butter (cacao butter) Cocoa butter is extracted from cacao seeds (cocoa beans) and is used in making chocolate. The butter is slightly yellow and solid at room temperature, yet melts easily at body temperature, which creates a creamy effect in the mouth. It contains antioxidants which help to naturally preserve it. The fats in cocoa butter are healthy since they are primarily oleic and stearic acid.

Cocoa powder Cocoa powder is derived from fermented cacao beans. During processing, cocoa powder may be exposed to high heat and chemicals, which lessen its levels of antioxidants and vitamins and minerals. According to FDA guidelines, cocoa powder and cacao powder are interchangeable terms except for one detail: *Cacao powder* specifically refers to raw, unsweetened powder. *Cocoa powder*, on the other hand, may still have a very small amount of cocoa butter present to subtly enhance the flavor. *Hot cocoa* products typically have combined sugar and cocoa powder together. In the 19th century, Dutch chocolate makers discovered that they could treat cocoa powder with alkaline salts to reduce its bitter taste. This "Dutching process" created a product that should not be confused with cocoa powder. Dutch cocoa provides fewer antioxidants than natural cocoa powder because the alkali process destroys some of the flavanols (the powerful antioxidants found in raw cocoa powder). When using a recipe that calls for cocoa powder, make sure you buy natural cocoa powder, not Dutch process. If you are making a recipe that will be exposed to heat, choose cocoa powder, since it is considerably less expensive. If you are making a dessert that is not exposed to high heat, consider using raw cacao powder, due to its increased health benefits.

Cocoa powder, raw (cacao powder) There has been some confusion between the terms cocoa and cacao. Cacao is technically the name of the bean from which cocoa is derived. Historically, cocoa powder referred to the product that was created from the cacao bean. But in today's market, we have access to the raw ground cacao powder. Raw cacao powder is ground, fermented cacao beans that are put through a cold-pressing process, during which the fat (cocoa butter) is removed. With the fat removed, cacao powder becomes hydroscopic, so it dissolves easily in liquids. Raw cacao retains more vitamins and minerals, and is high in antioxidants, which is one of the reasons it is classified as a "superfood." Superfoods are rich in a number of essential minerals, including magnesium, sulfur, calcium, iron, zinc, copper, potassium, and manganese. To make chocolate, you add the cocoa butter back in, along with a sweetener like agave nectar. Raw cacao powder is also great in smoothies and raw treats.

Coconut butter Coconut butter is made from coconut flesh and is creamy in color. It is solid at room temperature and begins to melt above 80°F. It can be added to smoothies, candies, and chocolates.

Coconut cream There is a distinction between coconut milk and coconut cream. Coconut cream forms at the top of coconut milk when refrigerated. Sometimes recipes will call for coconut cream; if you can't find it in the market, simply place coconut milk in the fridge and remove the cream from the top once it has separated from the milk.

Coconut oil—*See oils*

Coconut, shredded Shredded coconut, or desiccated coconut, makes a great coating for raw treats, and can be added to dishes to add protein and good-quality fat.

Corn flour and cornmeal—*See flours*

Cream of tartar Cream of tartar is the common name for potassium hydrogen tartrate, an acid salt that has numerous uses in cooking and baking. Cream of tartar is obtained when tartaric acid is half neutralized with potassium hydroxide, transforming it into a salt. Cream of tartar is a white powder that looks like baking powder. In fact, it is often an ingredient in baking powder, combined with baking soda, which helps the baking mixture to react when moistened and rise well. Tartaric acid is found in grapes, so cream of tartar is obtained from sediment produced in the process of making wine. Cream of tartar is well known for helping stabilize and give more volume to beaten egg whites. If you are beating eggs whites and don't have cream of tartar, you can substitute white vinegar (⅛ teaspoon per egg white), but that can be problematic, as it may cause cakes to shrink. Cream of tartar will last about one year, so be sure to date it and replace it in your pantry yearly.

Crème De Cacao Crème De Cacao is a chocolate flavored liqueur that often has vanilla tones.

Date sugar Date sugar is not a processed sugar. Instead, it's made from very finely chopped dry dates. Date sugar contains calcium, sulphur, iron, potassium, phosphorus, manganese, copper, magnesium, volatile oils, Vitamin B6, and folic acid. A drawback is that it can clump, which makes it an impractical substitution for the sweeteners in certain types of baked goods. Date sugar doesn't dissolve in liquids so it can't be used in beverages. However, it is wonderful for sprinkling on cereal or yogurt, throwing into a smoothie, dusting on cinnamon toast, or for the filling in a cinnamon roll.

Essential oils An essential oil is a concentrated compounds of a plant, usually made by distillation. Essential oils are used in perfumes, cosmetics, soaps, and other products, for flavoring food and drink, and for scenting incense and household cleaning products.

Flax seeds Flax seeds are the tiny brown or yellow seeds of the flax plant. They contain several essential nutrients, including calcium, iron, niacin, phosphorous, and vitamin E. Flax seeds are a rich source of omega-3 fatty acids and are best consumed immediately after grinding, since ground flax can be volatile and lose its properties soon after grinding. Flax seeds can be added to cereals, energy bars, smoothies, or porridge. Ground flax seeds can be used as an egg replacer. The seeds can also be sprouted and used in salads. They produce flaxseed oil (also known as linseed oil), which is great on vegetables and salads. Flax seeds are prone to rancidity and should be purchased in small quantities and stored in the freezer.

Flaxseed oil—*See oils*

Flours

Whole Grain Flours

Typically, baked goods contain processed flours, like unbleached white flour or pastry flour. While it's certainly tricky to bake with whole grain flours, it is well worth it. Whole grain flours are rich in nutrients and healing qualities, as well as a slew of vitamins and minerals that white flour does not contain (unless synthetic vitamins are added back in to "enrich" it). Below is a list of whole grains with their distinct properties and qualities. I recommend filling your pantry with a variety flours and storing them in glass mason jars in a cool, dark place, like a root cellar, refrigerator, or freezer to keep them fresh. Fresh ground flours are the most nutritious, healthful, and flavorful choices. Use a flour mill or Vita-mix to grind the grains.

Amaranth flour Amaranth looks more like a seed than a grain. It is an ancient food of Central America that only recently has become available in the U.S. Amaranth is very high in protein — nearly 16%. It is high in iron, calcium (more than milk), fiber, vitamin C, B vitamins, and minerals. A gluten-free grain, it is an excellent dietary addition for those with sensitivities to gluten. It is also high in lysine, which makes it useful in the treatment of herpes. In Chinese medicine, amaranth benefits the lungs, and is good for nursing or pregnant women and those who do heavy physical work. Amaranth is a suitable grain for those with type-2 diabetes due to its low glycemic index. Amaranth flour has a distinct, delicious, nutty flavor that works well with other grains, such as whole wheat pastry flour, barley, and spelt. It adds an interesting sponginess to recipes. When used by itself, amaranth flour is dry and gummy.

STORAGE: Amaranth seeds contain fairly high levels of polyunsaturated fat, so once ground into flour, it can easily become rancid. Therefore, keep it in the freezer in an airtight container for up to six months.

Barley flour Barley originated in North Africa and Southeast Asia. Before wheat and rye, it was the chief grain in Europe. Barley can be found whole or "pearled." Pearling removes the outer bran layer which makes it easier to cook, but removes the nutrients as well. The whole grain contains 10-15% protein and is high in niacin, folic acid, magnesium, B vitamins, calcium, iron, potassium, and phosphorus. It is high in gluten.

In Chinese medicine, barley strengthens the spleen and pancreas, regulates the stomach, fortifies the intestines, builds the blood, and benefits the gall bladder and nerves. Barley is deeply nourishing. It is easy to digest, so barley water is often given to sick and weak people. It treats diarrhea, soothes inflamed membranes, and alleviates painful and difficult urination. It helps reduce tumors, swellings, and water accumulations like edema.

Barley flour works very well with oat flour (especially for cookies) but can also be mixed with other whole grain flours. It is very good in cobblers, muffins, pie crusts, and breads. By itself, the texture of barley flour can be gummy and thick. Be sure to select whole grain barley flour, as opposed to flour made from pearled barley.

STORAGE: Barley flour has a short shelf life when stored in a cabinet, but will last up to four months in the freezer in an airtight container.

Brown rice flour Rice is the second highest consumed grain in the world and a staple crop for over half of the world's population. Rice is not as high in protein as wheat. To make brown rice flour, a flour mill uses dehulled grains. Most of the time, the flour is a bit gritty, though sometimes you find mills selling finely ground brown rice flour. Gritty flour is better for breads and muffins, while finely ground can be better in desserts. Whether you use gritty or fine is more a matter of personal preference than anything else. Brown rice flour contains bran so it is higher in nutrients than white rice flour. Brown rice is a gluten-free flour and can be used alone or in combination with other whole grain flours.

Brown rice is high in most B vitamins, magnesium, manganese, potassium, zinc, and iron.

In Chinese medicine, brown rice is said to strengthen the spleen and pancreas, soothe the stomach, expels toxins, and increase energy. The high concentration in B vitamins makes it good for the nervous system and increased focus and concentration.

STORAGE: Like wheat, brown rice flour can go rancid very quickly due to its high oil content, so it should be stored in the refrigerator for up to four to five months or up to one year in the freezer.

Buckwheat (kasha) flour While buckwheat is similar in nutrient content to other grains and looks like a grain, it is actually a fruit! It originated in Siberia and northern India, and later spread to the rest of Asia. It contains 15-20% protein and contains B vitamins, vitamin E, potassium, some iron, calcium, manganese, phosphorus, and fiber. Buckwheat is also high in flavonoids, particularly rutin and quercitin, which extend the action of Vitamin C and act as antioxidants. Buckwheat can lower the risk of high cholesterol and high blood pressure, which in turn can help prevent heart disease. Buckwheat's makeup is similar to sunflower seeds, with a single seed inside a hard outer hull. The starchy endosperm is white and the seed coat is green or tan, which darkens buckwheat flour. The hull is dark brown or black, and some may be included in buckwheat flour as dark specks. Buckwheat is famous for its use in pancakes, but also works very well in cookies, muffins, breads, dumplings, pastas (soba noodles are traditionally made with buckwheat), and baked goods. It is a gluten-free flour and can be used alone or mixed with other whole grain flours.

STORAGE: Buckwheat flour has a shelf life of about three months in the refrigerator or six months in the freezer. Whole buckwheat can last up to one year.

Corn flour and cornmeal Corn is the only grain that is native to the Americas. Corn is rich in vitamin A, and contains 10-20% protein. It also contains vitamin C, folic acid, B vitamins, potassium, magnesium, iron, zinc, and selenium. The five basic types of corn developed by native farmers are still available: popcorn, sweet corn, flint corn, dent corn, and flour corn. Today you can commonly find white, yellow, and blue varieties, all of which are interchangeable in recipes. In Chinese medicine, corn nourishes the heart, improves appetite, helps regulate digestion, promotes healthy teeth and gums, and tonifies the kidneys. Whole kernels of corn are milled into *cornmeal* (grittier) or *corn flour* (finer). The different mills of corn will have slightly different effects. For example, when making cornbread with cornmeal, the cornbread will be more dense and more crumbly than with corn flour. Avoid "degerminated cornmeal" which is more heavily processed, then enriched with artificial vitamins. Be aware that in the UK, corn flour refers to cornstarch. *Cornstarch* is made from only the endosperm of the corn and is used primarily as a thickening agent.

STORAGE: Corn flour and cornmeal will keep up to one year in a cool, dark cabinet if stored in an airtight container. The shelf life increases if the flour is stored in the freezer.

Kamut flour Kamut is actually a trademark owned by Kamut International, Ltd., used to market a variety of Khorasan wheat with certain guaranteed attributes. These attributes include certified organic production, preservation of the variety in its ancient form without hybridization or genetic modification, and high quality standards. The use of kamut is thought to have flourished in Egypt 5,000 years ago and was later replaced with higher yielding but less flavorful varieties of wheat. Compared to wheat, kamut is higher in protein and many minerals, especially selenium, zinc, and magnesium. I prefer the heirloom varieties of wheat such as kamut and spelt, since they have been preserved in their ancient forms and often do not trigger food allergies like wheat is known to do. Kamut has a particularly nice sweet flavor and is lighter than whole wheat, making it an excellent choice for cookies, breads, cakes, and baked goods.

STORAGE: Kamut flour stored in an airtight container will keep for up to one year in the freezer. It lasts considerably longer than wheat flour due to its low moisture content.

Millet flour Millet is the "queen of grains." It is the most ancient cereal grain used in history—predating rice, barley, wheat, and rye. Millet contains nearly 15% protein and is overall a very nutritious grain. It is a gluten-free grain and contains high amounts of fiber, niacin, thiamine, riboflavin, iron, magnesium, potassium, as well as calcium, zinc, and little vitamin E. In Chinese medicine, it is warming, diuretic, strengthens the kidneys, soothes morning sickness, and is beneficial to the stomach, spleen, and pancreas. Millet also sweetens the breath and has anti-fungal qualities, making it useful for those with candida. As a whole grain flour, it adds wonderful flavor, texture, and rich nutritional content to recipes.

STORAGE: Millet flour will keep in an airtight container for about two months in the refrigerator or six months in the freezer. Millet flour can go rancid quite rapidly if it is not properly stored. It is usually best to grind millet as needed to ensure the best flavor.

Oat bran Oat bran is the outer part of the oat kernel. It is a concentrated source of soluble fiber and serves as a slow-release, low-glycemic carbohydrate. It can replace flour to lower the glycemic index of a recipe.

STORAGE: Oat bran has the potential to go rancid, although it has a longer shelf life than flour. If you only use a little bit at a time, keep it in the freezer.

Oat flour Oats are the fourth highest consumed grain in the world. Oats do not contain gluten, but are often contaminated by gluten during processing. Recently, gluten-free oats have become available. After oats are hulled, the inner grain is scoured, which removes some bran. They are then steamed at 200°F or higher to kill fungus. The final product is the whole oat groat. Oatmeal is typically the rolled and flattened whole oat, which is much quicker to cook but more processed than the whole groat (although oat's nutritional value is less affected by processing than other grains). Oats contain 10-15% fiber, are high in protein, and are a good source of B vitamins. Oats contain folic acid, niacin, pyridoxine, panthothenic acid, as well as significant amounts of iron, magnesium, zinc, potassium, manganese, calcium, and copper. In Chinese medicine, oats restore the nervous system and reproductive system and build and regulate energy. Oats remove cholesterol from the arteries and digestive tract, strengthen cardiac muscles, and help renew bones and connective tissues. They also contain phosphorus which is important for brain and nerve formation in children. Oats can even help prevent infections and infectious diseases, especially in children. Now we know why they said, "Eat your oatmeal!" In baking, both rolled oats and oat flour are commonly used. Oat flour can be an excellent whole grain flour base in flour mixtures. It adds nice flavor and moistness to recipes, especially when combined with wheat, barley, millet, and brown rice flours. If you use oat flour by itself, it can be viscous. To maximize health benefits, avoid "quick cooking" oats, which contain considerably fewer nutrients.

STORAGE: Oat flour will keep for up to three months in an airtight container in a cool, dark cabinet, or up to six months if stored in the freezer.

Quinoa flour Quinoa, known as "the mother grain" among the Incas, has been cultivated since at least 3,000 B.C. It is a complete protein, and is high in iron, calcium, B vitamins, lysine, and minerals. It is gluten free. Quinoa looks like a cross between a sesame seed and millet. Quinoa is the highest in protein and fat of all the grains, and it contains more calcium than milk. It is available as a whole grain in yellow, white, pink, black, orange, red, and purple varieties. In Chinese medicine, quinoa tonifies the kidneys and is considered strengthening to the entire body. Quinoa flour works well as a base in flour mixtures, but should be used in smaller quantities due to its slightly strong and bitter flavor.

STORAGE: Once ground into flour, it has a tendency to oxidize fairly quickly, so buy small quantities and keep them fresh in a cool place. Quinoa flour will last four to six months in the freezer.

Rye flour Rye is a close relative to wheat and barley. It is a very hard grain and is best suited in breads. However, it can be employed in morning cereals and grain dishes, too. Rye contains nearly 20% protein and is rich in B vitamins. It is also a good source of fiber. In Chinese medicine, it is said to increase strength and endurance, clear liver stagnancy, aid in muscle formation, clean and renew the arteries, and aid in fingernail, hair, and bone formation. Rye is quite dense on its own, but can be mixed with other whole grain flours to lighten it up.

STORAGE: Whole-grain rye flour should be stored in the refrigerator in an airtight container, where it will keep for a few months. It will keep in the freezer for up to six months.

Spelt flour Spelt is an ancient relative of wheat and is said to have been an important staple in parts of Europe from the Bronze Age to medieval times. Recently, there has been a revival of spelt in the health food industry as an alternative grain to wheat products; many people who are allergic to wheat are not allergic to spelt. Like wheat, spelt flour is available in whole and white processed forms. For the greatest nutritional content, I recommend the whole grain flour. Spelt flour has a nuttier and slightly sweeter flavor than whole wheat flour, and the protein in spelt is easier to digest. Spelt contains about 58% carbohydrates, 17% protein, and 3% fat, as well as gluten, which makes it useful in baking. It is an excellent source of vitamin B2, a very good source of manganese, and a good source of niacin, thiamin, and copper. Because the outer hull is thicker than that of wheat, vitamins and minerals are better protected; it is also better protected against pollutants and insects, so the impact of pesticides is lower. When working with spelt, be aware that gluten from spelt proteins is weaker and can easily be overworked, so it is well advised to mix bread dough for a short time. Spelt flour can be used in place of whole wheat flour in recipes, and is especially good in bread and pizza dough. Be aware that spelt has a lower water absorption rate, so if using spelt in a recipe that usually calls for wheat, use less water.

STORAGE: Spelt flour will keep for a few months in a cool, dry cabinet and six to twelve months in the freezer.

Teff flour Teff is a species of lovegrass native to Ethiopia. It is high in dietary fiber and protein, and contains balanced levels of essential amino acids, such as leucine, phenylalanine, valine, isoleucine, threonine, and lysine, as well as important vitamins and minerals such as iron, calcium, potassium, phosphorus, Vitamins C and A, niacin, and thiamin. It is a gluten-free grain, which is why it is getting more attention in the health food community. Teff seed flour is used to make a staple bread in Ethiopia and Eritrea called "injera." It has a sweet, malty flavor and light quality, tasting a bit like hazelnuts. It is available in brown, red, and white varieties. The darker teff has more of a molasses flavor, while the white teff is more subtle. Because it is gluten free, teff needs to be combined with whole wheat, spelt, or kamut for yeasted breads. Note, however, that one of teff's unique culinary attributes is that, like grapes, it contains its own symbiotic yeast and is therefore not always well suited for yeasted breads. It combines well with amaranth, millet, and quinoa flours, especially for muffins and flat breads. You can experiment with it. It can be added into grain mixtures up to 20% and contributes its unique healing qualities and flavor to recipes. Teff flour can also be used as a thickener for gravy, soups, and stews.

STORAGE: Teff flour is best kept in the freezer, where it will last up to four months.

Whole wheat flour Wheat is the most highly distributed grain in the world. It forms a foundation in diets across the globe. Forms of wheat available include whole wheat berries, wheat bran, wheat germ, bulghur wheat, cracked wheat, wheat flour (white flour), and whole wheat flour. In Indian and Chinese medicine, wheat is considered greatly strengthening. Unfortunately, most wheat is employed in a highly processed form (white flour), which is greatly compromising to one's health. But if you choose whole wheat flour, you can retain the positive healing qualities of this popular grain. Whole wheat berries contain 10-20% protein and are high in all the B vitamins with the exception of B12. It also contains selenium, potassium, magnesium, iron, zinc, and phosphorus, as well as some calcium and copper. In its whole form, it has been shown to reduce the incidences of colon and breast cancer and regulate bowel function. In Chinese medicine, whole wheat tonifies the kidneys, calms and focuses the mind, nourishes heart energy, increases circulation, and is good for palpitations, insomnia, irritability, menopause,

416 | SWEETEN IT WITH AGAVE

and emotional instability. It encourages growth, weight gain, and fat formation. It should not be consumed by people with growths, tumors, or weight problems. Wheat often provokes allergic reactions, especially with flour products, which are typically rancid. Whole wheat flour has a tendency to go rancid much more rapidly than white flour because the germ has not been removed. There are a few options: grind the wheat berries yourself in a flour grinder or Vita-Mix; buy your flour from a co-op or store that freshly grinds their own flour; or, at the very least, purchase your flour from a store with quick turnover and that keeps flours refrigerated.

STORAGE: Whole wheat flour will keep in an airtight container in the refrigerator for up to three months, or six months in the freezer.

Whole wheat pastry flour This variety of whole wheat flour is ground from "soft" wheat and is a lighter, finer-textured flour with low gluten content. It creates a more refined quality similar to white flour, which makes it more ideal for use in pastries, cookies, cakes, and baked goods. Fortunately, not all of the bran and germ portions of the wheat kernel have been removed during the milling process, which makes whole wheat pastry flour a more nutritious choice than the standard white flour. In comparison to white flour, it will produce a slightly denser cake, though not nearly as dense as whole wheat flour would be. If you are baking bread, whole wheat flour is a better choice due to its higher gluten content and density. But if you are making more delicate desserts, whole wheat pastry flour is ideal.

Other Flours

Arrowroot flour Arrowroot flour is an easily digested powdered starch flour extracted from the roots of a plant also known as the "obedience plant," which grows in tropical regions. It is used for thickening sauces, juices, soups, syrups, and jellies, or to make a clear gloss. Unlike other thickeners like cornstarch and flour, it does not impart a flour taste and is thereby more neutral. It can also be preferable to cornstarch because it leaves a clear finish as opposed to a cloudy paste. It works very well with fruits, adding a nice sheen effect. In herbal medicine, arrowroot is regarded as a demulcent, and is made into a drink for bowel complaints, or as a pudding for invalids and children. Arrowroot can be added to recipes where you are substituting gluten grains with non-gluten grains, as it has a binding nature (just like guar and xanthan gum). Arrowroot dissolves instantly in cold water, making it easier (and cheaper) to use than kudzu root, which is another commonly used thickener with healing qualities. It is a better value to purchase arrowroot flour or powder in bulk in a health food store than in the little spice jars in the supermarket.

STORAGE: Arrowroot has a shelf life of about one year.

Chickpea (garbanzo) flour Chickpeas are high in protein and one of the earliest cultivated legumes. They contain zinc, folate, and protein and are low in fat, most of which is polyunsaturated. Because they are high in dietary fiber, they are a healthy source of carbohydrates for diabetics and those with insulin sensitivities. Chickpea flour is used in many cultures across the globe. The flour has a nutty and sweet flavor and is made from lightly roasted chickpeas that are ground. In Southeast Asia, it is known as "gram" or "besum" and is used to make flat breads, pancakes, and pakora (fried vegetable fritters). In Greece, traditional bread called "Eptazymo" is made with chickpea flour, as is a flat bread called "Socca," made in the south of France. Chickpea flour has gotten more attention in the health food community as another gluten-free flour alternative that is high in protein. When using it in muffin and bread recipes, mix small amounts of chickpea flour with other grains such as whole wheat or spelt in a one to four ratio. Chickpea flour can also be used to thicken soups and stews, and is especially good for binding veggie burgers. Chickpea flour can be substituted for the less desirable soy flour in most recipes.

STORAGE: Chickpea flour has a shelf life of about one year.

Garfava flour Garfava flour is a combination of chickpea flour and fava bean flour, and can be used just like chickpea flour.

STORAGE: Garfava flour has a shelf life of about one year.

Nut flours Nut flours are made by finely grinding nuts into a powder or "meal." They are gluten free, and high in protein and fat. You can easily make your own nut flour by adding nuts to a dry blender and blending on low until you get the desired texture.

STORAGE: Nut flours contain oils and have a shorter shelf life. Keep refrigerated for six to twelve months.

Potato flour Potato flour is made from cooked, dried, and ground potatoes. It is used in potato-based recipes such as potato bread to enhance the potato flavor and is often mixed with other flours for baking breads and rolls. It can also be used as a thickener for soups, gravies, and sauces. Potato flour is low in fat and is a good source of iron, manganese, potassium, copper, and Vitamins C and B6. Potato flour is often confused with potato starch, but potato flour is produced from the entire dehydrated potato whereas potato starch is produced from the starch only.

STORAGE: Potato flour has a shelf life of about two years.

Potato starch flour Potato starch flour is produced from the starch of the potato. It is a very fine powder and can be used with other flours for baking, especially in gluten-free baking. It can also be used as a thickening agent similar to arrowroot flour or cornstarch. For the best results, mix with water. Potato starch flour is often confused with potato flour, but note that potato flour is ground from the entire dried potato and is much heavier and more dense.

STORAGE: Potato starch has a shelf life of about three years.

Tapioca flour Tapioca flour is a slightly sweet, easily digestible starch flour extracted from the root of a plant native to the Amazon, otherwise known as "cassava," "manioc," "mandioca," "aipim," "macaxeira," "manioca," "boba," or "yuca" (not yucca, the vegetable). Grain free and gluten free, tapioca flour provides minimal vitamin and mineral content. In baking, tapioca flour can be added to recipes to lighten up wheat-free breads. It should be added in a proportion of 25-50%. It is possible to use tapioca flour by itself, such as in a traditional Brazilian bread called "Pao de Queijo," which contains butter and cheese. It also works if you add lots of beaten egg yolks and egg whites. But, generally, tapioca is best used in combination with other flours.

STORAGE: Tapioca flour has a shelf life of about two years.

Framboise Framboise is a French clear brandy made from fermented raspberries. It can impart a delicate raspberry flavor to desserts and drinks.

Fragoli Fragoli is an imported wild strawberry liqueur. Fragoli is excellent in delicate desserts and candies.

French Rose Absolute French Rose Absolute is a flavoring used in candies. It is made of vodka and French Rose essential oil. See page 342.

Garfava flour—*See flours*

Grain beverage (coffee substitute) Grain beverages are used as a healthy alternative to caffeinated coffee and tea. They are usually a combination of roasted barley, carob, dandelion, and chicory root. Well-known brands include Pero, Teecino, Cafix, and INKA. Instead of flavoring a dessert with coffee, try using a grain beverage for a similar roasted taste without the caffeine.

Grain-sweetened chocolate chips Grain-sweetened chocolate chips are sweetened with malted grains (barley and corn) instead of sugar. Sunspire is the main manufacturer. Use these in place of traditional sugar-sweetened chocolate chips to maintain the integrity of an agave-sweetened dessert.

Grapeseed oil—*See oils*

Goji berries: Goji berries, also known as wolfberries, grow on an evergreen shrub and have been used as a medicinal herb for 6,000 years in China, Mongolia, and in the Himalayas in Tibet. They look like red raisins when dried. Goji berries have been shown to protect the liver, help eyesight, improve sexual function and fertility, strengthen the legs, boost immune function, improve circulation, and promote longevity. Goji berries are rich in antioxidants, particularly carotenoids such as beta-carotene and zeaxanthin. They are great in smoothies, raw treats, hot cereals, granola mixes, power bars, or just by themselves as a colorful snack.

Guar gum Guar gum, also called guaran, is a galactomannan. It comes from the seed of a bean-like (legume) plant, sometimes referred to as the Indian tree. The guar seeds are dehusked, milled, and screened to obtain guar gum, which is a pale, off-white powder that is used as a thickener. It is high in soluble fiber. It also has eight times the thickening power of cornstarch. When added to dairy-free ice creams, it enhances the creaminess. It is particularly useful in gluten-free baking to bind, thicken and emulsify gluten-free ingredients. As with xanthan gum, measure guar gum carefully when using it in gluten-free recipes — otherwise, you may end up with heavy, stringy baked goods. Guar gum and xanthan gum can be used interchangeably in recipes.

Hemp seeds Hemp seeds are derived from the commercial production of Cannabis and the seeds are typically sold hulled. (Hulled hemp seeds are what are called for in the recipes in this book.) There is no drug impact from eating hulled hemp seeds, in case you were wondering. Hemp seeds are a highly nutritious source of protein, and are better tasting and more digestible than soybeans, for example. The seeds contain all the essential amino acids and essential fatty acids necessary to maintain healthy human life, including omega-3 and -6. Enjoy hemp seeds raw, ground into flour, sprouted, or added to baked goods, protein bars, trail mixes, smoothies, raw treats, or in granola. They can also be made into milk and from there processed into cheese, sauces, dips, or ice cream.

Irish moss Irish moss is a traditional, highly nutritious food from Ireland. It has appeared recently in raw food recipes as a healthy thickener. It is a species of edible sea vegetable, *Chondrus crispus,* and is a rich source of the emollient and moisture-binding substance carrageen. It also contains many micronutrients. Irish moss helps with radiation poisoning, cancer, hypertension, and cholesterol build-up. It also acts as a stabilizer in dairy products. You can use it in mousses, ice creams, shakes, pies, yogurt, nut yogurt, and nut cheese. When you purchase it, you will notice that you can buy purple flakes, powder, or a yellowish whole plant. The lighter varieties simply indicate that it has been bleached in the sunlight or exposed to light, which helps make the carrageen more available. For the best results, choose the whole plant, not the flakes or powder, and be sure to prepare it properly to avoid a fishy taste in your dishes.

PREPARATION: To prepare Irish moss for use in your recipe, start by using a scale to measure the dry weight needed for the recipe. Rinse it under cold water to remove sediment and sand completely. Place the moss in a quart mason jar, add fresh cold water until the jar is ¾ of the full, shake, and rinse three to four more times, or until the water runs clear. Make sure all of the sand and sediment are removed. Drain and add fresh water, then allow to soak for 24 hours in the refrigerator. Do not change the water or rinse the soaked Irish moss. It should have doubled in size and have a whitish color. Now it's ready to blend with water to create a creamy mixture, or to use according to your recipe. In general, 1 ounce of dry Irish moss will gel 1 cup of liquid so, if you want a mousse effect rather than a gel effect, add more liquid.

STORAGE: Dry Irish moss will stay fresh up to one year in a cool, dry place, as the salt will preserve it. If you have soaked more Irish moss than you need for a recipe, you can keep it in the fridge for up to a week in its original liquid. You may also use up extra moss by making a paste to use for impromptu recipe creations. Simply blend the moss with a little water until you get a thick, creamy consistency and store it in a closed glass jar in the refrigerator for up a week.

Kamut flour —See *flours*

Kelp One of the largest species of seaweeds, kelp is common part of Japanese cuisine and is used to flavor broths and stews or eaten as a simple snack. Kelp is an excellent addition to your diet, providing vital minerals including iodine.

Maca Maca is a Peruvian root that grows high in the Andes Mountains. It is dense in essential minerals, especially selenium, calcium, magnesium, and iron. It also contains fatty acids, such as linolenic acid, palmitic acid, and oleic acids, and 19 amino acids, as well as polysaccharides. Maca is used as an overall adaptogen and energy tonic.

Maccha (Matcha) Powder This finely milled green tea powder is used for Japanese tea ceremonies and is used to flavor mochi, green tea ice cream, and soba noodles. Green tea provides an excellent source of antioxidants.

Mango butter Mango butter is a tropical butter made from the kernels of the mango tree. It smells sweet and nutty and has a creamy consistency that is solid at room temperature. Mango butter is high in oleic and stearic fatty acids, just like cocoa butter and shea butter. For those allergic to cocoa butter, mango butter can be used as an equal-ratio substitute, particularly while making chocolate. Others just like to use mango butter to add some variety and gourmet distinction to their recipes.

Maple syrup An all-time favorite with pancakes, maple syrup is made by concentrating the sap of sugar maple trees. It was first collected and used by Native Americans and was later adopted by Europeans. Maple syrup is a rich source of manganese and zinc. Manganese produces energy and is an antioxidant. It also acts as an immuno-stimulant and aids in the production of hormones. Maple syrup is a precious sweetener (often called liquid gold) that imparts a lovely maple taste. It is especially tasty when added to sauces and frostings where you want the maple taste to stand out. It also works well in baking, and can be used instead of or in combination with agave nectar. It will impart a nice maple flavor to your baked goods, which is especially delicious in muffins and sweet breads.

Milk

In many recipes throughout the book, I leave it to you to choose the milk that you desire in the recipe. See below for more details.

Dairy milk Dairy milk adds depth and richness to recipes. Like so many foods, commercial dairy products are highly refined and there is growing concern and debate about their safety. Choosing a quality product is essential. Select raw, unpasteurized, and organic whenever possible (see Chapter 3 for more details on organic). For further information on raw milk versus pasteurized milk, see the Resources section. If you find you don't have access to raw milk in your area, consider some of the non-dairy milk options. Some prefer goat's milk over cow's milk, but goat's milk is also commonly pasteurized.

Non-dairy milk Non-dairy milks are made from, nuts, seeds, or grains and can be commercially purchased or made yourself. Examples of non-dairy milks include almond, oat, hemp, soy, rice, and coconut milk. See pages 79 and 80 for recipes. These milks can be delicious and satisfying additions to your diet. Usually less creamy and dense than dairy milk, they each have their own distinct flavor and nutritional properties. They lend themselves well to baking and cooking, so explore the variety and see what suits you best.

Coconut milk Though it would be logical to assume that the liquid found inside a coconut is coconut milk, the truth is that coconut milk is made by squeezing the grated flesh of coconut with hot water. Coconut milk contains saturated fats that are easily metabolized by the body and have even been used in weight loss programs. There are several notable health benefits of coconut milk: it is anticarcinogenic, antimicrobial, antibacterial, and antiviral. The main saturated fat that it contains, lauric acid, is also found in mother's milk and has been shown to promote brain development and bone health. Coconut milk makes a fantastic base for dairy-free ice cream. See pages 79 and 80 for instructions on how to make coconut milk.

Medicinal Mushrooms Mushrooms such as shitake, maitake, cordyceps, reishi, chaga, and turkey tail are considered valuable for medicinal purposes and can be purchased in powder form and thrown into smoothies, superfood balls, and raw candies. Research has show that fungi may inhibit tumor growth, increase immunity, and act as an antiviral and antibiotic. When adding medicinal mushrooms to your recipes, such as those listed in this cookbook, it is recommended to buy powders that have been pretreated with heat to break down the indigestible "chitin" and release the active compounds in a more concentrated and bio-available form.

Millet flour—*See flours*

Molasses, Blackstrap Molasses is a viscous byproduct of the processing of sugar cane or sugar beets into sugar. The sugar cane is crushed to remove the juice, which is then boiled vigorously. Centrifuges are then used to extract the sugar crystals from the syrup. The remaining syrup becomes molasses. It has a very strong, somewhat bittersweet flavor. It is best used in recipes rather than as a straight sweetener due to its potent flavor. It is typically used in recipes for ginger cookies, BBQ sauce, and baked beans. Molasses boasts many nutrients including manganese, copper, calcium, potassium, magnesium, and iron. For this reason, it is a useful ingredient in herbal iron tonics for women. Purchase unsulphured molasses since added sulphur can be harmful to health.

Nutritional Yeast Nutritional yeast is a deactivated, yellow, flakey yeast that is used as a condiment. It contributes a nutty and cheesy effect to dishes, making it popular with vegans. It's cultivated by culturing *Saccharomyces cerevisiae* with a mixture of sugarcane and beet molasses, and then harvesting, washing, drying, and packaging up the yeast. It is an excellent source of protein and vitamins, and is especially high in B vitamins. In addition, some brands are fortified with vitamin B12.

Oat bran—*See flours*

Oat flour—*See flours*

Oils

Coconut oil Coconut oil is made by pressing the coconut meat. Coconut oil has gotten a bad reputation over the years, due to a misunderstood study on animals. Researchers were not using unadulterated, pure coconut oil, but rather hydrogenated coconut oil that was purposefully altered to make it completely devoid of any essential fatty acids. Soon after that came the anti-saturated fat campaign and the promotion of polyunsaturated fats, such as canola, soybean, safflower, and corn. In follow-up studies, coconut oil was found to *not* cause high serum cholesterol and coronary heart disease. Instead, it has been shown to contribute to healthy hair and skin, weight regulation, increased immunity, bone strength, proper digestion, and healthy metabolism. It has also been shown to offer relief from kidney problems, heart disease, high blood pressure, diabetes, HIV, and cancer, to name a few. The benefits of coconut oil can be attributed to the presence of lauric acid, capric acid, and caprylic acid, as well as its antimicrobial, antioxidant, antifungal, and antibacterial qualities. Coconut oil becomes solid at temperatures under 76°F, so, it may be liquid or solid, depending on the temperature of the place where you store it. Coconut oil is excellent for cooking and baking and can be used in place of butter in baking, though you will use a little less coconut oil. For a recipe that calls for 1 cup of butter, use ¾ cup of oil instead. Coconut oil is perfect as a substitute for commercial hydrogenated and partially hydrogenated vegetable shortenings, which use low-quality oils like canola and soybean.

Grapeseed oil Grapeseed oil is a vegetable oil made from pressing the seeds of grapes, an abundant byproduct of winemaking. Grapeseed oil has a neutral flavor, which makes it a good dairy-free choice for baking and pie crusts. Other vegetable oils, like sunflower and safflower, have a tendency to go rancid, whereas grapeseed oil is rich in Vitamin E which preserves it. For that reason, grapeseed oil is my top choice for a neutral-tasting oil in baking.

Flaxseed oil Flax is a blue flowering plant that is grown for its oil-rich seeds. Flaxseed oil, also known as linseed oil, has gotten much fame for being a rich source of omega-3 fatty acids. It is one of the most volatile oils, and must be purchased fresh regularly from a store that carries it in the refrigerator section due to its tendency to go rancid within six to twelve months from purchase. Always check the manufacture date on the bottle, get the freshest one possible, and store it in the refrigerator. Flaxseed oil should not be heated, but instead added to dishes that are uncooked, such as salad dressings, smoothies, or raw treats.

Olive oil Olive oil is fruit oil that comes from olives. Olives are ground into paste and pressed to remove the oil. Olive oil is rich in monounsaturated fat and antioxidants like chlorophyll, carotenoids, and vitamin E. Scientists have identified a compound in olive oil called oleuropein which prevents LDL cholesterol from oxidizing. It is the oxidized cholesterol that sticks to the walls of the arteries and forms plaque. Using olive oil can significantly lower blood pressure and reduce the risk of heart attacks. It has also been shown to reduce blood pressure, inhibit the growth of some cancers, benefit people at risk for or with diabetes, and lessen the severity of asthma and arthritis. Olive oil definitely imparts a distinct flavor, and is probably not the best oil to use for baking, except for savory dishes and breads. Always select organic, cold pressed, extra virgin olive oil.

Sesame oil Sesame oil is made from pressing sesame seeds. It has been used as a healing oil for thousands of years. The presence of high levels of polyunsaturated fatty acids in the oil makes it excellent for controlling high blood pressure. Sesame oil also contains two unique chemicals called sesamol and sesamin, which are powerful antioxidants. It is available in regular and roasted flavors. When baking with sesame oil, use regular organic sesame oil, which has a mild taste. Roasted sesame oil imparts a very strong flavor that is more typically used in savory Asian dishes.

Vegetable shortening, organic (palm or coconut) Instead of using hydrogenated and partially hydrogenated vegetable shortening (which use low-quality oils like cottonseed, canola, and soybean oil), you can now purchase organic vegetable shortening made with palm oil or coconut oil. Palm oil is extracted and refined through pressing and crushing the fruit of the oil palm, rather than through using chemical solvents such as hexane. It contains a balance of polyunsaturated, monounsaturated, and saturated fatty acids. In addition, palm oil contains essential substances such as linoleic acid (an essential fatty acid which the body cannot manufacture) and tocopherols and tocotrienols, which act as natural antioxidants against damaging free-radicals. Palm oil, like coconut oil, has gotten bad publicity as a dangerous oil. As an informed consumer, do your research and be aware that many of these campaigns are driven by industries that stand to benefit from such accusations. I have found that organic vegetable shortening is delicious in cookies and cakes. Unlike butter, it is soft at room temperature, so whipping up a batch of cookies on short notice is no problem. It is also fantastic in pie crusts. If you are dairy free, organic vegetable shortening is probably the best and tastiest option.

Olive oil—*See oils*

Pomona's Universal Pectin Kit A sugar-free and preservative-free pectin kit that is activated by calcium water.

Potato flour—*See flours*

Potato starch flour—*See flours*

Quinoa flour—*See flours*

Rye flour—*See flours*

Salt Most people don't put much thought into salt; but having a high-quality salt in your diet is actually important. Commercial table salt can cause health issues that are avoidable by replacing it with a high-quality salt. When choosing salt, I recommend looking for ones that are unrefined and have some sort of color besides bright white. The reason: these salts have higher mineral content, enhanced flavor, and have not undergone the commercial processing that table salt does. Commercial iodized salts are typically stripped of naturally occurring minerals and contain additives such as aluminum silicate to keep it powdery and porous. Celtic sea salt or Himalayan salt are great alternatives and are easily found in a health food stores or online. Even when selecting a natural sea salt, look for those that have some variation in color instead of the less expensive, pure white types.

Sesame oil—*See oils*

Spelt flour—*See flours*

Spirulina Spirulina is a blue-green algae that thrives in warm, alkaline bodies of freshwater. This superfood is rich in protein, vitamins, minerals, and carotenoids (a type of antioxidant that can help protect cells from damage). It contains nutrients, including B complex vitamins, beta-carotene, vitamin E, manganese, zinc, copper, iron, selenium, and gamma linolenic acid (an essential fatty acid). Spirulina is 65-70% percent complete protein, with all essential amino acids in perfect balance. In comparison, beef is only 22% protein. This makes it a great supplement for vegetarians. Spirulina is easily incorporated in any diet by adding it to smoothies or raw-food treats. I even used it to add a little green color to the *Mint Chocolate Chip Ice Cream* on page 321! Spirulina can boost energy and cellular health, and consistent use can even help reduce cholesterol.

When selecting a spirulina, buy it from a trusted brand. Spirulina can be contaminated with toxic substances called microcystins; it can also absorb heavy metals if they are present in the water where it is grown. Look for a quality company that is attentive to these concerns.

Sweeteners *See agave nectar, date sugar, maple syrup, and molasses.*

Tahini Tahini is ground sesame seed butter. It is used commonly in Middle Eastern dishes and is the base of the popular candy, halvah. It can be added to candies, smoothies, and baked goods, and can also top muffins and breads just like peanut butter. Sesame seeds are high in manganese, copper, calcium, magnesium, iron, phosphorus, vitamin B1, zinc, and dietary fiber.

Tamari Tamari is a dark, rich, Japanese soy sauce that is generally thicker than soy sauce and provides better flavor for cooking. Tamari is available wheat free and provides niacin, manganese, protein, and tryptophan.

Tapioca flour—See *flours*

Teff flour—See *flours*

Vegetable shortening, organic—See *oils*

Whey powder Whey powder is dried whey, a byproduct from cheese making. Whey is the clear liquid that separates from curds when clotted milk or yogurt is strained through a cheesecloth. It contains approximately 50% of the lactose of the milk, proteins, vitamins, and minerals. Whey protein powders are made by separating the fat and lactose from the proteins. This protein powder is sold as a supplement for weight loss and body building.It is sold in the form of whey concentrate (70-85% protein) and whey protein isolate (90-94% protein). I recommend using pure whey protein isolate, especially if you are lactose intolerant. Whey protein isolate is a magical ingredient in gluten-free baking, adding the elasticity to recipes that usually require gluten. It also works great in pancakes. Whether you are buying whey powder or whey protein isolate, be sure to get them pure with no additives. Whey has been shown to have immune-boosting qualities.

Whole wheat flour—See *flours*

Whole wheat pastry flour—See *flours*

Xanthan gum Xanthan gum is a polysaccharide used as a food additive. It is produced by fermentation of glucose or sucrose by the *Xanthomonas campestris bacterium*. Xanthan gum can be used as a thickener in baked goods and as an ingredient in ice cream that will provide a creamier texture. In pastry fillings, it prevents "weeping" of the water in the filling, thus protecting the crispness of the crust. When mixed equally with guar gum, the viscosity is more than when either one is used alone. You often find xanthan gum in gluten-free baking due to its ability to give the dough or batter a "stickiness" that would otherwise be achieved with gluten. I recommend combining equal amounts of xanthan gum and guar gum and storing it in your pantry for the ideal gum combo.

Yeast *Saccharomyces cerevisiae* is the most common yeast used in baking. It is used as a leavening agent, where it converts the fermentable sugars present in the dough into carbon dioxide. This causes the dough to expand or rise as the carbon dioxide forms pockets or bubbles. When the dough is baked, the yeast dies off and the air pockets "set," giving the baked product a soft and spongy texture. You can buy active dry yeast in granulated form in any supermarket or health food store.

Yogurt Yogurt is a milk product. It's made by adding live bacteria cultures to milk, which causes it to ferment, coagulate, and thicken, adding a tangy, slightly astringent flavor. You can make your own yogurt using raw milk or non-dairy milks; it is easier when using a yogurt maker. When purchasing, consider choosing organic, plain yogurt; you can always add your own sweeteners, like agave or fresh fruit, later. Flavored yogurts often contain unhealthy ingredients, including so-called "natural" flavors, high-fructose corn syrup, and artificial sweeteners.

RESOURCES

Agave Supplies

Visit Sweeten it with Agave at: www.SweetenItWithAgave.com

Shop on our website for bulk agave, baking tools and supplies, whole grain flours, hard to find ingredients, and much more!

Organic and Local Foods

Visit www.organic.org

A consumer-friendly site with easy-to-understand explanations about the benefits of organic and ways to involve the whole family.

Visit Organic Center at www.organic-center.org

Organic Center's website is friendly to both novice and experienced readers. Their mission is to "advance credible, evidence-based science on the health and environmental benefits of organic food and farming and communicate them to the public"

Visit Organic Consumer's Association at www.organicconsumers.org

A giant flea market of activities, news, tidbits and events happening in the organic community

Visit Local Harvest at www.localharvest.org

Provides a handy map to find farmers' markets, family farms, and other sources of sustainably grown food in your area. They have links to seeds and organic growing tips as well.

Raw Dairy Resources

Visit A Campaign for Raw Milk at www.realmilk.com

A site that connects consumers with local farms producing raw, organic dairy products.

Visit RAW USA at www.rawusa.org

RAW USA is an organization dedicated to the promotion and production of safe, healthful, and delicious raw milk.

ENDNOTES

1   C.P. Khare, *Indian Herbal Remedies* (New York: Springer, 2003).

2   M. D. García, A. M. Quílez, M. T. Sáenz, M. E. Martínez-Domínguez, and R. de la Puerta, "Anti-inflammatory Activity of *Agave Intermixta* Trel. and *Cissus Sicyoides* L., species used in the Caribbean Traditional Medicine," *Journal of Ethnopharmacology* 71:3 (August 2000), 395-400.

3   García, Quílez, Sáenz, Martínez-Domínguez and de la Puerta, ibid.

4   Daniel F. Austin, *Florida Ethnobotany* (Boca Raton: CRC Press, 2004).

5   Margot Blum Schevill, Janet Catherine Berlo, and Edward Bridgman Dwyer eds., *Textile Traditions of Mesoamerica and the Andes: An Anthology* (Austin: University of Texas Press, 1996).

6   M.G. López and J.E. Urías-Silvas, "Prebiotic Effect Of Fructans From Agave, Dasylirion And Nopal," ISHS International Symposium on Human Health Effects of Fruits and Vegetables (Québec City, Canada) 2007 (http://www.actahort.org/books/744/744_45.htm).

7   The American Chemical Society News Release, "Ingredient in Tequila Plant May Fight Osteoporosis and Other Diseases,", March 23, 2010 (http://portal.acs.org/portal/acs/corg/content).

8   http://en.wikipedia.org/wiki/Agave_nectar (last accessed June 2010).

9   National Honey Board, "Honey Bee Products," http://www.honey.com/nhb/about-honey/honey-and-bees (last accessed June 2010).

10 Theodore L Brown, H. Eugene LeMay, Jr., Bruce E. Bursten, *Chemistry: The Central Science* (Pearson Education, 2006) p.1099-1100.

11 http://www.thepaleodiet.com/nutritional_tools/fruits_table.html (last accessed June 2010).

12 Theodore L Brown, H. Eugene LeMay, Jr., Bruce E. Bursten, *Chemistry: The Central Science* (Pearson Education, 2006) p.1101.

13 International Union of Pure and Applied Chemistry "Disaccharides,"*Compendium of Chemical Terminology* Internet edition.

14 http://www.thepaleodiet.com/nutritional_tools/fruits_table.html (last accessed June 2010).

15 http://en.wikipedia.org/wiki/Polysaccharide (last accessed June 2010).

16 "Study Finds High-Fructose Corn Syrup Contains Mercury," *HealthDay News*, January 28th, 2009.

17 Corn Refiners Association, "The Process." PDF available to download at http://www.corn.org/theprocess.htm

18 http://www.madehow.com/Volume-4/Corn-Syrup.html (last accessed June 2010).

19 Annemarie Colbin, *Food and Healing* (New York: Random House, 1986), 58-59.

20 Figures are collected from mostly from USDA Nutrient Database http://www.nal.usda.gov/fnic/foodcomp/search/ with supplemental data from http://www.thepaleodiet.com/nutritional_tools/fruits_table.html), except honey.

21 USDA National Nutrient Database data published in September 1987, http://www.nal.usda.gov/fnic/foodcomp/Data/Other/herr48.pdf (last accessed June 2010).

22 Warren Labs Analysis of Madhava's agave supplier, Nekutli: http://www.sweetenitwithagave.com/resources/warrenlabanalysisagave/, (last accessed February 2011).

23 Warren Labs Analysis of Madhava's agave supplier, Nekutli: http://sugarfreeagaverecipes.typepad.com/sweeten_it_with_agave/warren-labs-report.html, (last accessed June 2010).

24 Report from Wholesome Sweeteners about basic facts: http://www.sweetenitwithagave.com/resources/wholesome-sweeteners-facts/, (last accessed February 2011).

25 Compiled using data from the USDA National Nutrient Database http://www.nal.usda.gov/fnic/foodcomp/search/) and the International Database of Glycemic Index http://www.glycemicindex.com/ except for the can of cola which was taken off the Coca-Cola website: http://productnutrition.thecoca-colacompany.com/products/coca-cola#nutrition, (last accessed June 2010).

26 http://www.sweetenitwithagave.com/resources/warrenlabanalysisagave/, (last accessed February 2011).

27 https://www.aibonline.org, (last accessed June 2010).

28 http://www.madhavasagave.com/FAQ.aspx, (last accessed June 2010).

29 Warren Labs Analysis of Madhava's agave supplier, Nekutli: http://www.sweetenitwithagave.com/resources/warrenlabanalysisagave/, (last accessed February 2011).

30 Aveline Kushi, *Complete Guide to Macrobiotic Cooking for Health, Harmony, and Peace* (New York: Warner Books, 1985), 318.

31 Elaine Gottschall, *Breaking the Vicious Cycle* (Baltimore, Ontario, Canada: Kirkton Press, 2004), 11-16.

32 University of Sydney Glycemic Index Foundation, *Glycemic Index and GI Database*, http://www.glycemicindex.com, (last accessed June 2010).

33 A.E. Jarvi, B.E. Karlstrom, Y.E. Granfeldt, I.E. Bjorck, N.G. Asp, and B.O. Vessby, "Improved Glycemic Control and Lipid Profile and Normalized Fibrinolytic Activity on a Low Glycemic Index Diet in Type 2 Diabetic Patients," *Diabetes Care*, 1999, 10-19, http://care.diabetesjournals.org/cgi/content/abstract/22/1/10.

34 Barclay AW, Petocz P, McMillan-Price J, et al. Glycemic index, glycemic load, and chronic disease risk–a meta-analysis of observational studies. American Journal of Clinical Nutrition 2008; 87:627–37.

35 M. R. Weihrauch, and V. Diehl, "Artificial Sweeteners – Do They Bear Carcinogenic Risk?" *Annals of Oncology*, October 2004.

36 Glycemic Index Foundation, 7/20/10, http://www.glycemicindex.com/, (last accessed June 2010).

37 Robert Dare, *Food, Power, and Community* (Kent Town, Australia: Westfield Press, 1999), 78.

38 Antar, M. A., Ohlson, M. A., and Hodges, R. E., American Journal of Clinical Nutrition, 1964, 14, 169.

39 Stephen Haley, Jane Reed, Biing-Hwan Lin, and Annetta Cook, "Sweetener Consumption in the United States," United States Department of Agriculture *Electronic Outlook Report from the Economic Research Service*, August 2005 http://www.ers.usda.gov/Publications/EIB33/EIB33.pdf, (last accessed June 2010).

40 Janice R. Hermann, PhD., "Dietary Sugar and Alternative Sweeteners" (fact sheet), Oklahoma State University Division of Agricultural Sciences and Natural Resources, 2007 http://osufacts.okstate.edu/docushare/dsweb/Get/Document-2397/T-3157web.pdf, (last accessed June 2010).

41 Thornley S, McRobbie H, Eyles H, Walker N, Simmons G. The Obesity Epidemic: Is Glycemic Index the Key to Unlocking a Hidden Addiction? Med Hypotheses 2008,71.709–14.

42 Keith Connors, PhD., *Feeding the Brain: How Food Affects Children* (Cambridge: De Capo Press, 1989), 81.

43 David Ludwig, Karen Peterson, and Steven Gortmaker, "Relation between consumption of sugar-sweetened drinks and childhood obesity," *Lancet* (February 17th, 2001).

44 http://www.ams.usda.gov/AMSv1.0/NOSB, (last accessed June 2010).

45 Steven R. Schechter, N.D., *Fighting Radiation with Foods, Herbs & Vitamins* (Brookline: East West Health Books, 1988), 56.

46   Christine Horner, M.D., F.A.C.S., *Waking the Warrior Goddess: Harnessing the power of Nature and Natural Medicines to Achieve Extraordinary Health* (North Bergen: Basic Health Publications, 2005), 130.

47   Sally Fallon and Mary G. Enig, Ph.D., *Nourishing Traditions* (Washington, D.C.: New Trends, 1999), 35.

48   "Shopper's Guide to Pesticides," http://www.foodnews.org, (last accessed June 2010).

49   Charles Benbrook, Xin Zhao, Jaime Yanez, Neal Davies, and Preston Andrews, "New Evidence Confirms the Nutritional Superiority of Plant-Based Organic Foods," *State of Science Review: Nutritional Superiority of Organic Foods*, March 2008, http://www.organic-center.org/reportfiles/5367_Nutrient_Content_SSR_FINAL_V2.pdf, (last accessed June 2010).

50   Schechter, 58.

51   Mark Percival, M.D., "Antioxidants," *Clinical Nutrition Insights,* 1998, http://acudoc.com/Antioxidants.PDF, (last accessed June 2010).

52   Enrique Cadenas, "Understanding the process of Aging: The Roles of Mitochondria, Free Radicals and Antioxidants," Ivor E. Dreosti, ed., *Trace Elements, Micronutrients, and Free Radicals* (Clifton: The Humana Press, 1991).

53   Benbrook et al., http://www.organic-center.org/reportfiles/5367_Nutrient_Content_SSR_FINAL_V2.pdf, (last accessed June 2010).

54   Benbrook et al., (http://www.organic-center.org/reportfiles/5367_Nutrient_Content_SSR_FINAL_V2.pdf, (last accessed June 2010).

55   G. P. Sparling, D. Wheeler, E.T. Vesely, and L.A. Schipper, "What is Soil Organic Matter Worth?" *The Journal of Environmental Quality*, March 1st 2006, http://jeq.scijournals.org/cgi/reprint/35/2/548.

56   George Kupper, "Pasture, Forage and Sustainable Organic Production," The United States Department of Agriculture http://www.ams.usda.gov/AMSv1.0/getfile?dDocName=STELPRD3576887.

57   Agency for Toxic Substances and Disease Registry, "Nitrate/Nitrite Toxicity What Are Nitrate and Nitrite?" *Case Studies in Environmental Medicine (CSEM)*, http://www.atsdr.cdc.gov/csem/nitrate/nitrate.html, (last accessed June 2010).

58   Food and Agriculture Organization of the United Nations, "Organic Agriculture," Committee on Agriculture Fifteenth Session (Rome, Italy), January 25-29, 1999, http://www.fao.org/unfao/bodies/COag/cOAG15/X0075E.htm, (last accessed June 2010).

59   Edward O. Gangstad, *Weed Control Methods for Rights-Of Way Management* (Boca Raton: CRC Press, 1982), 153.

60   W.E. Chappell, "Multiflora Rose Control Studies With Soil Applied Herbicides," *Transportation Research Board Publications Index*, 1981, http://pubsindex.trb.org/view.aspx?id=173323, (last accessed June 2010).

61   Transportation Research Board/National Research Council, *Best Management Practices for Environmental Issues Related to Highway and Street Maintenance* (Washington, D.C.: National Academy Press, 1999), 24.

62   Rachel Carson, *Silent Spring* (New York: Houghton Mifflin, 1962), 112-113.

63   S. A. Khan, R. L. Mulvaney, T. R. Ellsworth and C. W. Boast, "The Myth of Nitrogen Fertilization for Soil Carbon Sequestration," *The Journal of Environment Quality,* 2007, http://jeq.scijournals.org/cgi/content/abstract/36/6/1821, (last accessed June 2010).

64   Elizabeth Stell, *Secrets to Great Soil: A Grower's Guide to Composting, Mulching and Creating Healthy, Fertile Soil for Your Garden* (North Adams: Storey Publishing, 1998), 176.

65   Annemarie Colbin, Ph.D., "SUGAR! Delicious and Deadly," www.foodandhealing.com, 2005, http://www.foodandhealing.com/articles/article-sugar.htm, (last accessed June 2010).

66   Annemarie Colbin, Ph.D., "SUGAR! Delicious and Deadly," foodandhealing.com, 2005, http://www.foodandhealing.com/articles/article-sugar.htm, (last accessed June 2010).

67   Paul Pitchford, *Healing with Whole Foods: Asian Traditions and Modern Nutrition* (Berkeley: North Atlantic Books, 1993), 14-16.

68   United States Department of Agriculture, *Table 4: Minimum Requirements and Specifications for Supplemental Foods*, 2010, http://nal.usda.gov/wicworks/Learning_Center/FP/Minimum_Req.pdf, (last accessed June 2010).

69   Fallon and Enig, 22.

70   Annemarie Colbin, *Food and Healing* (New York: Random House, 1986), 37-41.

71   Annemarie Colbin, Ph.D., "Frankenstein Food," foodandhealing.com, http://www.foodandhealing.com/articles/article-frankensteinfood.htm (1999), (last accessed June 2010).

72   Katherine Czapp, "Against the Grain," The Weston A. Price Foundation, 2006, www.westonaprice.org/against-the-grain.html (last accessed June 2010).

73   United States Center for Disease Control and Prevention, *U.S. Obesity Trends,* 2007, http://www.cdc.gov/obesity/data/trends.html#State, (last accessed June 2010).

74   Fallon and Enig, 4-7.

75   Alan L. Watson, *Cereal Killer,* (Minneapolis: Diet Heart Publishing, 2008), 11-14.

76   Fallon and Enig, 8.

77   Fatty Acid Chain, http://homepage.smc.edu/wissmann_paul/humanbiology/lipids.html, (last accessed June 2010).

78   Schechter, 58-60.

79   Sally Fallon and Mary G. Enig, Ph.D., "Splendor From the Grass" The Weston A. Price Foundation, http://www.westonaprice.org/Splendor-From-the-Grass.html (2000), (last accessed 2010).

80   Fallon and Enig, 8.

81   Fallon and Enig, 13-14.

82   Fallon and Enig, 19.

83   Jacques de Langre, Ph.D., *Seasalt's Hidden Powers,* (Magalia: Happiness Press, 1994), 29-34.

84   Pitchford, 198.

85   Colbin, 186.

86   de Langre, 46-47.

87   Chart, http://www.organichealthforlife.com/v/vspfiles/assets/images/chart.jpg, (last accessed 2010).

88   Real Salt Elemental Analysis, http://www.realsalt.com/images/realsalt_analysis.pdf,(last accessed 2010).

89   Certificate of the Analysis of Himalayan Crystal Mineral Rock Salt, http://www.biodistributors.com.au/ProdInfFiles/hcs.php, (last accessed 2010).

90   Analysis of commercial salt from WA Salt Supply, http://www.wasalt.com.au/Table.html,(last accessed 2010)

INDEX

A

Açaí powder 78, 407
Agar-agar 114, 240, 252, 278, 281, 286, 299, 407
    Apricot Agar-Agar Jam 121
    Gelatin-Free Agar Jello 370
    Instant Easy Fruit Jam with Agar-Agar 118
    No Cook Freezer Jam with Agar-Agar 117
Agave Nectar 13-31
    Flavored Agave Nectar Base Recipe 94
        Cayenne Black Pepper Agave Nectar 94
        Chocolate Agave Nectar 94
        Geranium Ginger Agave Nectar 94
        Lemon Balm Lime Agave Nectar 94
        Lemony Agave Nectar 94
        Orange Agave Nectar 94
        Orange Clary Sage Agave Nectar 94
        Peppermint Agave Nectar 94
        Rose Agave Nectar 94
Almond
    Almond Flax Nut Bar 359
    Almond Orange Cake 211
    Almond Milk 75, 76, 77, 252, 366
    Flourless Almond Cookies 234
    Marzipan (Almond Paste) 107
    Parozzo 200
    Raw Almond Chocolate Milk 76
    Vegan Almond Macaroons 236
Aloe vera juice 407
    Refreshing Aloe Tonic Drink 86
Amaranth
    Amaranth Apple Waffles 402
    Amaranth Cornbread 152
    Amaranth flour 411
    Amaranth Oat Bran Muffins 162
Angel Food Cake 212
Apple
    Amaranth Apple Waffles 402
    Apple Butter 120
    Apple Crisp 308
    Apple Cider Sauce 105
    Apple Pie 279
    Sparkling Apple Cider 81
Apricot
    Apricot Agar-Agar Jam 121
    Apricot Bread 149
Arrowroot flour 240, 252, 253, 278, 416

B

Baking powder 187, 190, 408
Baking soda 186, 187, 190, 408
Banana
    Banana Bread 148
    Banana Chocolate Chip Bread 157
    Banana Chocolate Crunch Popsicles 378
    Banana Coconut Muffins 181
    Banana Coconut Snack 365
    Banana Cream Pie 282
    Banana Cream Pudding 250
    Banana Rice Bran Muffins 177
    Chia Banana Coconut Pudding 255
    Fried Bananas with Chocolate Sauce 366
    Torta de Banana 251
Barley
    Barley Apple Muffins 163
    Barley Combo Crust 272
    Barley flour 411-412
    Barley Pudding 250
Base Recipes (Easily modified and customized)
    Beverage Base Recipes
        Juice Soda 81
        Live Water Crystal Soda 82
        Nut and Seed Milk 74
        Smoothie 78
    Cakes Base Recipes
        White Cake 193
        Chocolate Birthday Cake 195
        White Birthday Cake 194
        White Cake, gluten-free 209
    Candies Base Recipes
        Raw Chocolate 326
        Simple Chocolate 340
    Cobblers, Crisps and
    Crumbles Base Recipes
        Cobbler 304
        Crisp 307
        Crumble 309
    Extracts Base Recipe 95
    Flavored Agave Nectar Base Recipe 94
    Granola Base Recipes
        Granola #1-Oil-Free 388
        Granola #2-Bran-Style 388
        Granola #3-Combo Granola 389
    Ice Cream Base Recipes 314
        Dairy Ice Cream 314
        Gelato 316
        Coconut Milk Ice Cream 318
        Cashew Milk Ice Cream 322
    Jams, Jellies, Marmalades, and Preserves 113
    Base Recipes
        Fruit Jam with Pomona's Universal Pectin Kit 115
        Instant Easy Fruit Jam with Agar-Agar 118
        Jelly made with Pomona's Universal Pectin Kit 116
        No Cook Freezer Jam with Agar-Agar 117
        Raw Jam 119
    Muffin Base Recipes
        Muffins 161
        Gluten-Free Muffins 173
        Pastry Muffin Base 170
    Pie Crust Base Recipes
        Oil Crust 268
        Butter Crust 268
        Organic Vegetable Shortening Crust 269
        Combo Crust: Half Shortening, Half Butter 269
        Egg Crust 269
        Cheese Crust 269

Pie Filling Base Recipe
    Fresh Fruit Pie — 278
Popsicle Base Recipes
    Fruit Juice Popsicles — 375
    Herbal Popsicles — 379
Pudding Base Recipe — 242
Raw ChocolateCandy Base Recipe — 326
Snack Base Recipe
    Homemade Protein Bar — 358
Superfood Balls Base Recipe
    Dried Fruit Bon-Bons — 328
Berry Almond Crumble — 310
Berry Jam — 124
Beverages / Chapter 6 — **73**
Blackberry Sauce — 101
Blueberry
    Blueberry Bran Oatmeal — 391
    Blueberry Muffins — 164
    Blueberry Pie — 280
Bran Muffins — 165
Breads / Chapter 10 — **127**
Breakfast Foods / Chapter 22 — **385**
Brown Rice
    Brown Rice Bread, yeasted — 154
    Brown Rice Crispy Treats — 372
    Brown rice flour — 412
Brownies
    Brownies, Gluten-Free — 235
    Cocoa Brownies — 231
    Rich Chocolate Brownies — 232
Buckwheat
    Buckwheat flour — 412
    Buckwheat Muffins — 182
    Buckwheat Pancakes — 397
    Buckwheat Pancakes, Fermented — 400
Butter — 187, 216, 261, 408
    Butter Cookies — 225
    Butter Crust — 268
Buttermilk — 137, 186, 207
Buttermilk powder — 110, 130, 137, 140, 143, 144, 145, 161-167
    196, 205, 223, 226, 272, 371, 403, 408
    Buttermilk Teff Waffles — 405
    Kamut Buttermilk Bread — 136
    Whole Grain Buttermilk Pancakes — 398
    Whole Wheat Buttermilk Shortening Crust — 272

C

Cacao
    Cacao nibs — 90, 409
    Cacao powder, Raw — 76-78, 86, 255, 298, 300, 314,
    326-328, 409
**Cakes, Birthday Cakes, Cupcakes,
and Cheesecakes / Chapter 12** — **185**
Candies With a Healthy Twist / Chapter 19 — **325**
Caramel Corn — 373
Cardamom Grits — 392
Carob — 408-409
    Carob Balls — 336
    Carob Banana Frosting — 110
    Carob Bread — 140
    Carob Sauce — 103
Carrots
    Carrot Bread — 150
    Carrot Cake — 206
    Carrot Rice Muffins — 178

Cashews
    Cashew Milk Ice Cream Base Recipe — 322
    Chia Seed Raw Ice Cream — 322
Cayenne Black Pepper Agave Nectar — 94
Chai Chocolate Chip Coconut Ice Cream — 318
Chai Tapioca — 249
Challah — 142
Cheese
    Cheese Crust — 269
    Cheesecakes — 207
    Cream Cheese
        Cream Cheese Frosting — 110
        Cocoa Nut Frosting — 110
    New York Cheesecake — 207
    Ricotta Cheese Pancakes — 399
Cherry
    Cherry Pie — 281
    Dried Fruit Bon-Bon Base Recipe — 328
Chia Seeds — 329, 333, 350, 359, 360, 409
    Chia Banana Coconut Pudding — 255
    Chia Chocolate Pudding — 254
    Chia Fresca — 87
    Chia Raisin Cookies — 222
    Chia Seed Raw Ice Cream — 322
    Chia Sports Drink — 87
Chickpea (garbanzo bean) flour — 173, 416-417
Chocolate
    Chai Chocolate Chip Coconut Ice Cream — 318
    Chia Chocolate Pudding — 254
    Chocolate Agave Nectar — 94
    Chocolate Birthday Cake — 195
    Chocolate Bundt Cake — 213
    Chocolate Chip Bundt Cake — 197
    Chocolate Chip Cookies — 218
    Chocolate Chip Oat Bars — 356
    Chocolate Covered Cherries and Strawberries — 341
    Chocolate Framboise Rose Truffles — 342
    Chocolate Fudge Popsicles — 382
    Chocolate Ginger Cake — 199
    Chocolate Halvah — 351
    Chocolate Lavender Truffles — 345
    Chocolate Mint Truffles — 344
    Chocolate Peanut Butter Cups — 346
    Chocolate Pudding — 244
    Chocolate Raspberry Layer Cake — 204
    Chocolate Syrup — 103
    Chocolate Tahini Balls — 331
    Chocolate Zucchini Cake — 210
    Dark Chocolate Cake with Orange Ganache — 202
    Eggless Chocolate Chip Cookies — 219
    Fried Bananas with Chocolate Sauce — 366
    Irish Hot Chocolate — 89
    KC's Chocolate Chip Coconut Cookies — 233
    Mexican Chocolate Elixir — 90
    Mexican Hot Chocolate — 89
    Pomegranate Chocolate Truffles — 343
    Simple Chocolate Base Recipe — 340
    Raw Chocolate Candy Base Recipe — 326
    Red Velvet Cake (Chocolate Beet Cake) — 205
    Rich Chocolate Brownies — 232
Citrus — 95, 114
    Citrus Marmalade — 125
    Citrus Raspberry Herbal Popsicles — 380
    Citrus Soda — 81
Cobblers — 304
Cobblers, Crisps, and Crumbles / Chapter 16 — **303**

Cocoa
    Cocoa Butter   326, 328, 329, 331-333, 340, 409
    Cocoa powder   89, 90, 103, 106, 189, 197, 199,
                 202, 204, 205, 207, 213, 235, 243,
                 244, 253, 255, 266, 314, 342-345, 347,
                 348, 351, 352, 366, 374, 382, 409
        Coco-Coconut Banana Popsicles   378
        Cocoa Brownies   231
        Coco-Cocoa Cookies   223
        Cocoa Glaze for Cake   104
        Cocoa Nut Frosting   110
    Cocoa powder, raw   409-410
Coconut   235, 236, 410
    Coconut butter   77, 78, 292, 295, 296, 298, 300, 322,
                 326, 328-333, 340, 347, 366, 382, 410
    Coconut Brown Rice Pudding   248
    Coconut cream   240, 250, 251, 282, 295, 410
        Coconut Cream Pie   283
    Coconut Crust   275
    Coconut Haystacks   332
    Coconut Melon Snack   365
    Coconut Milk #1   79
    Coconut Milk #2   80
    Coconut Milk Ice Cream Base Recipe   318
    Coconut oil   78, 109, 421
    Coconut Pudding   252
    Coffee Coconut Ice Cream   319
    Maté Coconut Ice Cream   319
    Mint Chocolate Chip Coconut Ice Cream   320
    Raspberry Coconut Milk Sherbet   320
    Strawberry Cacao Chip Coconut Ice Cream   321
    Strawberry Coconut Milk Ice Cream   320
Cookies and Bars / Chapter 13   **215**
Cold Cereal   386
Combo Crust: Half Shortening, Half Butter   269
Corn   412-413
    Corn Bread with Corn and Green Chile   151
    Corn Bread, yeasted   139
    Corn flour   412-413
    Cornmeal   412-413
    Corn Muffins   179
    Sweet Morning Grits   391
Cranberry
    Cranberry Muffins   180
    Cranberry Orange Sauce   102
Cream Cheese Frosting   110
Cream of Tartar   410
Creamy Apricot Popsicles   377
Creamy Coconut Frosting   109
Creamy Mango Coconut Popsicles   377
Creamy Piña Colada Popsicles   376
Creamy Rice Pudding   248
Crème De Cacao   204, 210
Crisps   307
Crumb Topping for Muffins   160
Crumbles   309

D
Dairy- See also butter, buttermilk, milk, and yogurt
Dairy-Free Recipes
    Beverages (dairy free) / Chapter 6   73
    Almond Milk   75
    Smoothie Base Recipe   78
    Chia Fresca   87
    Chia Sports Drink   87
    Coconut Milk #1   79

    Coconut Milk #2   80
    Fresh Lemonade   84
    Ginger Beer   84
    Golden Milk   76
    Instant Lemonade/Limeade   85
    Nut and Seed Milk Base Recipe   74
    Pumpkin Cream Drink   77
    Punch   85
    Raw Almond Chocolate Milk   76
    Raw Cashew Chocolate Milk   77
    Refreshing Aloe Tonic Drink   86
    Spiced Apricot Cider   88
    Superfood Raw Coffee Slush   86
    Traditional Root Beer   83
Breads (dairy free) / Chapter 10   127
    Amaranth Corn Bread   152
    Apricot Bread   149
    Brown Rice Bread, yeasted   154
    Carrot Bread, yeasted   150
    Orange Rye Bread, yeasted   138
    Potato Millet Bread, yeasted   153
    Pretzels, yeasted   146
    Spelt Oat Bread, yeasted   131
Breakfast Foods (dairy free) / Chapter 22   385
    Amaranth Apple Waffles   402
    Granola Base Recipe #1-Oil Free   388
    Granola Base Recipe #2: Bran-style   388
    Granola Base Recipe #3: Combo Granola   389
    Buckwheat Pancakes   397
    Hot Quinoa Breakfast   393
    Millet Waffles   405
    Oat Bran Cereal   393
    Oat Bran Cereal with Slippery Elm   394
    Quinoa Waffles   404
    Simple French Toast   395
    Sweet Rice Pancakes   399
    Whole Grain Buttermilk Pancakes   398
    Whole Wheat Apple Waffles   401
    Whole Wheat Pancakes   396
Cakes, Birthday Cakes, Cupcakes, and
Cheesecakes (dairy free) / Chapter 12   185
    Angel Food Cake   212
    Almond Orange Cake   211
    Chocolate Bundt   213
    Irish Boiled Cake   201
Candies With a Healthy Twist
(dairy free) / Chapter 19   339
    Easy Nutty Fudge   353
    Nougat Caramel Candy Bar   347
    Peppermint Patties   348
    Raw Chocolate Base Recipe   326
    Sesame Almond Candy   349
    Sesame Crunch Candy   350
    Simple Chocolate Base Recipe   340
    Tahini Candy   352
Cobblers, Crisps, and Crumbles
(dairy free) / Chapter 16   303
    Cobbler Base Recipe   304
    Peach Cobbler   306
Cookies and Bars (dairy free) / Chapter 13   215
    Chia Raisin Cookies   222
    Flourless Almond Cookies   234
    Macaroons   235
    Vegan Almond Macaroons   236
Flavored Agave Nectars and
Extracts / Chapter 7 (all recipes are dairy free)   93

Fun Foods for Kids (dairy free) / Chapter 21 369
Banana Chocolate Crunch Popsicles 378
Brown Rice Crispy Treats 372
Caramel Corn 373
Citrus Raspberry Herbal Popsicles 380
Coco-Coconut Banana Popsicles 378
Creamy Apricot Popsicles 377
Creamy Mango Coconut Popsicles 377
Creamy Pina Colada Popsicles 376
Elderberry Blueberry Herbal Popsicles 380
Fruit Juice Popsicles Base Recipe 375
Gelatin-Free Agar Jello 370
Green Tea Popsicles 381
Herbal Popsicles Base Recipe 379
Lemonade Popsicles 382
Milky Lavender Herbal Popsicles 380
Mint Apple Herbal Popsicles 380
Peach Blueberry Fruit Popsicles 376
Peanut Butter Rice Crispy Treats 372
Rose Pomegranate Herbal Popsicles 380
Sweet Red Bean Popsicles 381
Ice Cream (dairy free) / Chapter 17 313
Cashew Milk Base Recipe 322
Chai Chocolate Chip Coconut Ice Cream 318
Chia Seed Raw Ice Cream 322
Coconut Ice Cream Base Recipe 318
Coffee Coconut Ice Cream 319
Ginger Mango Lime Ice Cream 319
Mango Coconut Sherbet 320
Maté Coconut Ice Cream 319
Mint Chocolate Chip Coconut 321
Raspberry Coconut Milk Sherbet 320
*Strawberry Cacao Chip Coconut Milk
Ice Cream* 321
Strawberry Coconut Milk Ice Cream 320
**Jams, Jellies, Preserves, and Marmalades /
Chapter 9** (all recipes are dairy free) 113
Muffins (dairy free) / Chapter 11 159
Banana Coconut Muffins 181
Pies and Tarts (dairy free) / Chapter 15 259
  Crusts
    Coconut Crust 275
    Egg Crust 269
    Kamut Oat Butter Crust 272
    Kamut Oil Crust 271
    Millet Corn Kamut Oil Crust 271
    Millet Sorghum Corn Crust 274
    Oil Crust 268
    Organic Vegetable Shortening Crust 269
    Raw Date Nut Pie Crust 293
    Raw Pecan Almond Date Crust 294
    Raw Pecan Pie Crust 292
    Raw Pistachio Crust 292
    Raw Walnut Crust 294
    Simple Brazil Nut Crust 291
    Simple Raw Macadamia Crust 291
    Sweet Amaranth Crust 274
    Tapioca Rice Crust 273
    Whole Wheat and Barley Oil Crust 270
  Fillings
    Apple Pie 279
    Blueberry Pie 280
    Fresh Fruit Pie Base Recipe 278
    Mango Key Lime Pie 286
    Pumpkin Pie 288
    Raw Banana Cream Pie Filling 297
    Raw Chocolate Banana Pie Filling 298
    Raw Chocolate Cream Pie Filling 298
    Raw Chocolate Rose Pie Cups 300
    Raw Coconut Lime Pie Filling 295
    Raw Key Lime Filling 295
    Raw Lemon Filling 296
    Raw Meringue Pie Topping 296
    Raw Strawberry Pie Cups 299
    Strawberry Pie 280
Pocket Pies and Toaster Pastries 276
Puddings and Custards (dairy free) / Chapter 14 239
Banana Cream Pudding 250
Barley Pudding 250
Simple Vanilla Pudding 243
Chia Banana Coconut Pudding 254
Chocolate Pudding 244
Coconut Brown Rice Pudding 248
Earl Grey Pudding 245
Maple Pumpkin Custard 246
Mocha Amasake Pudding 253
Mocha Chia Pudding 255
Rose Delight 245
Strawberries and Cream Parfait 247
Tapioca Pudding 244
Torta de Banana 251
Vanilla Amasake Pudding 252
Raw Food Treats / Chapter 18 (all recipes are
dairy free) 325
Snacks (dairy free) / Chapter 20 355
Almond Flax Nut Bar 359
Banana Coconut Snack 365
Coconut Melon Snack 365
Fried Bananas with Chocolate Sauce 366
Green Power Bar 360
Homemade Protein Bar Base Recipe 358
Maca Power Bar 359
Oat Bran Bars 361
Oat Prune Bars 362
Sesame Bars 363
Spirulina Chia Power Bar 360
Sweet Chipotle Cashew Crunch 364
**Syrups, Sauces, and Frostings
(dairy free) / Chapter 8** 99
Apple Cider Sauce 105
Blackberry Sauce 101
Carob Banana Frosting 110
Carob Sauce 103
Chocolate Syrup 103
Cranberry Orange Sauce 102
Creamy Coconut Frosting 109
Easy Fruit Syrup 100
Fluffy Frosting 108
Raspberry Sauce 101
Strawberry Sauce 102
Vanilla Meringue Frosting 108
Dark Chocolate Cake with Orange Ganache 202
Dark Rye Bread 137
Dates 18, 20, 21, 29, 63, 291, 293, 294, 322, 334, 335,
347, 357, 387, 390
Date Nut Pastry Muffins 171
Raw Date Nut Pie Crust 293
Raw Pecan Almond Date Crust 294
Date sugar 18, 46, 147, 226, 394, 144, 266, 274, 251, 374, 410
Digestive Biscuits for Toddlers 371
Dill Bread 133
Dried Fruit Bon-Bons Base Recipe 328

E

Earl Grey Pudding 245
Eggs 46, 55, 186, 240, 261
    Egg Crust 269
    Eggless Chocolate Chip Cookies 219
Elderberry Blueberry Herbal Popsicles 380
Empanadas 290
English Muffins 143
Essential Oils 94, 95, 410
Extract, Base Recipe 95

F

Fermented Buckwheat Pancakes 400
Flavored Agave Nectars and Extracts / Chapter 7 **93**
Flax seeds 74, 78, 218, 240, 371, 391, 401, 402, 410-411
    Almond Flax Nut Bar 359
    Flaxseed oil 349, 422
    Sweet Flax Sauce 105
Flour 411
    Amaranth flour 411
    Arrow root flour 416
    Barley flour 411
    Brown rice flour 412
    Buckwheat flour 412
    Chickpea (garbanzo) flour 416
    Corn flour and cornmeal 412-413
    Garfava flour 417
    Kamut flour 413
    Millet flour 413
    Nut flour 417
    Oat bran 413
    Oat flour 413-414
    Potato flour 417
    Potato starch flour 417
    Quinoa flour 414
    Rye flour 414
    Spelt flour 414-415
    Tapioca flour 417
    Teff flour 415
    Whole wheat flour 415
    Whole wheat pastry flour 416
Flourless Almond Cookies 234
Fluffy Frosting 108
Fresh Lemonade 84
Framboise 101, 204, 320, 342, 418
Fragoli 102, 418
French Rose Absolute 342, 418
Fried Bananas with Chocolate Sauce 366
Fruit Juice Popsicles Base Recipe 375
Fruit Jam with Pomona's Universal Pectin Kit 115
Fun Foods for Kids and The Young at Heart / Chapter 21 **369**

G

Garfava flour 417
Gelatin-Free Agar Jello 370
Geranium Ginger Agave Nectar 94
German Chocolate Cake 196
Gingerbread Men & Women 226
Ginger Beer 84
Ginger Mango Lime Ice Cream 319
Gluten-Free 40, 41, 50
Gluten-Free Flours 40, 41
Gluten-Free Halvah 352
Gluten-Free Recipes **50**
    Beverages / Chapter 6 (all recipes are gluten free) 73

Breads (gluten free) / Chapter 10 127
    Banana Chocolate Chip Bread 157
    Brown Rice Bread, yeasted 154
    Pizza Crust, yeasted 155
    Potato Millet Bread, yeasted 153
    Pretzels, yeasted 156
Breakfast Foods (gluten free) / Chapter 22 385
    Amaranth Apple Waffles 402
    Buckwheat Pancakes 397
    Buttermilk Teff Waffles 405
    Cardamom Grits 392
    Fermented Buckwheat Pancakes 400
    French Toast 395
    Hot Quinoa Breakfast 393
    Millet Waffles 405
    Quick Rice Cereal 392
    Quinoa Waffles 404
    Sesame Yogurt Waffles 403
    Sweet Morning Grits 391
    Sweet Rice Pancakes 399
    Whole Grain Buttermilk Pancakes 398
    Whole Wheat Apple Waffles (variation) 401
Cakes, Birthday Cakes, Cupcakes, and Cheesecakes (gluten free) /Chapter 12 211
    Almond Orange Cake 211
    Angel Food Cake 212
    Chocolate Bundt Cake 213
    Chocolate Zucchini Cake 210
    Ricotta Cheesecake 208
    White Cake Base Recipe 209
Candies With a Healthy Twist (gluten free) / Chapter 19 339
    Chocolate Covered Cherries and Strawberries 341
    Chocolate Framboise Rose Truffles 342
    Chocolate Lavender Truffles 345
    Chocolate Mint Truffles 344
    Chocolate Peanut Butter Cups 346
    Easy Nutty Fudge 353
    Gluten-Free Halvah 352
    Nougat Caramel Candy Bar 347
    Peppermint Patties 348
    Pomegranate Chocolate Truffles 343
    Sesame Almond Candy 349
    Sesame Crunch Candy 350
    Simple Chocolate Base Recipe 340
    Tahini Candy 352
Cobblers, Crisps, and Crumbles (gluten free) / Chapter 16 303
    Berry Almond Crumble 310
    Cobbler Base Recipe 304
Cookies & Bars (gluten free) / Chapter 13 215
    Brownies 235
    Coco-Cocoa Cookies 223
    Flourless Almond Cookies 234
    KC's Chocolate Chip Coconut Cookies 233
    Macaroons 235
    Vegan Almond Macaroons 236
Flavored Agave Nectars and Extracts / Chapter 7 (all recipes are gluten free) 93
Fun Foods for Kids and The Young at Heart (gluten free) / Chapter 21 369
    Fudgesicles
Ice Cream / Chapter 17 (all recipes are gluten free) 313
Jams, Jellies Preserves and Marmalades / Chapter 9 (all recipes are gluten free) 113
Muffins (gluten free) / Chapter 11 173

Banana Coconut Muffins — 181
Banana Rice Bran Muffins — 177
Buckwheat Muffins — 182
Carrot Rice Muffins — 178
Corn Muffins — 179
Cranberry Muffins — 180
Gluten-Free Muffin Base — 173
Nutty Rice Bran Muffins — 176
Rice Bran Muffins — 175
Pies and Tarts (gluten free) / Chapter 15 — 273
    Crusts — 268
        Coconut Crust — 275
        Empanadas — 290
        Millet Sorghum Corn Crust — 274
        Sweet Amaranth Crust — 274
        Tapioca Rice Crust — 273
    Crusts, Raw (all recipes are gluten free) — 291
    Pie Fillings (all recipes are gluten free) — 259
Puddings and Custards / Chapter 14
(all recipes are gluten free) — 239
Raw Food Treats / Chapter 18
(all recipes are gluten free) — 325
Snacks (gluten-free) / Chapter 20 — 355
    Almond Flax Nut Bar — 359
    Banana Coconut Snack — 365
    Coconut Melon Snack — 365
    Fried Bananas with Chocolate Sauce — 366
    Green Power Bar — 360
    Homemade Protein Bar Base Recipe — 358
    Maca Power Bar — 359
    Sweet Chipotle Cashew Crunch — 364
Syrups, Sauces, and Frostings / Chapter 8
(all recipes are gluten free) — 99
Goji berries — 78, 326, 328, 332, 334, 340, 387, 418
    Goji Chocolate Power Balls — 329
Golden Milk — 76
Golden Yogurt Raisin Muffins — 168
Grain beverage — 141, 418
Grain-sweetened chocolate — 195, 197, 198, 200, 204, 218, 223, 231, 233, 235, 244, 254, 314, 316, 318, 321, 322, 346, 356, 418
Granola — 378, 386, 387
    Granola Bars — 357
    Granola Base Recipe #1: Oil-Free — 388
    Granola Base Recipe #2: Bran-Style — 388
    Granola Base Recipe #3: Combo Granola — 389
Grapeseed oil — 421-422
Green Power Bar — 360
Green Tea Popsicles — 381
Guar gum — 153-156, 165, 168, 173, 175, 180, 182, 190, 196, 197, 202, 206, 211-213, 224, 228, 235, 240, 273, 290, 297, 300, 318-322, 402-405, 418

H
Halvah — 351
Hazelnut Chocolate Chip Bundt Cake — 198
Hemp seeds — 78, 328, 329, 333, 352, 360, 418
    Hemp Chocolate Fudge Bars — 333
Herbal Popsicles Base Recipe — 379
Homemade Protein Bar Base Recipe — 358
Hot Bran Cereal — 394
Hot Cereal — 390
Hot Chocolate—see also beverages — 89
Hot Quinoa Breakfast — 393

I
Ice Cream / Chapter 17 — **313**
Instant Easy Fruit Jam with Agar-Agar — 118
Instant Lemonade /Limeade — 85
Irish Boiled Cake — 201
Irish Moss — 296, 298, 419

J
Jams, Jellies, Preserves, and Marmalades / Chapter 9 — **113**
Japanese Water Crystals — 82
    Live Water Crystal Soda Base Recipe — 82
Jelly Made with Pomona's Universal Pectin Kit — 116
Jello
    Gelatin-Free Agar Jello — 370
Juice Soda Base Recipe — 81

K
Kamut — 413
    Kamut Oil Crust — 271
    Kamut Buttermilk Bread — 136
    Kamut flour — 413
    Kamut Oat Ricotta Muffins — 169
    Kamut Oat Butter Crust — 272
KC's Chocoloate Chip Coconut Cookies — 233
Kefir—see Japanese Water Crystals — 82
Kelp — 153, 419

L
Lemon —
    Fresh Lemonade — 84
    Instant Lemonade/ Limeade — 85
    Lemon Balm Lime Agave Nectar — 94
    Lemon Bars — 230
    Lemon Cashew Cookies — 336
    Lemon Meringue Pie — 284
    Lemonade Popsicles — 382
    Lemony Agave Nectar — 94
Live Water Crystal Soda Base Recipe — 82

M
Maca — 78, 86, 334, 419
    Maca Balls — 330
    Maca Power Bar — 359
Macaroons — 236
Maccha (Matcha) — 315, 419
Madeleine Cookies — 228
Mango —
    Mango butter — 326, 328, 329, 333, 340, 419
    Mango Coconut Sherbet — 320
    Mango Key Lime Pie — 286
Maple syrup — 420
    Maple Pecan Pastry Muffins — 172
    Maple Pumpkin Custard — 246
Marmalades — 114
    Citrus Marmalade — 125
Marzipan — 107
Maté Cocido Ice Cream — 315
Maté Coconut Ice Cream — 319
Meringue —
    Lemon Meringue Pie — 284
    Orange Meringue Pie — 285
    Raw Meringue Pie Topping — 296
    Vanilla Meringue Frosting — 108

Mexican Chocolate Elixir	90
Mexican Hot Chocolate	89
Milk	420
Coconut milk	420
Coconut Milk #1	79
Coconut Milk #2	80
Dairy milk	420
Non-dairy milk	420
Almond Milk	75
Golden Milk	76
Nut and Seed Milk Base Recipe	74
Raw Almond Chocolate Milk	76
Smoothie Base Recipe	78
Milky Lavender Herbal Popsicles	380
Millet	413
Millet flour	413
Millet Waffles	405
Millet Corn Kamut Pie Crust	271
Millet Sorghum Corn Crust	274
Mint	
Mint Apple Herbal Popsicles	380
Mint Jelly	123
Mocha Amasake Pudding	253
Mocha Chia Pudding	235
Molasses, black strap	226, 420
Muffins / Chapter 11	**159**
Mushrooms, medicinal	420-421
Goji Chocolate Power Balls	329
Maca Balls	330
Smoothie Base Recipe	78

N

Natural sodas—See also beverages, sodas	81
New York Cheesecake	207
No Cook Freezer Jam with Pomona's Universal Pectin Kit	117
Non-dairy milk—See also milk	
Nougat Caramel Candy Bar	347
Nuts—See also almonds, Brazil nuts, and cashews	
Nutmeg Cream	106
Nutritional yeast (Brewer's Yeast)	352, 374, 421
Nutty Fudge, Easy	353
Nutty Rice Bran Muffins	176

O

Oats	160, 307, 310, 357, 362
Chocolate Chip Oat Bars	356
Kamut Oat Ricotta Muffins	169
Oat bran	413
Oat Bran Bars	361
Oat Bran Bread	135
Oat Bran Cereal	393
Oat Bran Cereal with Slippery Elm	394
Oat Brown Rice Butter Crust	271
Oat Butter Oil Crust	270
Oat flour	414
Oat Prune Bars	362
Oat Raspberry Thumbprint Cookies	220
Oatmeal Raisin Cookies	221
Spelt Oat Bread	131
Steel Cut Oatmeal	390
Oils	421
Coconut oil	421
Grapeseed oil	421
Flaxseed oil	421
Olive oil	422
Sesame oil	422
Vegetable shortening, organic palm or coconut	422
Orange	
Cranberry Orange Sauce	102
Orange Agave Nectar	94
Orange Clary Sage Agave Nectar	94
Orange Meringue Pie	285
Orange Rye Bread	138
Organic Vegetable Shortening Crust	269

P

Pastry Muffin Base	170
Pazorro	200
Peach	
Peach Blueberry Fruit Popsicles	376
Peach Cobbler	306
Peanut butter	
Chocolate Peanut Butter Cups	346
Peanut Butter Cookies	224
Peanut Butter Frosting	109
Peanut Butter Ice Cream	314
Peanut Butter Muffins	166
Peanut Butter Rice Crispy Treats	372
Peasant Bread	141
Pecan Pie	287
Peppermint	89, 95
Peppermint Agave Nectar	94
Peppermint Patties	348
Pies and Tarts / Chapter 15	**259**
Pizzelles	227
Pocket Pies and Toaster Pastries	276
Pomegranate Chocolate Truffles	343
Pomona's Universal Pectin Kit	423
Popcorn	
Caramel Corn	373
Sweet and Cheesy Corn	374
Popsicles	375
Banana Chocolate Crunch Popsicles	378
Chocolate Fudge Popsicles	382
Citrus Raspberry Herbal Popsicles	380
Coco-Coconut Banana Popsicles	378
Creamy Apricot Popsicles	377
Creamy Mango Coconut Popsicles	377
Creamy Piña Colada Popsicles	376
Elderberry Blueberry Herbal Popsicles	380
Green Tea Popsicles	381
Herbal Popsicle Base Recipe	379
Fruit Juice Popsicles Base Recipe	375
Lemonade Popsicles	382
Mint Apple Herbal Popsicles	380
Milky Lavender Herbal Popsicles	380
Peach Blueberry Fruit Popsicles	376
Rose Pomegranate Herbal Popsicles	380
Sweet Red Bean Popsicles	381
Potato	
Irish Boiled Cake	201
Potato Millet Bread, yeasted	153
Potato flour	417
Potato starch	417
Preserves	114
Pretzels	
Pretzels	146
Pretzels, yeasted, gluten free	156
Puddings and Custards / Chapter 14	**239**
Pumpernickel Bread	134

Pumpkin
 Pumpkin Cream Drink   77
 Pumpkin Pie   288
Punch   85

Q

Quick Rice Cereal   392
Quinoa
 Hot Quinoa Breakfast   393
 Quinoa flour   414
 Quinoa Waffles   404

R

Raisins 20, 21, 82, 83, 144, 149, 167, 206, 248, 294, 330, 349,
    352, 357, 359, 361, 387, 388, 393, 390, 394
 Chia Raisin Cookies   222
 Golden Yogurt Raisin Muffins   168
 Oatmeal Raisin Cookies   221
Raspberry
 Chocolate Raspberry Layer Cake   204
 Citrus Raspberry Herbal Popsicles   380
 Framboise   418
 Oat Raspberry Thumbprint Cookies   220
 Raspberry Coconut Sherbet   320
 Raspberry Gelato   316
 Raspberry Sauce   101
Raw
 Raw Food Treats / Chapter 18   325
 Pie Crusts and Fillings, Raw   291, 295
  Banana Cream Pie Filling   297
  Chocolate Banana Pie Filling   298
  Chocolate Cream Pie Filling   298
  Chocolate Rose Pie Cups   300
  Coconut Lime Pie Filling   295
  Date Nut Crust   293
  Lemon Pie Filling   296
  Pecan Almond Date Crust   294
  Pecan Crust   292
  Pistachio Crust   292
  Strawberry Pie Cups   299
 Raw Chocolate Candy Base Recipe   326
Red Velvet Cake (Chocolate Beet Cake)   205
Refreshing Aloe Tonic Drink   86
Rhubarb Yogurt Swirl   256
Rice Bran Muffins   175
Rich Chocolate Brownies   232
Ricotta
 Ricotta Cheese Pancakes   399
 Ricotta Cheesecake   208
 Ricotta Gelato   317
Root Beer, Traditional   83
Rose
 Chocolate Framboise Rose Truffles   342
 Rose Agave Nectar   94
 Rose Apple Jelly   122
 Rose Delight   245
 Rose Pomegranate Herbal Popsicles   380
Rye
 Pumpernickel Bread   134
 Rye flour   414

S

Salt   43-44, 423
Sesame 74, 129, 265, 330, 331, 336, 351, 352, 358,
    359, 364, 371, 374, 387, 390

Sesame Almond Candy   349
Sesame Bars   363
Sesame Crunch Candy   350
Sesame oil   422
Sesame Yogurt Waffles   403
Simple Brazil Nut Crust   291
Simple Chocolate Base Recipe   340
Simple French Toast   395
Simple Raw Macadamia Crust   291
Smoothie Base Recipe   78
Snacks / Chapter 20   **355**
Sodas—See beverages
Sparkling Apple Cider   81
Spelt
 Spelt flour   414-415
 Spelt Herb Bread   132
 Spelt Oat Bread   131
Spice Muffins   167
Spiced Apricot Cider   88
Spirulina 46, 78, 295, 328, 329, 333, 358, 360, 374
 Spirulina Chia Power Bar   360
Steel Cut Oatmeal   390
Strawberry
 Fragoli   418
 Raw Strawberry Pie Cups   299
 Strawberries and Cream Parfait   247
 Strawberry Cacao Chip Coconut Milk Ice Cream   321
 Strawberry Coconut Milk Ice Cream   320
 Strawberry Gelato   316
 Strawberry Pie   280
 Strawberry Sauce   102
Superfoods—See also açaí, chia, goji berries, maca,
  mushrooms, raw cacao, and spirulina
 Coconut Haystacks   332
 Dried Fruit Bon-Bon Base Recipe   328
 Goji Chocolate Power Balls   329
 Hemp Chocolate Fudge Bars   333
 Maca Balls   330
 Raw Chocolate Truffles   334
 Superfood Raw Coffee Slush   86
Sweet and Cheesy Popcorn   374
Sweet Amaranth Crust   274
Sweet Chipotle Cashew Crunch   364
Sweet Flax Sauce   105
Sweet Morning Grits   391
Sweet Potato Pie   289
Sweet Red Bean Popsicles   381
Sweet Rice Pancakes   399
Sweeteners—See also agave nectar, date sugar,
  maple syrup, and molasses
Syrups, Sauces, and Frostings / Chapter 8   **99**

T

Tahini 78, 334, 351, 352, 394, 423
 Chocolate Tahini Balls   331
 Tahini Candy   352
Tamari   294, 423
Tapioca
 Chai Tapioca   249
 Tapioca flour   417
 Tapioca Pudding   249
 Tapioca Rice Crust   273
Taralli   229
Teff flour   415
Torta de Banana   251
Traditional Root Beer   83

Truffles 342
   Chocolate Framboise Rose Truffles 342
   Pomegranate Chocolate Truffles 343
   Chocolate Lavender Truffles 345
   Chocolate Mint Truffles 344

V
Vanilla
   Simple Vanilla Pudding 253
   Vanilla Amasake Pudding 252
   Vanilla Ice Cream 314
   Vanilla Meringue Frosting 108
Vegan Almond Macaroons 236
Vegetable shortening, organic- See oils

W
Water kefir—See Japanese water crystals
Waffles 401
   Amaranth Apple Waffles 402
   Buttermilk Teff Waffles 405
   Millet Waffles 405
   Quinoa Waffles 404
   Sesame Yogurt Waffles 403
   Whole Wheat Apple Waffles 401
Warm Hug 89
Wheat-Free Recipes
   Beverages / Chapter 6 (all recipes are wheat free) **73**
   Breads (wheat free) / Chapter 10 **127**
      Amaranth Cornbread 152
      Apricot Bread 149
      Banana Chocolate Chip Bread 157
      Brown Rice Bread, yeasted 154
      Carob Bread, yeasted 140
      Carrot Bread, yeasted 150
      Challah, yeasted 142
      Cinnamon Rolls, yeasted 147
      Corn Bread, yeasted 139
      Corn Bread with Corn and Green Chile 151
      Dark Rye Bread, yeasted 137
      Dill Bread, yeasted 133
      English Muffins, yeasted 143
      Kamut Buttermilk Bread, yeasted 136
      Oat Bran Bread, yeasted 135
      Orange Rye Bread, yeasted 138
      Peasant Bread, yeasted 141
      Pizza Crust, yeasted 145
      Pizza Crust, gluten free 155
      Potato Millet Bread, yeasted 153
      Pretzels, yeasted 146
      Pretzels, yeasted, gluten free 156
      Pumpernickel Bread, yeasted 134
      Spelt Herb Bread, yeasted 132
      Spelt Oat Bread, yeasted 131
      Stollen, yeasted 144
      Whole Grain Bread, yeasted 130
   Breakfast Foods (wheat free) / Chapter 22 385
      Amaranth Apple Waffles 402
      Blueberry Bran Oatmeal 391
      Buckwheat Pancakes 397
      Buttermilk Teff Waffles 405
      Cardomom Grits 392
      Fermented Buckwheat Pancakes 400
      French Toast 395
      Granola Base Recipe #1: Oil-Free 388
      Granola Base Recipe #2: Bran-Style 388

      Granola Base Recipe #3: Combo Granola 389
      Hot Bran Cereal 394
      Hot Quinoa Breakfast 393
      Millet Waffles 405
      Oat Bran Cereal 393
      Oat Bran Cereal with Slippery Elm 394
      Quick Rice Cereal 392
      Quinoa Waffles 404
      Ricotta Cheese Pancakes 399
      Sesame Yogurt Waffles 403
      Steel Cut Oatmeal 390
      Sweet Morning Grits 391
      Sweet Rice Pancakes 399
      Whole Grain Buttermilk Pancakes 398
      Whole Wheat Apple Waffles (variation) 401
   Cakes, Birthday Cakes, Cupcakes, and Cheesecakes
   (wheat free) / Chapter 12 **185**
      Almond Orange Cake 211
      Angel Food Cake 212
      Carrot Cake 206
      Chocolate Birthday Cake Base Recipe 195
      Chocolate Bundt Cake 213
      Chocolate Chip Bundt Cake 197
      Chocolate Ginger Cake 199
      Chocolate Zucchini Cake 210
      Dark Chocolate Cake with Orange Ganache 202
      German Chocolate Cake 196
      Irish Boiled Cake 201
      New York Cheesecake 207
      Red Velvet Cake (Chocolate Beet Cake) 205
      Ricotta Cheesecake 208
      White Birthday Cake Base Recipe 194
      White Cake Base Recipe 193
      White Cake Base Recipe, gluten free 209
   Candies With a Healthy Twist / Chapter 19
   (all recipes are wheat free) **339**
   Cobblers, Crisps, and Crumbles
   (wheat free) / Chapter 16 **303**
      Apple Crisp 308
      Berry Almond Crumble 310
      Cobbler Base Recipe 305-305
      Crisp Base Recipe 307
      Crumble Base Recipe 309
      Peach Cobbler 306
   Cookies and Bars (wheat free) / Chapter 13 **215**
      Butter Cookies 225
      Brownies 235
      Chia Raisin Cookies 222
      Chocolate Chip Cookies 218
      Cocoa Brownies 231
      Coco-Cocoa Cookies 223
      Eggless Chocolate Chip Cookies 219
      Flourless Almond Cookies 234
      Gingerbread Men & Women 226
      KC's Chocolate Chip Coconut Cookies 233
      Lemon Bars 230
      Macaroons 235
      Madeleine Cookies 228
      Oat Raspberry Thumbprint Cookies 220
      Oatmeal Raisin Cookies 221
      Peanut Butter Cookies 224
      Pizzelles 227
      Rich Chocolate Brownies 232
      Taralli 229
      Vegan Almond Macaroons 236

Flavored Agave Nectars and Extracts / Chapter 7
(all recipes are wheat free)   93
Fun Foods for Kids and The Young at Heart
(wheat free) / Chapter 21   369
   Banana Chocolate Crunch Popsicles   378
   Brown Rice Crispy Treats   372
   Caramel Corn   373
   Citrus Raspberry Herbal Popsicles   380
   Coco-Coconut Banana Popsicles   378
   Creamy Apricot Popsicles   377
   Creamy Mango Coconut Popsicles   377
   Creamy Piña Colada Popsicles   376
   Elderberry Blueberry Herbal Popsicles 380
   Fruit Juice Popsicles Base Recipe   375
   Gelatin-Free Agar Jello   370
   Green Tea Popsicles   381
   Herbal Popsicles Base Recipe   379
   Lemonade Popsicles   382
   Milky Lavender Herbal Popsicles   380
   Mint Apple Herbal Popsicles   380
   Peach Blueberry Fruit Popsicles   376
   Peanut Butter Rice Crispy Treats   372
   Rose Pomegranate Herbal Popsicles   380
   Sweet and Cheesy Popcorn   374
   Sweet Red Bean Popsicles   381
Ice Cream / Chapter 17 (all recipes are wheat free) 313
Jams, Jellies, Perserves, and Marmalades /
Chapter 9 (all recipes are wheat free)   113
Muffins (wheat free) / Chapter 11   159
   Amaranth Oat Bran Muffins   162
   Banana Coconut Muffins   181
   Banana Rice Bran Muffins   177
   Barley Apple Muffins   163
   Muffin Base Recipe   161
   Blueberry Muffins   161
   Bran Muffins   165
   Buckwheat Muffins   182
   Carrot Rice Muffins   178
   Corn Muffins   179
   Cranberry Muffins   180
   Crumb Topping for Muffins   160
   Gluten-Free Muffin Base Recipe   123
   Golden Yogurt Raisin Muffins   168
   Kamut Oat Ricotta Muffins   169
   Nutty Rice Bran Muffins   176
   Peanut Butter Muffins   166
   Rice Bran Muffins   175
   Spice Muffins   167
Pies and Tarts (wheat free) / Chapter 15   259
   Crusts
      Barley Combo Crust   272
      Coconut Crust   275
      Kamut Oat Butter Crust   272
      Millet Sorghum Corn Crust   274
      Oat Brown Rice Butter Oil Crust 271
      Oat Butter Crust   270
      Pocket Pies and Toaster Pastries 276-277
      Raw Date Nut Pie Crust   293
      Raw Pecan Almond Date Crust 294
      Raw Pecan Pie Crust   292
      Raw Pistachio Crust   292
      Raw Walnut Crust   293
      Simple Brazil Nut Crust   291
      Simple Raw Macadamia Crust   291
      Sweet Amaranth Crust   274
      Tapioca Rice Crust   273

Fillings (all recipes are wheat free)
Puddings and Custards / Chapter 14
(all recipes are wheat free)   239
Raw Food Treats / Chapter 18
(all recipes are wheat free)   325
   Snacks (wheat free) / Chapter 20   355
      Almond Flax Nut Bar   359
      Banana Coconut Snack   365
      Coconut Melon Snack   365
      Fried Bananas with Chocolate Sauce 366
      Green Power Bar   360
      Homemade Protein Bar Base Recipe 358
      Maca Power Bar   359
      Sweet Chipotle Cashew Crunch 364
   Syrups, Sauces, and Frostings / Chapter 8
   (all recipes are wheat free)   99
Whey powder   69, 78, 143, 161-167, 170-180, 223, 226, 424
Whipped Cream   106
White Birthday Cake Base Recipe   194
White Cake Base Recipe   193
White Cake Base Recipe, gluten free   209
Whole grains
   Whole Grain Bread   130
   Whole Grain Buttermilk Pancakes   398
   Whole grain flours   411
   Whole Grain Pie Crust Recipes   270
   Why whole grain flours?   39-41
Whole Wheat Apple Waffles   401
Whole Wheat Buttermilk Shortening Crust   272
Whole wheat flour   415-416
Whole Wheat Pancakes   396
Whole wheat pastry flour   416
Whole Wheat Barley Oil Crust   270

X

Xanthan gum   69, 153-156, 165, 168, 173, 175-180, 182, 190, 196, 197, 202, 206, 207, 211-213, 224, 228, 235, 240, 273, 297, 318-322, 402-405, 424

Y

Yeast   128, 424
Yeasted bread- See also Breads   63, 69, 130-147, 153-156
Yeast-free bread—See also Breads   148-152, 157
Yogurt   69, 77, 133, 187, 424
   Golden Yogurt Raisin Muffins   168
   Rhubarb Yogurt Swirl   256
   Sesame Yogurt Waffles   403

Join the Community!

Join Jen, author of "Sweeten It With Agave" and an online community of people interested in cooking and baking with agave nectar at:

www.SweetenItWithAgave.com

Here you will find:

- ✓ The latest news about agave nectar
- ✓ Forum for discussing baking and cooking with agave nectar and other agave topics
- ✓ Store with helpful kitchen tools and ingredients found in this book
- ✓ Member profiles, enabling connection with the community
- ✓ Recipe sharing from members and a recipe blog from Jen
- ✓ And much more!

If you create a new recipe or variation from this workbook/cookbook and want to share it with the community, take the opportunity to submit it to the website and even have other people rate it! Or simply drop in to read about other people's culinary discoveries and learn from their experiences. This site is perfect for people who are committed to their health and want to find new recipes that are both good for you and mouth-watering delicious.

Join us in this unique online cooking community, where we can collaborate, make new friends, and create cooking magic! In the old days, we used to work alone at recipes through countless rounds of trial and error. Either that or we'd inherit recipes from ancestors. But now we can transform our favorite recipes into healthier versions using agave nectar, whole grains, quality fats, good salt, and organic ingredients — and then utilize the creative genius of the community to refine them until we have tons of winners! Some of those winning recipes will be included in updated editions of "Sweeten It With Agave," making this a dynamic, live cookbook project.

Made in the USA
Charleston, SC
26 April 2011